WITHDRAWN

HARVARD LIBRARY

WITHDRAWN

A Harvest of
Medieval Preaching

A Harvest of Medieval Preaching

The Sermon Books of Johann Herolt, OP *(Discipulus)*

Ian D. K. Siggins

BX
1756
.H4493
S54
2009

Copyright © 2009 by Ian D. K. Siggins.

Library of Congress Control Number: 2009909591
ISBN: Hardcover   978-1-4415-8042-9
             Softcover   978-1-4415-8041-2

All rights reserved. No part of this book may be reproduced or transmitted in any form or by any means, electronic or mechanical, including photocopying, recording, or by any information storage and retrieval system, without permission in writing from the copyright owner.

This book was printed in the United States of America.

To order additional copies of this book, contact:
Xlibris Corporation
1-888-795-4274
www.Xlibris.com
Orders@Xlibris.com
67350

Contents

Introduction
Johann Herolt, His Sermon Books 1

The Catholic Faith
1. Preaching The Catholic Faith 17
2. Falsifying The Faith: Heresy And Superstition 23
3. Grace And Merit 37
4. Contrition 52
5. Sin 64
6. Church, Priesthood, and Monasticism 80

Godly Use Of the Creation
7. The World and its Inhabitants 97
8. Human Nature 112
9. The Soul and the Body 117

Morality In The Family
10. Sex 135
11. Marriage 149
12. Women 159
13. Children 180

Virtue and Vice in Society
14. Society 193
15. Wealth 210
16. The Poor 218
17. Speech 229
18. Food and Drink 239
19. Amusements 245
20. Trade and Commerce 256

21. The Jews 263

The Last Things
22. Death and Judgment, Heaven and Hell 273

Appendix 1: Herolt's Sermon Books 293
Appendix 2: Abbreviations, Editions, Bibliography 311

Acknowledgements

This study was made possible by a grant from the US National Endowment for the Humanities. I express my deep gratitude to the many librarians throughout the United States and Europe who generously helped me locate manuscripts and books and prepare microfilm copies of rare sources—in particular, my colleagues in the Houghton Library at Harvard University, the Stadtbibliothek Nürnberg, and the Staatsbibliothek München.

Johann Herolt, His Sermon Books

Johann Herolt, OP, (?1386-1468), a Dominican friar of Nürnberg, was the most prolific, skillful, and honored writer of sermon books in fifteenth-century Europe. It was a time when enormous energy was devoted to the preaching task in the mendicant orders and when hearing sermons was regarded as a lay Christian's pious duty. Herolt's library of homiletic aids was the most thorough and shapely preacher's guide and was used very widely. He gained a deserved reputation as the outstanding sermonist of his century in Germany and teacher of the best models for parochial preaching.

The Brethren of the Common Life praised him as "pre-eminent among modern sermonists":[1]

> Humble things please humble people. This outstanding teacher exemplifies this truth in the way he has suppressed his own name, and these offerings are entitled "Sermons of a Disciple" because he preferred to be known by an alias, even though it is as clear as day that he graduated from his own preceptor's instruction as a master teacher. No one should be surprised that this man is lauded, that praises are heaped on him, that he is acclaimed, since he is most certainly held in common esteem as pre-eminent among modern sermonists. Wishing, then, to become partners in this man's zeal, we the brothers, priests, and clerks of the Green Shoot at St. Michael's in Rostock, not with the preached but instead the written word, have brought this distinguished man, once hidden among a few behind closed doors, out into the open by the art of printing which, of all the arts of holy church, is now mistress in gaining the attention of the many, to the praise of the all-powerful God. (A.D. 1476 3 kal. Nov.)

---

[1] Johann Herolt, preface to *Sermones* (Rostock: Fratres communis vitae ad S. Michaelem, 1476), Hain 8478.

The lasting output of his long career was a complete library of pulpit materials. These works circulated very widely in manuscript in the first two-thirds of his century (at least 500 manuscript copies still exist). When printing began, eager printers published edition after edition of Herolt's books—up to 186 separate editions before 1500 and 60 or more thereafter, including republication in the seventeenth and eighteenth centuries.

Despite the wide circulation and repute of Herolt's work, he has all but disappeared from view in the modern period. Only one of his books—a collection of miracles of the Virgin Mary—has been republished in the past century, and the last article devoted solely to his work was published in 1903. One purpose of this book is to make Herolt's achievement readily accessible to students of the period and to offer an ordered exposition of the themes heard from hundreds of urban pulpits as a result of his work. It seems a pity that the most influential and widely published sermonist of his time should be virtually unknown to students of the period. I have therefore gone to some lengths to represent the content of his books in a form the modern reader can conveniently use.

My interest in Herolt's life and writings has several starting points. First, the sources from which he draws are rich and diverse—he gathers a veritable "harvest of medieval preaching."[2] Secondly, he is a very skillful shaper of homiletic materials. His sermons have intrinsic interest as shapely examples of the *ars praedicandi* at its fullest development and as an extraordinarily thorough attempt to apply the teachings of church fathers, canonists, schoolmen, and learned preachers to the pastoral care of lay parishioners. In the process, Herolt's moral observations are useful source of insights into social life and morals in the cities of fifteenth-century Europe. Thirdly, the thoroughness of his enterprise makes his corpus the best source I know for the religion and morality preached to the burghers of the empire on the eve of the Reformation and to a generation of reforming theologians, Catholic and Protestant.

The tendency of recent scholarship has been to look for the theological roots of the Reformation in the debates about grace and repentance in the scholars and academic preachers of the preceding period; but anyone familiar with the works of the Brethren of the Common Life, or Erasmus, or the young Martin Luther and his colleagues will recognize palpable links between the pastoral theology in Herolt's sermons and the religious ideas that shaped the Reform.[3] Herolt's explicit purpose

---

[2] With acknowledgment to Heiko A. Oberman, *The Harvest of Medieval Theology: Gabriel Biel and Late Medieval Nominalism* (Cambridge: Harvard University Press, 1963). Published 2nd rev. ed. in Grand Rapids by W. B. Eerdmans Pub. Co., 1967.

[3] "'Scotism' and 'Ockhamism' suggest too strongly a merely academic setting, whereas the ideas of the *via moderna* are on a wide scale absorbed by non-Franciscans, infiltrating even the doctrinally well-disciplined Dominican Order and shaping the piety of thousands of sermons preached all over Europe—a source still largely

is to avoid the complexities of scholastic theory in favor of a direct, accessible, pastorally useful address to lay Christians. He makes abundantly clear how different the pastoral teaching of the preachers was from the doctrines of the schools. In this way, Herolt (and writers of some other parish sermon books) are a far richer and clearer source of understanding of late medieval Catholic culture than the elite academic theologians whose works have received the lion's share of attention.

I have pointed out elsewhere that the fifteenth century ill deserves its reputation as a low point of preaching in the Western tradition.[4] The century certainly had its share of derivative, uneven, and fatuous preaching, but it is not alone in this. What is far more impressive is the quality of pastoral care displayed by the best of its sermonists.

Each half of the century made its diverse contribution to a period of vigorous homiletic effort in the cities of northern Europe. The first half displayed a renewed commitment to the preacher's task, spurred by conciliar conviction, the New Devotion, and the growing movement for strict observance of the rule in the mendicant orders. The training of preachers was a central strategy of the observant reform, especially among the Dominicans, the Order of Preachers. Dozens of churchmen wrote or compiled sets of sermons for use throughout the liturgical year. Some were learned sermons for the academies and cathedrals, others contemplative and mystical homilies for the cloisters, and yet others the flamboyant oratory of itinerant missioners. But the books most in demand and most often reissued were those designed for the needs of parish preachers, dealing with the daily concerns of pastoral care and lay morality. Since that was their purpose, they adopted simplicity of style and content which would make their sermons immediately useful to unassuming preachers and accessible to urban congregations. Herolt's success in achieving this goal was unrivalled.

The Life of Johann Herolt, OP

Johann Herolt, OP, was a lector and prior of the Dominican cloister in Nürnberg in the mid-fourteenth century and vicar of the Katharinenkloster, the Dominican sister house. His works comprised a series of catechetical tracts: *Liber Discipuli de eruditione Christifidelium* (1416); a massive set of *de tempore* sermons

---

untapped by scholarship." Heiko A Oberman, *The Dawn of the Reformation* (Edinburgh: T. & T. Clark, 1986; Grand Rapids: W. B. Eerdmans Pub. Co., 1986, 1992), 26.

[4] Ian D. K. Siggins, *Luther and His Mother* (Philadelphia: Fortress Press, 1981; repr. Eugene, Oregon: Wipf & Stock, 2003), 54-60; George Yule, ed., "Luther and the Catholic Preachers of His Youth," *Luther: Theologian for Catholics and Protestants* (Edinburgh: T. & T. Clark, 1985; repr. 1986, 1988), 60-64. E. F. Jacob called the fifteenth century "a century of the sermon." E. F. Jacob, *The Fifteenth Century 1399-1485.* The Oxford History of England VI (Oxford: Clarendon Press, 1961), 280.

(1418, additions 1430); *de sanctis* sermons (1432); a complete Lenten series, *Quadragesimale* (1434); sermons on the Epistles for each Sunday (1444); three *Promptuaria exemplorum* or treasuries of exemplary stories (one thematic, one of miracles of the Virgin, and one of legends of the saints) containing altogether about 1,200 stories; in manuscript only, two delightfully colourful works, a series of Advent sermons, *Der Rosengart*, preached to the sisters of St. Katharine's in 1436; and a collection of natural illustrations, *Applicationes rerum naturalium ad sermones* (1463). Also ascribed to Herolt by the manuscripts are three sets of *Postils* according to the literal sense (1437-39), one of which was later republished as the pseudonymous *Postil of Guillermus Parisiensis*.[5]

Herolt called himself simply "a disciple." The pen name *Discipulus* was his only identification on the spate of writings that flowed from his pen. Modestly, he claimed no authorship, merely the task of a loyal compiler. This pious desire for anonymity did not blunt the impact of his books in the fifteenth century, but it left the events of his long life shrouded in obscurity.

Neither the date nor the place of Herolt's birth is known with any certainty. Since his active career spanned more than half a century, from his first composition in 1416 until his death in 1468, we may suppose that he was born sometime around 1386.[6] His birthplace has been the subject of conjectures that have been repeated as fact: on no good grounds, Robert Gery suggested in 1685 that Herolt perhaps sprang from Basel, and he was followed in that guess by a number of others.[7] G. W. Panzer, by contrast, admitted that Herolt's birthplace was unknown and suggested that he might always have been a Nürnberger, since it was certainly in Nürnberg that he lived and worked.[8]

Not only are Herolt's origins obscure, but little detail is known about his long career, in spite of the respect he certainly enjoyed. In the literary record of the

---

[5] A full account of the content of each work may be found in appendix 1.

[6] W. Stammler suggests "between 1380 and 1390" (*Die Deutsche Literatur des Mittelalters—Verfasserlexicon*, Berlin & Leipzig: de Gruyter, 1936, Bd II, 424), and J. B. Schneyer says "c.1386" ("Winke für die Sichtung und Zuordnung Spätmittelalterlicher Lateinische Predigtreihen," *Scriptorium* XXXII/2, 1978, 237).

[7] Robert Gery, "ad Historiam Literariam Clarissimi Viri" in the appendix to William Cave, *Scriptorum ecclesiasticorum historia literaria* (London: Richard Chiswell, 1688, 1689, and 1698); W. Walther, "Das sechste Gebot in J. Herolts Predigten," *Neue kirchlichen Zeitschrift* III (Erlangen 1892), 487; R. Cruel, *Geschichte der deutschen Predigt im Mittelalter* (Detmold: Meyer, 1879), 480.

[8] G. W. Panzer, *Älteste Buchdruckergeschichte Nürnbergs* (Nürnberg: J. E. Zeh, 1789), 56. See also Nicolaus Paulus, "Johann Herolt und seine Lehre," *Zeitschrift für katholischen Theologie (ZkTh)* 26 (1902), 418; Stammler, *Verfasserlexicon*, II, 424, and 2nd fully revised edition, Kurt Ruh, ed., Berlin and New York: de Gruyter, 1981), III/4, 1124.

Dominican Order itself, Quétif and Echard admitted that his esteem as "a pious, modest man, learned and at the same time avid for the salvation of souls" was known almost only from his writings.[9] What may be known with some clarity is as follows.

Herolt's output spanned almost half a century, from the catechetical writings of 1416 to the collection of sermon illustrations from nature in 1463. In this time, there were periods of especially intense productivity. The catechism and the first collection of Sunday sermons were issued within the years 1416 to 1418, both of them immense works already displaying a prodigious breadth of reading; but nothing is known about the circumstances of their compilation. Again in the 1430s and 1440s, a series of works suggesting still greater versatility and maturity came from his pen.

During this second period of flowering, we catch occasional glimpses of Herolt's other activities. He was by then (if not earlier) a member of the Dominican cloister at Nürnberg, the center of observant reform in Germany.

The Nürnberg cloister played a seminal and pioneering role in the spread of the observance, or strict return to the rule, not only in the province of Teutonia but also in Saxonia and Polonia. It had adopted the reform itself in 1396 as a result of the zealous efforts of Conrad de Grossis of Prussia, formerly the pope's penitentiary and reformer of the convent at Kolmar. With the blessing of both the general of the order, Raymond of Capua, and Pope Boniface IX, Conrad became the first prior of the observance at Nürnberg, and brought with him a number of friars from Kolmar to implement the reform.[10] (Raymond of Capua himself was visiting Nürnberg "out of love for the holy observance" when he died in October 1399, and he was buried in the choir before the high altar.)[11]

From the outset, a fervent commitment to preaching and training in preaching went hand in hand with restoration of the rule at Nürnberg. Prior Conrad was "a very fiery preacher and a most ardent zealot for souls."[12] His longest-serving successor, prior Eberhard Mardach, though inhibited from preaching by a speech impediment, used his inspiring personal influence and his devotion to scripture to secure perpetual endowments of preaching offices in parish churches. He ensured

---

[9] *SOP* I/2, 762. They also explain how the name "Berolis" (later attached to Herolt or to a hypothetical second writer) arose as a mere corruption.

[10] Johannes Meyer, OP, *Buch der Reformacio Predigtordens* IV and V, QF (1909), 3; Meyer, *Liber de Viris Illustribus Ordinis Praedicatorum*, 36-37, QF 12 (1918), 56-58; Meyer, *Chronica brevis Ordinis Praedicatorum*, QF 29 (1933), 92; Gabriel M. Löhr, OP, "Das Nürnberger Predigtkloster im 15. Jahrhundert: Beiträge zu seiner Geschichte," *Geschichte des Vereins für Geschichte der Stadt Nürnberg* 7 (1947), 223.

[11] Meyer, *Liber*, f. 37, *QF* 12, 56-57.

[12] Meyer, *Liber*, f. 37, *QF* 12, 56.

that the incumbent preachers had sufficient access to books and provisions and urged his friars to move out of the cloisters into the secular parishes.[13] What he could not achieve by speech, he made up by training, writing, and private counsel; and if (as seems likely) Herolt's first productions were penned under Eberhard's leadership, they were probably intended for this purpose.

In 1427, Johannes Nider, perhaps the most influential Dominican of his time, became prior of Nürnberg, an office he held for two years until he became vicar general of all reformed priories and monasteries in Germany. Nider too was a formidable preacher and writer and used the cloister at Nürnberg as a source of reforming manpower to spread the observance to other centers. Nider himself undertook the reform of the Basel convent during the Council of Basel, at the behest of the general chapter at Lyons in 1431.[14] Friars sent out from Nürnberg eventually won over to the observance Dominican houses at Cologne, Vienna, Leipzig, Erfurt, Magdeburg, Halle, Regensberg, Basel, Krems, Eichstätt, Bamberg, Landshut, Bern, Worms, Pforzheim, Bolzano, Wimpfen, Stuttgart, and others, carrying their commitment to pastoral preaching—and manuscript copies of sermon books—with them.

The Cloister of St. Katharine

Another initiative Nider undertook at Nürnberg also had special significance for the balance of Herolt's career. In 1428, Nider renewed the effort to reform the sister house in Nürnberg, the cloister of St. Katharine. Earlier, in 1397, Conrad of Prussia had obtained papal authorization and the support of the city council to put an end to the "unspiritual and gross laxity" of the sisters by demanding their obedience and the closure of the house, but the delegation of councillors and monks retired in disarray at the women's "shrewish and obscene" resistance, one of the sisters even violently attacking her father, a city councillor, with furious kicks. An attempt by the monks, with the help of some tradesmen, to break into the cloister by stealth and subdue the women by throwing flour in their eyes was soon detected, and two nuns counterattacked by trying to strike the prior on the head with a large crucifix: the blow was fortunately deflected.[15]

In spite of a series of instructions imposed on the sisters under threat of excommunication, and continuing supervision from the order, the need for reform was not greatly different when Nider became prior thirty years later. Abuses and deviations from the rule, defiance of the order's authority, lax observance of the vows, and breaches of enclosure were still normal. But Nider succeeded where Conrad

---

[13] Meyer, *Liber*, f. 37, *QF* 12, 58-59.
[14] Löhr, "Das Nürnberger Predigtkloster," 223.
[15] Walter Fries, *Kirche und Kloster zu St. Katharina in Nürnberg. Mitteilungen des Vereins für Geschichte der Stadt Nürnberg*, 25 (Nürnberg: J. L. Schrag, 1924), 19-23.

had failed. He used the strategy that was to prove so effective elsewhere: in 1428 he gained approval to import ten nuns from the reformed cloister at Schönensteinbach in Alsace and appointed one of them, Gertrud Gwichtmacherin, as first prioress of the observance.[16] (She remained forty-one years in that office until her death in 1469, surviving Johann Herolt by just one year.) Eight of the thirty-five sisters already at St. Katharine's chose to leave rather than submit to strict observance of the rule. The twenty-seven who remained joined with the ten emissaries in a reform, which "rejuvenated both their religious life and their intellectual activity."[17]

Over the next forty years, Johann Herolt was closely associated with this renewal as teacher, preacher, confessor, administrator, and advocate of the sisters of St. Katharine's. Because of the catalytic role of the men's cloister in the strategy of reform, its membership changed constantly as preachers were trained and sent out to spread the movement. St. Katharine's also played its part. Ten sisters were sent to reform the convent at Tulln in Austria in 1436, and in 1442-43 ten or eleven more went to Pforzheim for the same purpose. Herolt's role, by contrast, seems to have been to stay at the center, generate and refine the materials for training preachers, and fill senior administrative and pastoral offices of the twin cloisters in Nürnberg.

We know some of the years in which he held various offices, although precise information is sometimes obscured by confusion of the friars' names.[18] It is beyond

---

[16] Fries, *Kirche und Kloster*, 22, 26.

[17] William A. Hinnebusch, OP, *The History of the Dominican Order. Volume Two: Intellectual and Cultural Life to 1500* (Staten Island, NY: Alba House, 1973), 203.

[18] The records of the order show members at Nürnberg whose names were Joh. Her, Joh. Gerolt, Joh. Gernolt, Joh. Herolt, and Theod. Herolt (sometimes with variant spellings). It is not always possible to tell exactly who is meant. The only serious confusion surrounds the name *Theodericus* (or *Theodoricus*) *Herolt* (or *Heroldus*). There are at least two midcentury manuscripts of works undoubtedly by Johann Herolt which are attributed to "Theodoricus Heroldus de Nuremberga ord. pred" (Uppsala, Univ. C. 414ª, f.880; Wroclaw, Bibl. Uniw. IF 696 (xv), f. 329ª, not "in pluribus codicibus" as Kaeppeli claims, *SOPMA* 2, 450). Similarly, the fifteenth-century historian of the order, Johann Meyer, in 1466 assigned the whole corpus of Herolt's writings to "fr. Theodericus dictus Herold" (*QF* 19, 76-77). These contemporary identifications may well suggest that Theodericus and Johann were one and the same, in which case we should know that Johann Herolt was certainly in the cloister by 1431 at the very latest and was a Nürnberg delegate to the general chapter.

The modern Dominican historians Gabriel Löhr and Thomas Kaeppeli both reject the identification. Kaeppeli interprets the two manuscripts to mean that Theodoricus collected Johann's sermons, and Löhr asserts bluntly that Theodericus and Johann had nothing to do with each other, and that Johann had not arrived

dispute that Johann Herolt was vicar and cursor of St. Katharine's in 1436. When he preached to the sisters a heartfelt series of Advent, Christmas, and New Year sermons on the monastic virtues, *The Rose Garden*,[19] the handwritten catalogue the sisters made of their rapidly growing library listed the *"gut predigt, die unser liber vater vicarius, Johannes Herolt, predigt, do er noch kursor was."*[20] The sisters' catalogue eventually listed 370 codices in fourteen categories, a remarkable collection of books gathered by gifts and by copying, including German bibles, Psalters, Gospel books and other biblical materials, tractates, lives of the saints, works of the German mystics, Dominican and other sermons, including some delivered by their spiritual directors Johannes Nider, Gerhard Comitis, Michael Hecht, and Johann Herolt.[21]

Herolt became prior at Nürnberg in 1437. The city archives contain a notarized letter of 3 August 1437 to George, bishop of Bamberg, about the capacity of the monastic houses of Nürnberg to observe their rule. It was signed by the Benedictine abbot George of St. Egidius; Johannes N., prior of the Carthusians; and Johann Herolt, prior of the Order of Preachers.[22] He remained prior until 1443, when Andreas Reinfall succeeded him.

Shortly thereafter, we hear of Herolt's intercession on behalf of his charges at St. Katharine's. In December 1444, the Nürnberg City Council had obtained a bull from Pope Eugene IV requiring that the abbots of St. Egidius or the pastors of St. Sebald should make no convent visitations without the consent and presence of

---

in Nürnberg by 1431 (Kaeppeli, *SOPMA* 2, 450; Löhr, "Das Nürnberger Predigtkloster," 231, n. 23). Neither Löhr nor Kaeppeli, however, seems to have any other basis for this belief than an entry in Würfel's eighteenth-century necrology of St. Katharine's (based, he says, on an earlier Necrologium), which names both men as confessors to the nuns, and gives Theodericus's death as July 1448 and Johann's (correctly) as August 1468 (Andreas Würfel, *Totenkalender des Katharinen Klosters*, Altdorf, 1769. Löhr's knowledge of this entry is from Fries, *Kirche und Kloster*, 43, n. 108ª). The evidence is not conclusive, and it may well be that there was only one Herolt at Nürnberg.

[19] Nürnberg Stadtbibliothek, Cent. VII, 57, f. 2-114.
[20] Nürnberg Stadtbibliothek, Cent. VII, 79, 2: 0, XXIV.
[21] Nürnberg Stadtbibliothek, Cent. VII, 79, 2: E, XLV; M, XII; 0, XXIV; and see Franz Jostes, *Meister Eckhardt und seine Jünger*, Anhang II: Die Handschriften des Katharinenklosters in Nürnberg nach einem Verzeichnisse des 15. Jahrhunderts (Freiberg, Switz.: Universitätsbuchhandlung, 1895), 147, 158.
[22] Nürnberg Stadtbibliothek, Cent. V, 73, f. 110-111ᵛ. See also Friedrich Bock, *Das Nürnberger Predigtsklosters: Beitrage zu seiner Geschichte. Mitteilungen des Vereins für Geschichte der Stadt Nürnberg* 25 (1924), 147-187.

the civic councillors, nor make any further intrusions or changes.[23] In the following three years, the sisters of St. Katharine's were deeply disturbed by this requirement, which threatened the observance they had so laboriously developed, especially when it gave the city fathers occasion to impose financial exactions on the convent. In November 1447, the prioress and sisters wrote a letter of appeal to the procurator general of the order to take action in their difficulties, "lest the regular life, which for seventeen years until the present has been achieved in our monastery by means of immense toil and innumerable austerities and trials, be lost." The reform had been achieved "through the vigilance of our reverend vicars and fathers in Nürnberg, who have nurtured us generously and richly in spiritual things and maintained us in the regular life." The gross exactions the city was demanding were not only difficult but also impossible, they said.[24]

Four weeks later, on 19 December 1447, Johann Herolt supported the sisters' plea in his own impassioned letter to Fr. Guido Flamocheti, provincial (and soon to be general) of the Dominicans.[25] It is the only extant document in Herolt's own hand. He recounts the very great disturbance, anxiety, and distress the bull had inflicted on the nuns at St, Katharine's. "Unless the bull is revoked, I earnestly fear that the observance maintained by the sisters unbroken for seventeen years will be destroyed . . . Would not the vicar who has been with them constantly, and the confessors, and indeed the sisters themselves, have better knowledge of the fitness of these women than outsiders?" Herolt describes for Fr. Guido the perseverance of the nuns in and above their duties and the reforming works they had achieved elsewhere. The exactions demanded of them were against the authority of the order, inimical to the convent, and beyond the meager resources of the sisterhood to sustain. As their "unworthy vicar ardent but inexpert in this sort of cause," he begs for Fr. Guido's intervention. The bull was revoked, but similar crises were to recur.

For example, on 27 November 1459, Prioress Gwichtmacherin and her nuns wrote another protest to the Holy See about the effect on their cloistered life of externally imposed exactions—in this case against extra taxes and doubled tithes demanded of St. Katharine's by Bishop George of Bamberg.[26] Again, Herolt came to their aid, this time in a notarized deed of appeal against the bishop's demands by "Johann Herolt, confessor, and Ulrich Immerdorfer, chaplain, as the spiritual custodians of the cloister and sisters of St. Katharine's."[27] In this case, as in the earlier glimpses of Herolt's official actions, there is an abiding and consistent defense of the observance and its spiritual importance.

---

[23] Stadtsarchiv Nürnberg, Rep. 89, 183.
[24] Stadtsarchiv Nürnberg, Rep. 89, 184 (13 Nov. 1447).
[25] Stadtsarchiv Nürnberg, Rep. 89, 185 (19 Dec. 1447, in Herolt's own hand).
[26] Stadtsarchiv Nürnberg, Rep. 89, 193 (27 Nov. 1459).
[27] Stadtsarchiv Nürnberg, Rep. 89, 192 (27 Nov. 1459).

In recognition of his decades of commitment to the sisters' life of godliness, when the general chapter of the order met at Novara in Lombardy in June 1465, Herolt was appointed visitor to St. Katharine's with plenary powers "both in spiritual and temporal matters, in head and in members" for the sake of the "conservation, reformation, and regular observance of your convent."[28]

Johann Herolt died in August 1468, during a visit to the convent of St. Blasius in Regensberg. The work of reform among the Dominicans of Regensberg was shortly to begin, and was undertaken in the years that followed. Though Herolt did not live to see it, he was buried with honor in the Dominikanerkirche in Regensberg, where a bronze relief shows him with book and staff, and a plate records the year of his death.[29]

But the true monument to Herolt's long life is found in the sermon books. A full description of the huge scope of his enterprise and its extraordinary circulation may be found in the appendix, with a bibliographical listing of manuscripts and editions.[30] Here I shall make only a few introductory remarks about the style and presentation of his life's work.

The Sermon Books

The sermon books are written in Latin (the only German work, *The Rose Garden*, was taken down by the nuns as Herolt preached). Herolt's Latin is clear, grammatical, straightforward but not inelegant. For all its plainness, Herolt's style is distinctive. He is capable of passionate intensity and eloquence, but consciously avoids sophistication and pretentiousness. For his ultimate audience, the parish laity, his stated object was to "teach simple things to simple people," but the intermediary was the living voice of preachers who delivered or adapted these sermons. The arrangement, language, and apparatus of the books were therefore designed to ease the transformation of Latin sources on paper into lively, persuasive vernacular speech.

As we shall see, the content of Herolt's massive *vademecum* for preachers ranges from sublime reflections on grace to banal anecdotes, from heartfelt appeals to a life of sanctity to bizarre threats of death and hellfire. The preacher often repeats traditional views of society and nature uncritically, but sometimes he freely questions accepted moral opinion and takes distinctive positions on contemporary issues of doctrine or canon law. There is a pastoral purpose behind much of this diversity.

In Herolt's view, the preacher's task is to pitch the call to salvation to the various levels of spiritual understanding among the hearers. There are several

---

[28] Stadtsarchiv Nürnberg, Rep. 89, 197 (12 Jun. 1465).
[29] Hilarius M. Barth, OP, *Regensberg: Dominikanerkirche. Schnell Kunstführer* Nr. 48. 2. vollig neu bearb (Aufl., München & Zürich, 1973), 18.
[30] See Appendix 1: Herolt's Sermon Books.

broad classes of potential listeners who need their own form of appeal. Many people who live worldly and dissolute lives may attend only rarely and need a sharp sermon of reprobation to start them on the way to repentance. Beginners on the path of grace sometimes grieve over past sins, want to avoid them, and hope to do good. Others go on and examine their consciences, lose their thirst for worldly pleasures, and strive to love their neighbors. Some of them progress to a point where they fear only God, do not complain in adversity, but long for the life to come.

In practical terms, this mixture leads the preacher to deliver messages addressed to particular sections of the congregation. For example, part of a sermon may be specifically framed for a subgroup of married couples who, if it were not for their married state, might well have aspired to enter the religious life, and they are advised how to emulate that devoutness while remaining in the world. Special appeals are made to fervent young people to consider a monastic calling as the surest channel of grace. By contrast, many sermons expound austere moral rules for the everyday issues confronting the mass of a typical congregation in their lives in the cities and towns. The overview of the sermon books that follows attempts to reflect this diversity of topic.

The arrangement of Herolt's model sermons follows the traditional rules of the manuals of preaching method, the *artes praedicandi*. There is usually a very brief introductory exordium, often based on a biblical or philosophical epigram, and an outline of what will follow in point form. The major topics of each sermon, which may be loosely associated but more often form a connected series, are numbered. Within each topic in turn, numbered points and subpoints are nested and made memorable with distinctions, images, mnemonic devices, and above all exemplary stories. Patristic and scholastic authorities are cited constantly, in very many instances from the sources themselves rather than chrestomathies, and traditional clusters of images or even whole outlines may be imported and adapted without hesitation.

It is not unusual for a single chapter to contain thirty or more patristic and ecclesiastical authorities (including the decretals of canon law, which Herolt cites often) and twenty or thirty biblical texts. Biblical quotations are drawn from many parts of the Old and New testaments, but especially from the Psalms, Gospels, prophets, and Wisdom books. They are used on the whole out of context, as proof of points the preacher has already expounded. With a few exceptions, biblical passages are quoted with accuracy.

To aid the preacher's task of translation, Herolt early adopted the practice of including German equivalents for uncommon Latin expressions, or where the precise vernacular idiom was essential to his purpose. They may be sayings from popular superstition or folk custom, terms of the dance or of gambling games, contemporary approximations to age-old ethical terms, medical equivalents, and the like, many instances will be cited in the chapters that follow.

In other ways, too, the apparatus Herolt added to his books was intended to make them flexible and easy to use. In the largest books—the catechetical and *de tempore* series—the numbered sermons are interspersed with capital letters in alphabetical order as an indexing device, and a topical index uses these letters to guide the user to the desired subject. In some cases, too, appended tables suggest ways in which sections drawn from several sermons may be reordered to create a new sermon outline. An elaborate system of cross-referencing between the sermon books and the collections of exemplary stories allows the user to vary the choice of leavening images.

Although *The Rose Garden* and parts of the *Quadragesimale* reveal that Herolt was capable of tropological allegory, and the *Applications* show him a master of imagery drawn from nature and the bestiaries, his chosen pastoral style for parish preaching was largely explanatory, literal, and instructive rather than allusive or evocative. Nevertheless, as I hope the pages that follow will show, there is a fervent doctrine of salvation and a clear and unmistakable unity of purpose, which guides and shapes all Herolt's work.

This book begins with that doctrine of salvation, then turns to Herolt's exposition of the nature of the world, his instruction in life and morals, and finally his graphic vision of the last things.

Herolt's Achievement

My intention is to allow Herolt to speak for himself, but there can be no doubt about his importance as a harvester of the Augustinian homiletic tradition, as a contributor to an energetic monastic and pastoral reform movement, and as a presage of the immense religious changes to follow in Germany. In the course of this study, I have increasingly come to appreciate Johann Herolt for the quality of what he attempted and (like his English confrere, John Bromyard[31]) for his skill as a communicator.

---

[31] G. R. Owst, *Preaching in Medieval England: An Introduction to Sermon Manuscripts of the Period c. 1350-1450* (Cambridge: Cambridge University Press 1926) and *Literature and Pulpit in Medieval England: A Neglected Chapter in the History of English Letters & of the English People* (Cambridge: Cambridge University Press, 1933; 2nd rev. ed. Oxford: Blackwell and New York: Barnes & Noble, 1961).

Generations of devout and committed Christians were exposed to spiritual instruction of this quality. Its impact on the Brethren of the Common Life and on the religious upbringing of (for example) Erasmus, Staupitz, Zwingli, or Luther has not been examined in depth. To a great extent, the Reformation, in its religious beginnings, was a response to the deep concerns of late medieval spirituality.

THE CATHOLIC FAITH

1

PREACHING THE CATHOLIC FAITH

It is not surprising that Herolt, the compiler of model sermons for a brotherhood of preachers, gives preaching the central place in the church's promulgation of the faith.

God calls people to himself by placing the words of life in the preacher's mouth.[1] Preachers cast the net of the word of God to catch souls.[2] They are like the angels in informing and admonishing people by the word of God.[3] A single sermon may be enough to convert even a gross sinner.[4] Preaching is the display of the "goods for sale in God's market."[5] God's word is the spiritual bread that feeds the soul:[6] hearing and retaining it makes a person the disciple of Christ.[7] This word is such that whoever captures it is captured by it: we must make the heart meek and soft and tender for the word to be inscribed on it. The soul is clarified by the word more than by fasting, vigils, or any other discipline.[8] The preached word cleanses the soul because it is a mirror in which we recognize the stain of our sins and apply cleansing grace, it illuminates the mind, and it effects God's presence in the soul and frees us from death for eternal bliss.[9]

The catholic faith is therefore to be preached constantly to the Christian faithful and guarded and retained by them.[10] On the part of the hearers, this means that they must first of all attend sermons, and especially on feast days and in Lent. One of the tests people may apply to themselves to judge whether they are worthy to communicate, or indeed predestined to salvation, is willingness and

---

[1] T.74.1/2 (H).
[2] T.93.0 (before P).
[3] T.111.1/7 (Y).
[4] P.V.: 2-4 "Verbum Dei" (589, 590, 591).
[5] E.14.2/1.
[6] T.35.2/3 (Y), T.149.2 (C), Q.26.1.
[7] Q.9.1.
[8] E.24.3.
[9] T.35.2 (Y), T.68.2/6 (G), T.70.2/7 (Q), 9.25.1/2.
[10] T.41.0 (F), E.21.2/1.

delight in hearing the word preached.[11] On the other hand, it is a sign of spiritual malaise to avoid sermons: to flee the light of preaching is like the photophobia of the dying.[12] There was a rustic, Jacques de Vitry tells, who always left the church the moment the priest began his sermon and waited in the cemetery until he was done; but during his funeral, as the clergy sang the office for the dead, the image on the crucifix took its hands from the cross and blocked its ears.[13] Blatant sinners deliberately avoid sermons for fear they will have to amend, like the cripple who fled from village to village before St. Martin's preaching lest he be cured and lose his handouts.[14] Those who will not hear the word of God are openly of the devil, for they deny Christ entrance to the camp of their being: "the gate to a man's heart is the word of God."[15] Rather, Christians must listen to their preachers reverently and devoutly, hearing Christ in his preachers as if their words came directly from his lips. They must listen attentively, as closely as animals attend to the ground where they graze, and retentively, not like a sieve that comes out of the water as empty as it was before. They must listen with gladness for the many blessings they will gain by heeding and retaining the word of God.[16] It is self-deception to imagine that one can be cured of an illness or deformity merely by hearing the prescription; but those who hear, retain, and fulfil the word in their deeds will be blessed.[17]

On the part of the preachers, they should make the faith known by crying aloud, not so much with a shouting mouth as with fervor of heart. God instructs his preachers what to preach to the common people: useful, not subtle, things; simple matters for instruction, not profundities.[18] Herolt gives several versions of the basic content: "what is to be fled—sins; what is to be preserved—the commandments and the virtues; what is to be desired and sought—grace and virtue now, glory in the future."[19] Again, "their sins, and things useful, not subtle—the Ten Commandments; the articles of faith; the seven mortal sins; the seven sacraments; the punishments of hell and the joys of heaven."[20] Or in the form of the first work of spiritual mercy, "instruct the simple, ignorant and erring, urging them to come back to their senses from the way of error, now for the sake of avoiding offence to God, now for the sake of escaping the penalty, or now for the sake of gaining heavenly glory, recalling them to notice how momentary is what they delight in

---

[11] D.3.5/3 (Q), T.47.3/3 (F), T.149.2 (C), E.20.1/1.
[12] D.3.5/3 (Q), T.129.2/2 (Q).
[13] T.35.3 (B), P.V.: 8 "Verbum Dei" (595).
[14] P.V.7 I "Verbum Dei" (594).
[15] E.25.1.
[16] T.35.1 (U and Y).
[17] E.25.1.
[18] S. preface, Q.3.1.
[19] D.16.2/3 (G).
[20] Q.3.1.

and how eternal is what they kill."[21] As a summary of the principal lessons of scripture, "the catholic faith, to be believed . . . divine precepts, to be observed . . . mortal sins, to be repented (as to past) and avoided (as to future sins) . . . the last judgment, to be feared . . . the example of the saints, to be imitated . . . the pains of hell . . . and the rewards of the elect, to be desired."[22] The ground plan of Herolt's two earliest collections, the catechetical and *de tempore* sermons, fulfill this prescription precisely.

The doctrinal content of Herolt's exhaustive expositions of the Ten Commandments,[23] the Apostles' Creed,[24] and the Lord's Prayer[25] need not detain us here, since it is summarized in other chapters. What is of interest here, however, is his comments on the nature and efficacy of catholic tradition, his cautions on a misconceived faith, his strictures on heretics, and above all his elaborate catalogues of the superstitious, magical, and demonic opposition to the faith.

For the task of preaching the faith in all the world, the apostles received an overflowing measure of the Holy Spirit, and from this flood they irrigated the whole world. The holy doctors (such as Ambrose, Augustine, Gregory, and Jerome) were rivulets from this torrent, and the doctors of modern times are trickles from their streams.[26] Christian faith is the only faith attested by miracles: Christ, the first teacher of the Catholic faith, corroborated his teaching by miracles.[27] If there are fewer miracles in the modern church than in the primitive church, it is because at first the church needed to be inducted into faith and strengthened in it and because the church had so far accumulated little in its treasury of merits.[28] The twelve articles of faith contained in the Apostles' Creed were composed by the twelve apostles at the first council in Jerusalem, each apostle contributing one article.[29] One article pertains to the Father, six to the Son, and five to the Holy Spirit. Since faith is the foundation of all good, and the starting point of all salvation, in order to please God we must have a correct, complete, and firm faith; and the twelve apostolic clauses identify the articles of faith, which no Christian must doubt.[30] For this reason, the Creed is to be preached to the laity often, and every Christian of the age of discretion is bound to learn and know it. Parents and baptismal sponsors

---

[21] D.20.2/1 (H).
[22] E.2.2.
[23] D.1-10, T.142-143.
[24] D.22, T.146-147.
[25] D.21, T.65.
[26] T.71.2/3 (S).
[27] S.18.2/7.
[28] Q.8.1.
[29] D.22.0 (A), T.146.0 (A), S.2.1/9, S.6.1/2, S.8.1/14, S.12.2/6, S.19.1/5, S.20.1/8, S.24.1/8, S.28.1/5, S.33.1/5, S.36.1/5, S.38.1/6.
[30] D.22.0 (A), T.146.0 (A).

have a duty to instruct children in these articles of faith.[31] The sharpest trials of life, the preacher says, are not those that afflict us from without but the temptation from within to hesitate in the catholic faith and despair of God's mercy.[32] This trial reaches its climax at the moment of death, when the demons assail and impugn the faith—a microcosm for every man of the great persecution at the end of the age. The best defense against this frantic assault is to ask the dying whether they believe the twelve articles and to read or recite the Creed to them.[33]

The Christian must hold this faith integrally—that is, believe each one of the articles and all that mother church believes. The catholic faith is so concatenated that to deny one article is to dissolve the whole— like breaking a ring.[34]

In essence, the heart of the faith is the Trinity and Christology:

> "This is the victory that overcomes the world: our faith." We are speaking, then, about the catholic faith; and here the first question is, "What is true faith?" Answer: it is to believe that the Father and the Son and the Holy Spirit are one God, and that in these three persons is indivisible deity, coequal glory, and eternal majesty. The true faith also bids us believe that the Lord Jesus Christ is true God and man, eternally born of his Father according to his divinity, temporally born of his mother according to his humanity.[35]

Even though "every Christian is bound to believe the trinity of persons and the unity of the divine essence," the Blessed Trinity must nevertheless be simply believed, not curiously scrutinized.[36] Dangerous speculation about the inscrutable articles of faith is like smiting Christ's head.[37] Such inquisitive people belong to the generation of evil, who will not believe unless they see miracles.[38] It is only the presumptuous who falsify the faith by demanding evident reasons.[39] They vaunt themselves by trying to solve the inscrutable: they want to investigate the Holy Trinity and the articles of faith rationally, which is both prohibited and exceedingly perilous.[40] Christians must therefore expel from their minds thoughts about the abyss of God and his hidden things. To be familiar with God and think many things

---

[31] T.23.2/1 (H), T.41.0 (F) and .2 (G).
[32] T.29.1 (O).
[33] T.134.2 (S), T.135.2/1 (C).
[34] E.21.2/2.
[35] E.21.2/1.
[36] T.75.3 (S), T.146.0 (A).
[37] Q.31.2.
[38] Q.8.1.
[39] T.41.3 (G).
[40] D.1.5 (G), T.54.2 (R-S), E.6.4.

about him is surely good and salutary, but to question how God can be three and one, this ocean depth is too perilous. So it is to investigate the incarnation, how a virgin could conceive and deliver, or the Eucharist, how the whole Christ hanging on the cross can be present under the form of bread. Those who engage in such subtle and fruitless speculations fall into great errors, complacency, and spiritual pride and dig a deeper pit of damnation for themselves.[1]

Rather, the faith is a light that makes us aware of ineffable truths and allows us to assent to those gifts, which we could not possibly have known naturally—the perpetual virginity of Mary, that God became man, that so large a body hung on the cross is under so small a host. These exceed all human sense and cannot be grasped except by faith.[2]

Overinquisitiveness is only one of the obstacles people throw up to block the light of faith. Christ, the true light, illumines all men by his words of promise just as a visible light manifests itself by its rays; yet all men are not illuminated. Some shut themselves up in a house of shadows; they affect ignorance, scorning to know what they could and should know in order to be free from sin. Some close their eyes, suppressing the light of knowledge by neglect or crass ignorance. And some block the light of faith by deliberately interposing the obstacle of mortal guilt.[3] Though invincible ignorance (the ignorance of the child or of mental impairment) is excused, ignorance of the faith from neglect, frivolity, or disdain is no excuse.[4] Indeed, Herolt says, the preaching of the word of God still has the same effect as the raising of Lazarus had on Christ's contemporaries. It makes some good people better, converts some evil people to good, and makes other evil people worse.[5] Evil men cannot hear the word of God because the truth seems too hard for them, or the truth is contrary to their deeds, or their hearts are elsewhere inclined, like vases with their mouths pointing down.[6] Even to hear the things that are for the soul's great blessing will cause a person in a state of spiritual lethargy to rankle and grow annoyed at the preacher.[7] Other hearers doubt whether the faith is really as the holy scriptures say or as the catholic doctors hold,[8] or say equivocally, "If it is as scripture and the catholic faith holds, so what?!" not contradicting outright but not believing firmly either.[9] Still others say that they believe in God, but by their actions show the opposite.[10]

---

[1] T.137.2/4 (U).
[2] E.40.3.
[3] Q.32.1.
[4] D.1.4 (G), D.12.11 (B-C), T.93.5 (T).
[5] 31.1.
[6] T.35.3 (A).
[7] D.16.2/3 (G).
[8] T.142.1/1 (R).
[9] D.1.3 (F), E.21.2/2.
[10] T.62.0 (before X).

By contrast, as the risen Christ showed five wounds to his disciples, so there are five marks of salvation through the catholic faith: a person's faith must be pure, with no admixture of falsehood or vanity; it must be certain so that nothing seems truer or surer; it must be strong and constant so that one is prepared to stake one's word, and in extreme circumstances one's life, on maintaining its truth; and it must be lively in good works, for a *fides non operans* is nothing but a dead corpse, a craftsman, without a tool, an armorer without metal, a ship without sailors.[11] Instead of a dubious or speculative or sterile faith, Herolt urges a heartfelt existential faith: the knowledge that "God is your creator and you his creature . . . he is your lord and you are his servant . . . he is your father and you his child . . . he is your redeemer and you must love him . . . he is your future judge and you must fear him."[12]

Because this faith is the foundation of all merit, it follows that all unbelievers are in a state of damnation and at the last judgment will immediately be consigned to the devil.[13] Of all unbelievers, the worst are heretics, for they corrupt the faith of a Gospel they have themselves professed.[14]

---

[11] E.21.2/2.
[12] D.30.3/2 (E), T.73.3/2 (D).
[13] D.1.1 (E), T.5.2 (E), T.142.1 (Q), E.21.2/1.
[14] E.40.3/1.

2

FALSIFYING THE FAITH: HERESY AND SUPERSTITION

Herolt makes only a few formal remarks about heretics in general. In his sermon on identifying heretics and hypocrites, he lists five telltale signs. First, heretics preach in secret—an obvious sign of malice. Truth does not seek corners, and a doctrine in a corner is suspect. Secondly, heretics slander the church's hierarchy and try to convince people that the clergy's resistance to their lies is merely envy. Next, they prefer to talk to "little women and the simple" who cannot understand their frauds and perversely set out to make broad the way to heaven Christ has made narrow. They oppose the ordinances and precepts of the church, misrepresent its festivals as moneymaking institutions, and mock the efficacy of its rituals and sacraments. And they assume a pose of highly visible sanctity, hoping to convince the gullible by their public devotions.[15] In one place only, he gives a rather idiosyncratic list of notable heretics in history:

> Arius who, acknowledging the three persons in the divinity, believed in three Gods . . . Saduceus who denied the resurrection of the dead [cf. Matt. 22:23] . . . Berianus who denied suffrages for souls; Manicheus who praised virginity and condemned marriage; and Jovinianus who on the contrary allowed marriage but despised the purity of virginity. And Johannes Hus of Bohemia, the greatest heresiarch, who was burned at the Council of Constance, but still has not had his full punishment, which accrues to him from day to day and from year to year![16]

But he usually identifies heresy with those sectarian challenges to the priestly religion that are more familiar to his listeners: "wretched heretics" who lyingly claim that matrimony is illegal or assert that mere fornication is no mortal sin; attack

---

[15] T.100.1 (Q).
[16] S.20.2/7.

the power of the hierarchy and clerical freedom from civil restraint; oppose the sacramental acts with their own magic and rituals; and scoff at moral regulations, claiming that the priests have confused custom with immorality.[17]

Herolt's treatment of heresy is not as energetic as the pastoral interest with which he catalogues "the classes of men who falsify the faith"—the superstitious practitioners of alternative magic. The most inclusive list is at the very beginning of his written output, in the 1416 exposition of those "many, many people" who transgress the first commandment in a multiplicity of ways;[18] but this list is amplified and expanded in the later sermon books.

What is noteworthy about Herolt's list is that the "heresies that falsify the catholic faith" are the folk rituals, animistic superstitions, women's lore and rustic traditions that formed the age-old, syncretistic, but organic folk religion of much of rural Europe.

He condemns as contradicters of catholic faith "those who observe times and Egyptian days"—days of evil omen which are believed inauspicious for certain actions. The "Egyptian days" proper were described by patristic tradition as inventions of the mathematicians of Egypt, who devised arcane formulae for identifying the dismal days of each month,[19] but Herolt uses the idea more broadly to include all forms of calendar-based superstition. So he speaks of "those who believe Innocents' Day and many other days to be Egyptian"[20]—that is, refrain from activities or expect bad luck on the Feast of the Holy Innocents (Childermas) and, for the coming year, the day of the week on which it fell.

It is, he says, quite legitimate to observe the calendar in performing actions which depend on natural causation. For instance, the celestial motions of the planets and the course of the stars influence the efficacy of medicines, sowing crops, planting trees, and the like, and observing the propitious and unpropitious times is not idolatry but sagacity and prudence; but to observe days and seasons in actions which depend wholly on human choice—doing business, marrying, collecting herbs, or other "inchoate" acts—is mortal sin.

Instead, one should regard every day as good because every day was made by God, and rather than obsessing over what day a task or journey starts, the Christian should begin every undertaking with the protective sign of the cross, say the Lord's Prayer and the Creed, and trust that everything will go prosperously with God's help.

---

[17] D.1.2 (F), T.25.0 (before K), T.100.1 (Q).

[18] D.1.1-24 (E-X).

[19] See Charles Dufresne Du Cange, *Glossarium Mediae et Infimae Latinitatis*, ed. D. P. Carpenter and G. A. L. Henschel (Paris 1842, II), 846.

[20] The edition at Strasbourg: Koberger 1492 also includes "Innovation Day" in the list, but the other editions omit it. It is presumably a misreading.

One seasonal practice the preacher singles out for special censure is the age-old celebration of the solstices as assimilated to the liturgical calendar: "Those who perform their incantations on the night of the birth of Christ or of John the Baptist sin reprehensibly."[21]

It is a falsification of the catholic faith to pay heed to dreams or to act on the basis of dreams. The Levitical prohibition of dream divination (Leviticus 19:26), together with their general ambiguity, is sufficient reason to pay no heed to our dreams, Herolt thinks; but he takes the opportunity to pass on the received wisdom about how dream images are formed.

First, dream images reflect bodily disposition: if the sleeper is cold, he may dream he is in ice or snow. They also reflect the dreamer's psychological characteristics and humors: choleric people have one sort of dream, sanguine people another, and so on. Anxious people, for instance, dream they are in dangerous situations, imagining that they are being chased by swords, eaten by wild dogs, or falling from a great height. Yet not all dreams mirror the external situations directly, but present reality by opposites. Thus a second factor affecting dreams is the fullness or emptiness of the stomach, as we all know from dreaming about food when we are hungry. A third factor is our preceding thoughts and preoccupations, an obvious and common experience, since the things we have been thinking about attentively often recur in our dreams.

But these physiological and mental influences aside, dreams can also be inculcated into our sleeping imagination either by God, directly or through the angels, granting visions tracing out future events ("but this happens rarely, except to specially good and perfect people"), or else by demons, who lead many astray by this device ("and this is not unusual at all"). However, as Gregory says in the *Moralia*,[22] dreams so interchange the qualities of objects that it is not at all obvious from what impulse they spring, and they are therefore far too hard to believe. Accordingly, anyone who undertakes to interpret dreams commits a double sin: they sin by trusting the dream in the first place and then compound it by involving others in their vanities.[23]

Chief among the falsifiers of the catholic faith are the patrons and practitioners of an alternative magic. Christians make themselves golden calves like the Israelites in the wilderness when they betake themselves to pythonesses, soothsayers, and spellbinders and treat them as if they were gods, when in fact they are violators of the faith, pagan, apostate, and enemies of God. Herolt describes the purposes that draw people to these deceivers.

In his terminology, a "pythoness" is usually a clairvoyant who claims to be able to locate hidden objects, such as lost property or stolen goods, or to foresee

---

[21] D.1.7 (H), T.41.4 (H), T.142.1/3 (R), Q.19.2, E.21.2/2.
[22] Gregory, *Moralia in Iob*, 5.46.
[23] D.1.8 (J), T.2.2/4 (M), T.41.5 (H), T.142.1/4 (R), Q.19.2, E.21.2/2.

the future. There are two errors in consulting them. First, it is a fatal error to seek counsel from the devil, who is the mortal enemy of us all and preserves an ill will toward us; and anyway, they cannot be believed, since the devil is the father of lies, and in practice their advice is often defamatory:

> A certain count had such a pythoness in one of the cities in his jurisdiction; she used to reveal hidden and secret information. The count went to her to test her, and asked about two horses he claimed had been stolen from him. She indicated who had stolen them and where they had gone. He said, "Oh, what a great liar you are! The people you name are innocent and blameless, for my horses are still in my stable!"[24]

Closely associated with the pythonesses are the diviners and soothsayers, from whom people not only make inquiries but also seek practical results. Sometimes a person will ask God or the appropriate saint for a cure for a headache or a toothache, and if it is not immediately forthcoming, they will impatiently go to a soothsayer instead. Or the motive may be to uncover the identity of a thief or to gain someone's love or to achieve material wellbeing or to find out some future event such as who will have to marry whom.

There are three different ways such an act of divination can be carried out, Herolt says, and they are not all equally serious. If a person really believes that by this act he will achieve the intended purpose, it is a very grave sin. If he does not believe it actually works, but out of curiosity experiments to see whether it has any efficacy or not, this too is a mortal sin, though less serious, because the sin consists in wavering in the catholic faith. If someone performs an act of divination out of mere levity or naivety, without intending or expecting to achieve anything by it, but just for fun, it is merely a venial sin in a layperson (though mortal in a cleric, who must know better).[25]

Particular forms of prognostication are singled out for description and censure. The casting of lots can take several forms. Sometimes dice are thrown and the point-score interpreted, or predictions are made from throws of the dice on a special book for the purpose called "the book of lots." Or people surreptitiously deposit a heap of salt and some strips of paper (with or without writing) and wait to see who picks them up or prearrange a bundle of sticks of varying lengths and see who takes the shorter or longer stick. Another method is to allow a book to fall open at random and remark what passage presents itself. A special form of this practice is the chance inspection of the Psalms, Gospels, or other passages of scripture.[26]

---

[24] D.1.9 (J), T.41.7 (I), T.54.2/2 (S), T.142.1/5 (R), Q.19.2, E.36.2/2.
[25] D.1.6 (G), E.36.2/2-3.
[26] D.1.14 (M), T.41.12 (L).

An even more serious confusion of the church's legitimate supernatural powers with popular distortions is the use of sacramental matter—baptismal water or an uneaten host—to perform divinations. The difficulty of making clear to the simple laity where the rights and wrongs of this practice lie is obvious in the story Herolt chooses as illustration. It makes three points: First, the attempt at divination is evil; secondly, the church's magic will not work for such unsanctioned purposes; and thirdly, that magic, if not transferable, is nevertheless very powerful indeed:

> A woman received the sacrament of the eucharist in her mouth, and let it fall from her mouth into a cloth, intending to perform her divinations with it. After she had carried it with her for four weeks but had not achieved what she had in mind, she was so provoked that she built a fire in her home, shut the door, and took the sacrament from her purse. Then Christ spoke to her: "Daughter, what are you going to do to me?" She said, "I am going to throw you in the fire!" Christ said, "Daughter, why do you want to burn me?" She replied, "Because I have carried you for a month now, and got nothing I wanted!" and threw the eucharist from her lap toward the fire. Thereupon Christ jumped back from the fire into her lap and said, "Even if you do not want to have me, yet I do want to have you and be with you." Immediately remorseful and afraid, she knelt down and begged forgiveness. Then she placed the sacrament in a dish, and ran straight to the priest and told him everything. So the priest went and carried the sacrament back into the church, and enjoined penance on the woman, who henceforth served Christ faithfully for the rest of her life.[27]

Yet another common form of illicit fortune-telling, the preacher says, is chiromancy, either by examination of the palms of the hand (and especially the lifeline to see how long someone will live) or by inspection of the fingernails to discover whether anything new is about to befall the person.[28]

Perhaps even more common than prognosticating the future is the attempt to influence it by magical means—a topic that gives Herolt the opportunity to explain that the appearance of other supernatural powers outside the catholic faith is illusory. This is his central pastoral lesson, whether the magic is the exotic spellbinding rituals of the "crones and crooners" or the banal superstitions of everyday life.

Most of the charms and spells he mentions are cures for human or animal ailments. Presumably as a remedy for headache, the charmers take the sufferer's

---

[27] D.1.19 (R), T.41.17 (O).
[28] D.1.20 (S), T.41.20 (P).

belt, circle and measure his head with it, then place the belt under his feet while he repeats, "Better I tread on you than carry you!" Some people even try to justify the action by claiming that the Virgin Mary once cast a spell on John the Evangelist when he had a headache, but it is false, the preacher says. As a cure for the eyes, the healers touch the earth with their hand, then touch the afflicted person's eyes with the same hand, reciting the appropriate formula. Others wash the sufferer's feet and then use the water to bathe the eyes—a practice that actually does more harm than good, Herolt comments. There are other healing methods in common use too. The enchanters lie people on the ground in the form of a cross and in this position measure them with a thread, then they burn the thread and give them the ashes to drink in water that has been drawn in silence. Sometimes they lead their clients through flowing water, or chant their spells with their backs turned to the sunrise, or lead people up to a tree and make them shake it. There are spells for healing wounds and others to stanch bleeding.[29]

A natural focus of the women's healing magic was childbirth, but the beneficial elements of emotional support and traditional midwifery enshrined in this lore are not exempted from the preacher's censure of superstition. If a woman is undergoing a difficult delivery, her husband's belt will be placed about her to ease the labor. A *carminatrix* will bless a woman in childbed with an unsheathed sword or blow out a lighted candle in her face or place a branch under the mattress where she is lying. Such charms are described as if they were of a piece with advice about contraception or abortion and are contrasted with the church's legitimate alternatives—incense, consecrated tapers, holy water, and the sign of the cross.[30]

There are other recurrent events in family life that also prompt people to have recourse to the spellbinders. It is a common practice, the preacher says, for women to take their sick, and especially their sick children, to the crones for cures and spells; and in so doing they falsify the faith of Christ. Such incantations have no healing efficacy, even if God sometimes allows it to appear otherwise because of the strength of people's trust. While the use of medicine and herbs for healing is good, since they have their effect by natural means, healing without medicines is a miracle that befits only God or the saints' intercession.[31]

The other occasion when there is grave danger for "the falsifiers and bereft of faith—enchantresses, sorcerers, soothsayers and proponents of fate" and those who trust them—is the deathbed. The faith of one in the midst of the death struggle is already violently assailed by the demons who wish to snatch the soul, and how can one who has already begun to stray from the catholic faith by recourse to such superstitions stand firm under that assault? Once again, the church has an

---

[29] D.1.16 (O), T.41.16 (O), T.142.1/9 (R), Q.19.2.
[30] D.1.15 (N), T.41.14 (N), T.142.1/8 (R).
[31] D.1.16 (O), T.41.16 (O), T.142.1/9 (R), S.27.2/2, Q.12.1.

alternative set of legitimate rituals—crucifix, candles, recitation of the Creed—that will strengthen the dying in their last agony.[32]

If it is a dangerous confusion to use the sacraments and sacramentals for divination, so it is foolish to use them as charms. People try to gain healing power from the palm fronds blessed on Palm Sunday by swallowing them. Oblations in masses or tapers, bread, or other objects offered over the crucifix on Good Friday are also used as charms or cures; and some people make themselves a ring from a coin offered over the crucifix, imagining that it will prevent their falling ill. Other abuses of sacral objects include measuring oneself with a consecrated stole or measuring the light thrown from St. Blasius's lamp.[33] Herolt agrees with Nicolaus Jauer's *Tractate on Superstitions*[34] that consecrated objects are not only abused by such practices, but what is more gain no healing power from being consecrated, since they were set apart to rouse people's reverence and devotion, not to be used as charms.[35]

Spells are often directed not at healing existing ailments, but at providing protection from future harm. Spells are cast on swords so that they cannot wound; some charms guarantee against fire or drowning, and spells are even cast on people—to allure a lover, protect a friend, or harm an enemy. Animals as well as humans are the objects of preventive or curative measures. There are spells for curing horses, cattle, or other stock of worms. There is a formula for blessing flocks when they are driven out in the morning so that wolves will not savage them and a similar spell for protecting lost animals from wild beasts. For human protection against dogs or wolves, people spell themselves with the wounds of Christ, and snake charmers cast spells on snakes to prevent them from biting.[36]

There are charms that take the form, not of incantations and rituals, but of letters—pieces of paper with various forms of writing on them, worn about the neck or kept on the person as a cure for toothache, eye ailments, or other illnesses, as a guard against death in childbirth, or as an insurance against death by fire

---

[32] T.134.2/1 (S).

[33] According to the Golden Legend, anyone who annually offers a candle in a church named for St. Blasius gains prosperity (Jacobus de Voragine, *Legenda aurea*, 3rd ed., ed. Th. Graesse, (Bratislava 1890, 169). According to the late but widespread legend (*MPG* CXVI 817-30), St. Blasius was bishop of Sebaste in the fourth century and was martyred under Licinius. He was said to have miraculously saved a child with a fish bone caught in its throat and hence became a patron of the sick, especially with throat ailments. He was one of the fourteen "auxiliary saints" and was very popular in Germany.

[34] See Adolph Franz, *Der Magister Nikolaus Magni de Jawor* (Freiburg im Breisgau: Herder, 1898), 151-196, 255.

[35] D.1.17 (R).

[36] D.1.16 (O), T.41.15-16 (N-O), T.142.1/9 (R), Q.19.2.

or drowning. They may contain sentences to be read or prayers to be prayed or characters merely to be carried about, perhaps with a prohibition against opening them. One such protective letter is called the *longitudo Christi* and contains only a series of incomprehensible names.[37] They are all gravely sinful superstitions, Herolt warns, and explains that any apparent efficacy they may have is simply a psychological effect of the credence placed in them by gullible people:

> A certain gentlewoman had an eye ailment, and went to the schools to ask if any of the scholars knew how to write something for her eyes; if any scholar should help her, she would buy him a new tunic. One of them came forward and said he knew how to write such words. He wrote a paper for her, wrapped it up in a piece of paper for her, and then wrapped it up in a piece of cloth and gave it to her to carry on her person. She was by no means to open it, but if she regarded it with the firmest hope, it would certainly help her. And so her eyes were healed. Then another gentlewoman who suffered from a similar eye condition asked how she had been cured, and she described how she had been made well by the letter. She begged her insistently to let her have the letter too, and grudgingly and with great resistance she yielded to her, on condition that on no account whatever would she open it, but return it to her in the same condition in which she entrusted it to her. This woman was similarly cured, and returned the letter. She gave the letter with the same stipulation to a third woman suffering the same eye ailment, and she too was cured and returned the letter to her. But meanwhile, the scholar who had written the letter, having received his new tunic, left the city. Finally the woman who owned the letter, overcome with curiosity to see what was in it, opened the letter and found nothing in the writing but the gibe, "*The devil tear out your eyes and throw mud in the sockets!*" Stung with remorse, she went straight to the parish priest and told him the whole story, showed him the letter, and told him how all three women had been cured by means of the faith they had placed in it.[38]

This is the burden of Herolt's quite elaborate argument against the efficacy of all forms of folk magic. It is particularly striking that this influential Dominican does not mention witchcraft, nor does he believe that collusion between the falsifiers and the devil represents deployment of real supernatural powers. Rather, the devil will use all sorts of trickery and illusion to encourage belief in the soothsayers' powers of persuasion, but they have no real efficacy, nor does the devil have carte blanche

---

[37] T.41.15 (N), S.27.2/2.
[38] D.1.16 (Q).

to perform genuine magic. The real danger is that sinful men and women will be diverted by superstition from the integrity of the catholic faith, and thus come to place their trust in the creature rather than God, and by loving something more than God miss their salvation.[39]

The demons, to be sure, have a stake in these bizarre forms of anti-catholic belief. To ask a pythoness for information about the future is to seek advice from the devil, but it is deceptive advice, both because the devil is invariably a liar, but also because demons have no supernatural knowledge of the future anyway. They know the secrets of people's hearts only by external signs and expressions, and their knowledge of the future is limited to what they can predict on the basis of observation. Even humans can do that: astronomers predict the weather from observing the skies, and physicians predict death or recovery from the appearance of the urine. But demons appear to have access to the future because their knowledge, though natural, is superior to ours owing to the subtlety of their angelic nature, their six thousand years' expertise in malice, and their access to unearthly services.[40] Therefore, those who want to predict the future by magic science or judge the secrets of people's hearts are not exercising numinous powers; they are merely overreaching themselves.[41] Demons may be the source of inspiration for the deceptive and perhaps nonsensical words some old hag uses for her spells, and as we have seen, demons often use their capacity to produce misleading dreams; but most of their energy, in Herolt's view, goes into maintaining the credibility of the charlatans and the credulity of their clients. For example, because of human sinfulness, God sometimes allows the devil to deprive someone of the use of one of his members or senses—sight or hearing or mobility. When the victim goes to an enchantress, the devil stops troubling the limb or sense concerned; and so the person thinks the spell has helped, even though it has no natural effect. This is precisely the same technique the demons used to gain sacrifices for dumb idols in ancient times.[42] Similarly,

> We read an example of a certain devout man who, on his way to the wood, recognized a devil in human form tending pigs (it was autumn, when pigs are driven to the woods to eat the beechnuts). The devout hermit asked the devil what he was doing there, and he replied, "I am guarding those pigs so that they are not harmed by wolves and wild animals. The enchanters have sung a spell over them, and I am guarding them very carefully so that people will persist in their error!"[43]

---

[39] D.I.23-24 (T-U), T.41.23-24 (P-Q).
[40] E.30.3/6.
[41] E.6.4.
[42] D.1.16 (O), T.41.16 (O).
[43] D.1.16 (O), T.41.16 (O).

The falsification of catholic faith lies not in possession of real magical power, but in the power attributed to magic.

Herolt is therefore concerned to explain at length why enchantments sometimes seem to help. The first reason, as we have just seen, is devilish sleight of hand, made possible by human sinfulness. The second is to test our faith: God allows spells or predictions to appear effective so that the authenticity of our faith may be proven. "Good Christians are not separated from Christ even by torments, but tepid and negligent Christians are sometimes separated from him by idle tales." The third reason is that people have meager confidence in God but firm though unwarranted confidence in the spells and enchantments. If it were not for people's confidence in such acts, they would be no help at all.[44]

The words of spells cannot possibly warrant this self-deceiving trust for three reasons. First, they have no natural efficacy, for if they did they would always help, whereas the opposite is often the case. Secondly, they have no intrinsic worth, for the words of some old woman are certainly not as worthy or effective as Christ's own words in the Lord's Prayer. And thirdly, they have no efficacy from their institution since God did not institute them, and therefore they do not possess the invariable power of the divinely instituted words of consecration. In other words, whatever competition there is in practice between magical rites and churchly rites, there is spiritual power only on the church's side.

But granted that they have no numinous power, someone may ask, if the words of a spell are good words, is there any harm in them? Yes, the preacher says, first because in practice there is hardly ever a spell whose good words are not mixed together with some vanity or falsehood; secondly, because even pure words are usually accompanied by a ritual action that falsifies them by attributing power to some created object; and thirdly, even if both words and actions were unexceptionable, it would still be sin because it is prohibited by the church.[45]

Herolt is determined not to ascribe genuine demonic powers to superstitious practice but to stress the pastoral consequences of dabbling in the arcane. There is no suggestion here of illicit pacts with the devil or of the potency of any resulting charisma. Herolt is engaged in a patient educational effort to debunk lay belief in any genuine power, other than psychological, in what the spellbinders perform. He brings the same corrective common sense to bear on reports of poltergeists and werewolves.[46] This is his approach even to the more exotic forms of divination.

He lists the practice of necromancy among the falsifications of catholic faith. It is performed, he says, by calling up the dead; "but since such necromancy is not in ordinary use among common folk, for the present we shall say no more about it." He will certainly avoid filling the minds of his audience with bizarre speculations

---

[44] D.1.16 (P).
[45] D.1.16 (Q).
[46] E.48.3/5-7.

that are not pastorally expedient. Instead, he takes the opportunity to lay to rest some more familiar myths about dying. When a person sweats during the death struggle, some people say that it is baptism, that on leaving life one exudes the same baptism one received on entering it. This is wrong. Some say that the departing soul will have no rest so long as the church bells are ringing, others that the soul should still be regarded as present so long as the bells ring. More elaborately, some people claim that the departing soul spends the first night with the Blessed Virgin, or with St. Gertrude, the second with the archangel Michael, and on the third night goes to its appointed destination. This too is wrong. Others again say that souls leave purgatory on Saturday evening and enjoy a respite until the moment the first person begins work on Monday morning. "And from this they want to infer that it is a sin to get up too early on Monday morning!" Yet others perform a superstition with the needle with which a corpse has been sown up.[47]

Herolt's instances of augury are also of the trivial, everyday sort. It is empty superstition, he says, to pay heed to the motion, song, or flight of birds, for instance, when a hen crows or a cuckoo cries *kuk-kuk* or ravens land on the rooftop (supposedly the signs of some special event). People also take foolish notice of when the dogs bark or whether a hare or a wolf crosses their path.[48]

The spiritual error of such auguries is made clear when Herolt turns to the popular notion of "fate." It is popular, he says, to ascribe both external events and inner dispositions to the constellations and the influence of the planets. People say, "It is fate," even when they are talking about their own sins. Herolt agrees with Chrysostom: "If someone were to become an adulterer or murderer because of a star, great would be the iniquity of the stars; but greater still his who created the stars." For if God had not foreseen what mischief the stars would do, he would not be omniscient; if he knew but was unwilling to make a change, he would not be good; if he wanted to but could not, he would not be omnipotent—all of which is contrary to Christian faith. God is all these things, and so it is a grievous sin against faith to ascribe responsibility to fate.

Yet all manner of everyday expressions do so. People twist their sins back on God by blaming the stars, cut the thread of human free will, make God's commandments empty, and rob good works of their praiseworthiness. Yet people explain their actions and passions by declaring, *"Das ist mir beschert"* (It's my portion), a saying Herolt counters with another: *"Das bescheren und das verdienen lauffent mit einander"* (one's portion and one's deserts go hand in hand). "If you don't steal, you won't be hanged," he says. But when someone does die an evil death by hanging or burning, people say, "That's how it had to happen," "God wanted it and arranged it," "He was born to this end," and "He was bound to do and suffer such things." This is

---

[47] D.1.13 (L-M), T.41.10 (K).
[48] D.1.12 (L), T.41.9 (I), T.142.1/7 (R).

to speak against the honor of God. Such events must be ascribed to human malice, not divine ordination.

It is true that particular temptations may prey on those tendencies of our animal sensuality that are under astral influence. One constellation may incline a person to a given vice or virtue more than another—for example, some inclination in one born under Venus to lust, under Mars to war, under Virgo to chastity—but to claim that birth signs control the vices or virtues is to contradict the faith. The stars impose no necessity to sin. Nor do they dictate people's occupations—money changers under Libra, fishermen under Aquarius, and so on. Man was not made for the stars, but the stars for man. No one sins unwillingly, and therefore no one must blame fate for his sins.[49]

People often deny the freedom of the will for extremely mundane reasons. When someone becomes embroiled in an illicit love affair, people say, "He's trapped. She has made him so that he can't be separated from her!" Or they explain mutual hatreds as quite involuntary. But no man, nor all the demons together, can so fragment the free will that anyone must unavoidably sin.[50] If a deterministic notion of fate attributes God's gifts and works to something other than God, so does a naive belief in chance.

Herolt condemns a series of popular superstitions about chance discoveries. A stupid credulity has grown up, he says, about finding a bird's nest with a mother bird sitting on eggs or chicks, to the point where some people take the nest home and keep it as a supposed source of fruitfulness and wealth. If the nest is preserved unbroken, they imagine that good fortune will never leave the household so long as the nest remains intact. If the mother bird is actually captured, it is believed to have wonder-working powers to effect reconciliation in love and to gain unparalleled prosperity. But there is no other author of fruitfulness and prosperity than God most high. Other versions of the same superstition include old women who believe that it is better to find a little scrap of iron than a whole lot of gold, or that it is very lucky to find a pin, or that it is better to find a nickel than a quarter. Again, they think it is very unlucky to find an egg or an ox but very lucky to stumble upon a wolf or snake or a lizard or a toad. Some also claim that a ring made from three iron keys which have been discovered by chance will protect the wearer from illness.[51]

The credulous also attach good or bad fortune to other quite natural events. They say that when a couple goes to bed on their wedding night, the one that falls asleep first will die sooner.[52] Or if a crone crosses your path early in the morning, you will have bad luck that day (some even contrive to have children cross their path when they begin a difficult task, Herolt scoffs, to avoid this superstitious effect). Some attribute bad luck to getting out of bed on the left side or putting

---

[49] D.1.11 (K), T.21.1 (S), T.41.8 (I), T.142.1/6 (R), Q.14.3, Q.32.2/2.
[50] T.41.11 (L).
[51] D.1.22 (S).
[52] D.1.21 (S), T.41.21 (P).

the left shoe on first or putting on a tunic or chemise back to front.[1] Women, he says loftily, are far more fascinated by this sort of nonsense than men, and a single woman is likely to know about more superstitions than a hundred men.[2]

Gullible people also give supernatural explanations of merely physiological events and thus falsify catholic doctrine. Once more, Herolt's instinct is to give a purely naturalistic account of the phenomena in order to deflate any spiritualistic meaning popularly attached to them, especially demonic notions about incubi:

> There are those who claim that people appear to them in the night and get on top of them and press down on them. But it is false—it is just the person's own blood. This is quite clear from the fact that it happens to people when they are lying awkwardly and on their backs, and as soon as they turn over it stops happening. And how could someone come in to you when the door is shut, seeing this is a characteristic of the glorified body alone?

Less colorfully, people say that if they hear a drumming in the left ear, it means someone is saying hateful things about them; but if they hear it in the right ear, someone is saying nice things. Or they say that someone is saying derogatory things about them if they get a pimple on the tongue.[3] People even try to give their superstitions an air of sanctity. They take stupid, invalid vows and then trust them to bring good fortune. For example, they will take a vow not to eat crabs, and this (they say) will make their eyesight stay as good as when they took the vow. Or they make it a rule not to eat the heads of animals, birds, or fish in order to be free of head ailments. Or they abstain from meat on Thursdays during the "fasts of the four seasons"[4] and believe that the plague cannot attack them. Others vow to abstain from meat on Christmas, Easter, and Pentecost for reasons that, as often as not, are foolish and superstitious and should be reviewed by their confessors. Some people will not go to the bathhouse on Tuesdays as a way of preventing fever. And there are a series of such prohibitions for Saturdays—people who will not cut their hair, or wash their head, or bathe on Saturdays, or women who do not sew or muck out the stables, and so on—which is doubly erroneous, Herolt says, since it also gives an appearance of judaizing.[5]

---

[1] T.41.22 (P).

[2] S.11.1/1.

[3] D.1.18 (R), T.41.18 (P).

[4] On the primitive *angaria* or *jejunia quattuor temporum* (variously observed as spring, summer, autumn, winter,or March, June, September, December respectively) and their denunciation by many church authorities, see *"Jejunium veniale"* in du Cange, III, 754.

[5] D.1.17 (R), T.41.13 (M).

An even more strongly prohibited form of misguided sanctity is the use of ordeals—establishing truthfulness or innocence by enduring some trial such as holding glowing iron, or plunging the hand in boiling water, or surviving a duel. This masquerades as faith but actually puts God to the test by demanding a miracle from him, and by attempting to adjudicate hidden matters reserved to God's own judgment as the only *perscrutator cordium*. Those who are killed in the process are eternally damned.[6]

All these forms of superstition displace onto some created object a trust that belongs solely to the creator and so constitute a weak and distorted faith. But there are practices that betray their idolatrous character more blatantly. Several common customs are tantamount to moon worship. At a new moon, people kneel to it and take off their hat or cap, or bow their head and address it. Many also fast on the day of a new moon, even if it is a Sunday, when fasting is forbidden. People try to palliate this apparent remnant of idolatry by claiming that by fasting they are honoring not the moon but all the saints whose feasts and fasts fall with that month's lunar cycle. "You can see what sort of an excuse that is!" the preacher exclaims, for if the new moon falls the day before an ecclesiastically sanctioned fast, people will keep the lunar fast and break the official fast before they will miss the first or go hungry on the second. There are some, too, who venerate the sun, Herolt says, and gives an example of an old woman who called the sun "holy mistress" and believed for more than forty years that she received cures and blessings from the sun until a preacher converted her.[7]

Others believe that Diana (vulgarly called *Fraw Berthe* or *Frauw unholt* or *die selig Frauw*) travels at night with her troop through many spaces, or they prepare a table at night and set out vases without lids so that the manes or penates must fill them and bring them fortune ("and so sacrifice to Mammon and become rich"), or they claim that the manes or penates ride their horses in the night and carry their children on their backs.[8]

Infidels, heretics, doubters, neglecters, speculators, idolators, and practitioners and patronizers of superstition—these are the falsifiers of the catholic faith, not only because they adulterate it with an "admixture of vanity and falsehood,"[9] not only because, if they do admit their errors, they are most likely to backslide,[10] but above all because they love and trust something other than God, "and whatever it is will be their god."[11]

To have a god other than God is to lose hope in his providence but above all to despair of his infinite mercy.[12]

---

[6] D.1.10 (J), T.41.6 (H).
[7] D.1.17 (Q), T.41.13 (M).
[8] T.41.19 (P).
[9] E.21.2/2.
[10] T.58.3 (F).
[11] D.1.24 (T), T.41.24 (Q).
[12] D.1.23 (T).

3

GRACE AND MERIT

Herolt's central tenet is that salvation is by grace alone; his pastoral message could be called "justification by sincerity alone." In the stained, guilty, and debilitated state of our fallen humanity, the preacher says, we have nothing worthy to offer God. We have no power to attain life except the residual freedom of will (in itself worthless) to want to accept the grace he offers in so many ways and to yield whatever self we have to yield—a movement however small of sincerity which recognizes who God is, what we are, and what Christ did and suffered for us. Even the good that flows from it is his gift and must be nurtured and guarded daily from the corrupt tendency of our nature to fall back into mortal sin.

Despite the single-minded clarity of this teaching, it may not always have been unambiguous to the hearers (or for that matter the preachers) of Herolt's sermons. Some uncertainty arises because the preacher must expound this doctrine of grace in a pastoral setting where all sorts and conditions of Christian men and women have more or less commitment to piety, zeal, probity, openness, or conformity.

The assumption must be that since the parishioners have been baptized and at least occasionally attend mass, hear sermons, or receive the sacraments, the efficacy of God's grace has touched them. But the histories of the flood and the exodus in the Old Testament and the story of the ten lepers in the New Testament are graphic examples of a universal conclusion:

> In the life of men few are saved, because only the just and good are saved . . . but alas! the majority are unjust and evil . . . . More are lusty than chaste, more proud than humble, more greedy than merciful, more deceivers and liars than truthful . . . . So "many are called but few are chosen," and no one knows whether he is of those who will be saved or those who will be damned.[13]

---

[13] T.126.0 (D).

With this somber assessment, the task of the conscientious pastor is to address the call of grace in all its diverse forms to the many spiritual conditions represented in any congregation.

Pastoral theology formally expressed this reality in a three-fold classification of beginners, proficients, and *perfecti,* drawn from the spiritual formation of religious. (In one sermon, Herolt realigns the formula to read "sinners, penitents, and proficients.")[14] God wills that we be converted, grow proficient in good, and be made perfect. The signs of the Holy Spirit's grace in beginners are grief over past guilt, an intention to avoid sin, and an inner desire to do good. In addition, proficients in the Christian life display "frequent and just conjectural examination of conscience," diminution of the thirst of worldly desire, a toleration of offenses and a heartfelt love of all. The *perfecti* are those who fear nothing but God, do not complain or murmur in adversity—indeed, their trials become sweet to them—and long to be released from this world, which has become their cross.[15]

To complicate matters further, progress in grace is not necessarily steady. There are three classes of people: those who never begin a good life (infidels and bad Christians), those who begin but do not go on in good life (they also are not saved), and those who begin and end in good life.[16] "But alas! there are many who were better and more prepared for death ten years ago than they are now."[17] Such inconstancy greatly offends God. It is like a recurrent illness, a reopened wound, a dog returning to its vomit, a snake swallowing its own venom.[18] It is like a servant who strikes his master in the jaw, seeks forgiveness, and then does it again.[19] It crucifies Christ afresh.[20]

In practice, this reality is brought home with greatest poignancy and frustration each year at Easter. The people have heard the passion retold, fasted, come (for possibly the only time) to confession, and communed at the Easter Eucharist but then go back to their lives without change. The devil loses many a man by the Lenten penance and regains him by backsliding after Easter.[21] Returning to sin after the feast totally obliterates the fruit of the earlier contrition—"even if one had as many good deeds as St. Peter, as many merits and good works as there are stars in heaven or sand by the sea, it is all annihilated and lost."[22] There are certain sorts of people

---

[14] T.102.3 (M).
[15] T.71.3 (T), cf. R.7.1-2 (101ª).
[16] E.32.3.
[17] T.102.3 (M).
[18] D.19.3/4 (J), T.52.2 (M), T.58.0 (before F), E.20.1/2.
[19] T.52.5 (M).
[20] T.1.3 (H).
[21] T.134.1/3 (R), E.32.2.
[22] T.52.1 (M).

who are marked out by their mean-spirited or vicious lifestyle as likely recidivists, but all Christians must persevere if they are to go on in the life of grace.[23]

Accordingly, the preacher, through whom God draws and calls sinners by every means, knows that he must address a multiplicity of spiritual needs. There are some who, whatever he says, will neither hear nor answer to the Lord's knocking; they are as hard as adamite, which cannot be softened by hammer or flame. There are some who reply humbly to Christ's calling, but then they make him go away and do not open to him, confess themselves to be sinners but have no will to change. There are some who hear Christ and answer and open to him—they turn from their sins through contrition and penance—yet they do not keep him long, do not let him stay with them but when other guests come they turn him out as a pauper, or their house is so cluttered with daily concerns there is nowhere for him to rest his head.[24]

There is only a minority who hear, answer, open, and let Christ abide with them; they persevere in a good beginning, and they want never to be separated from God.[25] Even they are at all points of proficiency along the path of grace.

Some listeners then need to hear the sharpest threats of death and hell, the denunciation of vice and sin; some need to be prompted to use the simplest external means of grace; some need to be chided or instructed or reassured; and some need to be incited by promises of heavenly bliss or moved by the appeal of Christ's passion or convinced by the shapeliness of faith.

So the message of grace alone—"we cannot think, consider, or begin anything good without God's help"[26]—had to share the pulpit with a profusion of themes on sins, deeds, duties, merits, strivings, penalties, and rewards, all with one common purpose but possibly confusing to a pious lay person who, uncertain of his or her final destiny, longed above all for that contrite sincerity of heart which gained God's grace.

By Grace Alone

Sola dei gratia—by God's grace alone—the preacher insists. No one will come to God's glory, or to God himself, unless God comes now in grace.[27] We cannot merit the tiniest droplet of his grace and goodness by ourselves or our own deserts. We must realize that grace is given to us from God's sheer goodness and liberality alone, not on account of our merits. Then "man will not trust in himself or his sanctity, or repute himself to be something when he is nothing."[28]

---

[23] T.58 passim.
[24] T.74.2/3 (L).
[25] T.74.2/3 (L).
[26] E.32.3/3.
[27] T.7.2/6 (R).
[28] T.72.1 (U).

There can be no restoration without grace. The human soul in its unfallen state gained its shapely grace from bathing in the vivid illumination of the divine light. But by turning from that light and sinning, the soul incurred a triple detriment: deformity in place of its loveliness, corruption and disorder in place of its goodness, and a duty to pay the fatal cost of its guilt. Thus damaged and helpless, the soul cannot escape unless God freely renews his grace, draws the will to himself, and discharges the penalty.[29]

Without God's intervention, there can be no escape. For as Anselm said, sin is like falling into a pit so deep that we can never get out except with another's help. As Augustine said, it is a spiritual wound which needs a healing physician; it is the chain or rope by which the devil leads men to hell, A fish can enter the net unaided, or the bird a snare, but once trapped, it cannot escape by itself.[30]

Can anyone merit eternal life without grace? No, says Herolt. God made human beings after his own image and likeness so that they would tend to him by natural inclination; but since they cannot now do so by their natural strength, God has conferred a better, higher strength—his grace—so that men and women would tend to him not merely by natural inclination but by a supernatural strength which makes up and helps the insufficiency of nature. Nothing can produce an effect disproportionate to its nature; none by their own power can make their actions deserve eternal life. "For by our natural capacities alone (*ex puris naturalibus*) we do not merit, and therefore without grace we can do nothing."[31]

Justice and Mercy

By our inadequacy, corruption, and guilt we are hopelessly lost without God's forbearance and mercy. Sometimes Herolt makes the contrast between justice and mercy as stark as possible. God's mercy and his justice are polar opposites, as far apart as east and west, his grace and his power as far apart as north and south. To move away from one pole is to approach the other; the farther one moves from God's grace, the closer one is to his power. "Accordingly, whoever wishes to return to God should retreat from God—that is, from God angry to God placated, from God punishing to God taking pity."[32]

For God's natural property is to show mercy, as the sun's is to shine. Isaiah 28 speaks of God's strange work of punishing (he is slow and reluctant to punish), but his proper office is mercy, like the bee, whose proper task is to make honey, but molested it can also sting: "So God, when he gives the honey of his mercy performs

---

[29] E.1.1/2.
[30] T.74.3 (N), E.1.1/2.
[31] E.34.3.
[32] Q.3.1.

his proper office, but when he applies the good of his justice he performs an office strange to him and involuntary, since he punishes unwillingly."[33]

Justice abounded under the old covenant, as it will again at the last judgment; but now, in this fullness of time, the time of Christ's incarnation and the outpouring of the spirit, the mercy of God abounds.[34] Even at a time like the present when "there is in the world neither truth, nor fidelity, nor true Christian life, but pride rules everywhere," God in his grace does not immediately punish, as he did the angels when he cast them from heaven for their pride or Adam from paradise for his disobedience. Instead, he forbears for the sake of repentance and emendation.[35] Divine mercy has made peace for the sinner with divine justice.[36]

Yet in another sense, God never shows one without the other.[37] Is there not a paradox, Herolt wonders, in melding mercy and justice as the doctors Thomas and Albertus do, arguing that God's mercy is his will to do his creation good, and God's justice the dispensing of his goodness? On the contrary, in the justification of the ungodly we seem to find mercy but no justice, since all justice presupposes some basis in merit, and in this case the sinner (as we have seen) has no merit at all.[38]

In his later homilies on the Epistles, where Herolt occasionally invokes the technical theological explanations he avoids in the *de tempore* sermons, he finds some help in Robert Holkot's account of this paradox. In the justification of the ungodly, Holkot says, there is a movement of free will and attrition, on account of which some basis for justice appears in God's pouring in his grace. Moreover, it would be an injustice on God's part not to do so, since in a certain sense God becomes the penitent's debtor through his own promise ("that thou mightest be justified when thou speakest," Psalm 51:4). Accordingly, in justification God acts from both aspects, mercy and justice.[39]

The only basis of this "certain sort of justice," Herolt insists, is a humble longing for salvation and the contrite confession that it is undeserved but for God's free promise. Although left as dead by the wayside with the wounds of sin, yet, however,

---

[33] T.97.1/1 (A), cf. Q.18.1.
[34] E.5.2.
[35] T.97.21/1 (C).
[36] T.52.5 (M).
[37] R.1.4 (19[a-b]).
[38] E.15.1/3.
[39] E.15.1/3. See Robert Holkot, OP, *Super Libros Sapientiae* C. III (Lectio 52 B). An English version of this passage translated by Paul L. Nyhus and edited by Heiko A. Oberman can be found in *Forerunners of the Reformation: The Shape of Late Medieval Thought Illustrated by Key Documents* (New York: Holt, Rinehart & Winston, 1966; Philadelphia: Fortress Press 1981, 144-48).

great a sinner one is, one is not deprived of that "mediating will" by which one can apply the medicine of penitence to oneself and be revived in grace.[40]

Reception of Grace

This and only this is what the sinner can do to cooperate with God's grace. (On a few occasions, Herolt uses the technical term *facere quod in se est*.)[41] Though all one has to offer is yearning, helplessness, and need, the movement of contrition is essential. In his sermons on the Epistles, Herolt explains the scholarly terms for the reception of grace. More often (and more clearly) he uses everyday language and images to make his meaning plain.

"No one can have the riches of grace unless they are donated by the liberal giver of grace. For just as a man cannot constitute himself in nature, so he also cannot bestow grace on himself. Hence it follows that man without God's grace cannot prepare himself for grace, nor keep himself in grace, nor guard himself from sin, nor perform any meritorious work." The saving grace which make these otherwise impossible tasks attainable is therefore described as fourfold: the preparation for grace by "*gratia operans*, which makes of the ungodly man a godly man"; keeping the soul in grace by "*gratia cooperans*, which makes of the good man a better man"; guarding from sin by "*gratia perseverans*, which transfers a man from this present life to the fatherland"; and enabling good works by "*gratia salvans*, which bestows merits."[42]

Our sufficiency is from God, who works in us *without* us, beginning good thoughts; *with* us, evoking good will and consent; and *through* us, giving us the capacity to do it.[43] That is why it is correct at once to say that all grace comes solely from God, and yet an individual person is inexcusable if he or she does not have grace. "For a man is freely given grace (*gratiam gratis datur*) by which, anticipated by God, he is always made ready to arouse and stir up his free will and do what lies within him and consent to it." If he does so, then he is "able to have the grace that makes him acceptable (*gratiam gratum facientem*)."

Can anyone from their own merits acquire this grace that makes one acceptable? No, says the preacher, because the grace by which we are justified from sins and acceptable to God, and which confers heavenly merit on our actions, we have from God. No one can deserve this grace by condign merit, only by congruous merit. In other words, we can still not do anything worthy to save ourselves, but we can do only what we can—to allow ourselves to be saved.[44]

---

[40] E.14.1/3, cf. Q.34.1.
[41] Q.4.2, Q.25.3, E.1.1/2, E.34.3/2, E.45.1/2.
[42] E.45.1/2.
[43] E.39.3.
[44] E.34.3/2.

This, Herolt tells the sisters of St. Katharine's, is why the cloistered pursuit of humility is so important. The foundation of the garden of the soul is the grace of God, which springs from humility because "humility is ready to receive the divine grace."[45] "You are admonished to fear God by the divine grace you have; but if you do not have the divine grace, you should acquire it by fearing God—we have nothing of ourselves."[46]

It is in this sense that the preacher can say in the same breath, "It is in man to follow God or the devil; and when the Lord draws some to himself it is from sheer divine grace."[47] For grace is an absolute bargain on offer in God's marketplace.[48] God is always ready to confer his grace. The Christ of Revelation 3:20 stands at the door and knocks: "If anyone open to me (that is, by removing the bolt of sin) I will come in to him (that is, confer on him my grace), because a man must do what is in him to do." Although a person cannot illuminate himself without grace, he can at least do something that will allow him to be illuminated—open a door or a window. Without the will, grace effects nothing; without grace, the will can do nothing. "The earth does not germinate without rain, nor the rain fructify without the earth."[49]

> God the father draws all, since he offers grace to all. Yet not all are drawn or come to Christ, for even though grace is offered to all, yet all do not accept it. But stretch out, man! Look, if this city (or some valley) were now full of fire or water or enemies and you could not possibly escape unless you were drawn up into the highest tower, and your friend standing on the tower, throwing a rope down, was ready to pull you up and anyone else who wished—if you then did not put your hand to the rope, or while you were being lifted you let the rope go in midair, surely the fault would be yours, and you would not escape. So it is with the rope of grace and love by which God is our true friend ready to draw us up on high.[50]

The Offer of Grace

Where is this grace on offer? Herolt notes in passing that there is a common prevenient grace which ought to allow an intellect unabused by emotion to be

---

[45] R.3.2 (30b-31a), cf. T.14.2/2 (L).
[46] R.1.4 (18b).
[47] T.74.3 (N).
[48] E.14.2/1.
[49] E.34.3/2.
[50] T.74.3 (N).

lifted up to God,[51] but this is too abstruse for pastoral purposes. More simply, God calls and draws people to himself in many everyday ways. He calls them by internal inspiration, "as often as you have good thoughts, you have been called by God . . . so there is never a day when God does not draw and call you to himself"; by external preaching, when he places the words of life in the preacher's mouth; by the example of the saints and virtuous people; by daily benefits—health, wealth, honor, food and drink, for he gives them all. If one ignores all these offers of grace, then God calls by the lashes of tribulation:

> For when someone does not wish to notice good inspirations or heed sermons, and neither examples nor God's benefits can soften him, then God in his mercy flagellates him so that he may be converted to God . . . . When God afflicts you with bodily weakness—toothache, eyeache, headache—understand this to be the voice of God. Similarly if poverty or misfortune or any adversity weigh upon you, receive the Lord's messenger and turn from your sins.

God calls people to grace by the promises of eternal, fruition and heavenly joys, and equally by the sharpest threats of eternal darkness, undying worms, inextinguishable fire, and the pains of the damned. Above all, he calls and draws us by his own bitter passion, with all its sweet signs of our acceptance.[52]

In practice, the offer of grace is made through the priestly ministry of the church.

First of all, grace is conferred in baptism. Grace is the matter of baptism, its point and content, and is given to all baptized infants equally (since they are all equally disposed to receive it) and to adult baptizands in proportion to their disposition. As the ritual use of salt before baptism intends, in baptism one receives sufficient grace to suppress the tinder of sin and preserve one from all mortal sin until death, if one wants to use it.[53] Grace is also conferred by the other sacraments. Confirmation, for example, confers not only the common cleansing grace of any sacrament but a special grace to commission the recipient for effective sanctity and the confession of Christ—from grace to make greater grace.[54] But if grace is sparse in the other sacraments, in the Eucharist, grace is found in its fount and origin, for here the Lord of grace himself is present in the fullness of all his graces.[55]

Other sacramental acts and devotions are also channels of grace. For example, there is abundant grace for those who honor Christ by genuflecting at the elevation

---

[51] E.40.3.
[52] T.74.1 (H-K).
[53] D.12.3 (M), T.66.3 (T-U), T.76.2/4 (X), T.77.2 (B).
[54] T.148.2 (T).
[55] T.79.1/1 (I).

in the mass, whether in church or at the sound of the bell in field or home.[56] In all the vicissitudes of life, devotion to the Blessed Virgin is an unfailing source of grace, for she is the mother of grace and the dispenser of graces.[57] More of the "goods for sale" are on display in God's market in Lent than at other times: preaching, vigils, prayers, fasts so that grace may be offered to each according to his or her individual need.[58] In general, because grace is so readily available, diligence in the life of faith gains grace; but slackness loses it, and the attainable goal is a life of grace marked by self-knowledge, warmth of love, and actions attesting to love.[59] Above all, by devout and continual meditation on Christ's passion, a person can seek more grace from God than if everyone on earth prayed for him.[60]

For the passion of Christ was *for us*. This supreme expression of God's mercy fervently underpins Herolt's doctrine of grace. "As a sign of his great love, for us he became man and entered this vale of misery, served us thirty years in hunger and cold, and after all underwent bitter death for us."[61] He who was immeasurably great, the noblest king of earth and lord of all, became a little child for us, lying in straw in a manger for us, travelling and toiling in weariness and interceding for us in prayers and vigils, stretching out his arms and yielding his whole body for us, sustaining bitterest death and descending into hell for us; and it is his satisfaction made for us that brings remission and grace, and opens heaven.[62]

> You would love one who gave property for you; more, one who gave up friends and relatives and left his own land; most of all, one who gave his body for you. Christ did all this . . . . Again, you would love one who for love of you poured out his tears, most of all if he shed his blood for you. Christ did this too . . . . Bernard: "Oh with what vehement embrace he embraces me on the cross, on which water flowed from his side, blood flooded from his heart, and the soul departed from his body." Again Bernard: "He did not suffer for himself, for he never sinned; and not for the good angels, who had no need of it, nor for the evil angels who will never possess glory; but for you" . . . Again, how much would you love one who gave a hand to be cut off for you when you were liable to have your head

---

[56] T.14.1/7 (C).
[57] T.161.3-4 (A-B), T.163.3/2 (S).
[58] E.14.2/1.
[59] R.2.5 (26), E.42.1/2.
[60] T.48.8 (K).
[61] T.79.2 (I).
[62] D.16.5/2 (M), D.22.5 (L), T.15.2/2 (P), T.27.9 (C), T.45.3 (H-J), T.75.2 (R), T.102.1 (I), T.119.1 (P), Q.6.2, Q.7.2, Q.10.2, Q.35.2, Q.37.2, E.5.0-1, E.6.1, E.13.2, E.18.1/1, E.22.1/1, E.23.2/2, E.38.1/4, E.39.0, &c.

chopped off; or an eye, or a foot, or some other member? But how much must you love and give thanks to him who gave not an eye or a hand or a foot for you, but gave his whole body to death? You would love one who freed you from death; more, one who also gave you a safe conduct; most of all, one who wanted to keep you always in the place of his own child. Plainly, we must deservedly love Christ who has done all this and more for you.[63]

There can, therefore, be no comparison or proportion between God's immeasurable mercy in offering us grace and the tiny movement of our will by which we acknowledge our helplessness and yield ourselves to that mercy. There is certainly no intrinsic merit in that movement:

He gives the justified the kingdom of heaven from his mercy; for he is scarcely obliged to us for our own deserts—indeed, they are nothing worthy of him (*immo nihil de condigno*). For if we achieve anything of good, yet we are bound to do more to God. So even if we have consumed all the powers of body and soul in God's service, and have acted to the limit of our ability, we must still say what Luke 17 [:10] says: "We are unprofitable servants: we have done what was our duty to do." That we cannot possess eternal life from our own merits in a worthy way (*ex condigno*), but only from the mercy of God, Bernard shows when he says: "If we had been born from the time when men first appeared on earth, and if our life were stretched out for a hundred thousand years, yet there would be no action of this whole time worthy to be compared with the future glory to be revealed in us."[64]

Even though in itself the movement of the will in contrition deserves nothing, it is essential, for otherwise the human soul would not be freely yielded. "God is so glorious a prince that he regards it as only worthy of himself that we serve him freely and voluntarily: he does not want to coerce or (as it were) drag anyone into the kingdom by the hair."[65] God wants the human heart given, not exchanged or sold.[66] Moreover, sin is by definition a voluntary action; merit and demerit are possible only insofar as an act is willed. The possibility of goodness is denied when people from a sense of determinism or helplessness deny the freedom of the will. Without this capacity to consent or resist even in the face of the most powerful inclination to sin, God's demand would have imposed an intolerable weight on us.[67]

---

[63] T.119.1 (P).
[64] T.97.3/3 (E).
[65] T.109.7 (H).
[66] T.8.1 (B).
[67] D.12.3 (M), T.21.1 (S), T.41.11 (L), T.77.2/2 (C).

God's Foreknowledge

Yet there are many people, the preacher warns, who foolishly use biblical statements about God's foreknowledge, election, and predestination as a reason for indifference to grace, or else despair, either because they say, "What will be will be: since I am predestined to life, I cannot perish and it is vain to strive!" Or the devil makes them think, "Whatever God wills must happen—if you must be saved, you will never be damned whatever you do; if you must be damned, you will never be saved whatever you do."[68]

What would happen if they applied the same argument to their bodies? "Don't prepare any food, don't mend any clothes—if God will, he will feed and clothe us!" But eternal things cannot be had without effort any more than temporal. The foreknowledge of God does not imply any necessity. God does not compel to good or evil; no one is damned except through the things that lie within his free will. How then does God's foreknowledge work?

Although predestination is true and certain and cannot be changed as to God, yet enough free will remains to us to go either way. A natural example: If I see someone blind at a crossroads, I know that if he goes by the way that leads to the ditch he will fall in it, but if he goes by the right way he will evade it. In the same degree as my sight is operative as to the blind person's way, to that degree God's foreknowledge is operative as to a man's damnation (except that I cannot know which way the blind person will go).[69]

Herolt illustrates the contingency of this foreknowledge by two examples. One is the story of a devout monk to whom divine revelations were often vouchsafed, who was asked by a brother from a neighboring monastery to pray for a revelation whether he was saved or damned. After earnest prayer, he saw that the brother was among the damned, and he avoided him; but eventually the friar demanded to know. When he was told, he rejoiced and said he would double and triple his penance until he received mercy and forgiveness. Later, the monk was shown that he was now in the number of the elect.[70] The other story is from Caesarius of Heisterbach:

> Ludwig, Landgrave of Thuringia, a learned man, was deceived by such error that he asserted he was necessarily saved if he was predestined or damned if that was foreknown. He also said he would neither flee nor anticipate the hour of his death. On this basis he used to indulge himself repeatedly in endless vices without any fear. Eventually he

---

[68] T.74.3 (N), T.93.7 (U).
[69] T.74.3 (N).
[70] T.74.3 (N).

became gravely ill, and when the doctor had been summoned he told him to administer a treatment which could make him better. The doctor, who was expert in both medicine and theology and was not unaware of his error, replied, "Lord, if the day of your death is coming, I would not be able to cure you. On the other hand, if it is not coming yet, it would be a waste of time for me to administer therapy, since you will get better without it." The count said to him, "What are you talking about? I know that unless I receive some relief quickly I shall die before my time!" Replied the doctor, "If you believe that life can be prolonged by the efficacy of medicine, why do you not believe it of penitence which is the medicine of the soul?" The Landgrave recognised the force of his words, and said, "Be the doctor of my soul from now on, since by your healing tongue the Lord has delivered me from the greatest error." [71]

In fact, Herolt says, it is quite clear what the will of God is for us—our sanctification. All good men are predestined to eternal glory, provided they keep faith, love, and the virtues. "For God foresees such people in the future whom he has predestined to life, and to bring about their predestination, it is as if he said to them, 'I indeed predestine you to life if you live in such and such a way' . . . and just as God foresees that someone will be saved, so he also foresees the means by which they must be saved (that is, through their merits and good works)."[72]

Of all the things which people long to know in this world, the most powerful is to find out whether they are children of the heavenly Jerusalem or children of darkness. Seneca tells a story about a man's two sons by two different mothers who were sent away for schooling. On their return they looked indistinguishable, and both wept with their "mother," so the father decided not to identify which was which so that the mother would take equal care of both. "So the Church, which is the mother of those of good conscience and the stepmother of the sons of perdition, does not know in the present who is the elect or foreknown child of God; but in the final harvest, the good and the evil will be discerned."[73]

Nonetheless, even though "no one knows whether he deserves hatred or love" (Eccles. 9 [:1]), it is only certainty one lacks—one may know with the knowledge of conjecture. For there are clear signs of election and reprobation. Adversity, a hunger for God's word, honor for those who fear the Lord, humility, avoidance of slander, compassion and mercy, ready dismissal of injuries, the desire to be better, frequent and grateful meditation on Christ's passion are all characteristic of the elect. Conversely, a life of unbroken ease, avoidance of God's word, dislike of

---

[71] T.93.7 (X).
[72] T.93.7 (U).
[73] E.17.2/2.

good men, pride, heartlessness, vindictive rancor, slackness, and disdain of what Christ has done for us are the telltale signs of the reprobate.[74] For the preacher, the pastoral consequences are clear. Those who make sincere and consistent use of the means of grace—and especially those who strive for a life of humility, patience, mercy, kindness, devotion, and penitence—may find assurance in God's promises of election. By contrast, those who live lives of backsliding, indifference, or outright vice must be brought sharply to the knowledge of their sins and their mortal danger.

There is a third response to God's grace which is the worst sin of all. It is the sin of Cain and Judas, the "sharpest trial from within" that tears the heart away from penitence and mercy, the one sin which by definition cannot be healed—despair. Herolt turns repeatedly to a solemn recital of authorities—Ambrose, Augustine, Jerome, Chrysostom, Gregory, Isidore, Bernard, Leo—to stress over and over again that despair denies God's mercy and refuses his grace. It is an inordinate grief, a demonic diffidence in the face of divine justice, which offends God and brings a curse on itself by rejecting forgiveness.[75] If neither Cain nor Judas could bring themselves to believe that God's mercy was greater than their heinous sins, the thief on the cross teaches us that even in the extremity of death, however depraved we are as sinners, we need not despair in any way of God's mercy.[76] And Peter, who bathed his threefold denial in his bitter tears and Christ immediately forgave him, is our example that no sinner, however grave the sins he has committed, must despair but should weep instead for his sins.[77]

Even though such tears have great power to blot out sins, extinguish purgatory, bring special consolation, and penetrate the kingdom of heaven, suppose that someone found his heart so tough that he could not weep for his sins, and whatever inner reflections and outer punishments he undertook, he was still not able to weep. What then? Should he despair that it was not in him to yield to God's mercy and grace? No, not at all. "If by no means he can provoke himself to weeping, he must not despair on that account, but let him grieve that it is so, and God receives the wish for the deed."[78]

Any opening, however small, is enough to admit God's promised grace, so long as it is the best the damaged will can do. But "for the one who does what he can, God will not withhold mercy."

---

[74] T.126.0 (D), T.149.0 (before A) and 1-9 (A-K), E.6.2.
[75] D.1.23 (T), D.16.2/5 (H), D.22.11 (T), D.30.2/1 (B), T.9.1/3 (H) and .3 (P), T.29.1 (0) and .2 (S), T.40.1 (A), T.44.6 (C), T.73.2 (A), T.122.2 (T) and .4 (X), T.131.9 (P), T.147.11 (0), Q.1.3, Q.26.2, E.14.3.
[76] Q.39.2/2.
[77] Q.14.2/2.
[78] Q.15.3.

Grace and Merit

For those who so receive the infusion of God's grace, a life of grace may follow. Now it is possible—indeed essential—for the Christian to do works of goodness and mercy and to grow in all the virtues in a way that acquires merit and brings reward. While it is necessary for salvation that our works be meritorious, without faith no good work or virtue has any merit or usefulness at all. "The least work in faith pleases God more than all the works by all the unfaithful."[1] Like those who labor in the night, like beasts of burden, those who do their works—even good works—in mortal sin offer a dead sacrifice and do not merit eternal life. "In order for our works to be acceptable to God and meritorious to us, we must do them in love and grace, without which no work avails whatsoever, even if it is generically good."[2]

God orders physical and temporal life in this world to give us the greatest opportunity to augment merit. The pains and tribulations of life in a defective body are the soul's opportunity to acquire merits; the poor, the weak, and the handicapped are allowed to survive so that their merit may grow through their sufferings (and so that the well-off may gain merits by their generosity); slander, abuse, exactions, and theft are all occasions for merit if they are borne patiently.[3] Ultimately the list of potential merits for the Christian in grace can be expanded to embrace all aspects of life. Herolt speaks of this in almost every sermon but summarizes all these endless opportunities in two common sermons for apostolic feast days.

We gain merit with our temporal substance by support to paupers in alms and works of mercy, patiently sustaining the depredations of violent men, forgoing wrongful acquisitions, sharing with our neighbors, and returning unjust property.[4]

We gain merit with our body by resisting the sins to which we are inclined; expending our energies in good deeds and serving God, especially visiting the sick and distressed, godly conversation, going to church, pilgrimage, hard beds, harsh clothing, castigating the body with vigils and flagellation, fasting, and early rising. Even more, we may gain merit by patiently bearing the infirmities God allows to befall us—"special gifts of God and signs of his love"—and enlarging our patience by recalling Christ's passion and the pains of purgatory.[5]

We gain merit with our soul by using its powers for God: memory, by remembering his benefits and giving thanks for them; intellect, by understanding

---

[1] T.41.0 (E-F).
[2] T.92.1 (K), T.140 passim, E.6.2.
[3] D.21.2/6 (L), T.34.3 (S), T.109.4 (D) and .6 (G), &c.
[4] T.150 passim.
[5] T.151.2/1-3 (C-H).

God as our creator whom we must obey, our redeemer whose bitterest death and passion redeemed us, our future judge whom we must fear in all our thoughts, words, and deeds; and by will, "being so conformed to the divine will that whatever he wants with us we want the same thing, whether sweet or bitter."[6]

The principal constituent of merits is the virtues (meekness, patience, humility, unity of spirit, and the rest). The exterior exercises (ceremonies, vigils, fastings) are chiefly instruments for proceeding to those interior acts of virtue.[7] For the elect who persevere in the life of grace, the joy each will have in heaven in his or her own merits will be a new gift and most precious course at the heavenly feast. It is a "certain and indubitable truth of the Christian faith" that one's place in the ranks of the heavenly choir will be in direct proportion to the merits one has attained here.[8]

Yet even these sempiternal rewards are gifts of grace. We attribute all the good works in us not to ourselves but to God's gift. One of the pastoral questions to be put to a dying person is: "Do you believe that you must go on to eternal life not on account of your own merits (which are still tiny in respect of eternal life) but on account of the merit of the passion of Jesus Christ, in whose merit consists the salvation of us all?"[9] Our confidence that God wishes to give us the kingdom of heaven comes not from our own merits but the merits of Jesus Christ our redeemer, whom the Father gave us to redeem us by his bitter passion.[10]

---

[6] T.151.3/1-3 (M-N).
[7] E.44.2/1.
[8] T.84.6 (L), T.88.0 (L).
[9] T.135.2 (C).
[10] D.1.23 (T), T.122.4 (X), Q.36.2.

4

CONTRITION

"How can I have a pure heart? Nothing from God is so useful for cleansing the heart as tears—the water of contrition and devotion." [11]

The tears of the penitent are like the rain on the earth cleansing, life giving, fruitful, refreshing, softening. Tears of contrition wash away the filth of sins. Trees seem dead in winter, but the spring rains give them new life. So tears revive those dead in sins, and a sinner without tears is a fish out of water, a mole out of the ground, a chameleon without air. As seeds lie dormant in the soil and sprout when they receive moisture, without tears of penitence the soul bears no fruit. Weary animals refresh themselves by splashing water, and tears comfort numb, weary, toiling sinners. Water softens hard things, and tears of compunction and devout prayer soften the severity of God. Tears of penitence extinguish the heat of guilt and purify the penitent's soul. Like the stillness of the air after rain, serenity and tranquillity of conscience follow the rain of tears.[12]

Sorrow for sin is the first sign that a person has embarked on the life of grace. As we have seen, it may be spontaneous, or it may need to be provoked, but "without contrition no sin is expunged." That contrition must proceed from a sincere and bitter heart.[13]

This is so much the burden of Herolt's message that he could also be said to teach a doctrine of justification by contrition alone. He explains why sin cannot be remitted without penitence, for sin is a wilful aversion from God and must be undone by a willing conversion back to God; and why even this returning would be worthless but for his grace anticipating, calling, drawing, healing, and sustaining us. All that we can do in our fallen state, and all that we are required to do by his promise, is the one thing within our capacity: to grieve for our sins.

The sinner, he says, is like Avicenna's elephant, which rested on a tree; the tree broke under its weight, and it fell in the pit. In its desire for rest, the soul relies on this transitory world. The elephant's trumpeting and bellowing for help is the

---

[11] E.51.1/2.
[12] A.L.: 1 and 2 "Lacrymarum compunctio" (118[b]-119[a]).
[13] T.8.2 (C).

clamor of our contrition to God and the voice of our confession to the priest—our only way of escape.[14]

Penance

While contrition is a transaction of the heart, and brings remission before any outward expression in oral confession, its pastoral focus is the sacrament of penance. Here the priest is not addressing a diversity of spiritual needs, but the standing and sincerity of a single person, elicited by careful questions and judicious counsel. To prevent the annual penance of most lay people becoming a formality—an obliged compliance but not an occasion for self-examination and growth—the preacher concentrates on the theory and practice of penance in sermons throughout Lent and other penitential seasons.

The intense contritionism of these sermons is already foreshadowed in the exposition of sacramental penance in Herolt's 1416 catechism.[15] The *de tempore* sermons for Lent borrow from the catechism and expand on it (though the call for penitence is a perennial theme, not confined to Lent).[16] By the time of the *Quadragesimale* of 1435, Herolt has expanded his practical answers to penitents' questions into a short tractate, to be preached as a daily series from Ash Wednesday to Holy Week, for those preparing to confess before the Easter communion.[17]

Penitence, Augustine said, is to grieve for past evils and by grieving not to commit them any more. In a gloss on Paul's discourse about love in 1 Cor. 13, Herolt declares that nothing in the sinner pleases God so much as repentance:

> If you were to give all the goods you have from God, and if you were to feed all the poor and build endless monasteries and churches, you would not please God unless you repented. And if you possessed all knowledge, so that you made peace throughout the world and disposed all good things in the world by your own counsel; and if you spoke the tongues of men and angels, so that you converted more sinners than all the preachers from the beginning of the world, you have become like a sounding brass, doing others good but destroying yourself, if you do not cease from sin. And if you give your body to be burned yet you will not please God unless you repent . . . .

---

[14] E.1.3.
[15] D.25.
[16] T.38, T.43, T.44.
[17] Q.1-26.

God loves penitence and contrition so much that for this he came from heaven to earth, from angels to sinners, from inexpressible delights to inestimable pains. Nothing else does the devil such harm or the sinner such good as repentance:

> If as many thousands of masses were sung for the sinner every day as there are stars in the sky, and all the saints interceded for him, and if the heavens opened to him every day and scattered at his bidding, and sun moon and stars followed their courses at his whim—indeed, if angels daily came down from heaven and talked with him and he was caught up in the air . . . and yes, if the blessed Virgin herself talked with him, it would not profit him as much as to repent.[18]

In a sense then, penance excels baptism (even though it has no indelible character). Baptism happens once, but penance may happen often; baptism removes original sin, but penance removes actual sin. Baptism is our spiritual generation, but penance brings spiritual healing. Penance can be done for every sin however great, save only despair, if one grieves from the heart, intends not to sin anymore, and is ready to obey and make reparation.[19]

Sacramental penance has taken three forms, Herolt explains—solemn, public, and private penance. Solemn penance, no longer in use, was when a bishop imposed a penance on a whole community for a public cause. Public penance may be imposed by a priest for manifest and scandalous wrongs such as open adultery, gambling, or blaspheming and may require church attendance, bare feet in procession, prostration at the church door, kneeling at the end of mass, and other visible censures. But most penance now takes place secretly in confession, where compensatory corrections may be aptly imposed.[20]

Can mortal sin be remitted without penance? No, for sin is a wilful turning from God and cannot be expunged without an equally deliberate turning back. What about forgotten sins? If self-examination does not bring them to mind, they may be confessed generally (unless remembered later). Can one sin be remitted without another? Venial sins, yes, but not mortal sins because any mortal sin excludes grace, yet remission requires grace and a real intention to abandon sin.[21]

Can one do true penance at life's end? Yes, as the thief on the cross showed, no repentance is too late while there is life. Yet to delay repenting to the threshold of death is extremely dangerous, not only because of the uncertainty of sudden death, but because when that time comes penance may prove impossible. "Although he promises you forgiveness at the end of your life if you have been truly penitent, yet it is exceedingly

---

[18] D.25.0 (A-B).
[19] Q.1.3.
[20] Q.2.3.
[21] Q.3.3.

difficult for penitence that arrives so late should be true penitence. For then torment binds the members, grief oppresses sense so that it can scarcely think of anything."[22] Herolt has a number of suitably graphic stories to illustrate the warning:[23]

> When the devil finds a person unprepared at death, it is like someone in bed hearing the *Stourmklock* [alarm bell] and leaping up but having barely a camisole or tunic to throw on and no other clothes to hand. So when illness strikes, people rush for a priest: there is nothing else to put on but to do true penance and confession. But such people rarely—hardly ever—repent truly.[24]

There is therefore no way to say with assurance whether such deathbed repentance is heartfelt, and so efficacious. Even if it is, one goes hence with punishments still to satisfy and no accrued heavenly merits.[25] Nevertheless, God looks at the intention of the heart, so the dying must resist the temptation to despair even if they have remembered a thousand unrepented mortal sins. If you have strength to speak, call a priest and confess; if you cannot, confess to the omnipotent God with a contrite heart and by no means despair, for God will not despise a humble and contrite heart.[26]

This advice again underlines the preacher's conviction that sincere contrition is the essence of true repentance and brings God's mercy before and apart from auricular confession or penances.[27] *In extremis*, it is enough to secure the soul's salvation. Even in ordinary circumstances, the penitent should go to the priest already justified by a contrition that wishes to confess and make amends. Normal penance has three integral parts—contrition, confession, satisfaction—but the keystone is the heart's sorrow.

Contrition is our spiritual conception, the intention that gives birth to confession and expiation.[28] How much grief must we willingly undergo? Must the sorrow of contrition be very great?

Our inward sorrow is to be very sharp—as bitter and laxative as absinth.[29] For we must find our joy in nothing so much as in God; this joy is destroyed by sin, and *contraria contrariis curantur*. The greater the love we have for one we have offended, the greater our sorrow. The better something is, the more we grieve for its loss:

---

[22] T.97.2/2 (D), cf. T.156.2 (Y), E.50.1/2.
[23] E.g., T.115.4 (J); T.134.3 (A); T.156.3 (A); P.M.: 56, 57 "Mors malorum" (335, 336).
[24] E.1.1/2.
[25] T.88.1 (L), T.156.4 and 5 (C and F), T.160.2 (D).
[26] T.134.2/2 (T).
[27] E.g., T.122.2 (T).
[28] T.87.1 (E).
[29] A.C.: 6 "Contritio" (114[b]).

Someone will grieve more for losing a florin than a denarius; but God is the highest and infinite good, whom we offend by sinning and lose him. It follows that the grief of contrition in its inner dismay should be greater than every other grief which can befall a person temporally—even the loss of all temporal possessions, or if father, mother, wife, all one's children were to die.[30]

Christ says to the "leper in our soul" that he wants us to wash by frequent outpourings of tears. When he wept on the cross, he showed us that we must weep (at least in our hearts) on account of our sins.[31] Even outwardly, Herolt says, tears and groans should be counted among the "common gestures of bodily reverence."[32]

Can our contrition be so intense that it expunges our entire liability for sin's penalty? Yes, in each of two ways, the preacher says. One aspect of our sorrow is a love for God that evokes our revulsion at sin; the other is the grief we feel at having betrayed that fervent love. In both respects, contrition may reach such intensity that it requites the whole penalty.[33]

But can it be too great, too intense? It is not possible for the "rational" aspect of our grief—our dismay at having offended God—to be too great. But "sensible" grief can grow too intense; it requires discretion, just as external disciplines require moderation, lest it become exorbitant and indiscreet. Such overweening distress offends God and like Cain or Judas runs the risk of despair:

> So it is when someone comes in inordinate grief, who says, to himself, "O God, why am I alive? Why was I born? Why do I not die?" and asks many counsellors the same questions. A person offends God more with these than with other sins—even if there is no sin at all!

The true contrite has humility toward himself, dismay at his own sin, but total trust in God.[34]

Sorrow for Sin

Should there be greater sorrow for one sin than another? (Herolt tries to allay commonplace lay anxieties without fragmenting his underlying message.) In general, yes, the greater the offense against God, the greater the remorse but with a fitting

---

[30] D.25.1/1 (E), T.43.1 (I), Q.6.3.
[31] T.102.2 (L), T.135.3/3 (D).
[32] E.43.2/3.
[33] D.25.1/3 (G), T.14.1/5 (F), Q.7.3.
[34] T.29.1/3 (Q-R), Q.7.3.

degree of emotive grief.[35] Is contrition demanded for each and every mortal sin? Yes, the actual aversion of will in every mortal sin must be reversed by an actual conversion for each remembered sin. Is a specific contrition then demanded for each sin? Yes, at the beginning of contrition, when someone reflects on their sins, a specific sorrow for each individual sin is fitting; but later on, when sorrow is informed by grace, then a common habitual contrition for all sins suffices.[36]

When should this sorrow be elicited? You are obliged to be contrite as soon as you recognize yourself to have sinned mortally (though not necessarily to confess immediately). But there are specific occasions—times of danger, the hour of death, preparation for mass or communion or ministry—which bring the question of mortal sin to the forefront, and then too contrition is evoked.[37] And is one bound to grieve for sins for the whole of life? One must detest one's sins as long as one lives, and without contrition no sin is expunged.[38] It is therefore good to rouse oneself to daily contrition by examination of conscience. As Peter Lombard says, for habitual contrition God forgives sins even before actual confession is made to a priest, so long only as one intends to confess. Like many another preacher of the period, Herolt quotes a gloss on Ezekiel 18 as if it were the prophet himself: "In whatsoever hour the sinner shall lament, he shall be saved (*in quacumque hora peccator ingemuerit, salvus erit*)" or "I shall remember all his sins no more (*omnium peccatorum eius non recordabor amplius*)."[39] Even if the mouth is silent, forgiveness follows; indeed, oral confession is useless unless the sin is forgiven. From Christ's instructions to the publicans, the lepers, and Lazarus, "it follows that before we confess our sins to the priest, we must be cleansed from sins by contrition . . .":

> Accordingly, anyone who wants to confess must be contrite before confessing, and thus come justified to confession (or at least in confession and before absolution). So it is expedient for every Christian . . . to return to his heart and dissect his conscience, by meditating diligently on what he has thought, heard, said, done and neglected to do . . . and grieve for those things he finds reprehensible in his conscience.[40]

---

[35] T.43.1 (K), Q.7.3.
[36] D.25.1/3 (G), Q.8.3.
[37] T.67.1 (Y), Q.8.3.
[38] T.43.1 (I), Q.10.3.
[39] T.97.2/2 (D); S.16.3; Q.9.3: cf. Jer. 31:34, Ezek.18:21-22, 27; Heb. 10:17 in the Vulgate.
[40] Q.9.3.

Priestly Confession

If contrition with a sincere heart brings remission and justification, is confession to a priest optional? No, Herolt says, though the diversity of his reasons suggests the answer is not self-evident. First, churchly authority says that confession is necessary to salvation. Christ instituted it in place of the general confessions and sacrifices of the Old Testament (Luke 17:14), and Ambrose said no one was justified without it. Secondly, it is a constituent mark of true contrition that the penitent intends to submit to this discipline and make amends. In this sense, contrition is incomplete without confession. Thirdly, it is a salutary discipline: heaven is opened through frequent confession with deep shame. It cleans out the heart in preparation for the Holy Spirit, a means by which hidden disease is opened to the hope of forgiveness, an opening of the tomb. It is good to confess in any stress. And "adding a felicitous oral confession to contrition, in due circumstances in a priest's hearing and omitting nothing relevant, augments merit."[41]

The characteristics of a worthy confession are summed up in a series of terms the preacher uses over and over for easy recall. Confession must be *premeditata, nuda, recta et integra, accusans, aspera, lacrymosa, cum spe et vera humilitate.*

First, it must be premeditated. But, you ask, how much diligence must a person devote to recalling sins? Certainly more than one would ever devote to anything transitory. When our responsibility to an earthly overlord places a hand or a foot or an eye at risk, we are most careful to render strict account; but in confession, our whole life is at stake. So we must devote enough forethought to our confession to allow the priest to know when and where, how often, and how severely the sins occurred. It will not do to say, "I committed this sin quite often." If we do not know exactly, we should say, "Ten or twenty or a hundred times over such and such a period," to give the priest a realistic sense whether we have sinned from ignorance and weakness or deliberate malice, how long we have lain in sins, from youth or for three or thirty years, so that he may apply an appropriate remedy.[42]

Next, it must be stark, unadorned, entire, and unexpurgated. The penitent has two duties here: to do everything he or she can (by listening to sermons and by active recall) to remember times, places, and frequency throughout the year; and to ask God to illuminate the heart to recognize sins, then go to the priest and disclose all sins baldly and openly so that he understands, not watering down, obscuring, or omitting any sin from human shame. Nevertheless, God's mercy is not divided. If you genuinely try to identify all your many sins but succeed in recalling only some of them, God will regard them all as confessed and expunged if you disclose

---

[41] D.25.2/1 (H), T.14.1/6 (G), T.43.2 (L), T.48.1/1 (I), T.68.2/1 (F), Q.12.2.
[42] D.23.2/2 (J), T.8.2 (C), T.38.0 (before C), Q.12.2.

them frankly; but if you have only a handful to confess and deliberately omit even one of them out of shame, none is forgiven.[43]

Humiliation, shame, and embarrassment are the great enemies here. They hold many back, yet ironically it is precisely the depth of the shame involved that is one of confession's chief values. Herolt even advises that one should not become too familiar with a confessor, since then the shame could diminish, and that would harm the confession; but on the other hand, one should not divide up a confession, running to other priests in order to reduce the embarrassment. He recommends three antidotes for this affliction. The first is plain reason. If you are not ashamed to *do* warped and dishonest things, why be ashamed to *confess* them, which is honest and beneficial? The second is divine intuition. God knows anyway, so why be diffident before his priest? The third is future confusion. If you do not disclose your misdeeds now, you will do so later before all humanity, the saints, and the angels.[44]

Confession must be of one's own sins, and another's name should not be given in confession unless it is essential to identify one's own sin. The priest who is a good physician of souls will not ask the identity of another person with whom one sinned. In confessing one of the alien sins—complicity in another's misdeed—the penitent should protect the other's repute as far as possible, but it is an even higher duty to purge one's own conscience.[45]

A worthy confession is self-accusing—that is, not mitigating the sin by claiming it was God's will or fate or someone else's fault or the devil's doing.[46]

Like the contrition it expresses, confession must be tearful; our sins must be confessed with grief and bitterness of heart so that mercy may follow. In practice, every confessor knows people who recite their sins as if they were telling the priest an anecdote, with no compunction at all about their sins. And those who weep for their other losses but do not weep for their sins betray the hardness of their hearts.[47]

Finally, confession must be made with good hope and true humility, for a penance made without humble confidence in God's mercy is useless and sterile.[48]

Tragically, Herolt says, of ten or twelve kinds of people who come to confession, possibly only one does true penance. One knowingly hides something, another discloses everything but intends to sin again, a third is sorry but will not make restitution, some confess but will not forgive others, some truly repent but

---

[43] D.25.2/2 (K), T.44.1 (R-S), Q.13.3.
[44] D.25.2/2 (K), T.14.1/6 (G), T.44.1 (S-T), T.113.7 (S), Q.13.3, Q.15.3.
[45] D.25.2/2 (K), Q.14.3, Q.23.3.
[46] D.25.2/2 (K), Q.14.3.
[47] D.25.2/2 (K), Q.15.3.
[48] D.25.2/2 (K), Q.16.3.

immediately backslide, and others confess but will not relinquish prohibited positions. Many penitents confess from custom or fear, not grace and love (often betrayed by the way they defer confession till the last week of Lent); and there are people who confess and accept a penance but never perform it. The all-too-rare true penitents are those who confess all the sins they are aware of, firmly intend not to sin again willingly, and are ready to make satisfaction according to the confessor's counsel.[49]

For this sobering reason, the preacher finds it necessary to address a number of more prosaic questions which beginners on the path of repentance may ask.

Who must confess? Every adult with the use of reason who has committed mortal sins after baptism. What is an adult? Someone of an age to know right from wrong in divine law. How does someone who is deaf or speaks a foreign tongue make a confession? In writing, or by nodding in response to questions, or through an interpreter sworn to secrecy.[50]

What are we bound to confess? Everything the church's instruction identifies as mortal sin, which has not been duly confessed before and which we can conscientiously recall (with due allowance for human frailty). In order to make this injunction even clearer, "a plain statement for simple people," Herolt lists the twelve commonest mortal sins "according to the usual course of the world" and then twelve rudimentary questions the confessor should ask parishioners to identify the commonest sins.

> For if those making confession have been led by shame to hide what they know they have committed, or from simplicity or ignorance so not know to confess completely, their confession may sometimes become inadequate, or useless, or harmful unless a prudent confessor and diligent investigator identifies their defect.[51]

Must one confess venial sins? There is no divine command to do so, but some recommend it annually for the sake of conformity and priestly absolution. Should you confess a sin if you are unsure whether it is mortal or venial? It is dangerous not to, but do not assert it as one or the other; just tell the facts and let the priest decide. What if the priest already knows about a sin? Confess it anyway; he knows as a man, not as vicar of Christ. Is it licit to confess sins one has not committed? No, one who was not a sinner becomes one by lying! But if you are uncertain? If the doubt is probable but you cannot be sure, then for security confess conditionally.[52]

---

[49] T.44.1-10 (R-E), cf. Q.26.2.
[50] Q.17.3.
[51] Q.19.2, Q.22.3.
[52] Q.20.3, Q.21.3.

How should you confess the sins you have forgotten? "Domine, it also seems likely to me that I may have committed many sins against God that I have forgotten through my negligence and inadvertence and cannot call to mind." That is enough, but if a sin is later recalled, it should be specifically confessed.[53] Must anyone who has sinned mortally confess straight away? Contrition and the intention to confess must be immediate; but there is no obligation to proceed to confession instantly, except at Easter or if one intends to take communion. Some say it is best to confess straight away, and there is some danger of letting sins pile up; nevertheless, confession may be deferred, and it is permissible for lay people to confess once a year in normal circumstances.[54]

Finally, to whom should one confess? Only to a priest and only one with competent jurisdiction. Confession may not be made to a lay person except in extreme necessity, and even then it is a counsel, not a requirement. Is the parish priest bound to believe a parishioner who claims he or she has confessed to another authorized confessor? If the issue is admission to communion, by all means, but not if a judicial issue such as excommunication is involved.[55]

As we have seen, the passionate high doctrine of contrition must descend through commonplace almost to banality in order to encompass all the sorts and conditions of Christians in the pastor's charge. Little wonder then that his image of the penitent as phoenix arising from the ashes of fervent humility to rebirth in confession and a new plumage of virtues gives place to another image. One who fears to begin penance is like the ass, very fearful of water on the ground or getting its feet wet or crossing bridges because of the weakness of its head![56]

Satisfaction

The third part of penance—satisfaction—occupies far less of the preacher's attention. The purpose of satisfaction is to excise the causes of sins and to prevent access to the things that prompt them. In principle, Herolt says, the penances imposed in satisfaction are supposed to bear some objective proportion to the severity of the sin in God's sight; but in practice, their imposition is today committed to the discretion of priests who can take into account the individual circumstances of the sinner and the situation. The objective is to find a realistic penance that will not drive the penitent to default or despair but will still have the intended effect of removing the causes and occasions of sins.

Herolt is prepared to take this principle of accommodation a very long way, while retaining his high view of the efficacy of discipline. If a penitent claims to be

---

[53] Q.23.3.
[54] T.67.1 (Y), T.68.2/1 (F), Q.24.3.
[55] Q.25.3.
[56] A.P.: 16.1 "Penitentia" (124ᵇ), A.P.: 18 "Penitentia" (124ᵇ).

contrite and to be firmly committed to persevere, but refuses a penance, what should the confessor do? Herolt's advice is not to send the person away, lest they despair, but to absolve: "It is proper for a pious confessor, in a warm and benevolent manner, not berating or rejecting but supporting and drawing, to hear such people confess in this fashion." Willingness, after all, is an essential aspect of any satisfaction.[1] Similarly, if the confessor believes the penitent may not perform a penance, he should not force an unwelcome satisfaction, but simply absolve without conditions on the undertaking that the penitent intends to make satisfaction.[2]

In light of this voluntary character, what satisfactions are appropriate? It remains the case that a work enjoined by a priest has more power in expiating sins than a self-chosen satisfaction, and the priest will generally make the satisfaction fit the sin, imposing corrections by opposites fasting for gluttony, alms for avarice, flagellation or hard beds or harsh clothing for lust, and so on. Restitution of any losses caused by one's sin is an essential and practical penance. Acts of pain are fitting if they serve the pastoral purpose, including flagellation if it is borne patiently for purging sins, but not if the purpose is vindictiveness rather than satisfaction. As far as possible, penances should have a preservative effect against the recurrence of besetting sins.[3]

Whatever the satisfaction, the penitent should know that the punishment owing to any sin must be expiated here or later; and as we shall see, it is prudent to fulfil it here. The rule is simply stated: If our penance here is equal to the gravity of the sin, then absolution is complete; nothing remains to be satisfied. If the penance exceeds the sin, we accrue merit in heaven. But if the penance falls short of the sin, then we shall make up the punishment in purgatory with a bitterness and sharpness that make our present penances seem as nothing.[4]

Here, as in every other respect, the pervasive context of the preacher's exhortations to repentance is the consciousness of death and all that follows it. On Ash Wednesday, when sinners come seeking the medicine of penitence for all the diseases of the soul, consecrated ashes are placed on their brows to warn them to remember death, with the words of the Memento: "Remember, man, that you are ash, and to ash you will return."[5] We do not know when, how, in what state, where, or by what means we shall die—in home or bed, in city or field, by water or fire, by day or night. "If, then, we have strayed by sinning, let us return to the path of salvation by repenting."[6] It is this urgency, and the example of Christ's humility and hope in his own death, which gives contrition its fervor:

---

[1] Q.27.3.
[2] Q.28.3.
[3] D.25.3/1 (L), T.14.1/9 (K), T.43.3 (O), Q.29.3, Q.30.3.
[4] D.25.3/3 (N), T.14.1/9 (K), S.24.2/5, Q.33.2, and see chapter 22.
[5] T.38.0 (before C).
[6] T.128.1 (J).

Fervent contrition is like blazing coals—first for its glow, for dead coal is jet black but when it burns, it glows red. Sins, like cold coal, show the blackness of sin. As Augustine says in *de doctrina christiana*, "The soul persisting in sin is as black as a crow, but when it is inflamed to repentance the blackness of sin is changed into the brightness of the love of God." . . . Secondly, coal has the power to conserve heat . . . so the ashes of humility and the memory of death conserve grace in a person and preserve him from the fall of sin . . . Nothing so powerfully recalls from sins as frequent meditation on death.[7]

Only the tears of repentance extinguish the fire of guilt and wash the soul of the penitent sinner.[8]

---

[7] A.C.: 7 "Contritio" (115ᵃ).
[8] A.L.: 1 "Lacrymarum compunctio" (119ᵃ).

5

SIN

"Sin consists in this: that a man, with premeditated reason, knowingly, voluntarily, and freely, without contradiction by his reason and with deliberate intention, turns himself from God to defective things."[9] The essence of sin lies in loving anything more than or as much as God.[10] Whatever absorbs a person's human energies, whatever it is one imitates, trusts, wants to serve, conforms to, labors for, fears to neglect, or loves and honors by words, acts, or sacrifices is one's god.[11]

The common characteristic of all the mortal sins is that each substitutes a creature for the creator as the object of devotion. Pride, for example, substitutes honor and adornment, avarice wealth and profits, gluttony, the belly, and so on. They do not allow God to be god and so deprive the sinner of the only source of grace and salvation. When Herolt discourses on the grave sins individually, his particular dissuasions—the reasons to detest each sin in turn, whatever its accidental features—come down to three things: Sin tries to rob God of his goodness, his glory, and his dwelling-place in the heart; it delights and aids the devil in destroying human life; and it devastates the sinner by robbing his body, soul, and spirit of all natural and supernatural blessings.[12]

Herolt's treatment of individual sins (and their manifestation in particular actions) is elaborate and extensive. Most of his moral judgments are described in later chapters. It is the pattern of his teaching about sin and sinfulness that concerns us here. A brief outline of his instruction may throw light on the message lay people heard in these sermons, which move directly from profound doctrinal formularies to moral commonplaces, from a profound analysis of sin as idolatry to a catalogue of everyday, even trivial, infractions.

The most concerted treatment of sins is to be found in the early catechetical book *de eruditio christifidelium* (1416). Much of this material is reproduced

---

[9] T.29.1/2 (P).
[10] E.37.1/2.
[11] D.2.24 (V), T.41.24 (Q), E.37.1/2.
[12] D.13.1 (A), D.14.1 (K.), D.15.1 (A), D.16.1 (A-D), D.17.1 (A-B), D.18.1 (A-B), D.19.1 (A).

verbatim, excerpted, adapted, or echoed in the *sermones de tempore* and *de sanctis* for regular parish preaching. The catechism begins with ten long chapters expounding the Ten Commandments, and each chapter contains a list of "the classes of people who break this commandment" or "modes of transgressing this precept." Thus there are twenty-four ways of "worshipping strange gods," fifteen empty uses of God's name, eight ways to break the Lord's day, seven ways to dishonor one's earthly and spiritual parents, ten forms of physical homicide and eight spiritual (one of which, detraction, has eight modes of its own), seven descending levels of sexual transgression, seventeen forms of theft (including twelve subcategories of fraud, ten of usury, and eighteen of gambling), eight ways to speak falsely, and ten ways to lust after one's neighbor's goods and four after his wife.[13]

The commandments, Herolt says, are the "path to eternal life." They declare God's purpose for human life, and God wants to befriend and dwell with those who keep them and to answer their petitions. They protect us from evil and bring a multiplicity of promised blessings.[14] Lest we forget God's commands, they are written on our very bodies as a constant reminder—on our ten fingers (to direct our actions), our ten toes (to direct our paths) and our five outward and five inward senses (to direct our thoughts and perceptions).[15] Furthermore, they are not burdensome, but light. How can they be light, seeing that to break one is to break them all? They weigh heavily on those with little love, but they are light to those with great love, which fulfils them all.[16] "All the commandments and their saving fulfilment flow originally from the root of love as from their wellspring and source, and are ultimately ordered towards love as their end and consummating goal."[17]

Despite this emphasis on love, the stronger emphasis is on innocence; and accordingly Herolt's expositions of the commandments catalogue all the common, everyday sins that in the church's eyes destroy that innocence. This catalogue is succeeded by another; now the framework is not the Decalogue but the traditional list (springing from Cassian and Gregory) of seven mortal sins. Each of the mortal sins receives its own chapter of the catechism, and these materials too are reused in the Sunday sermons. In turn, the preacher describes why each mortal disposition is to be hated, how many forms it takes, what children it begets, how it masquerades as virtue, and he usually adds practical advice about remedies.

---

13   D.1.1-14 (E-U), D.2.2 (B-L), D.3.2 (C-K), D.4.1 (A and H), D.5.2-5 (C-Q), D.6.1-7 (A-F), D.7.17 (A-JJ), D.8.1-8 (A-N), D.9.1-10 (A-C), cf. T.142-143, S.38.2.
14   D.1.0 (A).
15   D.1.0 (B), T.154.1/1 (E), S.39.2, E.2.2/2.
16   E.39.2/2.
17   D.1.0 (C).

Pride

Pride, "the beginning and foundation of all evil,"[18] takes both interior and exterior forms; and spiritual pride is potentially far more dangerous than outward pomposity.[19] Interior pride tries (like Lucifer) to rob God of his glory by supposing that you have your blessings from yourself or, if they are from God, that you deserved them for your merits, or you believe you have virtues you lack and esteem yourself (like the Pharisee in the Gospel) superior to others.[20] There is enormous peril in the complacency that springs from a conviction of one's own sanctity.[21] Exterior pride takes many obvious social forms; but the expressions of it that chiefly draw the preacher's ire are all the ostentatious, costly, self-indulgent, and newfangled fashions in dress, footwear, accessories, cosmetics, and headgear that seems to him such blatant expressions of contempt for God's handiwork, and female snares to catch male souls.[22] The children of pride, he says, are boastful and self-acclaiming and disobedience, and they have contention, hypocrisy, discord, and presumptuous novelty; and though such pride is most obviously a sin of the wealthy and respectable, it is equally reprehensible in the proud pauper (one who envies the ostentation of the rich).[23] In its most insidious form, it masquerades as spiritual zeal, holiness, and even humility, but in fact it is a sign of reprobation and a particularly intractable sin.[24] Pride is essentially mortal, since it refuses to be subject to God and makes vainglory its god instead.[25]

Envy

Frustrated pride gives birth to the mortal sin of envy. Not all envy is sin, Herolt says. There is an initial impulse to a sort of covetousness in our natures, but because it is not in our power to remove it, it is no sin unless we give it our consent. If we merely feel some unhappiness at a neighbor's good fortune without deliberation, that is simply venial sin. But if we experience grief at a neighbor's goodness, status, or good fortune out of deliberate hatred, that is mortal sin.[26] It makes the envious person terribly unhappy; everything he sees and hears seems to conspire together to his disadvantage. It is like a worm in wood, rust on metal, mold on bread; they

---

[18] T.31.3 (Q).
[19] T.72.1 (U).
[20] D.13.2 (B-C), T.107.0 (H).
[21] T.137.2 (R) and .3 (X).
[22] D.13.1 (E-L), T.83.2 (I), T.141.1 (J), and see chapter 12.
[23] D.13.17 (P-AA), T.21.3 (X), T.81.3 (B).
[24] D.13.8 (BB), T.58.7 (G), T.149.4 (E).
[25] D.1.24 (V), T.41.24 (Q), T.107.3 (O), E.30.1/2.
[26] D.14.2 (B), T.141.6 (O), E.29.2/2.

all feed on their host, and envy feeds on prior envy and does far more harm to the envier than the envied.[27] It is the diametrical opposite of love and gives birth to hatred, talebearing, joy at the adversity of others, sorrow at their prosperity, and detraction. Genuine hatred of vice is really not envy but love; yet envy often masquerades as this zeal and rectitude (it betrays itself by telltale signs—pale face, averted eyes, clenched teeth, and rigid posture). Or jealousy of the ideas or success of other groups may represent itself as fraternal loyalty to one's own group (an ever-present temptation to members of religious orders, Herolt thinks). Or in a specious display of loving concern for another's salvation, the envious person may decry coveted possessions as inexpedient. The entire disposition is the contradiction of that benevolence and innocence which forms the heart of neighborly love.[28]

Anger

Like envy, anger is not necessarily a mortal sin. But while the natural impulse to envy is always to be resisted, there is a good and praiseworthy anger, like Christ's anger at the envy of his opponents. Our capacity for anger has been given to us so that we may be legitimately enraged at vices and evil suggestions (our own and others'). There is also a venial anger. A sudden flash of unbidden anger may be venial if resisted, as may a trivial act of revenge which is not prepared to go further, or an inward impatient anger which resists outward expression. But as the severity of the expression escalates, so does the sinfulness of the rage. If the anger is nurtured inwardly and dreams of revenge, it is mortal sin even without outward action. Mortal anger may shown by outward gestures, by gestures and vituperative words, or ultimately by striking, wounding, seizing, or even killing another against God and justice; and this is a very great sin.[29] May one person abuse another in the course of fraternal discipline? May a husband strike his wife? Yes, in both cases, but only in moderation and only for correction, not for displaced rage.[30] The offspring of anger are strife, paranoia, and commotion, all mortal sins if they flow from habitual anger but venial if a result of choler or weakness; indigestion, for rage inflicts great harm on one's own body; and the always-mortal sins of contumely and blasphemy.[31] Blasphemy, the "provincial dialect of hell," is not ever excused by lack of deliberation, though a trivial, inadvertent oath may be venial if it goes unnoticed; but all execrable oaths which angrily ascribe to God what is not his own are a proof of mortal death.[32]

---

27 E.29.2/1 and 3.
28 D.14.3-4 (D-G).
29 D.15.2 (B-C), T.95.1-8 (G-M), T.141.5 (N), E.24.2/3, E.46.2/1.
30 D.15.7-8 (C), T.95.7-8 (I and N).
31 D.15.3 (D-F).
32 D.2.2/5 (D-E), D.15.3/6 (F), T.123 passim, T.129.2/4 (Q), T.139.1 (L), E.22.2/1, Q.17.2/2.

Anger, too, uses the device of self-righteousness to masquerade as virtue, representing itself as a zeal for justice and a fervent desire for the neighbor's well-being. It may even claim to be meekness and patience, especially (Herolt observes) in those who repress their anger, say nothing, but seethe inwardly.[33] The remedies he recommends against one's own anger are to reflect on Christ's passion, one's personal defects, and the virtue of patience and tolerance; to realize that one cannot harm another without harming oneself, like the bee who stings and then dies, or the mad dog who bites a rock and breaks his own teeth; and to keep silent.[34] Remedies against another's anger are a soft answer, a blessing, or again silence.[35]

Accidie

The mortal sin of accidie receives more perfunctory treatment. Much of the tradition Herolt repeats comes from the counsel given to monks when they succumb to tedium in the monastic round, and it must be stretched to describe a more commonplace weariness in doing good that the laity will recognize as a sin. So the preacher offers a selection of synonyms: accidie is torpor, aridity, nausea, spiritual (and often literal) oversleeping, coldness, tepidity, slackness, negligence, action out of habit rather than love, an inordinate bitterness of soul that snuffs out spiritual joy, the mind turning inward in a gesture of despair, a "badly lit fire that goes out quickly." As the body's natural humors are restored by adequate sleep but smothered by too much, so evil affections and noxious thoughts are multiplied by accidie and suffocate the warmth of spiritual love. Besides, it is a waste of useful time and energy.[36] The simplest definition is *tedium boni*, which has three grades. There is a certain physical lassitude after spiritual exertion, and this is no sin. Then there is a sense of weariness that may come from thinking how laborious spiritual work can be; even if one indulges this feeling, it is still only venial. But when tedium leads one to omit things necessary for salvation (such as hearing mass or completing imposed penances), then it is a mortal sin. If our efforts are acceptable to God, they must be done with diligence, gladness, and goodwill.[37] From accidie spring pusillanimity, malice, rancor (especially against those who urge a change of attitude), a toying with illicit pleasures, a state of torpor, and finally—the worst sin of all—despair. Yet it justifies itself in the name of fictitious contemplation. The remedies, the preacher says, are partly mental—consideration of how Christ labored, of how we are set in the time of grace, and of how our labors now free us

---

[33] D.15.4 (Q).
[34] D.15.5 (H), A.I.: 4 "Ira" (118ᵃ) and I: 6 "Iracundus" (118ᵃ).
[35] D.15.6 (J).
[36] D.16.1 (A), T.140.1 (A), T.141.7 (P), A.A.: 6 "Accidia" (111ᵃ).
[37] D.16.3 (J), T.140.1 (B-C), T.141.7 (P).

from labor hereafter and bring a reward. But the practical remedy is a diversity of occupations.[38]

Avarice

Avarice is a far more familiar vice. So familiar, in fact, that Herolt's catechism omits the usual list of ways to commit this sin. But he makes good this omission with a list of four varieties of avarice in his *sermo communis* on the seven mortal sins. A person commits the mortal sin of greed by desiring other people's possessions against God and justice; by acquiring property unjustly; by spending his wealth wrongly; and by first gaining, and then holding tight, his possessions with miserliness and insatiable cupidity.[39] Each of these themes—the dangers and deceptive security of wealth, slavery to riches, meanness and refusal to give, gambling, usury, fraud, conspicuous consumption—is elaborated in sermon after sermon, story after story.[40] The root of them all is an idolatry that takes earthly blessings and makes god of them, a sick craving that substitutes bondage to the creature for devotion to the creator.[41] Greed makes people hard hearted (but there will be no mercy to those who show no mercy); mentally perturbed and anxious; violent in gaining property by seizure, oppressing the powerless, or theft; traitorous, like Judas; deceitful in words and fraudulent in dealings; and forsworn.[42] Avarice often speciously represents itself as a necessary providence, or even as piety and liberality, claiming the motive for stockpiling wealth is to give generous help.[43] But greedy people are like the repulsive gryphons that guard the mountains where the gems are buried, lest anyone should mine and use them,[44] like toads that are frightened to lift their heads from the dirt for fear of losing ground.[45] The remedies for avarice are consideration of death, reminding a man of the contemptibility of all the things the world chases; confidence in the providence of God who will not forsake those who hope in him; separation from greedy and grasping associates; recollection of Christ's poverty; consideration that wealth acquired here will harm the soul hereafter, not least in the strict account in judgment of every last penny; comparison of the world's transitory wealth with the eternal riches; and recognition of how often possessions are the occasions of sin. They generate litigation and

---

[38] D.16.2 (E-H) and .4-5 (K-O).
[39] T.141.2 (K).
[40] See chapters 15 and 18.
[41] D.1.24 (V), T.41.24 (Q), T.118.0 (before J).
[42] D.17.2 (C-G).
[43] D.17.3 (H).
[44] A.A.: 14 "Anima" (112^b).
[45] T.82.4 (E).

dissension, backstabbing and malice; they place gluttony, ostentation, and lust within reach, and they make men arrogant.[46]

Gluttony

Avarice makes treasure its god; gluttony makes the belly god—meal times its holy days, the kitchen its temple, the table its altar, the cook its priest, meats its burnt offerings, and savory odors its incense.[47] Herolt reproduces from tradition two overlapping catalogues of gluttonous behavior: "seven reprehensible modes of eating and drinking to excess" followed by "five modes of sinning in gluttony." Gluttons eat before the due time. They have developed an excessive liking for delicacies. They devote too much energy and time to the preparation of meals, and they eat too avidly, too often, and too much, not only in quantity but also in the number and variety of dishes.[48] Gluttons ate like vultures that scavenge the ground for rotting food but have the greatest difficulty becoming airborne.[49] It is gluttony when you love your body so much that you are ready to eat on fast days against the church's precept or consume foods the church has prohibited (such as milk or eggs in Lent). It is gluttony when out of sheer delectation you deliberately ingest harmful substances that debilitate the body and shorten life. It is most obviously gluttony when you fall into so much excess, especially in drink, that you lose your reason and become nauseous, vomiting, and helplessly drunk—the worse the inebriation, the graver, (and more disgusting) the sin. In short, gluttony is when you love food so much that the appetite for delicious food becomes the final and chief cause of eating, "placing food before God who is the final and chief cause of all our acts." Enjoying food, to be sure, is not a sin—it is natural so long as it is done with gratitude and moderation—but to put such a sack of manure as the stomach in God's place is utterly despicable.[50]

Lust

In exposition of the sixth commandment, the preacher has listed the outward acts of lust. The basic list has five acts of increasing turpitude: fornication, defloration, adultery, incest, and unnatural acts. He sometimes adds two more acts: a breach of the vow of continence and abuses of the conjugal act.[51] Now he displays the spiritual nature of lust by listing seven or sometimes ten ways lust happens

---

[46] D.17.4 (J-O), T.118.2 (K-O).
[47] D.18.1/1 (A), T.41.24 (Q), E.50.2.
[48] D.18.2 (C-F), T.98.1/1-5 (F-K), and see chapter 18.
[49] A.G.: 5 "Gulosi" (117ª).
[50] D.18.3 (G-K), T.99.211-5 (M-P), T.141.3 (L).
[51] D.6.1-7 (A-G), T.25.2/5 (G), T.85.1-6 (O-R).

without any sexual act at all. For while the sixth commandment forbids the act of lust, the tenth forbids lustful desire.[52] However, it is simply a fact of experience that carnal concupiscence is the plainest expression of the tinder of sin, the *fomes peccati*, that remains in our soul as a result of the fall and in spite of baptism. That impulse of desire is not itself sin, but it prompts the suggestions that so readily ignite into sins, and in this sense our flesh that carries the kindling wood is our enemy.[53] Carnal concupiscence is a thirst, a fire that inflames the mind, a worm that gnaws at the innards, a cloud that darkens the reason, an unclean disposition so "one horse can pull more downhill than ten uphill."[54] Yet in spite of its strength, it is only a suggestion. It is not coercing, and those who claim otherwise blaspheme God and make themselves baser than the brute beasts.[55] It is only by yielding to the prompting and by indulging the desire that a man makes the flesh his god. So involuntary lustful thought without any pleasure is no sin at all; indeed, we can gain merit by resisting it.[56] The next step is a filthy thought that evokes some pleasure but without the consent of full reason: this is venial. For there are three steps that lead from temptation to sin: suggestion, pleasure, and consent. There may be an intermediate stage in which the reason sees that a thought is disgraceful, tries and fails to overcome it, and consent takes over, "like peeking through the fingers." But if a person chooses deliberately to indulge a lustful thought, consents to wallow in "morose delight," and imagines how pleasurable it would be to fulfil it, this is mortal sin, and so is an intention to do the act itself if opportunity arises. Mortal lust can also be indulged by intentionally looking at a woman with desire (or in a woman's case by adorning herself to evoke that desire), by speaking or joking seductively, by shameless touching of bodies or untoward embraces, and by giving trinkets and gifts designed to arouse passion. And refraining from consummating an act of lust merely for fear of scandal is tantamount to the act itself.[57] Lust, once indulged, produces blindness of moral judgment, precipitate behavior, thoughtlessness, inconstancy, self-absorption, hatred of God and love of the world, and helpless foolishness.[58] Lust makes a lubricious man into a goat—useless for productive work, always febrile and in heat, and fetid[59]—and such a man is not welcome at the heavenly feast.[60] Yet lust often disguises itself as affability and benevolence, charity and generosity, even (in the case of those who use pastoral contact as an opportunity

---

[52] T.143.6 (A) and .10 (X).
[53] T.88.4 (M), T.138.2 (B), E.2.2/3.
[54] T.2.1 (J), T.71.3 (T), T.138.2 (B), A.L.: 4-6 "Luxuria" (ll9ª).
[55] D.19.5 (N), T.58.5 (F), T.86.2 (D).
[56] T.151.1 (D).
[57] D.19.2/1-10 (B-H), T.86.1/1-10 (S-C), T.131.1 (F), T.141.4 (M), E.13.2/3.
[58] D.19.3 (J-L).
[59] A.L.: 7 "Luxuria" (ll9ᵇ).
[60] T.110.1 (M).

to indulge their fantasies) as sanctity and goodness of heart.[61] The remedies are to douse the fire of lust with the cold water and the thorns of tribulation and to starve desire by abstaining from food and drink and avoiding the occasions of lust (which in practice means avoiding the company of women, since Herolt addresses the sexuality of men only).[62]

What is striking about all these accounts of human sinfulness is how directly Herolt moves in every instance from a profound analysis of sin as idolatry (love or fear of a creature more than the creator, the refusal to let God be god) to a mundane, commonplace, even bathetic compilation of immoralities and foibles. By this conjunction, he implies that the divine will impinges directly on the minutiae of everyday life, but also that the goals and values of earthly life are meaningless apart from the pursuit of grace and heavenly reward. On the one hand, the "vilest thing in the world is every mortal sin—so vile that it is totally without profit either to body or soul";[63] but the "twelve commonest mortal sins"—that is, the infractions most commonly encountered in the confessor's questioning of penitents—are (1) false oaths in buying and selling, (2) superstitions, (3) working on feast days and eating on fasts, (4) disobedience to parents, (5) murmuring against God about trials and tribulations, (6) extramarital sex, (7) petty theft, (8) detraction and gossip, (9) dancing and proud dressing, (10) eating and drinking to excess, (11) anger and envy, and (12) marital discord.[64] These are not only the subject of the priest's interrogation during confession, but Herolt even pictures Christ, at the last judgment, asking cobblers whether they singed their leather or cellarers whether they gave full measure.[65] Indeed, sin is such an ordinary occurrence that it is very easy for the worldly wise to paint the mortal sins as urbane and commendable behavior:

> Nowadays, thanks to the social climbers, the vices have gained the name of virtues. Pride in clothing—girdles, shoes, all the external trappings—they call respectability: "How well this tunic suits you!" or "How good you look in that robe!" or "How prettily you move in that vest!" ... Avarice is called providence when someone labors night or day for temporal gain—whether just or unjust, however acquired, with or without God, they couldn't care less! ... Dissoluteness is called social merriment, going along with the crowd in things licit and illicit, good or bad, dancing, leaping, gambling, and all the rest ... Cunning is called prudence—especially wheeling

---

[61] D.19.4 (M).
[62] D.19.6 (O-Q), T.86.2 (D), and see chapter 10.
[63] T.119.1 (P).
[64] S.27.2, Q.19.2, Q.22.3.
[65] T.4.7 (X).

and dealing in trade and negotiation ... A lax conscience is called freedom of spirit—living free from care without any fear or thought of God ... Garrulousness is called affability—gossip among men or women, scurrilous talk not caring whether God is offended, but the sycophants call them merry fellows![66]

By the same logic, the worldly deride the virtuous. Anyone who lives austerely for God's sake is labelled stingy. Those who humbly imitate Christ are called hypocrites, serious-minded, avoidance of levity is called bitterness, quiet devotion is called laziness, simplicity and meekness are called stupidity, fear of God is a rigid conscience, avoiding bad company is insularity, pursuit of justice is severity and intolerance, someone respected for upright conversation is labelled "toady," and anyone who seeks his neighbor's edification is accused of presumption.[67] Such attitudes also reveal how easy it is to commit mortal sin at one remove—the so-called alien sins—by ordering, advising, consenting to, or even commanding another's misdeeds or by aiding and abetting, sharing in the profits, or failing to correct, resist, or disclose sinful acts.[68]

The Nature of Sin

Since Herolt's purpose is to address a simple, pragmatic description of everyday sins and their danger to the laity, the sermons contain far more of this sort of homely psychological observation than precise theological formulation of the doctrine of sin. As we saw at the outset, the definition of sin is "that a man, with premeditated reason, knowingly, voluntarily, and freely, without contradiction by his reason and with deliberate intention, turns himself from God to defective things."[69] Each of the elements of this definition receives separate treatment. The differences among original, mortal, alien, and venial sins are also spelled out, though always in a pastoral frame. Even in the 1444 *Sermones super epistolas*, where Herolt occasionally treats the doctrines of sin and grace far more technically than in his earlier works, the application to Christian living is never neglected.

There are two movements in mortal sin: a turning away from God and a turning toward the creature.[70] To these two movements correspond the inevitable consequences of sin, which have marked human life ever since our first parents took the path from temptation to sin—the serpent's suggestion, Eve's pleasure in

---

[66] D.11.4 (F), T.144.4 (K).
[67] D.11.4 (G), T.144.4 (L).
[68] D.11 (A-O), T.144-145 (H-R).
[69] T.29.1/2 (P).
[70] E.1.2.

it, and Adam's consent.[71] The immediate consequence is that man has lost God and is bereft of the vision of God, which none but God can restore. This privation in turn has had three devastating effects. First, man is deprived of the shapeliness of grace that flows from being bathed in divine light. Turned from that light, the soul becomes deformed, stained, wounded. Second, the soul not only loses its comeliness, but the goodness of human nature is intrinsically corrupted and disordered when its will is not subject to God. "Once man's order has been vitiated, the effects endure in the whole once-ordered nature of sinful man."[72] Even the elements from which our bodies are composed have been corrupted by sin,[73] and the proneness to desire which is the kindling of new sins is always in us.[74] "The human condition, from the prevarication of our first parents, has grown fragile and infirm, within and without, above and below, before and behind, to right and left, and the passions flow through all parts of the body."[75] The body thus corrupted by original sin serves as a weight dragging down the soul, its passions provoking a continual war in our members—flesh against spirit, affections against reason, and conscience against will.[76] Thirdly, man incurs the guilt of his sin. By turning away from God toward defective creatures, he merits eternal damnation and remains liable to pay this penalty unless discharged by God, against whom the offence was committed. By the sin of our mortal progenitors, the penalty of death attaches to our very nature— "man is by nature the child of wrath."[77]

Original sin is a deep pit into which man has fallen and he cannot get out, a net in which he is helplessly trapped like a bird or a fish, a rope by which he is led willy-nilly to hell, a chain bound so tightly about him that he cannot escape.[78] But God, through the mercy poured out for us in Christ, has provided a way of escape for those who are in the catholic faith by means of baptism. While all those who are outside the faith pay the penalty of original sin and are consigned automatically to damnation, the grace of God in baptism removes the guilt and with it the penalty of original sin. It restores primal innocence, frees from the devil's power, extinguishes the fire of hell, infuses grace to mitigate and overcome the tinder of sin, and impresses on the soul the indelible character of the children of God for whom heaven stands open.[79]

---

[71] D.19.2/4 (C), T.138.1 (A).
[72] E.1.1/2.
[73] T.60.3/6 (P).
[74] T.138.2 (B).
[75] E.31.0.
[76] T.34.3 (T), E.31.1.
[77] T.19.2 (D), T.27.10 (D), E.15.1/4, E.38.3.
[78] E.1.1/2.
[79] T.66.3 (U), T.76.2 (X), T.148.1 (S).

But the tinder of sin, the concupiscent desire that inheres in our bodily passions and appetites, is only dampened, not removed, by baptism. In itself, it is not sinful but is an ever-present catalyst that inclines us to sin, as the indwelling gifts of the Spirit incline us to goodness. In this situation, those who die in their baptismal innocence go straight to heaven. But for Christians of the age of discretion who must continue to live in the body amid the tribulations of the world, the choice that confronted our first parents is all but recreated. God's commandments still point out to us the path to eternal life and his will and purpose for us. On the other side, the concupiscence in our flesh and the graphic immediacy of the things that excite it play the serpent's role and constantly suggest a turning away from God toward the creature. And while we cannot do good without the aid of grace, we can do evil by ourselves.[80]

Can a Christian live without sin? Everyone sins venially—that is, commits those "everyday sins"[81] that require some punishment but are not weighty enough to deserve death. "If we are talking about someone who has reached adulthood, then from excellent and special grace, yes—one can live without venial sin. But if we are talking about the entire life of all saints, the answer is a unanimous No!"[82] Venial sin is committed four ways: something intrinsically trivial, a peccadillo—an idle word, an empty thought; an impulse which, if acted on, would be mortal but remains venial because cut off—a flash of sudden anger, a wave of involuntary desire; a mortal act immediately rendered forgivable by repentance; or an error of conscience, supposing something innocuous is sinful.[83] Venial sin is easily forgiven, but it should be avoided because it smears the soul (like dimming but not blotting out an image), diminishes fervor (like droplets of water that damp but do not extinguish a fire), and burdens good works (like piling on extra weights). It may delay heavenly glory for it is either satisfied easily here or far more bitterly in purgatory. It diminishes heavenly rewards. And most important, it predisposes us psychologically to many mortal sins.[84] The preacher graphically elaborates the pains of purgatory for unrepented sins, but the present remedies are ready to hand. Venial sins are dismissed instantly by the general confession, by devout breast-beating, heartfelt contrition, sprinkling with holy water, prayer (especially the Lord's Prayer), episcopal benediction, generous almsgiving, worthy communion, or for that matter any appropriate good deed.[85] But can one live without mortal sin? Yes, Herolt declares, with God's help. It would be Manichaean and heretical to say otherwise because if it were impossible to avoid mortal sin, baptismal grace would be of no

---

[80] T.138.2 (B).
[81] R.2.1 (21^b).
[82] T.110.1 (M).
[83] D.12.2 (M), T.110.1 (M).
[84] D.12.4 (M-O), T.110.2 (N-Q).
[85] D.12.6 (Q), T.110.3 (R-S).

effect, God's commands would be unsupportable, and free will and responsibility would be destroyed. Without freedom there can be no responsibility, but God's commands hold us accountable. No one sins involuntarily, and because mortal sin is voluntary, it follows that by the aid of grace one can live without mortal sin until death if one wills (as indeed John the Baptist, Thomas Aquinas, and many other *perfecti* have done).[86]

It comes as somewhat of a surprise then to hear the preacher say that mortal sin is first of all committed by ignorance.[87] Herolt has insisted that mortal sin is deliberate, premeditated, knowing, and intentional, and that children or mentally impaired persons cannot sin mortally if they have no discretion.[88] How then can it be committed in ignorance? His rather technical answer is that there are three sorts of ignorance—the invincible ignorance of those permanently or temporarily without the use of reason (it excuses from sin), the crass, neglectful ignorance of those who are too careless or too busy to find out what God wants (this does not excuse sin), and the affected ignorance of those who scornfully refuse to learn what is required in order to be able to sin freely (this is worse than well-informed sin, for it compounds the deed with contumacy).[89] Perhaps because this explanation is so technical, in a much later list of "ways to commit mortal sin," Herolt replaces ignorance with "awareness that one is doing something against the commandments of God or the precepts of prelates or church, or by any means commits a vice among the seven capital vices or against a vow."[90] A specious ignorance, in other words, is merely a means of committing intentional sin.

Mortal sin is also committed by performing a merely venial action but with an intentionally vicious purpose. For example, light-hearted words and gestures, trivial in themselves, are mortal sins when used seductively. The criterion is always intention. The act itself may even be omitted for fear of scandal or lack of opportunity, but the sin has still been committed if the will has granted consent. An erroneous conscience may commit mortal sin by believing that something one is doing, though not one of the seven sins, is mortally sinful—an extremely dangerous frame of mind, since it leads to despair. But the heart of the matter, as we have seen repeatedly, is that a person "loves or fears a creature more than the creator—as when someone loves wife, children, possessions, honor, beauty, or dress more than God, and so makes the creature his god. For whatever a man loves beyond God, this is his god."[91]

---

[86] D.12.3 (M), T.27.3 (D), T.77.2 (C), E.22.1/3, E.36.3/1.
[87] D.12.1/1 (A).
[88] T.23.2/2 (I), T.27.3 (D), T.29.112 (P), T.77.2 (C), E.36.3/1.
[89] D.12.1/1 (B-C), T.93.5 (T).
[90] E.41.2/1.
[91] D.12.1/2-4 (E), E.41.2/3.

The elements that must be present for a sin to be mortal are these: it must be a word, act, or desire that contravenes the law of God; the contravention must be deliberate; it must do actual or habitual despite to the face of God, consciously turning away from God and toward the creature; this aversion from God involves pride, contempt for justice, and perverted purpose, in which one "postpones the eternal God for momentary pleasure." Because this definition is so formidable, those who stand in fear of God and hope never to sin knowingly are able to do so, since God in his goodness will not let them fall. But also because it is so formidable, those of lax conscience who postpone the fear of God can easily and often sin mortally, simply because they imagine that only gross sins qualify as mortal. They suppose that adultery is serious but fornication is trivial; wounding or murder is wicked but giving offence is unimportant; they minimize fast-breaking, ostentation, dancing, gambling, swearing, and gossip as preoccupations of moralistic preachers.[92] There is a popular saying among the worldly: *"Der tufel ist nit als grulich als man yn malet"*:

> And such secular men also say: "Not everything is mortal sin which is preached as such. Once there were only four mortal sins—to betray one's master, to kill him, to commit adultery, and to murder one's neighbor." And then others chime in: "Anyway, who can love his enemy? Who can live chastely? Who can abstain from physical pleasures and earthly joys?" . . . But it is not enough for salvation to keep yourself from the greatest mortal sins—you must also keep yourself from the ordinary mortal sins, because you can be damned just as well with the least mortal sin as with the greatest.[93]

Hence the preacher's deliberate purpose in moving consistently from formidable definitions to moral commonplaces.

To be sure, there is a steady crescendo in the gravity of mortal sins. Herolt lists nine mounting grades: ill will; verbal expression of ill will; physical as well as verbal expression; habitual wrong; self-exculpation by blaming God or the devil or others for one's sin; delighting in—even boasting of—one's wicked deeds; teaching others to sin by word and example; presumptuous, knowing, and pertinacious sin; and finally—gravest, worst, and most perilous of all—sinning from despair. Quantitatively, the severity of the punishment will be proportional to the gravity of the sin.[94] One cannot be dismissed while another is maintained.[95] A single mortal sin has already expelled God and given place to the devil, for God hates mortal

---

[92] E.36.3/1.
[93] T.93.1 (P).
[94] T.93.1 (P), T.131.0 (F).
[95] Q.36.3.

sin more than anything in the universe.[1] Sin is a weight heaven cannot bear, nor earth. Finally, one mortal sin does more harm than a thousand demons, or a whole legion of demons, in the absence of sin.[2]

> A single sin is heavier than every weight in the world . . . if all the mountains were made of lead and were to fall on one just man, they could not drag him to hell. But mortal sin is so weighty that it dragged thence the noblest spirit of all—Lucifer.[3]

The cost to the sinner himself is immeasurable. It makes life wretched and death a fearful horror by destroying all the virtues it merits. Even if one's merits were as many as the trees of paradise or the stars of heaven, they are utterly despoiled by mortal sin. They are a dead sacrifice, a labor in the night, forfeiting all merit.[4] The sinner is like the ass; it is ponderous and resistant, cowardly and stolid (it thinks that when its head is among the brambles it cannot be seen by the wolf), but made for load bearing and constant toil. So the sinner is ponderous in falling, resistant to good, apt for bearing the load of sin in the present and the penalty in future, and patient only in sustaining the fruitless labor of this world.[5] But sinners are also like small boys—aware only of the moment and thoughtless of the future; puny and insignificant but think they are the greatest; and instantly filthy again after they are washed.[6] Mortal sin is like thunder, which shakes everything violently, rattles the head, and provokes terror; so sin destroys all merits, obfuscates reason, and strikes mortal fear. It is like absinth, so bitter and odiferous that it turns even the sweetest wine or honey sour. It is like a thorn: a person wounded by a thorn continues to suffer pain unless the whole thorn is extracted, and the sinner is not healed spiritually so long as a single remains.[7] And meanwhile, each sinful act is another whiplash in the scourging of Christ.[8] Mortal sin causes loss to Christ as well as the sinner, for the cost of the blood he shed is squandered.[9] "It would be better for a man to be infested with ten thousand demons, or transfixed with all the swords ever made, or burnt in fire, drowned in water, and rotated on wheels than to offend God knowingly and willingly with a single mortal sin."[10]

---

[1] E.46.3.
[2] Q.12.1.
[3] E.2.2/3.
[4] D.12.2/1 (F), T.92.1 (K), T.140.3 (F), E.6.2.
[5] A.P.: 5 "Peccator" (123ᵃ).
[6] A.P.: 7 "Peccatores" (123ᵃ).
[7] A.P.: 9-11 "Peccatum" (123ᵇ).
[8] Q.28.2.
[9] D.12.2/6 (K).
[10] T.137.1 (O).

What recourse is there for the Christian who has forsaken the restored innocence of baptism and by his idolatry has again incurred this penalty of perpetual death?

The answer is given intrinsically by the spiritual character of sin. Mortal sin cannot be remitted without penitence because mortal sin is the actual turning of the will from God, and remission is the actual turning of the will from sin to God in contrition.[11]

> Who is "in mortal sin"? One who has committed (or still intends to commit) a mortal sin and is not yet truly contrite. But if someone is contrite, even if he has not yet confessed but intends to confess and make satisfaction, he is no longer in mortal sin.[12]

The prior sincerity of the contrite heart, before and apart from sacramental penance, effects remission of the penalty of death in its grief over sin and its hope in God's mercy. To be sure, sacramental penance is the normal pastoral context in which this contrition is evoked, guided, and expressed. "The penance we do at this holy season [of Lent] works all these things in us: liberation from sin, the happiness of grace, opening of heaven's door, and the feasting in glory. That penance turns the thorns of vice into the roses of virtue."[13] But the decisive turning of will and deed from sin to God must take place in the soul. Unlike many of the scholarly writers of confessors' manuals at the time, who more and more assigned the effectiveness of penance to the sacramental grace of sacramental absolution,[14] Herolt (like other mendicant preachers in the parishes) persists in the older contritionist view that

> where there is true contrition, God dismisses sins even before their actual confession, if only there is intention to confess . . . And so anyone wishing to confess must possess contrition before confession, and thus come justified to confession, or at least during confession before the priest's absolution. Otherwise the confession would not be for his salvation: he would receive the sacrament of penance unworthily, and thus commit a new sin.[15]

---

[11] Q.3.3, Q.8.3, Q.10.3.
[12] T.140.3 (G).
[13] T.43.0 (H), Q.26.1.
[14] See Thomas L. Tentler, *Sin and Confession of the Eve of the Reformation* (Princeton: Princeton University Press, 1977), 233ff.
[15] Q.9.3.

6

CHURCH, PRIESTHOOD, AND MONASTICISM

Herolt's catechetical book on Christian doctrine, *de eruditione Christifidelium*, appeared in 1416. The Council of Constance was in midcourse, and one might have expected that ecclesiology would be an inescapable topic. But Herolt rarely mentions the doctrine of the church. No sermon is devoted to it, and the only formal definition appears in his exposition of the Apostles' Creed.[16] The church's life, institutions, laws, and moral authority are everywhere assumed as the framework for social and personal teaching, but the church itself is too much part of the given world to require justification to layfolk in sermons.

The church is "one, holy, and catholic." It is *one* because all the faithful, both before and after Christ, share one faith. Those before Christ believed in prospect, implicitly or explicitly, that the Son of God would be born, suffer, die, rise again, and ascend to heaven—the very same things that we believe in retrospect—even though they did not know the how or when of their salvation. "The church is therefore called one, since outside it no one is saved and inside it no one is damned."

It is called *holy* to distinguish it from the "congregation of evildoers" which is not holy but perverse, while the catholic church is pure. Just as a church building is cleansed and anointed when it is consecrated, faithful Christians have been bathed in virtue by the baptismal water and anointed with the unction of the Holy Spirit.

The church is *catholic*, that is, universal, in place (since the faith is preached throughout the world), in status (since no one, male or female, young or old, is excluded), and in time (since it includes all the just from Abel to the world's end, and remains utterly secure in face of all tyrannical attempts to destroy it).

Until the heavenly consummation, the church is divided into three parts: one part is still in the world in fear and anticipation; one part is already in heaven, without fear and without anticipation; and one part is in purgatory, still anticipating the glory it does not yet enjoy, but without fear. These three parts are represented

---

[16] D.22.10 (S), T.147.10 (N).

by the priest's fraction of the Eucharistic host into three, the portion held above the chalice being the church in glory.[17]

The Body of Christ

Herolt uses only two figurative images of the church, and they too are predictable. The church is figured "in Noah's ark: all those in it were preserved, and all outside it were drowned." Hence, the extreme danger of being outside the church.[18] The more powerful image is Paul's: the church is the body of Christ. Even this appears infrequently, but when it does the stress is on the mutual consolation and support Christians should show each other. "A human spirit does not quicken the members of a body unless they are connected. Similarly the Holy Spirit quickens those who are united in good in the body of the church."[19]

The nobler limbs and organs of the body do not despise the less noble, and love among Christians must cross class and status lines. The parts of a body do not envy each other but inescapably share joys and sorrows; so one Christian must not envy another's worth or fortune but be glad and beware of useless envy. The limbs of a body (like a fruit tree) do not perform their unique functions for individual advantage but for the corporate good—"the food the hand gets it gives to the mouth, the mouth gives it to the stomach, the stomach gives it to the liver, and the liver gives it to the other members." So the faithful should share their worldly goods. Bodily parts do not take revenge on each other; it would simply multiply pain if the head was hurt in a fall and took revenge on the foot that slipped, or the hand with a cut finger slashed back at the other hand; revenge between neighbors is equally stupid, and church members should not avenge harm done by others. Anything good or bad that befalls one part of the body is felt as happening to the whole organism, and so it must be in the church, as Christ shows by identifying with "the least of these my brethren."[20]

Failure of the mutual compassion that should exist among Christians is tantamount to amputation from the body of Christ.[21] When one part of a body is about to be excised, the whole body trembles; and any organ cut off from the others becomes withered, rotten, and useless. Any Christian living not in grace but in mortal sin is cut off from sharing all the goods that belong to the whole body— the benefits of the church's masses, prayers, and fasts, and the treasury of the merits of all the godly.[22] The power of excommunication from the church is too fearful a

---

[17] D.22.10 (S), T.147.10 (N), Q.17.1.
[18] D.22.10 (S).
[19] T.68.2/5 (F).
[20] T.120.2 (C-F), E.6.5/1-3.
[21] D.20.2/3 (M).
[22] D.12.2/1 (F), D.22.11 (T), T.147.11 (O).

prospect to be exercised lightly, since the person cut off from Christ the head, and from all the faithful his members, is of no use but for the eternal fire.

Excommunication

Even though the doctrine of the church does not deserve a sermon of its own, the subject of excommunication receives extended treatment, first in exposition of the third commandment (as an excursus on honoring one's spiritual parents, the priests), then as a sermon for the Sunday after Ascension, and more briefly as an instruction for the feast day of St. Peter *ad vincula*.[23]

Excommunication is twofold, major and minor. Minor excommunication bars a person from the sacraments or the kiss of peace. It is incurred when anyone knowingly communicates with an excommunicated person by speaking, eating, trading, or otherwise dealing with him. Herolt reserves the term "minor excommunication" for consorting with excommunicates, even though the elaborate index in his *de tempore* sermons lists over seventy other "inhibitions from holy communion" for breaches of divine precept, church regulation, or social morality. But the "leprosy of the soul" which is minor excommunication is contracted by contagion from excommunicates. There are only five cases where it is permissible to retain contact: if one speaks with an excommunicated person about his soul's salvation; if an orator, traveller, or pilgrim must obtain necessities in a territory under the ban; a wife is excused from shunning her husband; children still at home under parental authority are excused from shunning their father (as are servants who were in the household before the excommunication); or cases of genuine ignorance. But otherwise, if thirty men or women are dining together, or twenty men are drinking together in a clubhouse, and a publicly excommunicated person is present, they all incur minor excommunication. Even in church, if a known excommunicate cannot be removed, everyone else should leave. A nod of the head to an excommunicate may be permissible, but if he addresses you, the proper reply should be limited to "God correct you" or the like. If a husband invites an excommunicated person to a meal, the wife may eat too, but at a separate table. The only occasion when it is permissible to give anything to an excommunicate is in a case of life-sustaining necessity.[24] Any priest can absolve from minor excommunication.

Major excommunication not only excludes people from the sacraments, but also bans them from entering the church and expels them from the communion of the faithful. This is a fearful condition, for they are excluded from the consolation of all the faithful on earth and of God and the blessed in heaven. It is like leprosy but more fearful; it is a stab wound from a spiritual sword. It deprives the soul of all the church's spiritual treasures and leaves it as powerless as an amputated hand

---

[23] D.4.4 (J-P), T.69, S.29.2.
[24] T.69.1 (H) and .3 (L-M), S.29.3, Q 12.2.

or foot or ear. It hands over the soul to Satan and consigns it to the fire. Only a bishop may absolve from major excommunication, and in the case of certain major crimes against the church's personnel or property, only the pope or his delegate may absolve, and then "with misery and rods."

The real force of this sanction becomes clear when we hear that major or minor excommunication is incurred not only by public denunciation from the ambo, but automatically by major antichurch acts classified as "papal cases." (A bishop may absolve some of these acts if they have not been formally denounced, but they must be papal cases once they have been denounced in church)

Canon law imposes automatic excommunication on those who do violence to clerics or religious; heretics or those who patronize or receive heretics; accomplices of excommunicates in a crime; those who burn or vandalize a church, destroy an altar or a cross, steal a consecrated host, or desecrate a cemetery; those who forge apostolic letters; princes or patricians who forbid their subjects to sell to ecclesiastical customers or to perform commercial services for them (such as milling grain); authorities who demand tribute or tariff from church personnel; rulers or civic officials who either enact or enforce statutes restricting church liberty and clerical privilege, or sanctioning the payment of usury; or anyone who defies the authority of an ecclesiastical court, limits a subject's recourse to church tribunals, or encourages lay defiance of church officials carrying out a sentence of excommunication, suspension, or interdict. A further series of automatic major excommunication is imposed on clergy or religious who deliberately ignore these canonical sentences or act *ultra vires*.[25]

God has conferred the great dignity upon his priests that, while they are freed from all earthly jurisdiction, they exercise the power of excommunication in heaven and earth.[26] Thus a certain Count of Toulouse, automatically excommunicated as a patron of heretics, refused to be admonished by a godly abbot sent to warn him, so the abbot called for white bread and cursed it by excommunication. Instantly the bread turned black and rotten. Then the abbot absolved the bread and restored it to its pristine appearance.[27] When Pope Gregory IX excommunicated a rich man, all the cranes that used to rest on the rich man's roof transferred their nests to another housetop until he sought absolution. Flocks of sparrows were always flying into the church of St. Vincent the Martyr and soiling it and interrupting divine service; but after the bishop excommunicated them, any sparrow brought into the church instantly dropped dead.[28] A beautiful orchard, bought by the mother of a Duke of Burgundy from a priest, bore no fruit despite the high quality of the trees and soil; but the peasants explained that the previous owner had excommunicated it

---

[25] D.4.4 (J-L, P), T.69.1-2 (H-K).
[26] D.28.1/3 (A), T.111.1/3 (U).
[27] T.69.1 (J).
[28] T.69.3 (M).

when the young people in his church abandoned mass at harvest time to collect fruit instead.[29] More solemnly, an excommunicate who brashly entered a church of the Blessed Virgin was immediately struck dead by a bolt of lightning that left everyone else untouched.[30] And a fornicating priest, living in concubinage, who disdainfully ignored his suspension and excommunication by Bishop Elegius, was smothered by the devil the moment he approached the altar, fell backward, and expired before all the people.[31]

While the sentence of binding and loosing "is greatly to be feared by any Christian,"[32] the main targets of these cautionary examples are plainly the politically powerful who disdain clerical authority. The preacher shakes his head in disbelief at "those bigwigs who care not at all if they remain in major excommunication for four or five weeks, or even half a year or more," and contrasts this with the godly King Louis of France, who said that he would not take the whole world if he had to spend a single night and day knowing that he was excommunicated.[33]

The power of excommunication is the rejoinder to all threats to the immunities of the priestly caste, whether from the competing bureaucracies of the temporal order or from lay anticlericalism. The threats include personal violence against priests or religious, contravention of their immunity from arrest, theft of their possessions, and most of all imposition of taxes or tributes from which they are exempt.[34] But Herolt is also concerned about detractors of the clergy, who crucify Christ afresh and drive the thorns and nails into him by their sharp barbs against his priests.[35]

There are heretics who deliberately slight the pope, bishops, priests, and monks in order to incite the laity, claiming that the hierarchy's opposition to their unorthodox beliefs springs from vengeance and the envy of the churchmen. They impugn clerical privilege and power and challenge the power of the keys. They oppose church ordinances and defy its regulations, and they claim the celebration of so many festivals is merely an invention of the priests for raising revenue. They speak slightingly of the sacraments, and of holy water and consecrated places, and of prayers for the dead.[36]

But popular sentiment also takes less ideological forms. Some people sinfully believe, for instance, that they will not have good luck with any horse they buy

---

[29] P.E.: 41 "Excommunicatio" (125).
[30] P.E.: 40 "Excommunicatio" (124).
[31] T.111.3 (H).
[32] T.69.3 (M).
[33] S.29.2.
[34] E.g., D.28.1/3 (A), T.69.2/1 and 6 (K), T.104.6 (G), T.111.1/3 (T), S.22.2/2, S.30.2/2, S.36.2/4, Q.42.3.
[35] D.4.4/3 (V), T.111.2 (C).
[36] T.100.1/2 and 4 (Q).

from a priest or a monk.[37] Perhaps most widespread of all, people fail in their obligation to support God's ministers with their tithes and offerings. God wants priests provided with all their temporal necessities, yet people rob and defraud them by withholding their rightful support and tithes.[38]

Papacy and Episcopate

The sermon books contain only a few fleeting references to the pope and none at all to the papacy as an institution. Honor is owed to spiritual overseers in proportion to their charge, Herolt says. The parish priest has the care of all the souls in his parish, the bishop of all in his bishopric, and the pope in the whole world.[39] The only two instances he gives, however, are matters of formal jurisdiction. As we have seen, certain cases of major excommunication are solely within papal jurisdiction and others within a bishop's powers. Similarly, a bishop can dispense from many vows, but only the pope can dispense from four major vows—the vow of continence, the crusader's vow, and vows to visit the tombs of the apostles or the shrine of St. James.[40] Apart from an account of the papal custom of presenting a golden rose to the prefect of the city of Rome on *Laetare* Sunday,[41] only trivial references to the pope occur elsewhere.

The office of bishop, too, receives merely formal mention for the most part. Herolt speaks often of the duties of prelates but uses that term of superiors in both church and state (for the sake of good order, he says, in any collectivity spiritual or secular there must be one principal prelate.)[42] So the specific references to ecclesiastical dignitaries are fairly meager. The most striking feature of his account of the episcopal hierarchy is how little he mentions it.

The characteristic appropriate to prelates as pastors of Christ's flock, he says, is solicitude in guarding the souls committed to them. If churchmen go to such lengths to guard the relics of Christ, how much more care should they devote to the people he redeemed with his blood? Moreover, a prelate's own soul is in danger if a single person perishes by his neglect. Unless he brings the souls in his care to salvation, he will not see God's face.[43] Prelates are even culpable for their failure to prevent sins within their jurisdictions,[44] and they will give a strict account in the last judgment

---

[37] T.41.22 (P).
[38] D.4.4/2 (S-T), D.7.13 (N), T.59.3/3 (M), Q.19.2, E.3.1.
[39] D.28.1/9 (D).
[40] D.2.2/15 (N).
[41] T.43.0 (before H), Q.26.1.
[42] E.28.2/3.
[43] E.7.0-1.
[44] T.145.8 (R).

of their cure of souls.⁴⁵ Because the prelate acts in God's stead, Christians are under obligation to obey him and must always be ready to hear an order from him.⁴⁶ But for this reason, a prelate of the church must be such a man who knows how to feel compassion for the weaknesses of his subordinates.⁴⁷ Likewise, to despise prelates is to spit in Christ's face.⁴⁸ Yet, just as Christ was hated by the world, so the world still hates church leaders who preach the truth to it and correct its excesses.⁴⁹ It is a clear mark of heretics that they slight the church's hierarchy.⁵⁰

A rather darker view of powerful church personages, however, emerges from the preacher's use of exemplary anecdotes. It is a clear instance of hypocrisy, he says, if someone makes a display of sanctity to obtain an ecclesiastical dignity for which he is in fact unworthy.⁵¹ By sharp contrast with a mere handful of stories about devout bishops (such as Germanus, Paulinus, Martin of Tours),⁵² the usual role of a prelate in Herolt's exemplary stories is to illustrate just such unworthiness.

We hear of an ambitious archdeacon who gained a bishopric by murdering his predecessor, balancing a rock over the door of the church where the bishop was going to pray.⁵³ A proud and ambitious cleric in Burgundy usurped the church of St. Martin, and during mass, at the words "He who humbles himself shall be exalted" scoffed aloud, "Wrong, for if I had humbled myself before my enemies, I would not have so many tithes and churches today!"⁵⁴

Caesarius tells of the notorious Bishop Leopold of Worms, who was bishop in name only but in practice was a tyrant, without piety or religion. He scandalized the laity by his evil example, used the war between the kings Otto and Philipp as his chance to usurp the see of Mainz, despoiled its cemeteries, and mocked any pious warnings of hell.⁵⁵

From Magdeburg, we hear of the horrible Archbishop Udo, who had gained election with the aid of the Virgin Mary but was so corrupted by his high status that he began to indulge his every fancy, allowed the fabric of the churches to fall into disrepair, violated not only lay women but even nuns, and degenerated into every base form of flagitious behavior; and of yet another metropolitan of Magdeburg who was given over to madness, devastated his province, and wasted

---

45 T.4.2/8 (Y).
46 T.154.1/1 (F), E.24.2/2.
47 Q.14.2/2.
48 Q.20.2/2.
49 E.29.1/1.
50 T.100.1/2 (Q).
51 T.100.3/3 (X).
52 P.A.: 6 "Abstinentia" (6), P.C.: 5 "Caritas" (34), P.E.: 16 "Ecclesia" (100).
53 P.P.: 127 "Praelati" (519).
54 P.P.: 129 "Praelati" (521).
55 T.28.3 (M), P.E.: 42 "Excusatio" (126).

the property of his churches.[56] A cleric who had amassed the benefices of many churches as a canon and deacon is condemned as a blasphemer of Christ and a predator and slayer of the poor because he lived in luxury while the churches became a shambles, dressed splendidly while the church vestments crumbled, set his table with precious gold and silver dishes while the sacramental vessels were smashed or lost, surrounded himself with harlots and retainers while the poor went unaided, and forgot divine service and preaching to spend his time in bawdy plays and songs.[57]

In less detailed terms, we hear of dreams and visions where an archbishop is arraigned for dereliction by his patron St. Martin and dies suddenly, a lecherous canon is similarly denounced by his patron saint but repents in time and enters a religious order, and a bishop is struck down by heavenly fire as a leads a maiden in a wanton dance.[58] There is even a story of a monk of Clairvaux who refused election as a bishop in spite of the entreaties of his abbot and other bishops but suffered no detriment as a result of his disobedience. "If I had accepted the bishopric," he said, "I would have been damned eternally. For the church has come to such a state that it does not deserve to be ruled except by reprobate bishops."[59]

A great debate over ecclesiology was raging in Herolt's day among the elites of curia, court, and university. Intellectually and politically, the view of the church as a transcendent, unitary, spiritual power was challenged by a radically alternative model of church governance as a corporation of all faithful Christians on earth. But the lay congregation who listened to these sermons heard not a word of this debate.

Deliberately or not, the sermons convey an impression of the church as an inescapable source of vital numinous power and intricate moral authority, whose priestly caste has been endowed by God with sacrosanct powers and privileges and unique multiple access to heavenly grace; but within the life of the church on earth, the sincere Christian is far more likely to find true sanctity and salutary zeal among the devout, zealous, and sacrificial observants of a religious rule than among secular diocesan clerics, whose earthly entanglements dilute and even betray their high calling to nurture Christ's flock with correction and compassion.

In practice, this impression would influence such lay decisions as the choice of a confessor,[60] the duty to hear sermons, the giving of alms, and for some the contrite search for a life of inner grace modelled on monastic spirituality, and the fervent appeal for conversion to the religious life.

---

[56] P.P.: 123 and 124 "Praelati" (515, 516).
[57] P.P.: 128 "Praelati" (520).
[58] P.P.: 124-126 "Praelati" (516, 517, 518).
[59] P.P.: 122 "Praelati" (514).
[60] Q.25.3.

The Dignities of the Priesthood

In the face of such contempt for clerical status, the preacher responds with a lavish encomium on the dignities of the priestly office.

The nine dignities God has conferred on his priests correspond to the nine heavenly choirs of the angels. Priests are higher than all kings and princes of the earth. They consecrate and make kings, but all the kings of earth cannot make a single priest. No prince is so great that he does not bow his head in confession and humble himself before the priest who is God's vicar. God honors priests by granting them for their bodily sustenance all those temporal goods he has reserved for himself—the tithes, oblations, bequests, permits, and other elements of the *patrimonium crucifixi*. He grants them immunity from worldly jurisdiction, from arrest, and from taxation. He commits to them the souls of the faithful and above all the exclusive administration of Christ's gifts, the sacraments. God intends that strict obedience be paid to them as his deputies by all men of whatever status or condition. He gives his priests the power to bind and loose by excommunication, the spiritual sword, and absolution. They are like the angels in that they minister to God and man, they are chaste, they inform and admonish with God's word, and their office is his praise. They are like the Blessed Virgin in that, as she conceived the true body of Christ with five words (*Fiat mihi secundum verbum tuum*), so they confect it with five; as she carried Christ in her hands, so do they in the elevation of the host; and as her womb was sanctified before she conceived, so priests must be set apart and yoked by ordination before they consecrate the body of Christ. God honors priests above angels, and even in some respects above Mary, first in the dignity of their custody, the souls of many; secondly in consuming and touching the body of Christ; thirdly in consecrating Christ's body; and in this the least parish priest on earth can do what the greatest angel in heaven cannot.[61]

> Therefore priests are to be honored before all kings, priests, knights and nobles, for a priest is higher than kings, happier than angels, the creator of his creator; wherefore he is deservedly to be honored.[62]

Since God himself has so honored his priests, every man must also honor them.[63]

Unworthy Priests

But Herolt is not under any illusion that every priest is worthy of his exalted role. On the contrary, he is explicit in his denunciation of priests and religious who

---

[61] D.28.1/1-9 (A-D), T.28.1/5 (H), T.111.1/1-9 (T-B), S.42.2.
[62] T.28.1/5 (H).
[63] D.4.4/3 (V), T.111.2 (C), S.42.2.

besmirch their holy office; and on the principle *quanto altior gradus tanto sublimior casus*,[64] he assigns unworthy priests to a "most perilous estate."

A fornicating priest, or one living in mortal sin, not yet truly contrite nor doing true penance as he should, sins mortally as often as he performs any act pertaining to his order—baptizes, absolves, preaches, marries, administers communion or extreme unction, buries the dead, churches women, exorcizes water and salt on Sundays, sprinkles the people, or blesses the candles on Purification or palms on Palm Sunday or fire, wax, or font on Easter Eve or Pentecost, or—worse than all these—celebrates mass and consecrates and consumes the eucharist.[65]

Even putting on a priestly vestment condemns him. Any incontinent and fornicating priest whose sin is public is automatically suspended, and it becomes a mortal sin even to hear him say mass. There are priests whose turpitude leads them to spend the *patrimonium crucifixi* on concubines, actresses, and whores (both parties are duty-bound to repay it).[66] But Herolt's sense of what is unbecoming in a priest covers less obvious derelictions too. A religious seen leaping or dancing deserves excommunication, he says.[67] Laxity and inattention in saying the divine office with mumbled words and wandering mind is a mortal sin.[68] There are grasping churchmen and religious who conceal their avarice for earthly possessions behind the sanctity of shaved hair and a tonsured head, which are supposed to mean that their minds want to be free of the weight of worldly acquisition to fly up unencumbered to God, but their piety is a mask for greed.[69]

Herolt plainly invites his hearers to be discriminating in their choice of the priests and monks they support with their alms and to choose those who are faithful in saying their offices and zealous in the cure of souls.[70] He repeats a story told by his famous colleague, Johannes Nider, about a devout preacher in the collegiate church at York, whose fervent preaching and exemplary life won great favor with the people but so aroused the jealous hatred of his clerical brothers that they smuggled a whore into his room, set fire to it, and then shouted from his window for help, creating a public scandal and forcing him to leave in disgrace.[71]

The Cloistered Life

The empirical reality, Herolt points out, is that exposure to carnal delectations will inevitably lead to transgressions. For this reason, those who enter the cloistered

---

[64] D.28.2/2 (F).
[65] T.111.3 (D), S.42.2.
[66] D.28.2 (E), D.7.17 (TT), T.111.3 (E-G), S.42.2, Q.42.3, E.41.1/18.
[67] Q.32.2/2.
[68] D.16.2/6 (H).
[69] D.17.3/2 (H).
[70] T.150.1 (Q), E.29.3/5.
[71] E.29.3/6.

life of monastic religion receive richer grace and sweetness from God than do secular priests. The religious life is the best life, for it is already comparable to the life of heaven. Monks must live in the cloister as the saints and angels live in heaven.[72]

There are even parallels between the cloistered and the celestial life. The first is unanimity in willing, speaking, and working; this unity has great efficacy for monks in obtaining petitions from God, invoking his presence, and gaining forgiveness. Secondly, as the angels and saints are fed by divine sweetness, so too God feeds the religious, physically through alms and spiritually by grace. Thirdly, all things are held in common and shared freely, reinstating the law of nature before the fall. Fourth, the life of chastity is not a human but an angelic life. Fifth, the saints and angels sing God's praise continually, and the religious perform the canonical hours day and night. Sixth, as those in heaven give themselves totally to God, so those living in religion offer God the supreme sacrifice—that is, all they have: the good of possessions by the vow of poverty, the good of the body by the vow of chastity, and the good of the soul, the sacrificed will, by the vow of obedience. Hence finally, as the heavenly host always fulfils God's will, so religious submit their wills to obey their superiors *in loco dei*.[73]

Herolt acknowledges that this, too, is an idealized account, and that key elements of this high purpose have proved extremely knotty. Each of the three vows has its acute problems.

During the preceding two hundred years, the most public and controversial of these problems had been the issue of monastic possessions and the vow of poverty. In the older monastic orders, the poverty practiced was individual, not corporate; but first Francis, then Dominic, had instituted corporate poverty as the rule of the friars so that the order itself had no possessions other than monastic buildings and churches, no fixed income or property, but lived by charity and alms. The nature of evangelical poverty, and how zealously it should be maintained in practice, were questions that had split the Franciscan Order and threatened its very existence a century before Herolt wrote. The fierce, sometimes bloody, dispute had fomented spiritualist schism, preoccupied the inquisitors, engaged some of the outstanding minds of the period, and reached the highest levels of conflict between papacy and empire.

The same issues, in moderated form, were still lively in Herolt's time, in the movement for a "poor and tenuous use" of possessions among the Observant Franciscans. Amongst the Dominicans, the disputes over the extent of voluntary poverty were contained within the order, and it did not provoke the sorts of schismatic fragmentation that afflicted the Franciscans. Indeed, in 1425, shortly after Herolt first wrote on the subject of monastic possessions, Pope Martin V relaxed the rule of corporate poverty for some Dominican houses; and half a century

---

[72] T.121.1 (H).
[73] T.121.1/1-7 (H-M), T.159.3/2 (X).

later, Pope Sixtus IV extended the mitigation to the whole order, thus removing its mendicant character. Herolt, as a member of a reforming priory, would not have welcomed this development.

In his sermons, however, Herolt does not take an explicit position on the controverted question of corporate poverty. What he says about monastic poverty could apply equally well to individual or group commitments. But he makes unmistakably plain his adherence to a strict and rigorous understanding of evangelical poverty.

Not even a pope or an abbot can grant a monk dispensation to own property, he insists. A dispensation for the use of some property by a monk may be permitted but only for necessary cause and for an uncertain use (that is, there is no implicit guarantee that the monk will continue to have use of it, but the right to use it may be withdrawn at will). For this reason, a religious may speak innocently of "my book" or "my cap" for brevity's sake but sins mortally if asserting ownership. "Every religious must always be resigned to the loss of all things, or else he is a son of perdition," he declares, and excoriates the sin and perfidy of all religious who are not resigned to possessing nothing. They are idolaters, bound for hell, and they sin mortally whenever they perform any sacred duty. Families who provide material support for a son or daughter in a monastery must suspend those donations, on pain of mortal sin, if they believe the recipient is not willing freely to forgo everything altogether if the superior demands it.[74] Monks who are trustees of monastic foundations bequeathed as alms for the dead—a perennial source of material compromise for all the orders—grieve the souls of the departed if they fail to use them for the stated purpose.[75]

Herolt displays more compassion toward those monks and nuns who are subject to regular obedience but who have not assumed it gladly. A coerced obedience is a guilty obedience, he says,[76] and there is no consoling those who are in monasteries unwillingly:

> There are those who are shut up in obedience to the religious life yet in heart they wander in the world. They lead a harsh life, for everything to do with the service of God is a burden to them, and they perform it from coercion and fear. They feel no spiritual sweetness, and they are also deprived of physical pleasure and earthly consolation. It happens whenever children are placed in monasteries against their will, or because the father is poor, or the child is defective, or because there are too many children in the family, or because the child is presented to the monastery as part of a contract of simony. So no

---

[74] T.121.3 (J-L).
[75] T.160.6/4 (P).
[76] R.5.1/1 (64[b]) and 3/2 (69[a-b]).

one should even think of placing his child is a monastery against his will, or where religion will not be maintained, above all in its three substantial elements, poverty (that is, community), obedience, and chastity . . . It is better to be a drunkard than to be a bad, or possessive, or unchaste monk.[77]

Sadly, those divided people whose bodies are enclosed in the cloister but whose hearts are in the world offer a dead sacrifice, for death is the division of body and soul, and they lead a hard and grating life of enforced goodness.[78] Parents should not drive their children into a coerced obedience, but neither should they deter a child from a genuine desire to enter religion but should encourage and inform this impulse.[79] The rule of obedience sometimes chafes in very mundane ways. As despisers of the world, the religious must not be ashamed to imitate Christ in their humble clothing and solemn demeanor; they must learn to be content with convent food; and they must not object when, like Christ, they are sent from place to place, from prelate to prelate.[80]

One of Herolt's stories implies that the number of monastics who succeed in conforming their lives to Christ by obedience is only a small proportion of the religious. A good and assiduous novice in one of the orders, Rudolfus by name, saw a vision as he prayed after Matins one morning. In the brightening light of dawn he saw the crucified Christ in the air, and around him fifteen other men each hanging on a cross, and he recognized them as ten monks and five novices of his own order. In his stupefaction, Christ said to him, "Do you know who these men are?" He answered, "Lord, I know who they are, but I certainly do not understand what I see!" The Lord replied, "These alone of the whole congregation have been crucified with me by conforming their lives to my passion."[81]

The Monastic Virtues

Disobedience to a monastic superior is mortal sin because the love of God requires that we keep his commandments, and the superior is in the place of God. But a heartfelt obedience that is voluntary (without self-seeking or murmuring), joyful (not sullen or forced), and persevering to the end is "the key to paradise and the road to heaven."[82] Herolt's Advent sermons to the sisters at St. Katharine's, *Der Rosengart*, are a paean to the loveliness of the monastic virtues, godly fear, diligence,

---

[77] T.70.2/1 (P).
[78] E.6.2.
[79] Q.11.3.
[80] Q.24.2/2, Q.32.2/2, P.R.: 13 "Religiosus" (538).
[81] P.R.: 12 "Religiosus" (537).
[82] T.121.7 (N-O).

humility, patience, and obedience; but it is obedience that draws his most passionate praise. To the nuns, Herolt describes how obedience progresses from fear, through willingness, to single-mindedness, alacrity, gladness, courage, and finally to a point of unquestioning, all-inclusive, utterly humbled and permanent sacrifice of the will.[83] Such submissiveness, he says, ornaments and fortifies the soul, makes one's service wholly pleasing to God, brings God's indwelling, overcomes all enemies, and finally makes all things subject to the obedient soul.[84] For obedience excels the other virtues in heaven since all the others involve our own willing to some extent, but it is a greater virtue to live under another will. So monks and nuns who submit their wills to their superiors in a life of total obedience will gain the highest ranks of heaven.[85]

Whatever the burdens, trials, and dangers, the cloistered life remains to the preacher's mind the surest road to heaven. By the sacrifice of all worldly things, the religious gain title to a heavenly inheritance by right of exchange.[86] Conversion to the religious life brings remission of all sins: a profession that binds one totally to the divine service exceeds all other classes of satisfaction and public penance, and if going on crusade or pilgrimage or giving certain alms remits sins, how much more the entry into a whole life of religion, the highest sacrifice? As the *Vitaspatrum* says, those entering and professing religion obtain the same grace as the newly baptized, and those who remain in this grace by holy observance of their rule go direct to heaven.[87]

---

[83] R.5.3/1-9 (68^b-76^a).
[84] R.5.4 (76^a-82^a).
[85] T.56.10 (C), P.O.: 1 "Obedientia" (362).
[86] T.159.3/2 (X).
[87] T.13.1/4 (D), T.121.7 (P), S.24.2/3, S.30.2.

GODLY USE OF THE CREATION

7

THE WORLD AND ITS INHABITANTS

"The Lord dwells in all creatures, he inhabits them in their essence—otherwise they would all be reduced to nothing in the twinkling of an eye."[1] He has placed beauty, delight, and sweetness in his creatures so that they may draw men to the creator in whom all things exist.[2]

The preacher moves immediately from the beauties of this world to meditation on the world to come. The created world is by definition good for God made it, but it is also a mere passing shadow of the true heavenly world. The material boons of food and water, light and air are good and necessary sustenance for human life, but deceptively they always offer the temptation of inordinate use. For Herolt, affirmation of the world's goodness is a formality of sound doctrine, but in experience this world is a vale of tears, its offerings deeply disappointing.

The true path of godliness consists in renouncing the world. Herolt has a genuine interest in nature but displays it only fleetingly. For homiletic purposes, the world and its inhabitants are celebrated only to point away to other more enduring realities.

When the Holy Spirit gives understanding, it brings awareness of the magnitude and goodness of creation.[3] It is good to use the creation for good purposes—"the earth ministers food to man in produce and animals, water in baths and all sorts of fish, the air offers vital breath and every sort of bird, the sky grants us light to wake by day, darkness to sleep by night." But it is even better to use creation for praise and benefit—in tithing, alms to the poor, endowing prayers for souls, and support of one's neighbor in need. And it is best of all when creation allures man to a desire for the creator who made him and all creatures:

> So when you taste sweet wine and honey, think how sweet is the Lord of heaven. And when you see a beautiful person, or some other creature in his likeness, or a lily, think, "If these transitory

---

[1] R.0.1. (2ᵇ).
[2] E.24.1/1.
[3] D.22.1 (E), T.146.1 (C).

temporal things are so beautiful and sweet, and so delectable that the senses are individually refreshed by them in this life, how great will be the delight in bliss, where the whole creation will be displayed by its creator not under shadows but in reality, most perfectly and completely, and every sense will be filled up by delights by them.... In creation, we may recognize the trinity in its greatness of power, light of wisdom, and goodness of nature. This is why the creatures are called "traces of God."[4]

Herolt is so preoccupied with this godly use of the creation and its moral lessons that it is hard to reconstruct how he pictured the universe. He makes enough passing references to the shape of the world to show that, like most literate people of the period, he assumes the classic Ptolemaic model of the universe. A central, spherical Earth is surrounded by a series of concentric spheres. The innermost seven spheres each contain a planet: nearest to Earth is the moon, then Mercury, Venus, the sun, Mars, Jupiter, and Saturn. Beyond the planets is the sphere of the fixed stars, and beyond that, imparting motion to the whole, is the firmament, the Prime Mover.[5] The firmament's daily revolution from east to west inexorably rotates the lower spheres, too, but their circuits are slower because they tend naturally to revolve at various speeds from west to east but are forced by the firmament's motion to do otherwise.

Herolt says the sun has three planets above it and three below, and the moon is Earth's closest neighbor, close enough to exert power and effect on the tides of the sea.[6] He reflects the mechanics of the Ptolemaic model: "All creation needs time for its operation: the firmament requires a day to move from east to west, the moon needs a month to complete its circuit, and the sun a whole year."[7] These intricacies do not detain him, and when it suits his purpose better, he adopts a more primitive, three-storeyed cosmology. There are three places in the universe: the highest is the place of the angels and the elect; the lowest, the place of the damned; and the middle, this world, the place of the living.[8] But here he is speaking of souls: "No one in this life is free of sadness, for we are in the middle between the place of joy and hell."[9]

Herolt reflects several other standard assumptions of medieval cosmology. The spheres transmit downward not only motion but also influences. Astrological lore

---

[4] E.24.1/1.
[5] A. Pannekoek, *A History of Astronomy* (London: George Allen & Unwin, 1961; New York: Barnes & Noble, 1969), 176ff. Translated from De Groei van ons Wereldbeeld. Amsterdam: Wereld-Bibliotheck, 1961; C. S. Lewis, *The Discarded Image* (Cambridge: Cambridge University Press 1964), 96.
[6] T.162.1/9 (J), Q.4.3.
[7] D.22.3 (H).
[8] E.35.2/3, cf. T.50.1 (A).
[9] E.31.2/1.

had a measured response from the canonists and schoolmen, and Herolt reflects the church's attitude.[10] The reality of organic planetary influences on matter, on plants and animals, and on man both physically and psychologically, is not doubted; but observing the stars and astrological seasons for pagan, superstitious, predictive or determinative purposes is idolatry:

> If certain times are observed in those actions which depend on natural causation—for instance, on the influence of the planets and the circuit of the stars—such as taking doses of medicine, sowing fields, planting trees, and the like, of course this is not idolatry but wisdom and prudence, and is no sin.

Celestial effects on organic processes are simple common sense, but any predetermining effect on the human will is roundly condemned (with the odd result that planting, which is an organic action, may be done by the heavens, but harvesting, which is voluntary, may not):

But if, on the contrary, times are observed in other actions which depend solely on man's free will, for instance trading, taking a wife, gathering crops, and activities of this sort, to observe seasons and Egyptian days in such matters is mortal sin.[11]

Not that the planets have no psychological effect. Herolt quotes Henry of Hassia's judgment that "stars influence what is below them in various ways, such that men dispose themselves well or ill towards God."[12] But that influence must not be held to be coercive:

Those Christians who hold with fate, and base themselves on the constellations of the planets, do not recognize God in true faith. Blessed Gregory, in his homily for today, reproves them and shows that they are heretics and pusillanimous who say that fate, or the constellations under which they are born, rule and direct anybody in performing those actions in which they are influential.

To believe this would be to deny God's omnipotence, the merit of our actions, the meaning of God's commands, and our free will. Nevertheless, Herolt gathers authorities from Augustine, Aristotle, and Ptolemy to acknowledge that temptation may prey on innate inclinations of our animal sensuality produced by astral influence, predisposing us marginally to particular vices or virtues, yet these inclinations remain under reason's power: "This inclination or that constellation poses no necessity of sinning."[13]

---

[10] Lewis, *Discarded Image*, 103-04; Keith Thomas, *Religion and the Decline of Magic* (New York: Charles Scribner's Sons, 1971), 358-85.
[11] D.1.2/7 (H), T.41.4 (H), and see chapter 2.
[12] T.60.3/7 (P).
[13] D.1.2/11 (K), T.21.1 (S).

The conventional account of particular characters assigned to the planets appears again in Herolt's explanation of why human life has grown shorter since the days of the patriarchs. One reason, he says, may be the influence of "infecund planets," which certainly seem to be responsible for the greater virulence of disease and pestilence in recent days.[14] He does not identify the "infecund planets," but we may assume he has in mind Saturn, the *infortuna maior*. Illness, ageing, casualty, and plague were generally ascribed to this terrible planet's melancholy influence, not least in the recent onslaught of the Black Death.

The acknowledged terrestrial effects of the planetary spheres, the fact that their names were still those of pagan deities, and the tentative attribution of "souls" or "intelligences" to the spheres maintained the risk that some people would continue to worship the heavenly bodies. Herolt shares this suspicion with many canonists and inquisitors. He cites the warning of the decretal (25 q.5): "It is not permitted to a Christian to worship the elements [that is, the heavenly spheres], nor to observe the course of the moon or stars in contracting marriage or gathering crops, nor is it permitted to attend incantations [that is, the conjurings and prophecies of astrologers]."[15] The real threat was not out-and-out paganism but the difficulty of conveying to the laity (and even some priests) the clear but sophisticated distinction drawn by the schoolmen between astral science and astrological superstition. Herolt is all too aware of the room created for advertent or inadvertent confusion. He condemns those who attribute cures to the sun or those who worship the moon.[16]

The noblest of all the heavenly bodies is the sun. "God has commanded the sun to travel every single day from east to west, and every night to return to the east, it rests not day or night, summer or winter, from fulfilling that precept. Though it has toiled all one day, it rises next day and expects no special reward for its task."[17] The sun's special role is illuminating the whole universe; it is "the fount and origin of all light."[18] Though the sun's rays must pass through the atmosphere in order to illuminate the earth,[19] Herolt understands no more about the air's diffraction of visible light than his predecessors, but pictures the universe filled in every part by the light streaming from the sun with instantaneous speed, penetrating fineness, and inexhaustible power.[20] Our modern imagination, informed by journeys into space, pictures this earth as a tiny splash of color in a pitch-black void. The medieval imagination pictures a heavenly realm ablaze with sunlight, where the earth within

---

[14] T.60.3/7 (P).
[15] D.1.2/7 (H).
[16] D.1.2/17 (Q), T.41.13 (M).
[17] D.16.1/1 (A).
[18] T.50.4 (D).
[19] T.161.0 (S).
[20] T.50.4 (D).

the circle of the moon is the only realm of shadow on account of sin. Indeed, because of man's sin, sun and moon shine with only an eighth of their original brilliance and will be restored to full splendor at the final renewal.[21]

Meanwhile, the corrupted and corrupting aftereffects of the fall are quite literally in the air, the osmotic boundary between earth and the heavens, through which celestial influences must devolve. On account of sin, the atmosphere has become infected, and elements and influences that should have been beneficial have been turned banefully into their very opposites. (This alone is why the wild beasts, in their innocence, share our liability to illness.)[22] In the course of human history, this corruption has spread its infection ever wider. In patriarchal times, plants and animals were more plentiful and constitutionally stronger. Men lived longer, for the elements and humors from which they were formed were not yet degenerate.[23] Now the air is a realm of uncleanness, infested by demons, the smoke of sacrifice, and the virulence of sin. That is why Christ chose to suffer—raised up in the air—to cleanse and sanctify the impure air, as he had already cleansed the earth by walking on it, and water by his baptism.[24] This is why God tolerates the violent intemperance of the atmosphere: storms and thunder not only shakes sinners with fright that they may be converted, but they terrify the devils who now indwell the air, for "thunderclaps are the trumpets of Christ, the king of heaven."[25]

When that saving work is ultimately completed by the reforming of mankind, the world and all its creatures will also be renewed. The species will not change, but their properties will be transformed. There will be no dumb animals after the resurrection.[26] The sun, moon, and stars will be more brilliant; the air purer, without violent winds or black clouds, hail, thunder, or lightning; and the light of fire and the limpidity of water clearer and purer, but fire's heat and water's cold will be changed and their harmfulness removed. The earth itself will be purified and smoothed like a crystal, and its opacity and grossness forced downward to remain underground. Whatever deformity there is in all creation will be bound and driven below to aggravate the pains of the reprobate, while whatever it contains of beauty will be augmented and endure in enhanced delight in sensible creatures.[27]

Meanwhile, the present time is an exile and a vale of tears, a single daily regimen toward death, where weeping is more appropriate than mirth.[28] The world now corrupted and overshadowed by sin is a bleak midpoint between heaven and hell,

---

[21] Q.11.1.
[22] E.15.1/2.
[23] T.60.3 (O-P).
[24] Q.37.2/1, Q.41.1, cf. T.121.0 (G).
[25] T.108.2 (S).
[26] E.20.3/7.
[27] E.50.3/3.
[28] E.13.3.

where Christians are strangers, pilgrims, and wayfarers.[29] Justly we pray, "Deliver us from evil," for the whole world is full of dangers, and we are always surrounded by a multitude of snares.[30] We are truly wretched in this vale of tears, which is a place of calamities, full of bitterness and miseries—a lament that grows stronger in Herolt's later work.[31]

Accordingly, the preacher insists that love of this world is exceedingly perilous; it extinguishes love for God, it is the font of all vices, and it makes one an enemy of God and a servant of the devil.[32] Friendship with the world means enmity with God. They are diametric opposites, like hot and cold, fire and water, black and white.[33] The world's offerings are deceptive, and ultimately the world's servants have a harsher labor than Christ's. The world repays its servants with little, and its lovers with evil, finally leaving them nothing for all their toil but their sweat. They cannot attain the kingdom of heaven—it is an either/or choice.[34] Whole sermons are devoted to earnest dissuasions from worldly joys,[35] and Herolt never tires of urging his hearers to spurn this world's delights.[36] Like Elijah, the Christian should flee the rackets of the world into the contemplation of Christ.[37]

During our exile, good and evil are inextricably mixed in this world. Good men and evil men have lived together, and alike, since the beginning of the race. If it was true of Cain and Abel, of Noah's sons, and of the children of the patriarchs, even of the twelve apostles, it is still so in modern times and will be until the end:

> And this in every status—for among princes some are good and some bad, and likewise among knights and burgers and peasants, and among craftsmen, too. It is the same among priests and religious, and among servants and maids, and all the others . . . . For flowers grow with thorns, gold with copper, tin with silver, lees with wine, chaff with grain, and you cannot have one without the other. So it is with men in this world![38]

In the present age, the vast majority are unjust and evil: The lusty outnumber the chaste, the arrogant outnumber the humble, the greedy the merciful, and

---

[29] D.12.2/5 (K), E.31.2/2.
[30] D.21.2/7, T.65.212 (R), T.152.2 (G).
[31] T.105.0 (L), E.6.3, E.13.3, E.31.32.
[32] D.19.3/7 (L), T.152.1 (R).
[33] T.72.9 (U), T.136.1 (F), E.21.1/1.
[34] D.13.1/1 (A), T.136.3 (H) and 7 (L), E.21.1/2-3.
[35] T.94, T.136.
[36] E.g., T.1.1 (B), T.36.1 (D-H), T.70.2/1 (O), T.72.9 (U), E.8.1/2, E.11.3, etc.
[37] Q.20.1.
[38] T.30.1 (A).

tricksters and liars the truthful.[39] "Now there is in the world neither truth, nor fidelity, nor true Christian life."[40]

Even the good things of the world are all brief and small.[41] Natural life is short and transient, and Herolt amasses long lists of authorities testifying grimly to the brevity of life.[42] He cites a sermon of his Nürnberg colleague Johannes Nider that offers a series of somber explanations why God ordained that suffering should be the central reality of our life in this world: so that we may know we are not citizens here, but strangers and pilgrims, and have no hope in this world to slow our race to the fatherland; so that we may be spurred on by our sufferings to walk uprightly and hate the mortal sin for which all this has been inflicted on our race; and so that we may be purged as with fire and earn merit by bearing our wretchedness virtuously.[43] For man is placed in the world like a plant in a field to bear fruit; the meritorious fruit consists in the work we perform, but predominantly in the tribulation we patiently suffer.[44]

It is not surprising then that the preacher devotes little direct attention to the world of nature or that its chief use is as a source of warning and moral instruction. The clear-sighted observations of some early Dominicans, Albertus and his disciples, appear in mere fragments in these sermons, as axioms of natural philosophy for rhetorical polish or conventional tropes on the birds and the bees for moral edification. The physicists' premise that "nature is uniform in its operation"[45] becomes the metaphysical doctrine that "nothing whatever happens by chance," but everything without exception happens by God's true ordination. The listener's attention is directed not to the immanent chains of natural causality but to the hand of God in the minutiae of life's vicissitudes—a fire in a church, the death of a domestic animal, storms in the air, the precise span of a man's life.[46]

Images of exemplary creatures appear often in these sermons. Some are contrary examples, but on the whole Herolt has little consciousness of nature "red in tooth and claw," and the creatures' example shames the lethargy, ingratitude, and excess of humankind. "Irrational creatures are more obedient than slothful man": The heavens are tireless in their circuits, herbs and trees persevere from the tiniest beginnings to grow to huge size, Solomon commends the ant's prudence and toil, and Aristotle insists that nothing is naturally lazy.[47] Every creature praises

---

[39] T.126.0 (D).
[40] T.97.2/1 (C).
[41] T.136.04 (J).
[42] T.153.1 (A), E.11.1/3, E.42.1/1.
[43] E.31.2/2.
[44] T.153.0 (before A), Q.17.0.
[45] D.18.2.7 (F).
[46] E.15.2/1.
[47] D.16.1/1 (A).

its creator and urges the praise of God—water by its continual flowing, earth by germinating fruit and flowers, trees and plants by stretching high and growing upward toward their creator, the sun in its shining, and the birds in their singing. ("How absurd that man should lie abed in the morning and laze while the little birds praise God in the dawn!")[48]

Herolt's style is usually didactic and his exegesis literal; but in his examples from nature, more than anywhere else, he draws on the rich alternative strand of fanciful, symbolic, and spiritualizing pulpit rhetoric, represented (for instance) by his Franciscan contemporary, Johann of Werden.[49] Like other medieval preachers, Herolt depends less on the naturalists' observations, or even the common people's practical knowledge of animal husbandry, than on the credulous, fantastical, childish zoology of the Bestiaries.[50] The gullible travellers' tales or deliberate inventions of Herodotus, Aelian, Cicero, Martial, Juvenal, Pliny, and Lucan are all transmitted to the middle ages by Christian rapporteurs like Isidore of Seville (whose *Etymologiae* Herolt quotes), and then progressively allegorized by generation after generation of preachers, poets, and painters. The line between fact and fiction is not clearly drawn, if it is recognized at all.

The elements yield moral lessons. The air symbolizes our common humanity: "Physically each man has his own earth, his own water, and his own fire, but no one can have his own air."[51] Water by its incessant flow is our example of constancy.[52] Patience is like fire, for adversity toughens a man's softness and softens his hardness, as fire bakes tiles but softens iron for use; patience gives the light of self-knowledge as fire brightens a dark place. Suffering purifies the soul of sin as fire separates dross from gold and rust from iron and tests a man as fire tests precious metal. Fire prepares food, and adversity prepares the soul for love. Fire drives out moisture, and hardship dries up unclean desires.[53]

The most useful images are animals and birds. The whole animal kingdom is an example to mankind of mercy, for "by nature all animals maintain a mutual forbearance towards members of their own species."[54] Animals, too, are an example of a certain nobility, for they show gratitude to their benefactors. Witness the lioness who brought her ailing cubs to St. Macarius and after he prayed for their recovery

---

[48] D.2.2/5, T.112.1/2 (K).
[49] Johann of Werden (Verdena), *Sermones Dormi Secure*.
[50] See, e.g., Nikolaus Henkel, *Studien zum Physiologus im Mittelalter* (Tübingen: Niemeyer, 1976) Hermaea NF, Bd 38; Florence McCulloch, *Mediaeval Latin and French Bestiaries*. Studies in the Romance Languages and Literatures 33 (Chapel Hill: U. of North Carolina, 1960).
[51] Q.41.1.
[52] Q.41.1.
[53] R.4.4 (47ª-49ª).
[54] T.89.0 (0).

kept the saint supplied with sheepskins; and the wolf who carried a child off to the forest, and after the child removed a bone lodged in a wolf's mouth, the pack carried him back to the village.[55] The beasts are also examples to us of moderation in eating: They are generally healthy because instinctively they eat simple and appropriate food and only enough to satisfy their need.[56]

Individual animals may be object lessons of either laudable or reprehensible behavior. Pigs are instinctively compassionate by nature, and all rush together when any one of them is hurt or killed; and in this respect they are better than envious humans.[57] But pigs are more often a negative example. Detractors are like pigs, who "would rather have filthy mouths than filthy feet, and chose to lie in the mud than in the flowers."[58] The same conventional comparison is applied to lechers,[59] who like pigs "prefer the mire of lust to the flowers of chastity." But direct farming experience is applied to scurrilous charterers: "You judge a pig by its tongue, whether it is clean or dirty on the outside."[60]

Snakes also afford both positive and negative models. They routinely appear in horrid pictures of hell, and Herolt describes them as the most dangerous of beasts, lying coiled, moving tortuously, and striking silently. In this, detractors are also like snakes.[61] But Christians should imitate the wisdom of serpents if they are to live by the Spirit's wisdom. The snake will expose the whole of its body if it needs to protect its head, and so we should expose our bodies for the sake of Christ, our head. A snake fasts forty days and then sheds its skin by crawling through a narrow place, and so we should shed our old guilt in the narrow place of penitence. It protects itself from the music of the snake charmers by laying one ear to the ground and curling its tail round to block the other ear, and so we should protect ourselves from the world's blandishments by considering our earthiness and mortality, the instability and unfaithfulness of the world, and our own "tail"—death and the repayment the world offers its servants.[62]

This pun is applied to other creatures too. As cattle protect themselves from bothersome flies with their tails, Herolt says, and as both birds and fishes steer themselves with their tails, so man should consider his end![63]

---

[55] T.127.1/2 (H).
[56] D.18.2/7 (F), T.60.3/3 (P), T.98.5 (I).
[57] D.14.3/3 (F), D.20.2/3 (M).
[58] D.5.4/1 (P).
[59] D.19.1 (A).
[60] T.139.1/1 (K).
[61] D.5.4/1 (P), A.D.: 1 "Detractores" (115ᵇ).
[62] T.152.1 (Q), E.8.1/2, E.46.1/2, A.A.: 4 "Abstinentia" (111ᵃ).
[63] T.118.2/1 (K).

Another cliché is the ape's propensity to imitate whatever it sees. Thus "the hypocrite is the devil's ape, trying to imitate the children of God." Herolt's selection from a wide choice of ape stories is this:

> A poor cobbler was making some shoes. Whenever he was cutting leather for shoes, the moment he stood up and put down his knife, an ape which had been watching from a rich man's house opposite would immediately run across and cut some leather too, wanting to do just as the cobbler was doing; and it ruined the poor man's leather. The poor man often complained to the rich merchant about it, but the rich man took very little notice. So eventually, one day, the cobbler picked up a razor and shaved his beard and down his neck and throat. The ape watched, and after the cobbler left, it came over and picked up the razor, intending to imitate what it had seen. And so it cut its own throat![64]

Herolt has nothing good to say about the most familiar animal of all—the dog. Detractors (a favorite target) are again likened to dogs because a dog who gets a thorn in its foot will not stop yelping until it is out. Dogs are "the devil's"; they will not let even the smallest bird escape but bark and bite at it.[65] Dogs are short-lived because they are angry beasts, and irascibility will shorten a man's life too.[66] The dog is one of the few beasts that freely indulge in incest, unlike the camel, for instance, which will become violent to avoid it.[67] Even the dog's proverbial loyalty is given a monitory twist: When two men are walking along together and a dog is following at their heels, you cannot tell which is its master, but as soon as they part you can tell. And when you die, your wealth stays with the world.[68]

Some animal behavior reproves our lack of fidelity. If we claim we cannot live chastely, a fish can stop itself eating the bait if it sees the hook, and a bird will not eat the grain if it catches sight of the snare.[69] As horses, to run better, put down two hooves at a time, so the two affects of love and fear together are good for the soul.[70] The ruling classes should emulate the nobility of the lion, not the predatoriness of the shark. For the nobler a beast, the more tolerant it can afford to be. A lion provoked by its cub does not avenge itself because of its magnanimity and the cub's

---

[64] T.100.2 (U).
[65] D.5.4/1 (A), cf. A.D.: 2 "Detractores" (115ᵇ).
[66] D.15.1/4 (A).
[67] T.85.5 (Q).
[68] T.94.2 (C).
[69] D.19.5/1 (N).
[70] T.4.0 (before U).

slightness, but if one cub bites another, they tear at each other and trade bites.[71] Rulers who protect their own subjects from outside attack and then despoil them themselves are like the shark who protects sprats from other fish just to eat them itself. "The king of bees," Herolt tells us, "has no sting like other bees."[72]

Insects seem an anomaly in the goodness of creation. Following Proverbs, the ant may be taken as a model of provident wisdom;[73] but on the whole, such creatures are merely a troublesome spur to humility. Why did God make the flies and fleas and worms? On account of man's pride—the flies to bite him by day and the fleas by night, and even the greatest king cannot resist the tiniest worm.[74] The ludicrousness of human pride in ornate clothing is shown by the fact that the longer your train, the more fleas you collect.[75] To lie is to have flies in the mouth, like "someone who leaves his mouth open all the time for flies and any other unclean thing that likes to go in and nest there."[76] And ultimately, there is no escape from being eaten by worms.[77]

These creeping and crawling creatures are the chief symbols of our corruption. Herolt gives a characteristic account of a gravedigger who uncovered a body full of holes from which came worms that covered the body, a snake in place of its tongue as a sign of sinful speech, asps emerging from the liver because of lust, and a toad on the head because of pride.[78] Toads and worms, and dragons too, are standard elements of his grotesque vision of hell.[79] The loathsome toad also suits the preacher as an image of misers and tightwads: "We read of the toad that it eats dirt, but if it ever raises its head from the ground it gets frightened that it will lose some earth, so it doesn't dare eat more than it can touch or gather with one foot."[80]

By contrast, most birds provide improving models, and Herolt conveys some personal delight in his remarks about them. The dove is a fit exemplar for the soul that is why the Spirit took its shape. Like the dove, the soul must keen endlessly when it loses its spouse, Christ, and refuse to sit on a green branch till he returns; like the dove, it must lack the gall of malice and rather sustain than inflict harm; and like the dove, it must build its nest in the rock of Christ crucified and the good life.[81] Birds show an exemplary care for their parents. It is said of the crane

---

[71] T.97.1/2 (H).
[72] T.127.1/3 and 4 (H).
[73] D.16.1/1 (A), E.8.1/3.
[74] E.38.2/5.
[75] T.83.1/4 (H).
[76] T.133.1/1 (J).
[77] D.18.6/1 (P), Q.40.1, E.38.2.3.
[78] T.115.2 (H).
[79] T.125.9 (C), T.136.7 (N).
[80] D.9.6 (B), T.82.4 (E).
[81] T.72.2 (U).

that when the mother and father birds moult, the young gather the food until they grow new feathers, and of the stork that when its parents grow old it places them in its own nest and warms and feeds them next to its breast.[82] The stork, too, is Herolt's symbol for the sentry at the gate of the soul:

> It has the right attributes for the task: first, a stork is wide awake at night; it stands upright in case it hears anything, because it is concerned for its young. If it hears something, then it cackles so that everyone can hear it is alert. We likewise should also take good care of our garden [the soul] so that the evil one does not come and steal the noble roses. And because we are sentries who undergo temptation, we too should stay upright and display the fact that we are not asleep but awake, and exercise ourselves in good works.
>
> Secondly, when even the tiniest worm enters its nest and gets on top of it, the stork's character is such that it immediately has to leave. You should act the same way, for you should keep even the smallest worm out of the garden in constancy of godly fear, and similarly flee before all noxiousness.
>
> Thirdly, the stork is wont to live on top of men's houses, near people, who thereby gain a good example by your model and help. Thus you master the evil serpent who comes into the garden.[83]

The kinglet is a symbol of obedience. It flits nimbly from tree to tree and cannot be dislodged because it will sleep in the tiniest hole.[84] The warbler nests not in trees but in the grass and raises other birds' young: "The cuckoo does not raise its own young, but what it does is to bring the egg to the warbler and lay it in its nest, and the warbler hatches it. When it has grown big, the warbler has to be very watchful that it does not get swallowed up by it!" The warbler is an allegory of Christ who humbled himself for man, and the threatening fledgling cuckoo is our mortal sin.[85]

In Herolt's most figurative and florid work, *The Rose Garden*, natural imagery forms the almost rococo framework of an entire treatise on the virtues. The rose garden is the soul, and we are treated in turn to figurative elaboration of the enclosed garden itself, set on a hill and growing lily of the valley, sage, rue, and many noble spices; and in its center is an exceeding beauteous rose tree. There is a

---

[82] D.4.1/4 (A).
[83] R.2.3 (24ᵇ-25ᵃ).
[84] R.5.5 (83ᵃ⁻ᵇ).
[85] R.6.3 (93ᵃ-94ᵇ).

descant on each theme in turn: the wall of godly fear, and the symbolic meanings of its breadth, length, and height, and the gate of diligence hung on the hinge of constancy; the twelve layers of trenching that must be dug to prepare the soil of humility; the stem of the rosebush, namely patience, its six branches, obedience, meekness, goodness, mercifulness, friendship, and joy; on each branch, a rose and a bird with a characteristic song. There is enough delight in the color and fragrance of the roses, the blue and white of the lilies, the medicinal uses of rose water and rue, the moist cold freshness of violets, and the wreaths and garlands that may be culled to show that Herolt found a garden "a lovesome thing."

Herolt's sermons for other preachers' use of are far more literal and prosaic than *The Rose Garden*; yet occasionally he includes some time-hallowed zoological image of an allegorical sort. Finally, at the end of his long career, he gathered 151 *Sermon Applications from Characteristics of Natural Things* into one alphabetical collection, illustrating the vices and virtues from wondrous properties of the animal, vegetable, and mineral worlds. He points to the classic *Pie Pelicane*—the pelican drawing its own blood as an image of Christ;[86] he describes how a unicorn cannot be captured by violence, but if it lays its head on a virgin's lap it grows meek: so God, the fierce lion, resting in a virgin's lap, became a meek lamb.[87]

The most elaborate figure concerns the falcon, a noble bird, Herolt says, whose heart desires a reward when it has flown long for prey.[88] When Christ extended his hands on the cross to call the sinner to himself, he was the fowler recalling the hawk or falcon that has flown away. "For when the hawk flies off, the fowler stretches his hand out, and calls, and if it does not return he takes a piece of bloody meat and shows it to the hawk so that it will see the meat and come back." Christ himself was the bloodied lure, but "Alas! How absurd that a wild bird can be tamed in a month and trained to return to its master's hand, but the wild sinner sometimes cannot be tamed in twenty year!"[89] The reasons birds sometimes do not return, Herolt explains with spiritual corollaries, are three: They are overfed, sidetracked by carrion (like the crow from Noah's ark), or too accustomed to the freedom of the wilds to be domesticated.[90] The crow is like the devil. When it finds a cadaver, it goes first at the eyes.[91]

Allegory permits some of the more bizarre pseudozoology to enter as well. The longing of the soul for God, whom it has wronged, is like the harpies:

---

[86] E.18.311, A.I.: 2 "Ingrati" (118ᵃ).
[87] T.1.1 (B), A.X.: 1 "Christus" (130ᵃ).
[88] T.8.1 (B).
[89] T.49.1/2 (P), Q.41.1.
[90] Q.13.1.
[91] D.15.1/4 (A).

> The poets write that harpies are birds with human faces. Yet it is such a fierce bird that when aroused by hunger it will wound and kill a man. But then it grows thirsty and flies to water to drink, and when it sees its reflected face, and its likeness to the one it has just killed, it suffers such remorse that it dies too.

The soul is like the bird of paradise, incomparably beautiful of plumage and voice, which pales and keens incurably when captured.[1] And the phoenix, after it has lived five hundred years, gathers aromatic wood into its nest, sets fire to it, and rises renewed from the ashes. The application is self-evident—the resurrection will bring the glorification of our bodies. Herolt's series of instances of natural self-renewal illustrates the difficulty of knowing whether these images are intended literally or poetically for the phoenix is one of a list which also includes the snake shedding its skin by forty days' abstinence; the aged eagle, which

> when its beak grows too curved for it to open it and gather food ... grinds down its own beak on a rock until the curvature is gone and it is able to eat, then soars ... until its feathers are burning from the sun's rays, and immediately plunges down into a gushing fountain where it is wholly renewed;

or the deer which, when its pelt and antlers have grown too big from age, finds its natural enemy the snake. The snake hides from fear of the deer, but the deer drinks and flushes the snake out with the water; the snake bites the deer on the nose, and the poison drives the deer to drink at a fountain where its pelt and antlers are lost and new growth begins.[2]

Yet there is one piece of ancient fancy that Herolt firmly rejects. There are, he says, no such things as werewolves. The devil's work cannot transform people into wild beasts—wolves and the like. To believe that it happens is a pagan and faithless heresy. There are some natural transformations in the life cycle of creatures like snakes, worms, and frogs; but it cannot happen in this life to a human body except as an illusion. All the demons can do is to provoke real wolves to attack and eat men, in the hope of convincing the credulous and simple that people are turned into wolves, as the pagans once believed. Strangely enough, wolves come off as realistically in Herolt's treatment as any animal because in this case he does quote Albertus Magnus directly: the other reasons wolves attack humans are increased hunger in time of famine, ferocity in the breeding season, protection of cubs, rabies,

---

[1] T.7.2 (R).
[2] E.46.112, A.A.: 13 "Anima" (112ᵃ).

the unique sweetness of human flesh, or—in another more characteristic order of reality—as a hidden or manifest judgment of God.[3]

Ultimately, the preacher's purpose is to direct the listener's attention away from natural phenomena to urgent spiritual concerns. "Many people have more compassion for brute beasts torn by the wolves than for their brethren dragged to hell by the demons!"[4] Meanwhile, though it is sinful superstition to observe the flight of birds, the crowing of hens, or the barking of dogs in augury,[5] it is no sin to kill animals. For it is no sin to use something for its ordained purpose; in general, plants and animals exist for man's sake.[6] However brief and transient the life of nature, it revolves around man—a soul animating a body. Man is the chief inhabitant of this world.

---

[3] E.48.3/6-7.
[4] E.43.2/1.
[5] D.1.2/12 (L), T.142.1 (R).
[6] D.5.2/4 (D).

8

HUMAN NATURE

The first man was made from the dust of a Damascus field. Afterward he was placed in a garden of delight, where the weather was always temperate, the air pure, and the plants ever in bloom and the scent rich and sweet. There Eve was made from Adam's rib.[7]

It was a noble creation. God made man wise in reason, innocent in life, and powerful in dominion. Adam contemplated God with an inner aspiration, not as clearly as the saints in heaven but not as enigmatically as we do who are now on the way. He understood the natures of all animals, plants, trees, precious stones, and all visible, palpable things. He possessed all virtues. In his innocence he was without guilt, and his soul ruled his body so that he suffered no weakness from within, wound from without, or any deception. He did not yet suffer the penalties of hunger, thirst, cold, or heat nor live in expectation of death, since he would have gone alive into glory. He felt no shame at his nakedness, for he was vested with the stole of his innocence.[8]

If man had remained in paradise, reason would have ruled passion, and the only occasion for sexual intercourse would have been a rational, obedient intent to have children. There would have been no sterility; and since there was no death, and each man thus had only one wife, boys and girls would probably have been born in equal numbers. They would have been born, as we are, feeble, small in size, and without immediate use of reason; but they would have developed with a lucidity, depth, and insight far beyond ours. They would, in short, have shared some of the common deficiencies of our beginning but none of the deficiencies of our end.[9]

But why, indeed, did God choose to yoke a precious soul with a deficient body? The first answer is one of those formulas the modern mind finds artificial but whose symmetrical scheme so delighted medieval culture. God had already created pure spirits—the angels. He had created pure bodies—the elements, rocks, wood. So now, to complete his creation, he made the third thing—both physical and spiritual—a

---

[7] T.31.1 (L).
[8] T.34.1 (K).
[9] T.34.1 (M).

body and a soul. A second reason is tropological: the soul without a body could gain certain merits by loving, acknowledging, and remembering God; but it needed the body to merit by fasting, pilgrimage, martyrdom, flagellation, abstinence, and the like. God gave us a body and members for service so that our feet could serve him by walking, our hands by touching, our eyes by seeing, and our mouths by speaking, the sort of service the angels cannot perform.[10] But the ultimate reason is man's greater glory in the future, enjoying not only a spiritual vision of deity but a physical vision of humanity and divinity in one.[11] 'The principal cause of man's creation in the world is heavenly bliss and the beatific vision."[12]

Man is, in short, God's noblest creation.[13] The greatness of man's created dignity in God's eyes is shown nine ways: he is created in God's image; he has been made lord of all creatures; each man has an angel assigned to guard him; God desires man's praise here and in the future; God assumed human nature, not the angelic nature; God bought mankind at so dear a price; and feeds man with his own holy blood; man was created for eternal bliss with the angels; and nothing can satisfy man's desire but God, who is infinite and immense.[14]

Some of these items recur in another homiletic list—reasons to be thankful for God's blessings. In the dignity of man's creation, God shows that he loves man above all creation by making him in his image and likeness and by appointing him lord of all creatures. In assuming flesh, God shows that he loves man above all angels in honor, love, and vision: in honor by assuming human, not angelic, nature; in love by redeeming men, not the fallen angels; and in vision in that man, not angel, will see his nature joined to the divine. In undergoing the passion, God shows that he loves man more than himself, so to speak, since it was for man that he exposed his body and his life.[15]

Accordingly, man owes God gratitude for his creation, for "whatever we are or possess, we have from God."[16] Even our own nature reminds us to give thanks, for

> in the human body, the naturalists say, nature has reproduced as many members as there are days in the year. So even rational instinct teaches us that no day should pass without divine praise and thanksgiving, wherever a man catches sight of any part of his body . . .[17]

---

[10] T.155.1 (R).
[11] D.2201 (D), T.34.3 (S), T.146.1 (C), Q.17.1.
[12] E.44.1.
[13] D.5.2/9 (G).
[14] T.32.2 (S-U).
[15] T.102.2/6 (O), T.112.2 (N).
[16] D.22.1 (E).
[17] T.112.1/3 (L).

Though the body reminds us of God, it is the soul, not the body, which is created in the image and likeness of God.[18] Before the incarnation, the dignity of that image was motive enough for striving to keep human nature clean; but since the incarnation, an even higher motive has been added—the inseparable union of our nature with the divine.[19] How is man made in God's image? As God is immortal, so is the soul; as God is lord of all, so man is lord over all creatures; and in the powers of the mind, memory, intellect, and will, Father, Son, and Holy Spirit may dwell by recollection, knowledge, and love.[20]

Man is a microcosm of all creation. When Christ commissioned the apostles to preach to all men, he said "preach to all creatures" because "man shares the essence of every creature—being with the stones, living with the plants, feeling with the irrational animals, understanding with the angels."[21] The preacher repeatedly asserts man's lordship.[22] When the creed calls God "creator of heaven and earth," it makes us aware of the dignity of man, since "God created all creatures on man's account and subjected them all to man. Man's worth is so great that he must precede all creatures and come next behind God."[23]

But it is intrinsic to human dignity that man was created able to sin. God does not wish to coerce anyone into his kingdom and gave man reason to tell good from evil and free will to eschew evil and choose good.[24] Adam and Eve abused their freedom and sinned, and the effects on human nature have been devastating.

In place of the serene strength and beauty of man's first innocence, "the human condition, from the prevarication of our first parents, has become fragile and infirm, inside and out, above and below, in front and behind, to right and left, and the passions course through every part of the body."[25] Now what is a man like? The philosopher tells us he is like the morning rose, beautiful before sunrise, but later it stinks; he is like a bad apple, which often has a worm.[26] By sinning, man has incurred a triple detriment. He carries a blemish, for he is deprived of the shapeliness of grace by the deformity of sin. The goodness of his nature has been corrupted because man's nature is disordered when his will is not subject to God. Once the order of man's nature has been destroyed, disorderliness is the permanent state of

---

[18] T.132.1 (A), E.24.1/3.
[19] T.1.2 (G).
[20] T.75.1/2 (P).
[21] T.66.2 (T); cf. Gregory, *Moralia*, 6.16.
[22] D.22.1 (E), T.32.2/2 (T), T.34.1 (K) and 3 (S), T.66.2 (T), T.75.1/2 (P), T.102.2/6 (O), T.112.2 (N).
[23] D.22.1 (E), T.146.1 (C).
[24] T.109.7 (H).
[25] E.31.0.
[26] E.35.2/1.

sinful man. And he incurs the penalty of his guilt, for by sinning he merits eternal damnation.[1] Man is now by nature a child of wrath.[2]

The very matter out of which man's body is made is subject to the same corruption. Man is composed of the four elements: water in the humors, fire in the body's natural warmth and vision, air in respiration, and earth in the flesh and bones. But

> the infection and corruption of the elements by sin has grown greater now, and will increase even more in the future. Iniquity superabounds daily in the world, and dissipates the elements from which man is compounded.[3]

The result is that human nature now possesses twelve common defects (Christ assumed ten of them in willing to become man): human nature suffers cold and heat, hunger and thirst, weariness, sadness, fear, shame, grief and death, and (the two Christ did not assume) ignorance and sin.[4] Spiritually, it is now man's nature to be inconstant, and he must be on guard against his own innate instability.[5]

In God's purpose, the soul was to receive many benefits from its conjunction with the body, but now that union has many incommodious effects. The body now burdens the soul with the pollution of original sin, an inherent proneness to sin, difficulty in performing good works, dulling of intellect, the continuous onslaught of temptation, a multitude of sufferings, and the delay of heavenly glory.[6]

What then of man's present life in this world, stained, disordered, and guilty? It should make us aware of the solidarity of mankind, the brotherhood we all share in this sorry condition, and humility and mutual compassion. In one of Herolt's favorite set pieces (attributed in one version to Joannes Januensis), all men and women are said to have four things in common. Lords and ladies, servants and maids, rich and poor, noble and ignoble are all alike in their *beginnings*, for they are all made by one God, and from the same mud, and they are all born naked and poor. All are alike in *midcourse*, for they are all mortal, rich and poor alike, and have but a brief life. All share *a common end*, for all men are reduced to the same death and putrefaction; there is no distinction between the dried bones of noble and ignoble. And finally, all men without exception will stand before the *judgment* and will all be compelled to render account before one judge and be assessed by one justice.[7]

---

[1] E.1.1/2.
[2] E.38.3.
[3] T.60.3/6 (P).
[4] T.27.1/1-12 (A-D).
[5] R.0.3 (4ᵇ).
[6] T.34.3 (T).
[7] D.21.2 (D), D.30.3/3 (F), T.59.2 (L), T.65.1 (Q), T.73.3 (E), Q.2.2, E.7.3.

The implicit social commentary is clear enough. Our human similarity and common parentage should incite us to love of neighbor. In nature, there is natural love within species:

> If the bear, the wolf, the lion, and the snake—the cruellest of all the animals—hold no malice towards members of their own species, how much more should man withhold his malice from others men who are his own species? If nature teaches brute beasts to keep love and gentleness to those like them, what will be the excuse for those who fail to do so by the reason they possess?[8]

The fact that we are all born naked, helpless, and weeping is an object lesson.[9]

> We see earth clothed in grasses, herbs, and flowers, the green, trees clad in bark and leaves, the stars with light, the birds with feathers and wings. But man alone is born naked among creatures, and after a little returns naked to the earth and is buried.[10]

Every child does four things at birth that teach us our humble estate: it is born weeping, not laughing; it is born curved and as if four-footed, like the brute beasts; it puts its hand to its mouth, as if to say that it has come to such wretchedness because of our first parents' sin of the mouth; and it is born naked and poor, against pride and avarice. Only man is born naked. Other animals have skins to clothe them; only man must seek covering against cold and nakedness.[11]

No man may vaunt himself because he is highborn or spurn others.[12] This is the reason the Lord's Prayer addresses God as "*Our* Father."[13] Our common creation and redemption should lead us to forgive our neighbors' faults[14] and understand their frailty.[15] It should warn us against despising others for ignobility, poverty, sinfulness, or disfigurement.[16] The lesson of the human condition, above all, is humility.

---

[8] T.120.1 (A).
[9] E.38.2/3.
[10] E.45.3.
[11] T.76.0 (A).
[12] T.65.1 (Q).
[13] D.21.2 (D), T.65.1 (Q).
[14] T.154.2/1 (P).
[15] T.73.3 (E).
[16] E.7.3.

9

THE SOUL AND THE BODY

The coin shown to Christ had Caesar's image and superscription, but when he said we should render to God what is God's, he taught us to guard God's image and superscription in our own nature—our immortal soul.[17]

The soul, Herolt says, possesses nine dignities, nine signs of its eternal worth. The list is virtually identical with the nine dignities of human nature we have examined already.[18] In other words, the worthiness of human nature is the value of the soul to which the body is at best ancillary and at worst hostile. The soul, Herolt says repeatedly, is nobler than the body.[19] The soul's dignities are to be created in God's image; and whatever the body has of beauty, strength, speech, or motion, it derives from the soul. The soul excels every corporeal creature; indeed, one soul is more precious than all the kingdoms of the world:

> In men's esteem, there is nothing more precious than the blood of Christ, for one drop of Christ's blood excels infinite worlds in preciousness and worth. But in Christ's own esteem, the soul of man is so noble that he gave it equal value with his own blood when he exchanged the one for the other—his shed blood for the redemption of man's soul. The worlds were infinite, but Christ shed not a droplet of his blood for them. For man's soul, he poured out all his blood.

Christ deputed his angels to care for man's soul. He acquired his right to it by the mighty labors of his ministry; he feeds it with his own body. God chose the soul to live with him eternally. Nothing can fill it except God alone, who is its spouse, and it is ordained to enjoy eternal bliss.[20]

---

[17] T.132.0 (before A).
[18] See chapter 8.
[19] D.18.2/1 (C), T.98.1 (F), E.23.22.
[20] T.132.1 (A-D).

As the body is nothing without the soul, so the soul is nothing without God.[21] Other things may occupy it, but only God can fill it.[22] The light of grace shines about the rational soul;[23] the Word of God nourishes it.[24] He has given us the gift of the soul

> so that we may direct our entire intellect and affect and all the powers of the soul towards God, and occupy ourselves with godly and heavenly matters. So the soul begins through words to recognize God, through will to love the one recognized, and to rest sweetly in the Lord recognized and loved. And then it will be the best gift of all when the soul makes such progress that it is inflamed in God's love and is united with the Lord, to be one with God, as glass with fire.[25]

We may gain eternal merit through the soul by directing its three powers of memory, intellect, and will toward God: *memory*, by recalling his benefits and giving him thanks for them; *intellect*, by understanding God as our creator to whom we owe obedience, our redeemer who bought us by bitterest death and passion, and our judge whom we must fear in all our thoughts, words, and deeds; *will*, by being so conformed to the divine will that whatever he wants for us we are willing to have happen, whether sweet or bitter, and by having a constant good will to self-emendation and service.[26] So the soul becomes God's dwelling place: *memory* is the Father's chamber, in which he may dwell by continual recollection; *intellect* is the Son's chamber, in which he may dwell by the knowledge of the true faith; and *will* is the chamber of the Holy Spirit, in which he may abide by love.[27] Virtue is adornment of the soul, and "if the soul is decorated with virtues, the eternal wisdom, the eternal word will gladly live with his grace in any soul that wishes."[28]

The soul is the bride of Christ. Christ is the zealous suitor who makes his ardor known to the beloved soul he longs to wed by displaying the marks of his sufferings for it.[29] No one but God can satisfy the desire of this spouse.[30] The soul of any man "will be impregnated by him when good will and good intention are

---

[21] Q.24.0.
[22] D.17.1 (B), D.26.3 (F).
[23] T.80.2 (R).
[24] T.35.2 (Y).
[25] E.24.1/3.
[26] T.151.3 (M).
[27] T.75.2 (P).
[28] R.0.1 (2^b).
[29] T.144.1 (K).
[30] T.132.1 (D).

conceived." But that spiritual fetus may be smothered in the will: it is spiritual murder when by neglect or contempt good intention does not come to birth.[31] Those who rationalize about their good intentions for ten or twenty years before delivering a good work are bound to deliver a monster![32] Sometimes Christ, like a jealous husband, withholds his sweet presence from the soul to test its constancy; but like the dove, the soul that is Christ's bride should "keen after Christ when it has lost his sweetness, and wait mourning when he leaves until he returns."[33]

As a faithful bride of Christ, the soul must do five things to please him. It must honor its new family—God and the Blessed Virgin. It must love its husband, Christ. It must rule the home—the heart and conscience—keeping them clean and free of all filth and dust. It must run the household and family, for "the soul, Christ's spouse, has three noble serving maids inside and five less noble outside:" The inside maids are the three powers of the soul, memory, intellect, and will who must be directed to keep rooms fit for the habitation of Father, Son, and Spirit, while the five outside maids are the five bodily senses who must be regulated so that they admit no unwelcome impressions. And finally, the soul is to serve its spouse at table and in bed to prepare Christ the bed of a pure and secure conscience and the good food of works performed in grace.[34]

Herolt finds little homiletic use for the technicalities of scholastic psychology. As a rhetorical flourish, he says all our knowledge arises in sense impressions, and nothing appears in the intellect that has not first impinged on the senses.[35] But he reflects little of Thomas's subtlety on the reciprocity between intellect and will in the act of knowing.[36] In his treatment of temptation, he hints that bodily sense impressions first impinge on the soul as morally neutral suggestions and acquire guilt or merit only as the will then takes pleasure or displeasure in them and the reason yields or withholds consent.[37] In this linear progression, it remains the duty of reason to command the senses, to conquer the wilful proneness to sin that is innate in our corrupted sensuality.[38] In practice, the will is to be crushed, abandoned, and sacrificed. The highest ideal of spirituality is the total submerging of the will in obedience.[39] Herolt is far more committed to this monastic ideal than to the more

---

[31] D.5.3/2 (I).
[32] T.17.2 (I).
[33] T.72.2 (U).
[34] T.124.2 (L-M).
[35] Q.10.0.
[36] Thomas Aquinas, ST I-II q. 19 a. 3.
[37] D.10.4 (C), D.19.2/1 (B), T.138.1 (A).
[38] T.88.6 (M).
[39] T.18.3 (R), T.56.10 (C), T.121.6 (M), R.5.2 (67ª).

active view he mentions elsewhere that God wants only voluntary service, so gives man reason to discern good and evil and will freely to choose between them.[40]

If a person chooses the evil, he kills his own soul and becomes guilty of Christ's blood. To soil the soul, the image of God, with the filthiness of mortal sin is equivalent to throwing the image of the crucified Christ or the Blessed Virgin Mary into the mire. Mortal sin deforms the beauty of the soul, for it is most beauteous in grace.[41] But though the soul is so precious to God, and he shows its value in so many ways, evil men totally undervalue the soul. "They clean up their cellars if they get dirty sooner than their stained souls!" Some of them sell their souls for property or dissipation, some lose their souls from laziness or malaise, some pawn their souls by neglecting those they are pledged to care for, and some even give their souls away for nothing at all like the angry or the envious who get nothing for their bitterness and misery.[42]

There are even some people who deny the very existence of the soul. This popular sentiment was familiar enough to the Dominicans from their role in inquisition, but Herolt gives it little emphasis perhaps in order to avoid fuelling speculation. He dismisses the heresy with a monitory tale:

> A man was sitting in a tavern, and he asked his companions if they believed in the existence of the soul. He said he didn't believe there was a soul at all—he'd never seen one! The priests and monks had invented souls, and hell too, for worldly profit. "So," he said, "I don't believe in the existence of souls, or of hell either!" When his friends insisted that according to the true catholic faith there certainly were souls and a hell, and a heaven too, and that after the soul left the body it would either be in the pains of hell, or in purgatory, or in the joys of heaven, he exclaimed, "If someone wants to buy my soul, I'll sell it to him!" One of them answered, "I want to!" and he sold it to him for a quart of wine, which was soon drunk. And lo and behold, a devil in human guise came in, and he repurchased the soul from the man who had first bought it, again for a quart of wine. After that wine was drunk, the demon said to the man, "Give me the soul I bought—it's mine!" The onlookers agreed, "If someone buys something, by rights he should have it." Then and there the sot who sold his own soul was smothered by the devil, and the devil snatched him by the body as his companions looked on and carried off his soul to hell.[43]

---

[40] T.109.7 (H).
[41] E.33.2.
[42] T.132.2 (E-G).
[43] T.132.3 (H).

The heresy that medieval churchmen found most threatening of all, despite its antiquity, was Manichaeism because its dualism graphically expressed a deep-seated ambivalence that persisted at the heart of orthodox Christian belief. In Herolt's account of it:

> The Manicheans teach that the visible things were created by the prince of darkness, but the invisible things by God. This is a heresy hateful to God and to men—to God, because it diminishes his lordship by robbing him of dominion over visible things; to men, because it despises them by assigning them to the devil, at least that part of them that is visible.[44]

A thousand years before Herolt, Augustine of Hippo had abandoned Mani in passionate quest of a subtler, more sensitive insight into human suffering.[45] The same impulse led Augustine, late in life, instinctively to seek some deeper integration of the body—so often seemingly the instrument of our misery—with the goodness of the soul.[46] But the saint made only tentative moves in this direction and bequeathed to western Christendom no clear reconciliation between a wholesome acceptance of bodiliness as a boon of nature and grace and a fearful, humiliated, masochistic denigration of the body as a vehicle of self-contempt. It is a tension that Herolt cannot escape.

The Body

Human nature, he tells his hearers, consists of a soul animating a body. The soul intrinsically possesses the powers of intellect, memory, and will; the body, when animated, possesses the powers of sense, heat, and motion.[47] Herolt gives only a few inadequate hints of a reproductive theory about how this union takes place. Infants' bodies, he says, are "formed from two lines, that is, from the seed of both parents," and the substance of the maternal contribution is the mother's blood (though some people believe it is her humors).[48] It must be living blood for menstrual blood, which is dead, kills the male semen.[49] As the body is thus

---

[44] D.22.1 (D), T.146.1 (B).
[45] Peter Brown, *Augustine of Hippo* (Berkeley and Los Angeles: U. of California Press, 1969), 394-95.
[46] Margaret Miles, *Augustine on the Body*. AAR Dissertation Series 31 (Missoula: Scholars Press, 1979), 127-131.
[47] E.42.1.
[48] T.146.3 (E), T.162.1/2 (D).
[49] T.162.2 (T).

formed, the soul is created *ex nihilo*;[50] the form of the soul is not introduced into the mother's womb until the matter is arranged physically.[51]

At their first creation, human bodies were vigorous and healthy, compliant and obedient.[52] Adam's physique was strong and handsome;[53] he was created in the prime of his manhood, as if at the ideal age of thirty-three and without debility.[54] Amongst all the creatures, man's body is the noblest.[55] God chose to give men bodies to round out the perfection of his creative work. The culmination of heavenly glory will be the vision of man's nature, body and soul, eternally united with divinity.[56] Moreover, Christ's coming in the flesh has sanctified and ennobled the body: "God created our body, and served us for thirty years with his own."[57] And at the last day, the bodies of the elect will be recreated like Christ's glorified body, as brilliant, subtle, agile, and immortal as the sun.[58]

Meanwhile, the body itself should be an incentive to godliness. The body provides the soul with an indispensable instrument of virtue. Because it has 365 members, it reminds us that no day should pass without thanksgiving, and this transforms even such mundane corporal acts as eating, chewing, drinking, sleeping, rising, and toiling into acts of piety.[59] The preacher encourages layfolk to use the most obvious parts of their bodies as mnemonic devices. The Ten Commandments are inscribed as a reminder on our ten fingers and our ten toes.[60] The five fingers of a hand symbolize five memories (of death, the passion, the judgment, the pains of the damned, and the glory of the blessed) that will repel evil thoughts.[61] The shape of our bodies teaches us temperance in eating, "for man, of all the animals with large bodies, has the smallest mouth and the shortest teeth, and the mouth is not stooped to the ground."[62] Each part of the body has its own spiritual lesson to teach. The feet touch the earth with the soles—we should not love earthly things. The hands must be washed repeatedly—we should cleanse our words, works, and thoughts by daily contrition. We have only one mouth to teach us moderation in speech and temperance in food and drink. The tongue lives in a humid space,

---

[50] T.146.3 (E).
[51] T.7.0 (before P).
[52] E.24.0.
[53] T.60.3 (O).
[54] T.34.1 (K), E.20.3/7.
[55] E.24.1/2.
[56] D.22.1 (D), T.34.3 (S).
[57] T.151.2 (F).
[58] T.50.4 (D), E.50.3/2.
[59] T.112.1/2 (L).
[60] D.1.1/9 (B), T.154.1/1 (E), E.2.2/2.
[61] T.138.5 (H).
[62] E.11.2.

to show how easily one slips, and is doubly enclosed by teeth and lips because of its untameable propensity for havoc. The ears are always open—we must be readier to hear than to speak—and they are smaller than beasts' ears to teach us discrimination. We have right and left eyes to show that we must keep our spiritual vision in both prosperity and adversity. We have two sets of limbs but only one head to demonstrate the need for a single leader in any association, spiritual or secular, or else there will be no peace. Our unique uprightness of stance teaches uprightness of life, and the coordination of the body's members shows how we must love one another.[63]

In gratitude for God's good gift—"God made, assumed, redeemed, and glorified our body"—we worship with gestures and acts of bodily reverence.[64] But here the preacher's ambivalence appears. In another place he attributes outward bodily acts of worship to "a sort of overflow of the soul into the body, from the force of the soul's affection."[65] For however good the body, the soul is nobler.[66] Whatever worth, comeliness, beauty, strength, warmth, or capacity for speech and motion the body possesses, the soul confers and preserves it. The body is worthless without the soul.[67]

At first, this may seem to be merely a matter of definition. If a body without a soul is a dead body, then of course the body is worthless without the soul. But the preacher's repetition of this statement is meant to carry a far more pessimistic judgment. The body, Herolt says, is a good thing to the extent that, like other creatures, God made it; but now, because of sin, it fights against the soul.[68] Our own flesh is not to be loved inordinately but rather hated—it is the soul's enemy—and to love the body is to hate the soul. Flesh is the corruption of spirit. We should be glad even of illness because it "weakens our enemy, the body, the greatest of all our foes."[69] Because of the pervading fragility and weakness of the bodily passions since the fall, a continual war is waged in man between flesh and spirit.[70] The body burdens the soul and weighs it down.[71] All our service for God must now be carried out with debilitating effort and struggle because the soul is dragged down by the body. The battle is unending and victory is rare.[72]

---

[63] E.28.2/3.
[64] E.43.2/4.
[65] T.64.1/1 (I).
[66] D.18.2/1 (C), T.98.1 (F), E.23.2/2.
[67] T.71.1 (R), T.132.1 (A), 0.24.0.
[68] E.24.1/2.
[69] T.128.1/3 (K).
[70] E.31.0.
[71] E.34.0.
[72] T.158.4/2.3 (P).

By "flesh" Herolt does not mean the Pauline concept of "the fleshly man"; he understands the process of corruption quite organically. The familiar triad, "the world, the flesh, and the devil," becomes in Herolt's vernacular "the body, the world, and the evil fiend."[73] The four material elements of earth, air, fire, and water from which man's body is formed became infected when sin entered and have grown more and more corrupt and dissipated. Meanwhile, the plants and animals provided for men's sustenance have grown poorer and sparser, the air more polluted, gluttony more widespread, sexuality more degenerate, and disease more virulent. The result has been a dramatic and continuing decline in longevity.[74] The human body, once so noble and strong, has grown pale and deformed, heavy and lethargic, gross and inept, so fragile that hunger and thirst, heat and cold, lassitude and illness can harm it; and above all, it is now mortal, indeed, bound to die.[75] But in addition to these innate physical miseries, the corruption of our nature flowing from original sin causes other less-tangible passions to course through our bodies, setting flesh against spirit, emotion against rationality, and will against conscience.[76]

However much this sounds like a psychic process, Herolt represents it as a bodily one. What is distinctive about the seven deadly sins of pride, envy, anger, accidie, greed, gluttony, and lust is that they are "the sins to which our body is more inclined."[77] The concupiscence at the root of all these sins is a physical propensity, for "the kindling of sin remains in our body: even though the original sins from which this kindling results is totally deleted by baptism, the kindling itself is not wholly extinguished."[78] The kindling, though not itself sin, gives us a proneness to evil.[79]

The mortal sins are physical propensities in that they arise as cravings for sensual objects that please and delight the body and make inordinate or illicit use of those tangible objects—so much closer to hand than the heavenly joys of the soul—to indulge the pleasures of the bodily senses: feastings, rich clothes, soft wide beds with three mattresses and three cushions on which to satiate sensual pleasure and corporal delights.[80]

Pride indulges the desire of the senses of touch and sight for soft, refined cloth, unnatural colors, and ostentation and offends God by insolently trying to improve on his handiwork. It makes an idol of the body.[81]

---

[73] R.1.4 (20^b).
[74] T.60.3 (O-P).
[75] T.50.4 (D).
[76] E.31.1.
[77] E.24.1/2.
[78] T.151.1 (C).
[79] T.138.2 (B).
[80] T.11.3 (D), T.138.2 (B).
[81] T.83.213-34 (I), T.141.1 (J).

Gluttony intemperately indulges taste and smell and makes the belly its god. But overeating causes debility, ever since Adam ate the apple. Fat bodies cannot live long because they have too little blood, their natural heat is smothered by blubber, and their air passages are clogged. The belly is an unclean vessel that corrupts costly food. A taste for delicacies fuels the appetite and sets two against one—food and the body against the soul.[82]

And so for the other deadly sins, they are prompted by the bodily senses, craved by the bodily appetites, and indulged by the bodily pleasures. They are executed by hands and feet, by eyes and ears, by mouths and tongues. They aggravate bodily corruption. They even display their deleterious effects visibly in the body. Envy betrays itself by pallor, cast-down eyes, and grinding of the teeth; anger by whitening of the face; sloth by the suffocation of natural warmth; lust and rage both by the shortening of life; and gluttony by vomit, stench, belching, and nocturnal emissions.[83]

The conclusion is inevitable: the soul now experiences the body as an insufferable encumbrance and hateful impediment. The body burdens the soul with the pollution of mortal sin because it is the corrupted and coarsened vessel of the kindling of sin. It burdens the soul with an inherent proneness to evil because the delights of the senses crave inordinate satisfaction and provoke a continuous onslaught of temptation. The body's liability to all the mortal ills that flesh is heir to imposes on the soul huge difficulty in performing good works, dulling of the intellect, and a multitude of wretched physical sufferings. And because the body is also the instrument of the expiation of sin both here and in purgatory, it postpones the soul's entrance into heavenly glory.[84]

Hence, the strength of the preacher's language: "We are made of vilest clay."[85] "As Augustine said, 'If you diligently consider your own body—what comes out through your mouth, your nose, the rest of your body's orifices—you have never seen a viler midden!'"[86] How ironic that men should proudly encircle that place of humiliation, their midriff, full of abomination and uncleanness with bejewelled girdles![87] If we needed grounds for humility, we could find them in our own bodies, whose origin is rotting matter, whose birth is naked, impotent, wailing, whose end is dust and ashes, and whose final state is to be eaten by worms. "This is the very reason it is called a cadaver: CAdaver DAta VERmibus."[88]

---

[82] D.18.2 (D-F), T.98.2-5 (G-I), T.99.3-5 (N-P), Q.28.1.
[83] D.14.4/1 (G), D.15.1/4 (A), D.18.4/2 (L), D.19.1 (A), A.A.: 6 "Accidia" (111ᵇ).
[84] T.34.3 (T).
[85] T.158.4 (P).
[86] D.13.3/1 (E), D.18.6/1 (P).
[87] D.13.3/4 (K).
[88] E.38.2/3.

Whence then your pride, O man, whose conception is guilt, whose birth is pain, the labor of life to die, and after man a worm, and after the worm foulness and horror? Thus every man is turned into no man![89]

Bodily Castigations

Hence, too, the severity of the discipline Herolt prescribes for the body. He recommends unremitting castigation of the body—"maceration of the flesh"—by abstinence and fasts, harsh clothing, hair shirts, hard beds, early rising, prayers, vigils, physical toil and exhaustion, flagellation with whips and rods, bare feet, pilgrimages, groaning, tears, genuflections, and prostration in the form of the cross. It is the standard, time-tested battery of castigations in monastic self-discipline, the institutional form of the extreme, self-chosen mortifications of the desert fathers; but Herolt has no hesitation in urging this discipline on the laity or in holding up the exceptional men of the desert as models of pious austerity.

The ostensible motives for all these bodily castigations are many. The first is conquering the flesh. Albertus Magnus's *Tract on the Virtues* is the source of the definition, "True maceration of the flesh is when someone spontaneously castigates his own body by vigils, fasts, prayers, the discipline, abstinence from food and drink, so that in all things the flesh is subjected to the spirit." To attain such mastery, the Christian response to the body's desires must be to fulfil none of its pleasures but only its essential needs.[90] In clothing, for instance, the servants of this world seek pleasure and sheen and softness in their clothes, but the servants of Christ seek only to cover their nakedness and wear harsh clothing to quiet the flesh.[91] Castigation tames the vices of the flesh as Judith, for example, tamed her body with a hair shirt worn day and night.[92] Just as one scrubs the outward body with a rough cloth to wash it, so asperity of life avails for spiritual cleansing of the soul.[93]

Accordingly, there should be a specific concern to forestall or sublimate particular predilections, or if need be, to make the punishment fit the crime after the event. "Castigation aids the soul's health because it extinguishes the fire of lust."[94] Benedict in the brambles, Bernard in the freezing water, are hallowed examples of quenching lust.

One who falls into sin should punish himself in the very part of the body in which he sinned—abstinence for drunkenness, for example, flagellation for lust,

---

[89] D.18.6/1 (P).
[90] E.35.1.
[91] T.83.1/2 (G).
[92] T.7.3 (S).
[93] T.102.2/2 (L).
[94] E.11.2.

harsh clothing and sleeping on a hard bed for mollycoddling the body, going barefoot to church for dancing, and so on.[95] For if you do not castigate yourself, God will castigate you,"[96] or at least the priest will do so at confession:

> As to satisfaction, note that satisfaction should always be made by opposites. For instance, prostration, humiliation, and forgoing ornate clothes are to be enjoined on a proud man . . . abstinence and fasts on gluttons and drunks . . . on the lustful and adulterers afflictions of the body are to be enjoined, such as lying on a hard surface, wearing harsh clothing, and receiving disciplines with rods; and so for the others.[97]

Whether self-imposed, enjoined in penance, or inflicted by life itself (by "the lashes of life"), such expiatory exercises (*poenalia*) make satisfaction for sin, commute purgatorial torments, heal the soul, and open heaven.[98]

But since prevention is better than cure, such castigations of the body are better performed as a preparation for grace. Even a person in a state of mortal sin who afflicts his body with rods and fasts is made more fit for receiving grace than another sinner who does not do so.[99] Herolt's advice to the hardened, obdurate sinner who cannot force himself to weep by thinking of the passion or his sins or judgment or heaven or hell is to try applying external punishment to his body by whipping himself. (If even this does not work, he should still not despair but offer his regret for being so numb.)[100]

If chastening the body makes one ready for grace, it follows that castigations are the mark of the virtuous man.[101] They distinguish the children of God from the children of the devil.[102] Indeed, since adversity is a sign of election but its absence is the opposite, what can a fortunate person do to be saved? "Humiliate himself before God and repent of his sins . . . punish himself and impose tribulations on himself, castigating and flagellating his body with fasts and harsh clothing, prayers, vigils and other good exercises."[103] (Note that, following the Vulgate, Herolt sometimes uses "flagellate" figuratively, of bodily austerities or even involuntary afflictions, though more often he speaks literally of whipping or beating—a familiar enough practice

---

[95] T.156.4 (C).
[96] T.140.4 (H).
[97] Q.30.3.
[98] T.14.9 (K), O.29.3, Q.35.3.
[99] T.92.2 (M).
[100] Q.15.3.
[101] E.44.2/2.
[102] E.41.3/2.
[103] T.149.1 (B).

not only for monastic discipline but from flagellant bands that still accompanied the missions of some of Herolt's more flamboyant fellow preachers.)[104]

Moreover, not only do abstinence and castigations promote virtue, but they even have salubrious physical effects, he believes. They promote health: a sober, abstemious person lives a wholesome happy life, enjoys even his austerities, and is well disposed to meet any eventuality. A moderate diet makes for health, and it prolongs life, as the longevity of the patriarchs showed. What did they eat?

> From Adam until the flood they did not eat meat or fish, but vegetables, herbs, and fruit, and they did not drink wine. But after the flood, the potency of herbs and fruit grew weaker, and they were given God's permission to eat meat and fish . . . . You can tell that they had not drunk wine before then by the fact that when Noah planted a vine after the flood, he became drunk—he did not know about the strength of wine.[105]

However, Herolt cautions, the virtue of abstinence may be overdone, leading to debility and a shortening rather than lengthening of life. The body, after all, is to be nourished for its service.[106] One must strike a balance between too much food, which aggravates the body and suffocates reason, and too little, which weakens the body.[107] The same is true for other mortifications. Such worship must be reasonable. God sometimes even withdraws his grace from a man so that he will not weaken himself and debilitate his body too much by his castigations, for otherwise he might want to fast, pray, keep vigil, and perform other labors of self-discipline all the time because they seemed so sweet to him.[108] For spiritual joy makes burdens light that would otherwise seem heavy—early rising to pray, vigils, fasts, hair shirts, and scourging.[109] On the other hand, it is the experience of many who love God wholeheartedly that they undergo emotional suffering from the contrition of heart and castigated body they willingly offer in daily mortification.[110] As a seasoned spiritual director, Herolt is aware of the fierce energies that can be unleashed by this strong medicine and the diverse psychological extremes of self-destructiveness or dread that may result.

---

[104] For sources on the flagellants, see H. Haupt, "Geisselung (kirchliche) und Geisslerbruderschaften," *Realencyklopädie für Protestantische Theologie und Kirche*, 3rd ed., ed. A. Hauck, vi (1899), 432-444.
[105] E.11.2.
[106] E.28.1/2.
[107] T.98.3 (H).
[108] T.72.4 (U).
[109] E.4.1.
[110] E.31.1/3.

He feels obliged to caution that "sanctity does not consist in fastings and vigils and exercises, but in virtues." The externals are praiseworthy only insofar as the predispose one to the virtues.[111] And a man would gain more grace by one hour's recollection of the passion "than if he fasted for a whole year on bread and water, and daily underwent rods and whips until the blood flowed."[112]

Nevertheless, there remains one familiar inspirational motive for bodily castigation: the imitation of Christ and the saints. The poverty of Christ's birth is a compelling reproof of cosseting our bodies. The mean rags of Christ reprove costliness, the harsh straw on which Christ lay reproves softness, and Christ's narrow manger reproves big, wide beds and cushions.[113] He held to abstinence from his very entry into the world: he was born in winter, in the middle of the night, was placed in a manger on straw, in adult life never wore shoes or linen but only a seamless tunic, and never ate any meat except the paschal lamb.[114] We imitate Mary's carrying the infant Jesus in her arms when we afflict ourselves, for with the arms that serve God in enduring grief we carry Christ.[115] The magus's gift of frankincense becomes the vigor of our service in bodily castigation.[116] Most of all, of course, we carry the cross in imitation of Christ, and bear the marks of his wounds in our bodies, when we inflict such discipline on ourselves.[117] "As Christ's whole body, and all his members, were stretched out, so we also must stretch out all our members and the organs of our body in allegiance to Christ, by raising our hands to God in prayer, extending our arms in the manner of the cross, bending our knees within the mass, prostrating the whole body on the ground in the shape of his cross."[118] And we have the example of the saints: Judith's hair shirt; John the Baptist's austerity in food, drink, and vestment; St. James the Less, who developed hide like a horse's or a camel's on his knees and who refused to bathe; Lazarus, who afflicted his own body after he was raised; Martha, who lived on nothing but herbs, apples, and roots for seven years before her death and wore only tunic and hair shirt in summer or winter; St. Bartholomew, who genuflected one hundred times each day and again each night; St. Paul, who beat his body into subjection; Bishop Germanus, who practiced severe abstinence for thirty years; St. Nicholas, who even in infancy forwent his mother's breasts on Wednesdays and Fridays; St. Cecilia, who wore a hair shirt under her gold vest; a virgin who lived in a cave for

---

[111] T.18.3 (R).
[112] T.48.9 (K).
[113] T.11.3 (D).
[114] E.11.2.
[115] T.17.2/8.
[116] T.80.2/5 (R).
[117] E.41.3/2 and 3.
[118] Q.36.2/2.

thirty-seven years to serve God; and a multitude of other stories of the austerities of the desert fathers.[119]

So we must present our bodies as a living, not a dead, sacrifice in recompense to Christ for taking our body and offering it to God for us. But "a body is never a worthy sacrifice unless it is killed and decocted by the fire of tribulation." If such tribulation is patiently and willingly suffered, our body is not only a living sacrifice but is sanctified before God.[120]

In sum then, we gain merit for our souls by means of our bodies in three complementary ways: first, by resisting those sins to which our bodies are inclined because of the corruption of the fall and the persisting tinder of sin; secondly, by doing good works and expending the body's energies in the service of God—using our eyes for compassion, our ears for hearing good, our mouth for godly instruction, our hands in prayer, our feet for going to churches and shrines and on pilgrimage, or for visiting the sick, our whole body for flagellations, hardships, and austerities; and thirdly, by bearing patiently those griefs and infirmities God sends us, which may sometimes be even better than doing good deeds. For even illness is a special gift of God and a sign of his love.[121] In this life, the greatest part of merit and demerit consists in the exercise of the body.[122]

The Inevitability of Suffering

Where, finally, is the religious power of all these ambivalent justifications and exhortations concerning the human body? They are a wholly characteristic and deeply rooted attempt to make a virtue of necessity—to confront the inevitability of suffering ("If you do not castigate yourself, God will castigate you") and the inescapable wretchedness of life in the body. The misery that is the central experience of life is not to be displaced onto some distant, impersonal fate but is accepted into man's own moral accountability. The resulting anguish could be devastating to mind and emotion if the full sharpness of pain, cruelty, illness, and death could not somehow be deflected, transmuted, and controlled. This is the enduring power of the harsh disciplines of self-mortification: if passion can somehow be ritualized, if the forms of pain can be chosen, if self-humiliation and submission of will can be embraced as not only one's due but one's hallowed destiny, then in the midst of misery there may be security, a liberating passivity, a surcease from the dividedness of life in this body.

---

[119] T.7.3 (S), E.11.2, E.35.1, S.4.1/1, S.20.1/4, S.23.1/7, S.33.1/3, P.A.: 1-9 "Abstinentia" (1-9), &c.
[120] E.6.1-2.
[121] T.151.2/1-3 (C-L), E.24.1/2.
[122] E.6.0.

But the only joy this doctrine offers is sublimation, a joy of the soul in thus surmounting its enemy the body and turning its tortures to good account. There is no joy in embodiment, only a formal affirmation of the goodness of man's material being and feeling. Ultimately, the only way the preacher can escape a dualism as deep as the hated Manichaeans' is to set the body in the grand mythological sweep of fall and restoration.

For the vision of the end is a vision of bodies. To the damned, it is a vision of a hell of bodies, where the bodies of the reprobate will retain all the gross carnality of the present life; they will be crass, ponderous, obscure, and still able to suffer.[123] They will be grotesquely deformed, blackened by flames, weakened, heavy, naked and ashamed, and though suffering excruciating torments indestructible.[124] It is a vision of bodies twisted and tortured; of loathsome serpents and toads; of razors and hooks and chains of fire; of boiling oil; and of faces, hands, bellies, legs, and genitals bound and unendingly punished for the sins of the flesh.[125]

But the bodies of the elect will be recreated in beauty. Each child of God will be resurrected at the ideal age of thirty-three, the age of Christ at his passion; and his body will be the size it would have reached at thirty-three, irrespective of the age of death.[126] There will be no tailors or cobblers, for clothes will not be needed in the resurrection.[127] All defects will be made good, and the saints' bodies will be free of all vice, deformity, or corruption. They will differ in brightness according to the perfection of their life and merits, but the brilliance of these bodies will be like the sun. Bodies now pale and deformed will then be seven times as beauteous as the sun is now; bodies now heavy and lethargic will then be perfectly agile, swift as the sun's rays, swift as the angels, swift as thought itself ("as quickly as I can think 'the world's limit,' I could be there in body if I wished"); bodies now gross and inept will then be so subtle and fine, like the sun's rays, that nothing will be too dense for it to penetrate ("even if there were an iron curtain stretching from heaven to earth, the just could pass through it, body and soul, as easily as if it were not there"); and as nothing can damage the splendor streaming from the sun, so bodies now so frail and vulnerable will then be so fine, secure, and free from suffering that nothing can harm or ever slay them.[128] There will be no ageing, no illness, but perpetual dignity, beauty, and health.[129]

Then at last, when our body has been freed from all we know of corporeality, its goodness as the God-given companion of the soul will be unambiguous.

---

[123] T.147.12 (O).
[124] T.50.5 (E).
[125] E.g., T.101.2-4 (D-G) and see chapter 22.
[126] D.22.1/2 (V), T.50.3 (C), T.84.1 (K), T.147.12 (O), E.20.3/7.
[127] E.20.3/7.
[128] T.50.4 (D), E.50.3/2.
[129] T.57.9 (E), T.84.1-2 (K).

MORALITY IN THE FAMILY

10

SEX

In the state of innocence, Herolt says, when mankind's higher powers ruled the lower, the only reason for the sexual act would have been the generative function.[1] Even in original purity, sex was a lower power and, since the fall, a corrupted and corrupting power.

When we recall how little attention Johann Herolt has received in recent times, it seems ironic that the first modern essay to draw attention to him confines itself to quoting passages about sexual relations and disapproves of Herolt for the shameless freedom of his language.[2] The Lutheran author Wilhelm Walther claimed that few of Herolt's sermons were free of expressions concerning sexuality so explicit that they compared unfavorably not only with modern preaching but also with the sermons of Luther (not everyone's model of decorum).[3]

Walther's strictures drew a justified rejoinder from Nicolaus Paulus. He rightly pointed out that anyone who took the trouble to read Herolt's sermons would soon discover what a gross exaggeration this was. If his sermon books occasionally spoke about sex with a freedom unwonted from chancels at the turn of the twentieth century, they were after all addressed not to congregational audiences directly but to their preachers and confessors and contained explicit warnings against speaking incautiously or scandalously to the laity about sexual sins either in the pulpit or in the confessional.[4] (Walther had noted this caveat but dismissed it as exceptional.)[5]

Sanctimonious avowals of sexual morality have often disguised a fascination with the subject, but there is no such obsession in Herolt however narrow his prescriptions. His attitude toward sex seems coldly dispassionate. And notwithstanding Walther's hyperbole, Herolt's explicit discussion of sexual morality

---

[1] T.34.1 (M).
[2] Wilhelm Walther, "Das sechste Gebot in J. Herolts Predigten," *Neue kirchliche Zeitschrift* 3 (Erlangen, 1892), 485-99.
[3] Walther, "Das sechste Gebot," 488, 499.
[4] Nicolaus Paulus, "Johann Herolt und seine Lehre," 439-41.
[5] Walther, "Das sechste Gebot," 493.

is largely confined to a few dry, systematic expositions of the Ten Commandments and the seven cardinal sins. It will be a fairly simple matter to review his treatment as it is summarized in catechetical form in *de eruditione* and the parallel passages of the *sermones de tempore*.

The fifth commandment prohibits harm to another in his own person, Herolt says. Similarly, the sixth prohibits harm to a married man in the person of his spouse —a formula that reinforced the traditional sense of a wife as a possession of value. But the commandment against adultery also has a wider application. As the interlinear gloss paraphrases it, "You will not join yourself to any other person except by the covenant of marriage."[6] Accordingly, there are six groups of people who transgress this commandment or six ways the act of lust may be committed, each one graver than the last: fornication, deflowering virgins, adultery, clerical incontinence, incest, and the "sin against nature." (In the earliest version of this list, Herolt adds a seventh transgression of a rather different sort—conjugal love with too much libidinous desire—but it is omitted from the later versions of the passage.)[7]

The first act of lust is simple fornication between an unattached man and woman. Not surprisingly, there were proponents of the view that this was not a serious sin, so Herolt borrows a rebuttal from Heinrich of Vrimaria. Divine law proscribes only mortal sins, but it forbids fornication; and only mortal sins exclude from heaven, but St. Paul says the fornicator is excluded. Fornication is unusual in that it can never be anything but a sinful act. Homicide may not be mortal sin if justice demands it; theft may not be mortal sin in extreme need; work on feast days, oaths, or anger may all have justifiable occasions; but "no one knowingly fornicates without mortal sin":

Let us reflect that someone may have thought, said, and done no evil, and done all the good deeds he could think of, and fornicated just once: if he dies without penance, he is necessarily damned. Even if all the masses celebrated by the church till the world's end were celebrated for him alone, it would not free him from eternal death. And for that fleeting pleasure he kills his own soul, deprives himself of the company of Christ and Mary and all the saints and angels, and subjects himself to the power of all demons and to eternal torment. For one act of fornication he will burn in hell for as many years as Christ will reign in heaven—eternally!

The preacher brings his heavy artillery to bear on the apparently incorrigible nonchalance of so many lusty lay folk.[8] But if people were really of the faith, he declares, they would know that the apparent delights of fornication were poisoned and therefore avoid them at all costs. If you put bitter or poisoned food in front

---

[6] D.6.0 (before A).
[7] D.6.1 (A), cf. T.85.0 (N), T.143.6 (A).
[8] D.6.1 (A), T.85.1 (O).

of someone, of course he will refuse it point-blank; but the sensual pleasure of fornication is bitterer and more lethal than death, for it brings spiritual death.[9]

Herolt has special warnings against fornicating with prostitutes, not so much for social reasons as that he anticipates knotty canonical ramifications. Three considerations make it detestable. Unbeknown to her client, the harlot may be married. So that what seems to him to be simple fornication is in fact adultery. Secondly, if two members of the same family were by chance to sleep with the same whore, the effect would be incest (with the curious result that the first could be absolved by a priest for simple adultery but the second only by a bishop for incest). Thirdly, even when such situations do not arise, with a harlot one always exposes oneself to these risks, and therefore the sin is just as despicable.[10] There is no exception to the rule that frequenting harlots is mortal sin.[11] Accordingly, those who make it possible for harlots to ply their trade are implicated in the sin. Household heads who knowingly allow prostitutes to work in their houses are evil hosts who offend God.[12] Innkeepers who accommodate pimps and frequenters of whores are guilty of the alien sin of "recourse,"[13] and they will give a strict accounting at the last judgment for letting prostitutes and players operate in their taverns.[14]

As for the unfortunate women who sell themselves, they are not excused because they live in poverty and struggle to amass a few necessities. They do so unrighteously and are damned by it.[15] Because they also tend to pass themselves off as virgins, they run the extreme risk of exposing their own unborn children to abortion.[16] Nevertheless, Herolt does allow that in practice a harlot is entitled to keep what she receives from a secular client as payment, but she is bound to make restitution to the church of anything she receives from a cleric.[17]

The second act of lust is graver than fornication. It is *stuprum*, the illicit deflowering of virgins. There are four reasons to detest the violation of virginity. The first is the enormity of the sin, and the preacher's authority is the ghastly story in Genesis 34 of the male blood feud that ensued when the Hivite Shechem sought the hand of Jacob's daughter Dinah, whom he had loved.[18] The second and

---

[9] D.19.5 (N).
[10] D.6.1 (A), T.85.1 (O).
[11] E.13.23.
[12] E.26.3.
[13] T.144.5 (M).
[14] T.4.8 (Y).
[15] T.81.2 (A).
[16] D.1.2/15 (N), T.61.22 (T).
[17] D.7.17 (TT).
[18] D.6.2 (C).

obvious reason is the destruction of virginity, which is an incomparable treasure.[19] Spiritually, however, a virgin who is raped does not lose her virginity, so long as she resists and gives no consent;[20] and therefore, Herolt counsels, a woman is not to kill herself rather than be violated, for without consent she does not sin, and even with consent suicide is a graver sin than adultery.[21] The third reason is the likely aftereffect:

> Sometimes the man who illicitly deflowers some virgin is the occasion of a thousand fornications she later commits—just as one who first breaks the gate or hedge of a garden or vineyard is responsible for the loss caused by others who come later and otherwise would not have entered.

The practical motive of this patronizing forecast is destruction of the woman's marriageability. "A virgin so corrupted can sometimes never find a legitimate husband, but becomes common property." By the ordinary rules of jurisprudence, the man who first violates her is guilty of all the sins she then perpetrates.[22] There is, however, a clear distinction to be drawn between *stuprum* and rape. As we saw above, a virgin does not lose her spiritual virginity when she is raped for "*stuprum* is the illicit deflowering of virgins, yet in such a way that the girl spontaneously and voluntarily consents to her deflowering," whereas rape is a far graver act of violence demanding excommunication of the violator ("and all his accomplices," Herolt adds revealingly). He quotes the guidance canon law gives confessors: if a man deflowers a virgin without her consent, he is bound to marry her; but if she was willing he is not so bound, though in penance he should be instructed either to recompense the girl or marry her. If necessary, confessors are to make compensation the penance to be performed—not that she can really be recompensed for so great a loss.[23] Yet one is to make satisfaction before God to the best of one's ability, since her greatest treasure has been stolen.[24] The seriousness of the situation is underscored by a typically gruesome exemplary tale (whose first occurrence implausibly declares that the knightly protagonist "often corrupted a certain virgin," an assertion later rephrased):

> A certain knight had deflowered a virgin. After he died, while she prayed and wept for him, the dead knight appeared visibly to her

---

[19] D.6.2 (C), T.85.2 (P).
[20] T.157.1 (G), E.15.2.
[21] D.5.2/4 (D).
[22] D.6.2 (C), T.85.2 (P).
[23] D.6.2 (C).
[24] T.96.3 (U).

and spoke to her in a very hoarse voice. When she asked the cause of his hoarseness, he said, "Because 1 used to glory in the voice of sweetness, the singing of lusty and worldly songs." When she asked why his legs looked jet black and scabby and covered with ulcers, he answered, "Because I used to glory much in my legs, how handsome they were in the military fashion, stretching them and adorning them proudly. Now 1 go among thorns, 1 am wracked and wounded in those legs!" Again she said, "Milord, what is the state of the rest of your body?" He answered, "Open your eyes and see!" And he cast from his chest the cloak in which he seemed to be wrapped, and she saw a huge and hideous toad clinging to his breast with its arms clasped tight about his neck and its mouth joined to his mouth. With its belly hanging down against his belly, it grasped and—bound his genitals with its feet, as if with thongs. Asked why he suffered thus, he answered, "For the lascivious kisses with which I kissed you and other women, I suffer this kiss, and for the embraces the embrace of the toad, and for the deed of passion I am tormented in my genitals without ceasing." When the woman asked if he could not be freed from these pains, he replied, "Do not pray for me—it does nothing for me, for 1 am eternally damned. And it is so because I neglected the medicine of penitence." So saying, he vanished. The woman afterwards sought a cloister, and there wept for her sins.[25]

The third act of lust is adultery. The punishments to befall the adulterer surpass even the torments of the violator of virginity, for adultery is a still graver sin than *stuprum*. The unexamined reason, of course, is that there is greater injury in the abuse of a woman who is subject to another man's power.[26] Indeed, the proofs of adultery's gravity all concern the husband's viewpoint and the contravention of his honor. Herolt lists six such proofs. First, adultery contravenes the sacrament of marriage instituted by God in paradise. If it is a grave sin for a monk to transgress the rule of his order laid down by some human saint, how much worse to transgress an order which God himself founded.[27] Secondly, it is against the natural law, "Do unto others . . .": "Just as you do not want anyone else to sin with your wife, so you do not sin with another's wife."[28] Thirdly, adultery exceeds the theft of any earthly substance, since one is bound to love one's wife above all people and things in the world. That is why, the preacher adds innocently, many men would rather suffer material loss than knowingly endure this evil in their wives. Fourthly, adultery is a

---

[25] D.6.2 (C), T.96.3 (U).
[26] D.6.3 (D).
[27] D.6.3 (D), T.85.3 (Q).
[28] D.6.3 (D).

sort of murder, for as a man and wife are one flesh, to take away a man's wife is to take away his own person too. (This theme of the wife's exchange value is consistent throughout.) The fifth proof of adultery's gravity is the sorts of consequences that may flow from it. Murder, for instance, as when David had his loyal soldier Uriah killed to further his adultery with Bathsheba; or incest, if by chance someone were to marry a spouse who unbeknown was the illegitimate child of an adultery by one's own father or mother; or disinheritance, if it becomes known that such a bastard child does not share the legitimate heirs' right to his nominal father's estate.[29] Because of such dire consequences, it is one of the seven prime duties of marriage not to deviate sexually. Hence, too, the lengths of incarceration or even death to which a Joseph or a Susanna were prepared to go in order to avoid adultery.[30] Despite Susanna's example, however, a woman is not to kill herself to avoid adultery, since the very great and dangerous sin of suicide is even graver than adultery.[31] The final proof of adultery's enormity is the punishment inflicted on adulterers—physical punishment, like the plague Nathan declared on David's house, or the story of the adulterer who on entering church was immediately obsessed by demons, punished before all the people and taken to hell, temporal punishment, like the stoning required by the law of Moses ("But in this day and age, if all the adulterers were stoned, there would be no stones left!"); spiritual punishment, for adulterers will not enter heaven; and eternal punishment in hell (graphically illustrated by Herolt with a tale of bourgeois adulterers swimming in a demonic vat of fire "like peas in a pot of oil").[32]

On a more mundane level, Herolt gives a technical warning against betrothal to one woman followed by marriage to another. In the church's eyes, the resulting union is always adulterous and the fruit of the union illegitimate.[33] As to the woman's role in adulterous affairs, the emphasis (as we shall see shortly)[34] is on the sexual threat posed to men's souls by women, especially their alluring dress and behavior by which the woman becomes "her brother's murderer."[35] Confessors should inquire about the occurrence of such adulterous activity at penance, and a wife who has fostered an adulterous passion on a man's part is to make reparation to the best of her ability, especially repaying through the confessor any of her husband's property she has used furtively to give seductive love tokens to an admirer.[36] Herolt is not wholly sanguine, however, about the permanence of such penitential redress:

---

[29] D.6.3 (D).
[30] D.29.3/3 (F), T.25.2/3 (E), T.85.3 (Q).
[31] T.25.2/3 (E).
[32] D.6.3 (D), T.85.3 (Q).
[33] D.29.2/6 (C).
[34] See chapter 12.
[35] T.83.2/3 (I).
[36] Q.22.3, E.41.11, Q.40.2.

"Experience has shown," he says, "that the committers of lustful sins, especially adulterers and sodomites, are among the quickest to slide back into their sinful, incontinent ways after the Easter confession."[37]

The fourth act of lust is sacrilege, transgression of the law of religious profession—that is, violation of the clerical vow of continence to which priests and religious have bound themselves before God. This miserable sin is graver than the first three because in this case the breach of trust injures God himself.[38] So a fornicating priest is in a most perilous state for if he has broken chastity or is living in flagrant mortal sin, until he does penance in true contrition, he compounds his sin every time he performs a priestly act—"truly a horrendous and stupendous and exceedingly dangerous thing, in such a role and dignity to be enmeshed in so many and monstrous crimes." Accordingly, a fornicating priest is automatically suspended from the duties of his office (whose sacramental efficacy, however, is not destroyed by irregular performance). Nevertheless, Herolt argues, despite some ambiguity, canon law does give a bishop the power to dispense the priest—a pragmatic concession to the widespread practice of concubinage amongst a numberless proletariat of rustic supply priests.[39] A cleric who spends parish income ("the patrimony of the crucified") on harlots, or on disporting himself with actors, is required to make restitution to the church from his private resources, if any, or else earning it by handcrafts or manual labor;[40] while, as we saw above, any harlot is bound to return to the church what she has received from a clerical customer.[41] Such regulations are for Herolt a regrettable necessity. He greatly prefers, in collecting illustrations, to tell edifying stories of exemplary priests who withstood temptation, went to extraordinary lengths to snuff out the least spark of sexual desire, and led back to godliness the women who tempted them.[42] The power of sexual temptation is acknowledged, to the very highest ranks of the church, but the means to combat it are within reach:

> When Pope Leo was celebrating mass and communicating the people on the day of Christ's resurrection, a woman kissed him on the hand, and this caused a vehement temptation of the flesh to erupt within him. So the man of God cut the hand that was offending him right off and threw it from him. Meanwhile a murmuring arose among the people over why the supreme pontiff was not celebrating the divine things in the customary manner. Then Leo turned himself to the

---

[37] T.58.5 (F).
[38] D.6.4 (E), T.85.4 (Q).
[39] D.28.2/2 (E-F), T.111.3 (D-E).
[40] D.28.212 (F), T.111.3 (F).
[41] D.7.17 (TT).
[42] E.g., P.L.: 25, 26, 30, 310-32 "Luxuria" (268, 269, 273, 274, 275).

Blessed Virgin and committed himself wholly to her providence. But she was always near him, and restored his hand with her own holiest hands and remade it, telling him to proceed and offer the sacrifice to her son. Therefore Pope Leo told all the people what had happened to him, and showed them all his hand restored.[43]

The fifth category of lust is incest—"transgression of the law of the natural condition," when people commingle themselves with their own kin within the line of consanguinity. Even some of the brute beasts are ashamed to do so, Herolt says, and he retails Aristotle's account of the camel that was blindfolded and put to its dam but crushed and trampled its owner when it discovered what had happened. "It is a sin that makes a man like a dog, because the dog in its act does not preserve the line of consanguinity."[44] Only a bishop can absolve the sin of incest, which is graver than the first four sexual sins.[45]

The sixth act of lust is gravest of all. It is the sin against nature which "transgresses the law of natural inclination," the unmentionable vice of those who contaminate themselves unspeakably by perverting the natural use of intercourse by any artifice or device whatsoever. Even to name this most disgusting of sins would be to pollute the speaker's mouth and the hearers' ears. True to this conviction, Herolt speaks so circumspectly about the sin against nature as to be rather obscure and even then adds a warning against preaching openly on the subject. It seems incredible, he says, that men have perpetrated such an outrage, that human nature should even be capable of it. And just this was one of the reasons Christ deferred being incarnated so long, and on the night of his birth, all the then sodomites were wiped out. How can such a sin continue to exist in a nature he has so dignified? Sodomites are the worst of men, and the enormity of their sin is displayed in the lasting destruction of Sodom and Gomorrah and the five cities and even their innocent inhabitants. After four millennia, the region still cannot support bird or fish life and is rightly called the Dead Sea. Ever since, sodomy has been known as one of the four sins that cry out to heaven. One must not even think of it—remember what happened to Lot's wife when she looked back to Sodom.

After all these expostulations, Herolt finally and reluctantly addresses the question, What is the sodomitical sin and how is it perpetrated? For answer, he quotes the inclusive definition of Johannes's *Summa*, book 3, section 38, question 73: "Any act of lust performed in any manner whatever except between a male and a female in the regular way and in the proper vessel is adjudged a vice against nature and sodomy." Note, Herolt says, that this means one must preserve regular coitus and the proper mode as much with one's own wife as with a stranger, inside marriage

---

[43] P.L.: 26 "Luxuria" (269).
[44] D.6.5 (E), T.85.5 (Q).
[45] D.6.5 (E), T.85.5 (Q).

as outside; "for it is possible that one who thus perverts regular intercourse even with his own wife sins more gravely than if he knew his own mother." Perverting the proper mode apparently includes adopting anything but the male-superior position, since Augustine is cited as authority for declaring that "it would be most detestable for the woman to be girt with the sword and the man with the spindle." But if so many "perversions" are thus included under the umbrella of sodomy, are there any distinctions among sodomitical sins, and what is their relative gravity? Once again, Johannes's *Summa* (book 2, section 5, question 3) provides a fourfold answer: the first sin against nature is the sin of effeminacy, which consists only in omitting actual intercourse with the other. It is a worse sin when one does not keep to the proper vessel; worse still when one does not keep to the proper sex, namely intercourse between males; and worst of all, bestiality, when one does not keep to the proper species. Herolt will expatiate no further and warns his colleagues against doing so, "lest one cause scandal at it or occasion of sin."[46]

This then is the sum of Herolt's systematic exposition of the sins of lust; but it is also possible, he declares, to commit the mortal sin of lust without performing an act at all. Lust without a corresponding act happens ten ways, and eight of them are mortal sins.[47] Indeed, because this sort of lustfulness is so much more commonplace and public, the preacher feels free to express his disapproval much more explicitly and frequently.

The first instance is when a dirty thought enters one's mind but against one's will and without giving any pleasure. In fact, this is no sin at all; good men living chaste lives need not be greatly disturbed by it for it is the devil tempting them.[48] If the devil is the primeval source of such foul suggestions, one is clearly not liable for them unless one gives consent.[49] Indeed, the occurrence of such temptations is an opportunity to win merit by withstanding them. Our task is to drive them out. If we withhold consent, there is no pollution.[50] At the second stage, the thought is still involuntary but yields some pleasure. This is a venial sin. While unbidden thoughts do us no harm without our consent, yet the sweetness of grace may be lost if we do not quickly resist unclean or indecorous thoughts but instead somewhat enjoy them.[51] It is very dangerous to tarry in any disgraceful thought because it can so easily progress to mortal sin.[52] There is a regular progression from initial temptation to eventual sin: suggestion to pleasure to consent. These three elements were all present in the first sin: the serpent suggested eating the fruit, Eve ate with

---

[46] D.6.6-7 (E-F), T.25.2/5 (G), T.85.6 (R).
[47] D.19.2 (B), T.86.1-10 (S-C), T.141.4 (M).
[48] D.19.2 (B), T.86.1 (S).
[49] D.10.4 (C), T.88.4 (M), T.138.1 (A).
[50] T.67.3 (A), T.138.3 (C).
[51] T.72.7 (U).
[52] E.13.2/3.

pleasure, and Adam ate with consent.[53] Hence the third stage, which now is mortal sin, is to give consent to "morose delight"—to take deliberate pleasure in one's lustful thoughts, to involve oneself in them, to wish one could carry them out.[54] "Alas," Herolt says, "there are many men and women who, though they have no real intention of proceeding to action, nevertheless indulge their evil thoughts and delicious fantasies."[55] The most blatant example is the man who fantasizes about another man's wife—the commonest contravention of the tenth commandment.[56] But morose delight, excessive libido, can occur within marriage too.[57] And some, such as lepers, who are forced to abstain from sex become the devil's special target and must be doubly careful to refrain from morose delight.[58] Spiritually, we spit on Christ's face when we pollute our conscience with fetid thoughts.[59] Of course, there is an equivocal stage (which Thomas called "introspective consent") when one's reason recognizes the wrong and the danger in such immoral delectation but fails to escape it, so one yields a passive, acquiescent consent "like peeping through one's fingers"; but the mortal sin of real consent involves choosing with full reason to linger in the delight and to crave it.[60] Why are we so prone to slip from suggestion to pleasure to sinful consent? There are three reasons, Herolt says. The inherited corruption of our nature makes us more inclined to evil than to good. Secondly, the sensuous objects that arouse our concupiscence and delight our fantasies are all around us, but the things that incite us to good are far away in heaven. And thirdly, we can do evil by ourselves, but good only with the aid of grace.[61] But those who are full of the Holy Spirit receive the gift of "handling serpents"—that is, immediately rejecting evil suggestions from the devil or from neighbors and not yielding to unchastity at the shameful example of others.[62]

There is another, more bizarre, form of sexual fantasizing that Herolt dismisses as culpable superstition, namely the belief in incubi. In this, he is in agreement with the main line of medieval doctrine—a line that was tragically forgotten in the propaganda and witch-hunting of succeeding centuries. Among those who falsify the faith, he says, are those who claim people appear to them in the night and press down on them, whereas they are simply lying awkwardly and when they turn over it

---

[53] D.19.2 (B), T.86.2 (T).
[54] D.19.2 (C), T.86.3 (U), T.141.4 (M), Q.20.2/2.
[55] T.141.4 (M).
[56] D.10.4 (C), T.143.10 (X).
[57] E.13.2/3.
[58] E.44.3/3.
[59] Q.20.2/2.
[60] E.13.2/3.
[61] T.138.2 (B).
[62] T.67.3 (A).

stops.[63] Even alone then, we must beware of the vagaries of the sexual imagination. Indeed, the tropological lesson of the way Christ was stripped for flagellation is "that we guard ourselves from all physical nudity, lest we ever appear naked in the sight of God and the angels and men." Were not our first parents ashamed so to appear before God in the garden? Even if no one is looking, modesty before God and one's angel should deter one from nakedness.[64]

Thought leads to action; and the fourth variety of lust without act is when foul thought has led to pleasure, pleasure to consent, and a person is willing to translate the fantasy into action if opportunity arises. This intention is tantamount to the act itself, even if it never happens.[65] But there are several all-too-common methods of nurturing one's fantasies short of the sexual act itself. Lust can be committed by looking at another person lecherously; so one must keep a careful guard upon the eyes—they are swift as leopards to harm the soul. They are like two gates into the camp of the body, and one who controls the entrances controls the camp. As to woman, the object of lusting eyes, "there is no place from the soles of the feet to the top of the head of a woman adorned where the devil's net is not spread to trap souls."[66] Lust may be committed by speech, or by laughter, when someone speaks seductively to a woman or jests with her in the hope of enticing her.[67] Dirty language is a particular vice of the elderly and of women, Herolt says: "Some old people, and sometimes women and maidens too, often speak in scurrilous and lascivious language. It is utterly reprehensible, and it shows they have shameless hearts."[68] But it is a Christian's duty to refrain his tongue from filthy talk, which is not mere levity but corrupts the integrity of people's minds and provokes their desires.[69] Filthy talk and jesting progress easily to illicit and impudent touching and embracing, especially in those festive seasons of year, such as pre-Lent, when fun and games are the order of the day and when ostensibly lighthearted contact often conceals a lecherous motive.[70] Such shameless petting, hugging, kissing, and the like are what the apostle brands "turpitude."[71] This is at least part of Herolt's fierce opposition to the dance;[72] dancers inflame the onlookers to lust by their provocative costumes and by the bodily contact and embraces that form their movements.[73] So part of

---

[63] D.1.2/18 (R), T.41.18 (P).
[64] Q.28.2/2.
[65] D.19.2 (C), T.86.4 (U), T.141.4 (M).
[66] D.19.2 (D), T.85.5 (X), T.138.4 (G).
[67] D.12.14 (E), D.19.2 (F), T.86.6 (A), T.141.4 (M), E.41.2/4.
[68] D.19.2 (F), T.86.6 (A).
[69] D.8.8 (M), T.96.216 (T), E.25.2/1, E.16.2.
[70] D.12.14 (E), T.22.2 (B).
[71] D.19.2 (F), T.86.7 (A), T.141.4 (M).
[72] See chapter 19.
[73] T.37.2 (S).

the Christian's spiritual circumcision must be to circumcise his hands from illicit touch;[74] otherwise, the pains of hell will include inexorable bonds for the hands and feet that have been agents of worldly transgressions, kissing, embracing, petting, dancing, and leaping.[75]

The sin of lust is also committed, especially among women, by adorning the body or using other signals designed to arouse desire, "not only in the streets and at dances but even in church."[76] Herolt's preoccupation with the sins of ornamentation is described later.[77] There are women, he says, who crave a reputation for beauty simply to be attractive to men; if that is the motive, then it is a sin, though a natural desire for beauty may be innocent enough.[78] But there is no innocent way to perform the next enticing ploy—gifts and little presents of trinkets or money or jewelry intended to inflame the recipient to lust or even to sinful action. The volume of traffic in such love tokens is reflected in Herolt's strictures on artisans who fabricate such gifts in full knowledge of their intended use; they share the lovers' mortal sin as do the go-betweens who carry the gifts and mediate such liaisons.[79] Herolt is also aware that such gifts flow both ways,[80] that women as well as men send such allurement to their admirers, and any man who receives such a symbolic invitation to an act of turpitude must discreetly return it through the woman's confessor.[81]

The final form of the sin of lust without a sexual act is found in people who really wish to perform an immoral act and indeed could well do so, having opportunity of time, place, and partner; but they refrain, not from any worthy motive, but only from fear of the world and of scandal and embarrassment. Yet if they knew they could do it and stay hidden, no concern for God or the saints or their own souls' salvation would deter them.[82]

But we must always picture God as present and seeing all the secrets of our hearts.[83] Indeed, whatever remains hidden here will be published for all to hear at the judgment seat of Christ. That judgment will be exceedingly fearful for the strict accounting we must render of all our thoughts, words, and deeds; and "Oh! How many vengeful and lustful and other perverse thoughts are held in the heart with deliberateness and resolve, of which we shall give account!" The evil deeds to be

---

[74] T.19.3 (F).
[75] T.125.6 (S).
[76] D.19.2 (G), T.86.6 (A), T.141.4 (M).
[77] See chapter 19.
[78] T.118.17 (J).
[79] D.19.2 (H), T.86.9 (B).
[80] E.41.11.
[81] Q.40.2.
[82] D.19.2 (H), T.86.10 (C), T.141.4 (M).
[83] T.138.4 (F).

judged will include "illicit touch, or sight, or hearing; illicit petting or embracing yourself or others; . . . and how often you have committed acts of lust outside marriage." (This passage contains Herolt's only reference to masturbation.)[1] In anticipation of that judgment then the question, How often have you committed an act of lust? is to be a standard part of the confessor's interrogation of a penitent.[2]

Sexual lust is the form that concupiscence takes in our flesh. The original sin of Adam and Eve has issued in a corruption which takes the form of a tinder, a propensity for sin to take hold, that makes us more readily inclined to sin than to goodness. When the soul inwardly accepts the pleasurableness of some desire, and the reason consents, that is concupiscence. The promptings come from our chief enemies, the world, the flesh, and the devil; and the flesh works against us by provoking sexual desire and carnal concupiscence.[3] But Christ is "the true sun who dries up all the clouds of carnal concupiscence."[4] We must gain merit by resisting desire in our flesh; we must excise concupiscence by the spiritual circumcision of our hearts, our eyes, and our hands.[5]

It is simply false, the preacher insists, to claim as so many do that they cannot remain continent. Man's innate propensity to concupiscence is not a compulsion. True, a man's libido is as flammable as straw in a desert;[6] yet "those who say they cannot live chastely, nor are able to abstain from the act of lust, contradict the truth of the faith; for with the help of God, any man can keep himself from lust. To hold otherwise is heresy."[7]

Help is available to one who wants it, and Herolt offers practical remedies against importunate desires. First, one should immediately douse the flames of passion with the cold plunge of tribulation, in the form perhaps of physical discipline administered by oneself or others or at least recollection of earlier tribulations if one is reluctant.[8] The outstanding exemplars are Benedict, who assuaged his ardor by tearing his body amidst the thorn bushes, and Bernard, who plunged into freezing water.[9] Since fire needs fuel, the second remedy is to fast, especially avoiding those varieties of food and drink that stimulate the libido—strong wines and pungently flavored foods, which are "like blazing matches for igniting lust."[10] And the third

---

[1] T.3.2 (P-Q).
[2] Q.22.3.
[3] D.19.2 (C), T.88.4 (M), T.151.1 (C).
[4] T.2.1 (J).
[5] T.19.3 (F), T.151.1 (C).
[6] D.19.6 (Q).
[7] T.86.11 (D), cf. D.19.5 (N).
[8] D.19.6 (O).
[9] T.86.11 (D); cf. D.19.6 (O), where the saints' names are erroneously transposed.
[10] D.19.6 (P).

remedy is simply to stay away from the heat—to avoid the presence of women. If two stones collide, they give off sparks; excessive familiarity between two people will spark the fire of lust.[11]

So far from availing themselves of such remedies, however, people go to the opposite extreme. Herolt castigates young married couples who go to the old crones to ask for aphrodisiacs to increase the ardor of their lovemaking (whereas they should do it only for God's honor and in order to multiply).[12] In his judgment, he says, it is a mortal sin when married couples have sex simply in order to enjoy it greatly and use heated things or other stimulants to heighten their sensations.[13] Against such licentiousness, it is most commendable when we extinguish desire with virtue, use the Spirit's gift of discernment to expel lust, and subject our sensuality to reason.[14] To do so is to merit an eternal place in the angelic choir of the Dominations: "They are the greatest lords who know how to conquer themselves."[15]

Herolt never completely escapes the conviction that it is not only the abuse of sex but sex itself, which is corrupting. Lust, he says, shortens a man's life and debilitates his body; he cites Aristotle's declaration that "*coitus* is a destruction of the body and an abbreviation of life." This is the reason the biblical patriarchs lived such long lives: The ancients were far more chaste than we are and did not marry until eighty or ninety. And it is also the reason celibate monastics live above-average life spans.[16]

Celibacy, however, is not within every man's capacity. The chief provision made for the mass of men in order to avoid fornication is the institution of marriage, and Herolt has much to say about sex within marriage and about all the other duties of wedlock. To this subject we now turn.

---

[11] D.19.6 (Q).
[12] D.29.2 (B).
[13] T.25.2/5 (G).
[14] T.86.6 (F), T.73.7 (G).
[15] T.88.6 (M).
[16] D.19.1 (A), T.60.3/5 (P).

11

MARRIAGE

Marriage is an estate which God has honored in many ways—by instituting it himself, by choosing paradise ("the worthiest place under heaven") for its foundation, by establishing it in the solemn state of man's innocence, by choosing to be born of a virgin mother who was married, by attending and miraculously blessing the marriage at Cana, and by making it one of the seven sacraments. There are some wretched heretics, Herolt exclaims, who lyingly claim that marriage is no longer legal in the new covenant (he is thinking of the professed belief of Albigensian *perfecti*); but their deceit is plain: "St. Benedict founded the order of Blackfriars, St. Francis the order of Minorites, St. Dominic the order of preachers, but God instituted the order of matrimony." Since God has so honored married people, they in turn must honor God by their living together.[17]

Three things are essential if they are to do so. Before marriage, they are to prepare themselves spiritually to receive the sacrament. They must begin married life in the fear of God. And afterward they must continue to live together lovingly, peaceably, loyally, and patiently until their life's end.[18]

The preacher expounds this quite conventional doctrine at some length. More briefly, we may review his ideas about the social institution, moral duties, and personal relationship of marriage by ordering them chronologically from courtship until death.

First then, Herolt sketches a few of the proprieties to be observed in arranging a marriage; and the first consideration, he suggests, must be the social compatibility of the partners. For to marry someone who is not one's equal in age, wealth, and status is almost to guarantee the failure of the match. Marriage of a noble to one outside the nobility, of a young person to someone old, or rich to poor rarely leads to compatibility or harmony, and the daily workings of the relationship are constantly threatened by the inequalities between husband and wife. If there must be disparity in age, however, better an old man with a young wife than *vice versa*.[19]

---

[17] D.29.0 (A), T.25.1 (A).
[18] D.29.1-2 (B), 3 (E).
[19] D.29.213 (C), T.25.2 (O).

Herolt also disapproves of the current practice of early marriage. "These days," he says, "adolescents contract marriages, so now child begets child." It leads, he suspects, to a shorter life span. Though eighteen-year-old men and fifteen-year-old women may marry without sin, it was better in former days when people waited a long time before marrying.[20]

The few formal arrangements mentioned by Herolt reflect little marriage across class boundaries; they tend to be based on marriage practices within the upper, moneyed ranks of society. The desirable characteristics one seeks in the spouse, he says, are beauty, nobility, wisdom, wealth, health, and fidelity.[21] He paints a romantic, chivalrous portrait of the zealous suitor wishing to make his ardor known to the maid he wants to wed: the swain parades his zeal before her by wearing garlands, embroidered bracelets, cutoff shoes, ornamented belts, and courtly costume; he sings love ballads; he gives her some precious and beautiful gift; he undertakes some labor for her as her champion and hero; and he asks importunately by letters, in person, and by messengers.[22] But as a prelude to marriage, this fancied picture of courtly love is far less likely than the mundane negotiation of a contract between families.

Herolt approves such negotiations in principle, though he is nostalgic for the old days when they were more high-minded:

> Once the custom was that when a man wanted his daughter to be betrothed to someone, he would carry out an interrogation. First of all, was the groom born of good and upright parents who enjoyed a good repute, held the true faith, and feared God? Secondly, was the groom himself virtuous or vicious, humble or proud, irascible or mild-mannered? Was he a gambler, a drinker, a blasphemer, or did he himself fear God? Thirdly, how was the dowry acquired—justly or unjustly? By usury, or gaming, or fraud and lies? and so on. Similarly, if a person had to receive someone's daughter as a wife, he would ask the same set of questions.

This mutual cross-examination had the virtue of avoiding one of the great pitfalls of wedlock, marriage into a family corrupted by vice (especially the pecuniary vice of usury or unjust acquisition). Herolt fears, however, that his contemporaries use the very same procedure for just the opposite motive:

> But alas, nowadays they sell their children—they hold a market the way they usually buy and sell horses! They sell their children in

---

[20] T.60.3/8 (P).
[21] T.157.2 (H).
[22] T.124.1 (K).

just the same way. They do not ask how the property involved was acquired, but only how much there is to give—they say, "I will give my son so much and you will give your daughter so much." Their principal concern is property.

To marry one's son or daughter to a usurer, Herolt warns, is to consign him or her to eternal damnation. So the examination of a prospective bride or groom must be carried out with minute attention to the sources of the other family's wealth.[23]

There are other investigations to be completed before betrothal too. One needs to be as sure as possible of the parentage of one's intended, for otherwise there is a danger one may inadvertently marry a blood relative because of someone's past fornication, another likely cause of marriage breakdown.[24] A man also needs to be reassured that the woman he intends to marry has not at some earlier time vowed to remain a virgin spouse of Christ. Beware if he marries such as one, for if she thus disastrously spurns Christ, the highest king, he will vindicate himself in their marriage. So if the groom suspects that she may have taken this vow before the betrothal, he must interrogate her closely to determine the order of the two vows; and the earlier vow must take priority. Otherwise, "he would do better to marry a poor woman with no vow!" As for the woman, Christ may well allow her to have an angry, deformed, argumentative, drunken, gambling, and blasphemous husband for her fickleness.[25]

By the same token then, the bride must be certain that her prospective groom is not already committed to another woman. If a man is betrothed verbally to one woman but then takes another woman in marriage, Herolt warns, the church holds the union to be adultery, each conjugal act a mortal sin, and the children illegitimate; and the man cannot be absolved unless he leaves the second woman and returns to the first.[26]

The preacher is aware that couples try to escape the church's social control by marrying in secret. He censures two such forms of clandestine marriage: one that takes place privately and without witnesses ("in a stable or a barn or some other hiding-place") so that no proof of the union exists and one that takes place without the customary solemnities before the church so that the church is then in no position to enforce matrimonial duties in case of dissension.[27]

Above all, it is essential that people enter marriage for the right motive—the honor of God, their own salvation, and the procreation of children—and not merely to satiate sexual desire. The devil lives with couples who marry for lust. Herolt is

---

[23] D.29.7 (D), T.26.2 (S).
[24] T.26.7 (T).
[25] D.29.2/5 (C), T.26.3 (P).
[26] D.29.2/7 (D), T.26.5 (Q).
[27] T.26.5 (R).

specially scathing about May-December relationships where the ill-assorted couple have disparate but equally unworthy motives: "antique, barren old women who take up in marriage with young men in order to fulfil their sexual cravings, while the young men accept the old hags for their property!"[28]

After all these cautions have been observed, how is the marriage to be performed? Characteristically, the Dominican is more revealing in what he disapproves than in what he recommends. The parties must remember that matrimony is a sacrament, the only one of the seven sacraments that is both voluntary and repeatable.[29] So it must be approached, as any sacrament, in a state of grace. It is a prescription for marital disaster to contract marriage in mortal sin, which in practice means the couple must prepare for the ceremony by contrition and confession.[30] There are three seasons of the year when the church forbids weddings: from Advent I to the octave of Epiphany, from Septuagesima to the octave of Easter, and from three days before Ascension to the octave of Pentecost. Weddings, in other words, must not compete with the church's high seasons. With a lack of proportion not untypical of canonists of the time, a breach of this discipline is treated as an impediment as serious as those already mentioned.[31]

The celebrations themselves, Herolt admonishes, must not be the usual occasion for uproariousness. If the marriage is to begin in the fear of the Lord, "the nuptials must be celebrated devoutly—not with revelry in disreputable company, as is the manner of so very many, but amongst upright people." It is a mark of piety to invite the poor into the wedding feast so that they in turn may pray for the bride and groom.[32] Most people, Herolt regrets to say, take no notice and prefer music to godliness:

> They drive the poor out of the house and make them stand outside while they let in disreputable people like pipers, lute-players, and trumpeters.... Those who contract their marriage in mortal sin, and begin their nuptials without fear of God, with pipes and trumpets and actors, or what is worse, go to the town hall and dance, baring their heads and necks, decorating their bodies with proud robes and gilded girdles, long sleeves and trains, and inflame and wound the onlookers' souls with wicked desires—they sin gravely, and Christ is not present at such weddings as he was at Cana in Galilee.[33]

---

[28] D.29.2 (B, C), T.4.1/9 (A), T.26.1 (O).
[29] D.23.0 (A).
[30] D.29.2/4 (C), T.26.8 (T).
[31] D.29.2/2 (C), T.26.4 (Q).
[32] D.29.2 (B).
[33] T.26.8 (T).

If the preacher's austere desire to replace such festivities with pious solemnity was honored more in the breach than in the observance, that is no doubt also the case with his advice for the wedding night. Parents should give their children who are entering marriage the same instruction that the angel Raphael gave Tobias and Sara; they should abstain from consummating the union for the first three nights to devote themselves to godliness. This is, he adds, a good counsel, not a precept; but to follow it wins merit and promises a good beginning for the relationship.

Herolt deplores the fact that many marriages begin rather in superstition. As the bride first enters the bridegroom's house, he reports,

> She touches the lintel with her hand and says, "I am touching the top of the lintel—I'll have the upper hand in every battle! (*Ich griff uber das ubertur: mein krieg gang allwegen fur*)," and believes that by so doing she will win every fight. Then the husband says back to her, "I am touching the hinge—I'll bend your back and your haunches for you! (*Ich griff an die wenden: ich byeg dir deinen rucken und die lenden*)."[34]

Herolt makes no comment on the social implications of this custom, simply on the sinfulness of such superstition. So also with another piece of wedding-night lore that when a couple first comes together in marriage, the one of them who falls asleep first will die sooner. Such beliefs break the first commandment and are mortal sins.[35]

How is the now-married couple to live together until parted by death? The mutual obligations of husband and wife are seven in number, Herolt says.

The first is mutual love, a love that exceeds every love to be found in this world. It is symbolized by the ring given in marriage, which is gold, circular, and worn on the fourth finger. As gold excels all other metals, this love excels all other loves; circularity signifies a perpetual love ended only by death; and the fourth finger means a heartfelt love, for the physicians say a vein runs directly from the heart to the fourth finger. How is a husband to show his wife such love? By not unjustly distressing her by word or deed and (since they are one flesh) by providing her with all the material necessities, especially in pregnancy. And how is a wife to show her love? By honoring her husband, as Mary always honored Joseph, and by obeying him in all lawful matters.[36] We shall return shortly to the question of how mutual such "mutuality" really is.

Their second obligation is to live together as peaceably as the angels in heaven. Some people live in wedlock like cat and dog, like rooster and hen. They even

---

[34] D.1.2/21 (S).
[35] D.1.2/21 (S), T.41.21 (P).
[36] D.29.3/1 (E-F), T.25.2/1 (B-C).

get used to it! But the devil lives with a quarrelsome couple, and if they are both argumentative, they will go to live with him in hell. Yet even here an accommodating spouse has a spiritual opportunity:

If one of you is malicious, angry, impatient, venomous as a snake and discordant as the devil in hell, the other must sustain it patiently, and the intolerant partner will purge you of your sins—he will be your devil in the present, so the other devils will have no power over you in the future.

Such meekness is specifically the woman's duty. But woe to a husband if he is the henpecked one![37]

Thirdly, they must not deviate from each other and break faith and promise by adultery.[38] There is an obvious degree of anxiety about this subject. Husbands who love their wives must nevertheless labor under the uncertainty "that she perhaps loves someone more than you."[39] It is an anxiety often aggravated by the enforced or prolonged absence of husbands on business. God's testing of the soul is likened to a test a suspicious husband performs:

A husband wants to test his wife's constancy, her faithfulness and love—if a merchant, for instance, were to pretend to leave for the market fair, and instead stayed hidden in the house to see what his wife would do in his absence, and what she would say about it later, and if she was sad at his departure and happy at his return.

Such self-flagellating jaundice is used as an image of Christ who sometimes delays his coming to the soul "to test its constancy—to see if it wants to take another husband in his absence, or to be constant for his sake."[40] The preacher's New Year's garland for married folk is a garland of rue, which expels poison, so that it will drive the venom from their relationship and give them fidelity.[41]

The fourth duty of marriage is patience in labors. Husbands and wives should help each other to bear the cross.[42] They must help each other to acquire and keep honest property by their hard work, especially in the earlier years of their marriage when they are young. And they must help each other raise the children (which means the mother performs the domestic tasks of child care while the husband toils assiduously to earn their food).[43]

---

[37] D.29.3/2 (D), T.25.2/2 (D).
[38] D.29.3/3 (E), T.25.2/3 (F).
[39] T.119.1 (P).
[40] T.72.2 (U).
[41] R.7.2 (112^b-113^a).
[42] R.4.4 (58^a).
[43] D.29.2/4 (E-F), T.25.2/4.

We must devote more space to the fifth obligation, "temperance and uprightness in the conjugal act." The issues here go to the heart of the purposes and intentions of wedlock. Herolt lists four such intentions, three of which are good and the fourth wicked. The procreation of children, first of all, must be the principal intent, in obedience to the command to multiply. Secondly, the example of Mary and Joseph indicates that marriage is for mutual solace and aid without any physical union at all. The third proper intention is as a remedy for lust; and hence the fourth intention, to satisfy lust, can only be a devilish perversion.[44] Though the begetting of children is the principal good, and an act of piety,[45] one cannot overlook Herolt's preference for the second option—abstinence within marriage. If social constraints oblige one to marry, better within marriage to approximate the higher estate of virginity. In the *Storehouse of Examples*, the matrimonial stories that take pride of place are two long extracts from *The Lives of the Fathers* (*Vitaspatrum*) about couples who in one case remained virgin throughout their long years together and, in the other case, by agreement had come together only three times in thirty years to beget children.[46] Indeed, if mankind had not fallen, this duty would have been the only reason for intercourse;[47] and in the early days of the church, the fathers used the conjugal act only in great fear of God and purity of mind as an act of worship.[48]

For the mass of mankind, however, there is need for a remedy for lust, a means of avoiding fornication. Normally then, sexual responsibility in marriage is expounded as a debt owed to one's partner, a debt to be discharged on demand, place and time permitting. One sins gravely by refusing out of disdain, but to acquiesce is to perform an act of justice and meritorious.[49] Even during pregnancy, so long as there is no danger to the fetus, the debt may be paid or exacted without mortal sin, since (according to Petrus of Tarantasia) conjugal duty consists not only in offering service but also in providing a remedy. With casuistic nicety, however, marriage is defined as duty first and a remedy only secondarily so that compliant payment of the debt is meritorious; but providing sex only to prevent one's partner's fornication, though no sin, is not meritorious.[50]

There are only two exceptions to the general rule of sexual duty owed on demand. First, couples are to abstain from intercourse during sacred seasons, namely in Lent, on the four rogation days, and on holy days and nights (including Sundays, festivals, fasts and their vigils). Secondly, they are to abstain during menstrual periods ("the time of women's infirmity") and during confinement

---

[44] T.26.1 (N).
[45] D.6.7 (F).
[46] P.M.: 7, 8 "Matrimonium" (294, 295); cf. T.25.8 (U).
[47] T.34.1 (M).
[48] D.6.7 (F).
[49] D.6.7 (F), T.25.2/4 (G).
[50] D.6.7 (F), T.25.2/5 (I).

and the ten days of purification after it.[51] One of Herolt's favorite examples is the story from Gregory's *Dialogue* about a lawfully married couple who breached the first requirement by having intercourse on the night of the Sabbath, and during the procession on Sunday, the wife was seized and twisted by the devil before all the people.[52] But for those crass enough to ignore the second set of prohibitions, the direst consequences are foretold: children conceived during menstruation or purification may be leprous, epileptic, demoniac, or deformed, and thus display their parents' sin—if, indeed, further conception can take place, since "the man's seed is mixed with the woman's dead blood."[53]

The reason such transgressions occur, of course, is that all too many people marry to satisfy lust. Morose delight and its resultant pollution are as possible within marriage as outside it;[54] and in his first book, Herolt lists as unnatural a conjugal love that is too libidinous and one of the mortal sins of lust.[55] Certainly it is a sin when a couple engage in sexual activity only for its sensual pleasure. Once again, the sophistic calculus of intention is brought into play. The pleasurable feeling may be either "within matrimonial bounds" or "fornicating"—that is, it may be aroused by one's wife alone, and would not desire her if she were not one's wife (in which case it is merely a venial sin), or it may be the sort of lust that would desire her even if she were not one's wife (in which case it is fornicating, a mortal sin). But in Herolt's opinion it is always a mortal sin to perform the conjugal act "impetuously and from sheer libido, transcending the bounds of integrity and reason, with meretricious blandishments or . . . using stimulants to potency in order to heighten desire." (The earlier version of this passage goes on to condemn the person "who tries to perform the act when he has no desire for it (*conatur facere cum non appetat*)," but in the later transcription this is corrected to read, "Who tries to perform the act so that he will enjoy it greatly (*conatur facere ut multum appetat*)."[56] Finally, as we have seen, a man "sins most mortally when he knows his wife against nature or use" and perhaps even more disgracefully in marriage than outside it. Herolt tells a ghastly story of a man who sodomized his wife and died horribly after his bowels were prodigiously debauched in the midden.[57]

Those who have been married will give a solemn account in judgment of how they have discharged these sexual duties: "How the marriage began, for progeny or for lust? Second, if they have loved each other and lived peaceably? Third, if

---

[51] D.6.7 (F-G), T.25.2/5 (H-I), T.61.2 (T).
[52] D.6.7 (G), T.25.2/5 (I), T.117.2/6 (E), T.154.11 (G).
[53] T.61.2 (T), Q.29.1.
[54] E.13.2/3.
[55] D.6.7 (F).
[56] D.6.7 (F), T.25.2/5 (G).
[57] P.M.: 16 "Matrimonium" (303).

they have persevered in the conjugal act at the time of debt?"[1] But though sexual duties take the lion's share of the preacher's attention, there are a number of other practical obligations remaining on his list.

The sixth duty of matrimony is faithfulness to each other in temporal property. The stated basis of this mutual obligation is a theory of community property. "They must both be lords of their possessions," just as the apostolic church held all things in common. Indeed, they are one flesh, so "how could property be divided between them?" But this bold proposition is seriously undermined by the discussion that immediately ensues of wives who sin mortally by stealing from their husbands, not only by extravagance and illicit flirtation, but even by legitimate expenditure without his consent. Meanwhile, husbands are castigated for spending money on gambling or drinking in taverns when they ought to apply it to the family's support.[2] Herolt makes no attempt to reconcile such differences in financial freedom with his theory of community property.

Unwarranted expense in clothing and accessories is an area where, in Herolt's opinion, wives are often guilty of such derelictions. They do so for various reasons, he thinks. Sometimes they decorate themselves to be provocative in men's eyes; sometimes they claim they do it to please their husbands and to stop them being attracted to other women, "but vice has deceived them! The fact that so many women adorn themselves to go abroad in the streets rather than at home with their husbands proves it!" The only time such beautification is permissible is when it is genuinely intended for the husband's pleasure, ignores fashionable trends, springs from no inordinate impulse, and is applied with moderation.[3]

In legal practice, the chief effect of the community property principle is that matrimony confers the right of inheritance upon the death of the spouse.[4]

The final obligation of matrimony is the due and upright education of children. The subject of parents' duties toward their children is the matter of whole sermons, which we shall examine in detail later.[5] Here we simply note that parental duty consists above all in three things—instruction in godliness and virtue; correction of excesses and misdeeds; and (seemingly most serious) bequeathing of a just estate for if they pass on unjustly acquired property, they damn not only themselves but all their heirs.[6]

There is no reason, Herolt believes, why married folk should not maintain a spiritual state within marriage.[7] Only death need bring the faithful performance

---

[1] T.4.1/9 (A).
[2] D.29.3/6 (G-H), T.25.2/6 (I-K).
[3] D.13.5/1 (N).
[4] T.159.3/4 (X).
[5] See chapter 13.
[6] D.29.3/7 (G), T.25.2/7 (L).
[7] R.7.2 (105ª).

of all these duties to an end. Death dissolves marriage; so we hear that, if Lazarus had wished to resume marriage with his wife after Christ raised him, technically he would have had to remarry.[8] Herolt has equivocal advice for the widowed. He is harshly critical of the cynicism of children who, in order to protect their own inheritance, dissuade a widowed parent from remarrying, even though the parent knows fully well that he or she cannot be continent.[9] On the other hand, he is sure that widowed continence is a higher state than marriage. Ideally, one ought to do as the dove does: "After it loses its mate it will not take another, nor ever again sit on a green branch, but always keens for its mate."[10]

---

[8] D.23.0 (A).
[9] T.25.1 (N).
[10] T.25.0 (A), T.72.2 (U).

12

WOMEN

Eve, Herolt says, was made from Adam's rib, not from his head, lest she dominate the man, nor from his feet, lest she be despised by the man, but from his side so that the bond of love might be displayed between them.[11]

This traditional gesture in the direction of parity between woman and man is merely that. For the most part, Herolt faithfully repeats male prejudices about women—old dogmatic rationalizations of men's fear and distrust, vitiating any incipient Christian tendency to free women from incapacity, inferiority, or indignity. It would be foolish to underestimate the cultural role of the priests and preachers who have transmitted men's prejudice and women's self-hatred, sanctioned men's power and women's subjection, from generation to generation. Because of the thoroughness of his enterprise, Herolt stands squarely in this jaundiced succession.

But mendicant preaching also developed a special concern for the social expression of spirituality in women.[12] No vice is so excoriated in women as pride, no virtue so extolled as humility; but it is a humility cast on domestic lines and entails a characteristic image of the feminine as meek, modest, mollifying and obedient, soft of speech, and sweet of manner. Most of the church's counsel, as reflected in these sermons, perceives women as wives and mothers and in this and other respects evaluates them only as accessory to the world of men. It is a world of increasingly bourgeois values. In it, women gain value insofar as they honor a man's authority, respect his property, cushion his bad feelings, provide him service in bed and board, and remain suitably modest in speech and dress. They are belittled insofar as they exercise independence and autonomy and execrated insofar as their beauty provokes a man's desire or their resistance provokes his anger. The first set of postures is identified as humility, the second as the mortal fruit of pride. For all this, a firm foundation is claimed in human nature and divine justice.

---

[11] T.34.1 (L).
[12] Marina Warner, *Alone of All Her Sex: The Myth and Cult of the Virgin Mary* (New York: Alfred A. Knopf, 1976), 183-35.

The Sin of Eve

It all began with Eve. Why did the serpent attack the woman first? Herolt bases his answer on Chrysostom: "Women are incautious, soft and fragile." The devil attacked Eve first because woman is by nature the less cautious sex and thus more easily deceived; the softer sex, therefore more swiftly turned to good or evil; the more fragile sex, therefore more easily overcome.[13] The effect was that both our first parents sinned, yet the woman sinned twice as much as the man. Adam sinned twice by eating the apple and by excusing himself, but Eve sinned four times by her initial pride and unbelief, by eating, by inciting Adam to eat, and by excusing herself. Eve's sins were different in both quantity and quality. She sinned from sheer mental pride, blinded by desire for the preferred deity. But "the man did not really believe what the serpent said," so his was not an absolute but a sort of provisional desire, partly provoked by "a certain amicable benevolence towards his wife, whom he did not wish to trouble." Their sins were different in effect, for "if the woman alone had sinned, it would not have harmed us." Adam's sins provoke no generic comment from Herolt, but Eve's sins are all typical of her gender: "Still to this very day women imitate Eve in pride and unbelief . . . to this day they imitate her in doing more readily what is prohibited them . . . to this day women know best how to excuse themselves and defend their faults."[14]

Accordingly, the terrible punishment visited on Eve's sin of pride has passed to all her daughters. It was woman who expelled man from paradise, and men must be alert to that fact in all their dealings with women.[15] "By offering occasion, Eve drove Adam from paradise, deprived the world of life, and obliged the whole human race to hell—and it all sprang from pride." The penalty brought down on womankind by this pride is the grief of childbirth, pain so vehement that David likens them to the fires of hell, almost the fiercest to be found in this life. Herolt hastens to add that, of course, the pains of hell are greater—did not Bernard say that one little spark of hellfire was worse for a sinner than a thousand years in travail?—and that all women do not undergo the same degree of pain. But the comparison is apt for the intensity of distress involved.[16] The preacher's graphic account confuses the intensity of the body's work with an intensity of grief and pain and ratifies this travail and sorrow as a just affliction for women's pride:

> Such pains are given to women to be warnings to them not to be proud in any other respect. God especially detests pride in women, and conversely loves their humility. Here is the proof: no other sin

---

[13] T.34.2. (O), cf. T.116.2. (Q).
[14] T.34.2 (P-Q).
[15] D.19.4/3 (M), T.61.2 (S), T.97.3/1 (E).
[16] T.61.2 (S).

has ever been punished in the world as Eve's sin—she perpetrated it six thousand years ago and still today (and until the world's end) it is punished in Eve's daughters; so that women cannot execute judgment or give testimony, receive ordination as priests, preach, or hear confession; and furthermore they are to be subject to their husbands, and carry their children with heaviness and deliver them with pain.[17]

The transition is revealing. The preacher moves directly from identifying labor pains as God's unremitting punishment to justifying woman's exclusion from any socially powerful role. The protection of male prerogative becomes identical with God's fierce hatred of female presumption. And if a woman ignores this biological warning against overreaching herself here, "God intends to punish such a woman hereafter with infernal torment."

The Example of the Virgin Mary

So the countervailing exemplars for women are models of humility. If Eve is set before us as an example of sin, the Canaanite woman of Matthew 15 is set before us as an example of its remedy in penitence.[18] Some devout women, like Martha, St. Cecelia, and others, have provided outstanding models of austerity and self-castigation.[19] But Eve's counterpart *par excellence*, her true antitype, is of course the Virgin Mary. Herolt repeats the venerable typology that goes back to Justin Martyr and Irenaeus: "Perdition came through Eve the virgin; accordingly reparation came through the Virgin Mary." It was a theme long enshrined in hymnody: *"Death, that woman introduced, a woman put to flight,"* Herolt recites,[20] and *"The gate of paradise, through Eve closed to all, through the Virgin Mary is opened again."*[21] The grace found in Mary at the angel's greeting was the grace our first parents lost in the fall;[22] through the fall we were lost, but through Mary's presence at the passion we are no longer children of wrath.[23]

In theory, this transforms the status of womanhood. Why did Christ reveal his resurrection first to women? "As a mark of dignity—to give us an example that out of reverence for the glorious Virgin Mary we should honor all women, married, widowed, or virgins; for 'death, that a woman (Eve) introduced, a woman (the

---

[17] T.61.2 (S).
[18] Q.12.0.
[19] E.11.2.
[20] T.163.12 (P).
[21] T.50.6 (F), T.146.3 (F).
[22] T.50.6 (F), T.146.3 (F).
[23] E.18.2/4.

Blessed Virgin) put to flight.'"[24] (Herolt cannot resist adding that there was a second reason; women's native incapacity to keep a secret guaranteed that the news would be passed on.) But in practice, the consequences for women of Eve's sin are far more automatic, categorical, and inexorable than those of Mary's grace.

Eve sinned, and death entered the world. Otherwise, "bodily life would have passed over into eternal when God pleased."[25] The immediate effect was the fearful conjunction of sexual desire with procreation. In the state of innocence, when the higher powers ruled the lower, generative duty would have been the only reason for the conjugal act.[26] The longer consequence, already declared in Genesis 3, was the linking of pain and guilt in all women's reproductive functions and woman's subjection to men's desires. In this manner, the odious amalgam of sin, sex, and death marks woman as the embodiment of all that is vile, squalid, and corrupt in man's physical life. In particular, her creative functions in gestation, parturition, and lactation are branded perpetual signs of the curse of Eve.

The alternative model held out to women as an escape from Eve's curse is the humility of the Virgin Mary. The dogma about Mary, as it developed, exempted her in turn from each of the consequences of Eve's pride. Whereas Eve fell from innocence, Mary was cleansed and preserved from all sin—miraculously—by the action of the Holy Spirit in her mother's womb[27] and by Christ's guarding her in life from every sin.[28] Eve was made subject to her husband's desire and fated to carry her children in heaviness and deliver them in grief; Mary "conceived as a virgin, a virgin brought forth, and after the birth remained a virgin."[29] Her delivery was altogether painless and without difficulty; she was her own midwife.[30] In short, the Virgin's delivery excelled that of all other women because

> other women are fearful before the birth because so many women die in labor (and therefore women commonly prepare themselves for childbirth as if for death by receiving the sacrament); they have grief during the labor (Genesis 3) and languor after it. But the blessed Virgin did not have to fear because she had a guardian angel—the sanctifying father.... Likewise she had no grief during the delivery, partly because Christ stored up that grief until his passion (and then "the sword pierced her soul"), partly because she conceived without sin (and a woman is subject to that grief by reason of sin), and partly

---

[24] T.50.6 (F).
[25] E.49.12.
[26] T.34.1 (M).
[27] D.21.4/1 (N), T.1.2 (E), T.162.11 (D), S.5.1.
[28] Q.18.3.
[29] D.22.3 (K).
[30] T.11.3 (D).

because she was so glad to find herself giving birth to God's Son, bearing the redeemer, and retaining her virginity—such immense gladness excluded every other source of sorrow . . . . Nor did she undergo any languor after the birth because she bore the "medicine of God," the Son of God who heals all languor and every infirmity, and because "the power of the Most High overshadowed her" and made her cool and allowed her to suffer no molestation in her labor.[31]

Mary's virginity was an "integral" virginity of body, soul, and spirit. She had integrity of body because she always kept her body intact, of soul because inwardly she kept in check every tiny motive and desire, and of spirit because she was never divided from God by any sin.[32] In spite of the fact that she was the most beautiful of women, no man could lust after her, not only because of her modest bearing and devout countenance, but because God covered up in her all those things that could be incitements to lust.[33]

In all these respects, women are presented with a model that is by definition impossible of imitation. Granted that the preacher is swift to emphasize exemplary features of Mary's demeanor and behavior, it remains the case that Mary's role as the second Eve rests on her very uniqueness, her difference from all other women, and that that difference depends on miraculous divine intervention. The capacity to give birth chastely and virginally is simply the most dramatic instance of an unattainable criterion of ideal womanhood. Rather than leading to the ostensible outcome—"honor to all women out of reverence for the blessed Virgin"—the latent but enduring effect is to reiterate constantly the distance between hateful reality and idealized archetype. Mary's perfection both explains and illustrates her freedom from the ordinary laws of sexuality, childbearing, and mortality. Since her perfection must always elude other women, it underlines their despised and guilty condition and heightens the very anxiety and self-hatred it offers to relieve. It betrays a notion of goodness divorced from the material world and free from the trammels of the body. "Christ came to call us back through Mary to a state of immortality—that is, an angelic purity where there is no marrying or giving in marriage—so she had to be purest of all."[34]

In practice then, Mary's role is less an exemplar than a unique possessor of purity and dispenser of graces. Nevertheless, she is said to guide, enlighten, and instruct travellers across the sea of this world by her own examples. She instructs wives to obey their husbands and honor them as she obeyed Joseph and always loved him, widows not to remarry after their husbands' deaths but to remain in widowhood,

---

[31] T.162.13 (F).
[32] T.163.11 (N).
[33] D.21.4/5 (Q), T.163.11 (O).
[34] T.163.21 (Q).

and virgins to flee the companionship of men and to refrain from much talking.[35] Indeed, she is a perfect model to widows and virgins of modest, upright, and useful speech, since the Gospels only record that she spoke six times—twice with the angel, twice with Elizabeth, and twice with the Son.[36] For though garrulousness is reprehensible in men, Herolt declares, it is more so in women and most of all in widows and virgins.[37] "Sins of the tongue" are at the top of his list of the principal sins of women;[38] women can scarcely keep anything hidden but always pass on anything they have heard from others without delay.[39]

But the all-embracing lesson for women from Mary's example is the lesson of humility:

> The humility of women especially pleases God. He has rewarded the humility of one woman, the blessed Virgin Mary, above all the virtues of all the saints—indeed in a sense he has esteemed her humility above all the Virgin Mary's own virtues.[40]

Humility

Except for Christ only, Mary was the humblest human being ever to have lived on earth, so humble that although she was holier than everyone in heaven and earth, she attempted no miracle. Why did she have to be so humble? Once more the preacher accounts for Mary's role in formulas rather than personal terms. His answer is the reconciliation of opposites: to receive the all-highest, she had to be the lowest; to be exalted above all saints and angels, she had to be lowlier than all; to undo Eve's death-dealing pride, she had to restore life by her humility, for *contraria contrariis curantur*.[41]

A like humility is enjoined upon other women: "The humbler a woman, the closer she will be to the blessed Virgin Mary in heaven (and the prouder a woman, the further away from her she will be, and the closer to Lucifer in hell)."[42] But this humility has the most far-reaching consequences for a woman's personal life. Its chief expression is submissiveness, especially of wives to husbands:

---

[35] T.162.19 (J).
[36] T.116.2/1 (R), for consistency reading *sexies* for *septies*.
[37] T.116.2/1 (P).
[38] T.125.9 (C).
[39] T.50.6 (F).
[40] T.61.2 (S).
[41] T.163.12 (P).
[42] T.61.2 (S).

> Women must be patient and meek. As a sign of this women have gentle voices, and they tie soft veils around their necks to indicate that they are bound to answer their enraged husbands sweetly—to temper with their sweet responses the malice and irascibility of their bad husbands.[43]

Any departure from this meekness draws the scornful censure:

> If, by contrast, she is perverse and rebellious and angry, while her husband is good and kind, she will be tortured by demons in hell ... For it is a heavy weight to bear a litigious woman.[44]

> A woman who wants to lord it over her husband is a sick creature—it is not to be endured![45]

Once a man begins to bicker with his wife, he will never have any peace. Proverbs 19 compares a nagging woman to a leaking roof—when he tries to stop the dripping in one place, it starts in another.[46] A man would do better to have ten angry neighbors than one angry wife.[47] Accordingly,

> a woman must be signally careful not to be angry, because there is no anger above a woman's anger, on account of the fragility of that sex. It is really a poor man who has an angry and vexatious wife.[48]

Rather, a wife must show her love by honoring her husband—unlike those who despise their husbands for their age, infirmity, or poverty—or by obeying him in all things.[49] She is duty-bound to obey because "all power is of God."[50] Like all other subjects, she is bound to obey her lord in all licit and upright matters.[51] Even her capacity to make pious vows (fasting, early rising, abstinence, or pilgrimage, for instance) is strictly limited by her husband's consent.[52] This subject status flows, as we have seen, both from Eve's punishment and from Mary's example. Herolt

---

[43] T.95.8 (N), cf. D.25.3/2 (F), T.25.2/2 (D), S.27.2.
[44] T.25.2/2 (D).
[45] R.5.1 (63ᵇ).
[46] D.13.7/3 (S).
[47] D.29.3/2 (F).
[48] T.95.8 (N).
[49] D.29.3/2 (F), T.25.2 (C).
[50] T.33.1 (C).
[51] T.59.3 (M).
[52] T.2.2/15 (R).

compares a wife's obligation of acceptable service to her husband to the duties of attendants and servants to their masters. Like them, she must obey his lawful commands, not provoke him to anger, and do gladly what she knows will please him.[53] Herolt also likens the obligations of a wife to the soul's duty as Christ's spouse. The instructions to the bride Sara in Tobit 10 form the basis for this tropological treatment: a wife is to honor her in-laws, love her husband, rule her home and family, and serve her husband in bed and board.[54]

The Obligations of Husband and Wife

These duties, it is true, are often set in the context of mutual obligations between husbands and wives. The love between them is to exceed all earthly loves, as the symbolism of the wedding ring betokens,[55] yet there is a decided imbalance in the practical expression of this mutuality. There should be no occasion for conflict over household property, since ideally all material possessions should be held in common,[56] or at least the man should honor the woman's right to a share in all the necessities of life, especially when she is pregnant.[57] Yet Herolt feels obliged to deal several times with the social problem of wives stealing from their husbands. Even her giving an alms without her husband's consent is theft and a contravention of the seventh commandment, except in three circumstances: if she is independently wealthy, if she gives alms from her paraphernalia (the personal effects of a married woman outside the dowry), or if she gives—in moderation—from the domestic supplies of food and wine within her jurisdiction.[58] Even these exceptions (in areas where custom permits them) do not apply if the husband expresses any displeasure. She can also be guilty of theft from her husband by unjustified expenditures on clothing and accessories.[59] More glaringly, a wife sins doubly and mortally by stealing from her husband for illicit expenditures, for instance, if she makes a gift to an admirer to allure him to an immoral act or otherwise fosters adultery on another's part. In this case, she must make restitution (for obvious reasons secretly, by the agency of her confessor) if she can.[60]

The most explicit case of imbalance in a theoretically mutual relationship concerns violent provocation. In order to show love to his wife, a man must not

---

[53] T.33.1 (C).
[54] T.124.2 (L).
[55] D.29.3/1 (E-F), T.25.2/1 (B).
[56] D.7.8 (H).
[57] D.21.3/1 (F).
[58] D.7.8 (H).
[59] D.29.3/6 (G), T.25.2/6 (J).
[60] Q.40.2; E.41.1/1.

unjustly upset her by word or deed,[61] but the emphasis is on "unjustly." Does a husband who beats his wife sin mortally?

> I reply that if he does so for the sake of correction, and moderately, he does not sin mortally; for a superior has to correct an inferior, and the husband is the head of the wife, not *vice versa* (Genesis 3) ... But if he hurts and beats her from vindictiveness and anger and without good reason, he sins gravely. This is the situation with those men who, when they have been offended by others (say in the tavern or elsewhere) and cannot take their revenge directly, take it out on their wives without cause, and in this they gravely offend God.[62]

Part of the solemn accounting that a man will have to give in the last judgment will be the question, "How often have you struck or wounded your wife (or others) from anger or vindictiveness?"[63] In anticipation of that final reckoning, Herolt indicates that the issue of unjustified wife beating is a standard question at confession; the confessor is to ask a husband how often he has struck his wife angrily or vindictively. The corresponding questions to a wife, however, are whether she has disobeyed her husband or cursed him in her heart or deliberately provoked him to blasphemy, cursing, or anger.[64] It is explicitly a wife's responsibility not to provoke her husband to violence;[65] if she does, she shares responsibility for his sin, even though she is the victim.[66] Rather, her duty is to cushion her husband's wrath with her meek responses. And "the more blows or bad language she sustains patiently, the more crowns she will gain."[67]

Pregnancy and Childbirth

Any actual damage done to the woman, if undeserved, is thus subsumed under the heading of "salutary tribulation"; but if she is pregnant, then concern is aroused for the safety of the fetus. Herolt classifies as abortionists "those accursed men who distress their pregnant wives by words or actions, beating and shoving them and so committing the murder of their own children."[68] Men must spare their wives when they are pregnant and not terrorize or disturb or beat them; they should

---

[61] D.29.3/1 (F).
[62] D.15.2/8 (C).
[63] T.3.2/3 (O).
[64] Q.19.2; Q.22.3.
[65] D.1.2/15 (N).
[66] D.8.6 (L).
[67] T.25.2/2 (D).
[68] D.1.2/15 (N).

even deprive themselves of food and drink to provide for their expectant wives.[69] A pregnant woman, who is apt to be "picky about food,"[70] has a special claim on material support for the sake of the unborn child.[71] But should any damage befall the child in the womb, "women must not absolve themselves, if they become pregnant and then provoke their husbands to anger."[72] It is the mother, above all, who must be "solicitous of the treasure she carries in her womb."[73]

Women heard much from pulpits about the honor of parents, the powers and proprietary rights of husbands, and the protection of the unborn but very little about their own human needs. Sometimes they heard their legitimate fears and concerns discounted or misunderstood by the men who expounded moral law. In his recurrent attack on superstitions and abuses surrounding childbirth, Herolt dismisses the popular sentiment that "the perils undergone by women in giving birth are harmful to them." This, he declares, is false (unless they have been guilty of inducing a miscarriage) and goes on to talk instead about the danger to the soul of the unbaptized child.[74] The only peril worth discussing is the spiritual danger of losing the vision of God. This becomes explicit in another version of the same set piece:

> It is asked: If a woman dies in childbirth or immediately after it, is it harmful to her in the salvation of her soul? No, there is nothing prejudicial to her in childbirth if she is otherwise fitly disposed—indeed, usually speaking it is better for her, since all women prepare themselves before labor by contrition, confession, and reception of the sacrament.[75]

So, too, Herolt rejects the folk belief that a woman dying in childbed cannot see God's face directly but only through a veil, or that she loses her soul unless her body is brought into the church.[76]

Accordingly, Herolt fiercely rejects all those forms of folk wisdom, sympathetic magic, and midwives' lore that women had evolved to cope with this most intense of experiences. They are all superstitions, falsifications of faith, and breaches of the first commandment; and a woman who has placed any trust in them is certainly harmed in soul if she dies giving birth. Among the practices that draw

---

[69] T.16.1/1 (A).
[70] T.98.2 (G).
[71] D.29.3/2 (F), T.25.2/1 (C).
[72] D.1.2/15 (N).
[73] T.16.1/1 (A).
[74] D.1.2/15 (N), T.41.14 (N).
[75] T.61.2 (T).
[76] D.1.2/15 (N), T.41.14 (N), T.61.2 (T).

condemnation are these: "There are people who, when a woman is experiencing difficulty in giving birth, encircle her with her husband's belt to make her delivery easier" (sometimes, no doubt, an act of sympathetic magic, but possibly also a piece of crude midwifery, like the obstetrical girdles of more recent times). "Again, there are those who bless a woman in childbed with an unsheathed sword, or blow out a candle in her face—totally superstitious!—or place a branch within the mattress where the woman is lying for the delivery."[77] Also condemned are magic letters, charms written on pieces of papers and carried by women to preserve themselves from the dangers of childbirth.[78]

There are, of course, practices of a similar sort that the preacher heartily recommends. To burn incense, light a consecrated taper, sprinkle holy water, or make the sign of the cross over the woman in labor are all licit and godly. The issue is plainly between those gestures that have churchly sanction and those that do not. The efficacy of the midwife's repertoire in alleviating pain or anxiety is not an issue, however:

> such grief is natural for travailing women; yet if a woman orders this grief towards God and in patience of heart offers the pressure of grief to God omnipotent, and gladly suffers such grief for God's sake, it is to be hoped that through her sorrow she may earn a growth in merit and a diminution of the pain of purgatory.[79]

It becomes plain why the purposes of midwives and the supportive tradition of women's lore were so suspect to the preachers. They represented an alternative magic, an attempt to escape from the just curse of Eve, and a shirking of potentially meritorious suffering.

Midwives

Naturally, the confrontation became especially pointed when midwives entered the priests' special territory—the administration of baptism. The practical necessity of emergency baptism could not be gainsaid, so care is taken to spell out what is and what is not permissible. These precautions give us some glimpse of aberrant practices that were thought to occur. The proper minister of baptism is a priest, but in an emergency anyone—man or woman, believer or unbeliever—may baptize, so long as the intention is right and the churchly form and matter are used. However, a simple cleric may not baptize if a priest is present nor a woman if a man is present. A child cannot be baptized *in utero*, nor must the mother be cut to baptize an unborn

---

[77] D.1.2/15 (N), T.41.14 (N), T.61.2 (T), T.142.1 (R).
[78] T.41.15 (N).
[79] T.61.2 (T).

child unless the mother is already dead and the child still viable. If there is fear for the survival of a partially delivered baby, it may be baptized on a presenting head but not on other parts such as hands or feet ("though no harm is done if these parts are sprinkled with baptismal water, since divine mercy is not circumscribed"). If a baby is so baptized and later fully delivered, cautionary baptism is to be applied using a conditional formula. The matter of baptism is pure water—not wine or beer or urine or any other liquid—and the form of words must be "I baptize you in the name of the Father, Son, and Holy Spirit." The vernacular formulas of old women are not baptism at all when they say, "If you live, let this be your bath; but if you die, let it be your baptism, in the name of the Father, Son, and Holy Spirit (*Soltu leben so sey dir das ein bad. Soltu aber sterben so sey es dir ein tauff. in den namen des vaters und des suns und des heyligen geystes*)."[80] Herolt also rejects as superstition the curious custom of placing an infant before baptism under a stool.[81]

Herolt's sermons provide evidence of the church's growing mistrust of midwives, its suspicion that they often resorted to magic and its determination to bring midwifery under ecclesiastical licence and control. The forays of Dominican inquisitors into rural areas where the authority of the village healer-charmer-midwife was unmistakable no doubt heightened the order's alarm and sense of competition. In the later fifteenth century, when Herolt's sermon books were enjoying wide popularity in printed form, the Dominican authors of *Malleus Maleficarum* urged that midwives should be required to take an oath of orthodoxy in order to preclude their recourse to witchcraft and superstition.[82] It was but a short step from there to the steady growth of legal and professional regulation of midwives in the sixteenth and later centuries.[83] The ineradicable persistence of such mother-to-daughter folk wisdom and skill, in spite of the attempts of male authorities to suppress them, added much fuel to the horrible witch hunts of the early modern period.[84]

But the suspicion was already well established long before. In his earliest book, dated 1416, Herolt already labels the perpetrators of female superstitions "old crones" (*antiquae vetulae*) and accuses them as well of the far graver crimes of abortion and contraceptive advice. Those who provide means of contraception— "who make women sterile"—appear to be guilty of as many murders as the conceptions they have tried to prevent. To give help and advice about killing a child in the womb is "a very great sin that exceeds the murder of any baptized neighbor, for the simple

---

[80] D.23.1 (B), T.76.1 (U).
[81] D.1.2/15 (N), T.41.14 (N), T.61.2 (T).
[82] Malleus Malificarum, 3.34.
[83] For the development of such regulation in sixteenth-century England, see Keith Thomas, *Religion and the Decline of Magic*, 259.
[84] See T. R. Forbes, *The Midwife and the Witch* (New Haven: Yale University Press, 1966).

reason that in the child the soul is slain with the body," unlike a baptized victim.[85] Abortion thus shares with suicide the gravest category of homicide—"murder of both body and soul."[86] Popular sentiment was liable to deny that a fetus thus aborted had any soul, so this opinion is explicitly condemned: if the child was alive *in utero* and dies without baptism, its soul descends into the limbo of children where it suffers no pain of the senses.[87]

Alongside the "old crones," Herolt lists four other groups who are often guilty of the "double murder" of abortion: harlots who, though pregnant, pass themselves off as virgins, endangering the fetus;[88] husbands who "commit the murder of their own children" by beating, shoving, or harassing their pregnant wives;[89] innkeepers who adulterate their wine to increase profits, thus causing abortions and other maladies;[90] and pregnant women themselves, who (as we have seen) must be "solicitous of the treasure they carry"[91] and not provoke their husbands' violence. If a woman has a miscarriage, she is not damned on that account,

> so long as she is not responsible for the abortion and has been diligent in taking care of herself. Yet she should be contrite and confess as a precaution, lest it happened from her own negligence, or she herself provided the occasion, say by wearing broad girdles or squeezing herself into tight dresses, or by dancing or riding or the like.[92]

Albertus Magnus is cited as authority for the special risk of miscarriage by excessive movement just after conception and just before term. Gynecological logic also justifies a partial exemption from the severity of the Lenten fast during pregnancy for nutritional reasons[93] and mandates abstinence from intercourse where there is risk of miscarriage.[94]

If there is no such risk, the ordinary obligation of sexual service obtains, even in pregnancy. That ordinary obligation is another instance of the imbalance within the ostensibly mutual relationship of marriage. Of course, sexual compliance is one area where the example of the Virgin Mary's humility could not be applied. But it could be applied to the nurture of a child, for Mary was "a solicitous and

---

[85] D.1.2/15 (N), T.16.1/1 (A), T.41.14 (N), T.61.2 (T).
[86] T.142.5 (Y).
[87] T.41.14 (N).
[88] D.1.15 (N), T.61.2 (T).
[89] D.1.15 (N), D.15.2/18 (C), D.29.311 (F), T.61.2 (T).
[90] E.26.3.
[91] T.16.1/1 (A).
[92] T.61.2 (T).
[93] D.18.3/2 (H), T.39.4 (N).
[94] D.6.1/7 (G), T.25.2/5 (I).

attentive mother who caressed, fed, and carried her child in his infant frailty."[95] She fed, bathed, and wrapped him, kept him warm, rocked him to sleep, cradled him in her arms, and sang to him, as mothers do.[96] In sermons, as in poetry and iconography, the nativity was still movingly pictured in a gently domestic mode. In later centuries, the portrayal of Mary as a nursing mother virtually disappeared as her representation became more regal, more prudish, and more remote.[97] But the Dominican Order had been specially keen to promote this evocative image, and Herolt still has Mary pleading in heaven for a sinner, "O Son, remember that I cherished you with motherly love and fed you with my breasts, and condone this sinner."[98] In the "inestimable poverty" of Christ's nativity, the Blessed Virgin teaches women to breast-feed their children themselves; and the decretals repeat the injunction.[99] Failure to do so, in Herolt's view, is one of the cases where parents deserve to lose their children:

> Death sometimes results when a mother does not want to breastfeed her own child—like rich women who in the habit of using wet nurses. Sometimes the milk of the wet nurse is not as compatible with the child as its own mother's milk, with which it was nourished in the womb and to which it is accustomed. Sometimes children die in this way who might have lived if their own mother had suckled them.[100]

Accordingly, lactating mothers needing their strength are partially exempted from the Lenten fast.[101] If a mother from illness cannot breastfeed her child, she should find an upright and modest wet nurse, since children, it is said, imitate their nurse's character—as in the case of the noblewoman who had twins, fed one herself and gave the other to a wet nurse. But the wet nurse ran out of milk and, needing the money, put the child to suckle on a sow. The one grew up to be extremely courtly, but the other was rustic and gross, with disgusting table manners and a fondness for wallowing in mire! There is great merit, however, in the nurture of children if they are raised to be Christian: "As often as a mother gives her child milk, is wakened by the child, carries or bathes or otherwise tends the child, she always gains merit."[102]

---

[95] T.162.12 (D).
[96] T.17.2 (H-M).
[97] Marina Warner, *Alone of All Her Sex*, 204.
[98] T.161.4 (C).
[99] T.11.3 (D).
[100] D.23.3/5 (D), T.77.1/5 (C).
[101] D.18.3/2 (H), T.39.4 (N).
[102] T.61.3 (U).

One corollary of such child care (which is presumed to be the mother's role exclusively) is that "a mother naturally loves a child more than a father does."[103] Herolt gives several reasons why this is so. On Innocents' Day, he explains why the text says, "Rachel wept for her children" and not Jacob: "According to Aristotle, mothers are more susceptible and kinder than fathers, and therefore have more compassion for their children."[104] Why does a mother love a child more?

First, whatever we devote more effort to, we love more; but a mother devotes more effort than a father to children, in carrying them, giving them birth, and also in educating them. Secondly, we love more the thing we know more certainly to be our own; and a mother knows for certain that the child has been born from her, but the father, even if he believes so, is still not sure that the child is born of his seed . . . . Thirdly, we love more the thing in which we know we have a greater stake; but according to the Philosopher, a greater portion of the mother's substance than of the father's is in the child's body. Fourthly, Augustine says that friendship is founded on the habit of living, talking, and conversing together; and mothers are more accustomed to do these things with their children than fathers are.[105]

All these duties of wives and mothers occupy much of the preacher's instruction to women, but there is a minority of women who fall outside this normative role. Herolt makes special comment about three groups: widows, virgins, and single women of independent means.

Widows

If the life of a widow is to be meritorious and dedicated to Christ, it must have these seven characteristics. First, true widows learn to rule the households committed to them; God expects them to have families more devout and upright than other people, so they must be exemplary in their Christian practice. Secondly, a widow must have hope in the Lord for almost all widows are desolate and sad, even if they are wealthy, for they are often unjustly deceived since they have no man to counsel them, often molested since they have no man to protect them, and often sad since they have no husband of their own to console them. (Pastorally then, Herolt advises, it is a grave error to share the grief of grieving widows but a great merit to console them.) Instead, "they should take refuge in the wounds of Christ as the dove seeks the clefts of the rock." Thirdly, widows must not be lazy but constantly occupied in good deeds. It is dangerous for anyone in any estate to be idle but especially women; look what happened when the devil found Eve idle! Next, widows must not be talkative. Garrulousness is reprehensible in men, more so in women, but most of all in widows and virgins. It is particularly important

---

[103] T.116.1/1 (M).
[104] T.16.2 (E).
[105] T.116.1/1 (N).

for widows to be discreet and to hold their tongues. Fifth, widows should wear widows' weeds, not curious or ornate dress; they are so easily inveigled by the lure of beautiful clothes and thus trapped by demons. Such adornment is even worse in a widow than in a married woman, for there is some excuse for a wife to try to please her husband; but Christ is the widow's spouse, and she should be adorned inwardly with virtues. Sixth, a widow is to be active in works of mercy for the poor and sick. (In this, as in other respects, St. Elizabeth of Hungary is a special model for widows.) Finally, widows must subdue their bodies to the spirit and direct their souls to God in devout and attentive prayer. Accordingly, they must castigate their bodies with fasting and abstinence and make up for the devotional time they lost in domestic chores.[106]

As we saw earlier, Herolt adduces the Virgin's example as an instruction to widows not to remarry but to remain in widowhood.[107] There are four reasons, he says, why it is better not to remarry: as an indication of greater chastity, whereas multiple marriages are evidence of incontinence (though it is a sin to dissuade widowed parents from remarrying if they know they cannot be continent)[108]; as a sign of greater love to the departed husband by refusing to take another in his place; as a source of greater security, since a widow is her own mistress and lives in peace; and so also as a source of greater freedom to serve God. She can rise and retire when she likes, eat, drink or fast when she pleases, do works of mercy at her own discretion, and the like. A young widow still of child-bearing age may remarry without sin, but even in this case, it is better for her to remain a widow for the reasons given.[109]

Virgins

Christ went out of his way to reaffirm at Cana that marriage was a good and godly estate; still, it remains true that "the married are blessed, widows more blessed, but virgins most blessed of all."[110] Virginity, widowhood, and marriage differ in brilliance as the light of the sun, the moon, and the stars; they differ in worth as gold, silver, and lead.[111] We have dealt already with the issues of sexual sin and restitution in the violation of virginity;[112] here we consider Herolt's account of the dignities of the state of virginity, "the treasure above all treasures." Christ has privileged virgins with nine such dignities (corresponding to the nine choirs of the angels). They have

---

[106] T.116.21 (O-T).
[107] T.162.1/9 (J).
[108] T.26.1 (N).
[109] T.116.22 (U).
[110] D.22.3 (K), T.25.0 (before A), T.146.3 (F), T.157.1 (G).
[111] T.157.1 (G).
[112] See chapter 10.

an incomparable treasure, an angelic life, the kingdom of heaven since God lives in them, and inscription in the book of life; they are the adornment of heaven and the beauty of the Church. Christ has a special love for them; they receive a special aureola added to the common glory of the elect. They are spouses of Christ, and virginity holds the principate in heaven and earth.[113] Accordingly, Christ requires six things in his virgin spouses: beauty (that is, purity of conscience); nobility (uprightness of morals and guarding of the senses); wisdom (discretion in speech); abundance of riches (that is, of virtues); health (the agility of the soul in good works); and faithfulness in love (the desire to serve none but Christ).[114]

All of this is highly formal and receives little practical content apart from the standard injunctions to modesty of dress, appearance, and speech; avoidance of familiarity with men; and inner resistance to desire. It was not a topic of pressing relevance to the lay parishioners who were Herolt's chief targets, and the inclusion of a sermon on the topic was doubtless for the sake of completeness, and to provide an outline for preachers to communities of religious. Sadly, however, practical reality did demand that Herolt deal with the implications of the rape of a virgin. Thomas Aquinas, the decretals, and the legend of St. Lucia are his authorities for the reassurance that a virgin who is raped does not lose her virginity or her aureola, provided she tries to resist and at least keeps her mind from consent.[115] On the other hand, it is not enough for someone to be a virgin physically while inwardly she hopes to marry; she will receive the aureola only if she repents of the wish before she dies. So it is better to be a virgin with a vow than without in order to offer one's whole self to God. In practice then, the subject represents an exhortation to entry upon the cloistered life. Lest women disqualify themselves from this high option by unnecessary doubts, Herolt declares on Albertus's authority that little girls who do something carnal in their childish years do not thereby lose their virginity. At that age, there is no deliberation of counsel in them nor any impulse to delight.[116]

Unmarried Women

Unmarried women who do not fall into these sanctioned categories of widowhood and virginity receive only fleeting mention but in a highly revealing way. Expounding Mary Magdalene's fallen state, Herolt points to three causes: first, her physical beauty; second, her temporal wealth; and third, her independence and ownership of her own home:

These three things were to her, and still are to many other women, the occasion of sin. The first thing that is an occasion of sin to many women is beauty of body.

---

[113] T.157.1 (G).
[114] T.157.2 (H).
[115] T.157.1 (G), E.15.2.
[116] E.15.2.

For the beauty of women is like a glowing coal, a gleaming sword, an apple rotten and full of worms. For youths see the glowing coals, touch them and are burned; they see the gleaming swords, grasp them and are wounded; see apples outwardly beautiful but rotten inside, pick them and are deceived. But those who are wise guard themselves from these things . . . The second occasion of sin to women is wealth and abundance of temporal possessions . . . The third is when she is independent and her own mistress. For woman is soft fragile, and incautious, and therefore to be ruled and guarded.[117]

This eloquent account contains the classic elements of men's attitude to women: a patronizing tone, a refusal to allow women a self-determined place outside the reach of male proprietorship, and a perception of women as the embodiment of all that is sexually threatening and uncontrolled. The same elements appear in many of Herolt's asides about women. A similar condescension informs his remarks about the curiosity, lability, and garrulousness of women. So does his comment that "nuns are enclosed, not for actual evil or for evil intent, but on account of their sex's fragility"[118] or that "heretics prefer to talk to little women and the simple who cannot understand their frauds."[119] The principal sins of women, he loftily declares, are "sins of the tongue, superfluous adornment, soothsaying, and making false confessions out of embarrassment."[120] Women have no access to male authority either by nature or by aptitude: "If a woman is not chosen to be pope or king, it does not make her sad, for it was not open to her, nor was she adequate to such a dignity."[121]

Adornment

But the sexual threat embodied in women draws the most energetic treatment. The focus of this concern is the subject of adornment and "proud dressing," a theme to which these sermons return repeatedly. "There is no place from the soles of the feet to the top of the head of a woman adorned where the net of the devil is not spread to trap souls."[122] Herolt speaks scornfully of the "massive ingratitude, indeed contempt," of women who devote more care to their hair than they do to God—"if it is dark they want it blond, if it straight they want it wavy"—and who use the beauty of their hair as a trap to capture the unwary male (as Judith ensnared Holofernes).[123] When they make themselves up "in contempt of their creator,"

---

[117] Q.37.1.
[118] T.90.11 (U).
[119] T.100.13 (Q).
[120] T.129.9 (C).
[121] E.15.16.
[122] D.19.25 (D), T.86.5 (U).
[123] D.13.3/2 (G).

the way this offends God may be gauged from noticing how greatly offended expert artists become when someone presumes to improve their works. The same can be said of the creator of all creatures . . . These people are like Lucifer who wanted to be more beautiful than almighty God made him—those, for instance, who have pale faces and want to make them white and red; those with black hair who want to have blue-grey, or straight hair and want it to be curled; they don't want to be content with God's handiwork . . . . Such people want beautiful faces on the outside, but inside they wear diabolical faces![124]

Vain adornment deeply displeases God; clothing should be a vehicle for a woman's humility. She should veil her head "to show that privation began in and from her"—namely in Eve—so women should bear the veil rather than men; and "to show that she has a superior—her husband." For, as Aristotle said, "the masculine is by nature worthier than the feminine." By veiling herself, "a woman shows that she knows herself guilty and subject." There is a third reason—respect toward her guardian angel. Indeed,

in some countries there is such uprightness and modesty among women that they scarcely dare show themselves even to their own husbands with heads uncovered. But in some other countries, the opposite is the case, where married women are not only not ashamed to appear before their husbands uncovered, but go dancing and leaping before the entire population with bare heads—it is especially indecent in women who have been known by men![125]

A woman, married or unmarried, who adorns herself and paints her face so as to look desirable is "a murderer of her brothers" when she entices men to sin. Even if she has no deliberate intention of alluring some man to concupiscence, and has no wish to comply, she knows very well what the actual effect will be; but she prefers to damn her neighbor's soul than forgo her proud costume.[126] It is a signal designed to incite lust.[127] Herolt is mortified that not only in the streets and at dances, but even in church, women wound the hearts of the men who look at them, "now by using white color, now by red, now by conversing familiarly, now by joining hands, now by bringing their faces close." Some prink their cheeks by rubbing them with goat hair and paint themselves as an artist paints pictures, and

---

[124] T.83.2/3 (I).
[125] D.13.3/3 (H).
[126] T.83.2/3 and 2/5(I).
[127] T.86.8 (B), T.141.4 (M).

"by these devices offer their neighbors traps and occasions of ruin . . . . They are slayers of souls."[1]

What then is a man to do? Above all, he must guard his eyes.[2] But there are also some mental devices by which a man may shield his soul from a woman's physical beauty:

> Reflect that you yourself have never devoted the care and effort to adorning your eternally endangered soul so as to please God as this woman has to adorning her rotten and mortal body to please the world . . . . Reflect, too, how beautiful are the faces of the elect in heaven, and how they will be adorned in glory.[3]

In principle, of course, a man is not forced to lust by the devil or by the flesh, "nor by the woman either, for 'the masculine is by nature stronger than the feminine'";[4] but in practice a man is as liable to lust as the stubble in an arid desert is to flame, so "the remedy is for a man to keep distance from the fire of lust—that is, from the presence of woman."[5] "A bad woman," Herolt quotes, "is three times worse than a demon (*Femina demonia tribus assibus est mala peior*).[6] Proverbs 22 had forewarned that the mouth of a woman was a deep ditch: the devil specially likes to buy souls cheaply "when a fatuous woman gives her soul to the devil and her body to a lecher" for the mere price of a transitory pleasure.[7] Women, too, have perverse fantasies,[8] and there is a special danger confronting churchmen in lust masquerading as sanctity; one must beware (as Ambrose warned) of private conferences with "godly" women.[9]

All these classic male attitudes to women are perhaps most succinctly stated in the judgment Herolt quotes approvingly from Duns Scotus: "A man who induces a woman to an act of vice is duty-bound to make restitution of the loss, either personally or through an intermediary, by leading her back efficaciously to penitence and virtue."[10] Following Herolt's own homiletic method, we may conclude with an exemplary story about the fate in store for any woman who defies the curse of

---

[1] T.86.8 (B).
[2] D.19.25 (D), T.86.5 (X).
[3] T.86.5 (Y).
[4] D.19.5/5 (N).
[5] D.19.6/3 (Q).
[6] D.14.3/2 (E), T.96.23 (R): "a certain metrist."
[7] D.19.1 (A).
[8] D.19.2/3 (C), T.86.3 (U), T.141.4 (M).
[9] D.19.43 (M).
[10] E.16.36.

Eve, ignores the Virgin's example, and lives in feminine vanity. It is a horrid, and psychologically revealing, tale:

> A certain priest used to afflict himself greatly on his dead mother's behalf, praying and celebrating mass for her. One day, when he was celebrating for her and longing to know something of her state, he caught sight of her in a basket near the altar, stripped bare by two demons, and bound. From her head there seemed to come serpents of fire like hair, and there was a toad on her breast with its front feet around her neck, spewing fiery flames into her face. On her hands and feet were the chains of fire by which she was bound. And the priest was told that it was useless for him to pray for her, for she was damned. He was also told that she suffered these pains for decorating her head and hair—this is why she had the fiery snakes circling her head. She carried the toad on her bosom for baring her neck and breasts; and the toad spat flames of fire in her face because she had painted her own face. And because she had stretched out her hands for immodest caresses and touching, and offended God with her feet by leaping and dancing, her hands and feet were now bound with burning chains. Therefore Matthew 22 says of such sinners: "Bind their hands and feet and cast them out into the dark . . . [11]

The Storehouse of Examples offers the preacher a wide choice of such cautionary tales about the spiritual dangers posed to, and by, women. What was the visceral effect of these attitudes and images on the women and the men who listened to such preaching year after year? One can only speculate on its cumulative impact—on the women, with compassion, and on the men, with dismay.

---

[11] T.83.3 (I).

13

CHILDREN

Bearing and nurturing children "in heaviness and pain" are a woman's chief business. The preacher admonishes pregnant women to protect the treasure they carry and fulminates against any who endanger the unborn fetus by violence, carelessness, abortion, or the illicit magic of the midwife. Woman's inherited humiliation extends also to the duty of breastfeeding, a duty reinforced by the Virgin's example and made weightier by the belief that an infant imbibed character with its nurse's milk.

These conspicuous functions aside, Herolt has little to say about the importunate daily task of child care. It is, of course, the mother's task; she naturally loves a child more than a father does, for "she devotes more effort to her children in carrying them, giving them birth, and educating them."[12] Accordingly, the details can be left for women to deal with. Herolt has much to say about parents' later duties in disciplining their children as they grow and training them in godliness, but the sermon books only fleetingly describe the daily care of children in infancy. Interestingly, the best glimpse we gain of Herolt's feelings on the subject is the report in *The Rose Garden* of his own sermon on Christmas Day 1436, where he preached to a largely female monastic audience. He employs the long-hallowed device of urging his hearers to conceive, bear, and nurture the baby Jesus in their hearts; and in fashioning his allegory, he sketches the proper ways to handle an infant.

There are seven things, he says, that "help a child to thrive and grow strong and healthy." First, one should feed it appropriate food that is easily assimilated, namely milk. Secondly, food should be given a little at a time, not too much and not too little. Third, one should not give an infant wine, especially if it is still at the breast; for wine and milk in combination are liable to produce leprosy. The fourth requirement is to lift a child and move it about, dance with it, and swing it but gently, for otherwise one may easily harm it. Done correctly, this motion benefits a child greatly, sharpening its reflexes and physical agility. Herolt gives no encouragement to the practice, current elsewhere in Europe, of swaddling a child to restrict movement. His fifth recommendation is that one should gradually

---

[12] T.116.11 (M-N).

expose a child to the air, with discretion of course, a little more each time, so that it becomes acclimatized to variations in temperature. Sixth, one should sing to a child, lullabies and happy songs; and as it learns to talk a little, tell it stories. Last, Herolt advises, one should not let a baby cry very much, for a child is greatly harmed by the moisture and congestion of its crying, and then it will not grow strongly.[13]

Herolt's own preaching here closely follows one of his Christmas outlines in the *de tempore* sermons—imitation of Mary's care of the infant Jesus. Here the list of maternal actions to be reenacted spiritually includes feeding and bathing the babe, wrapping it and keeping it warm, putting it to sleep, cradling it in the arms, and singing to it "as mothers do."[14] Generally, however, the homeliness of Herolt's own sermon is not characteristic of his remarks about children in the model sermons he provided for others to use. In the sermon books, it is not the domestic particularity of child life that occupies him but the mutual obligations of parents and children and the moral status of parenthood in the eternal arbitration of sin and merit.

Parenthood

This preoccupation extends even to explaining differences in fertility between the rich and the poor. Sometimes people blame God for the fact that so often the poor have many children while the rich have few. But God does not do this without good reason. God blesses the poor with children, first as a sign of his special love for the poor; secondly, so that they may earn heavenly rewards for nourishing them; and thirdly, as an evidence of the blessedness of the poor in heaven. (There is no hint of any more material explanation.) "So the poor should not complain about the multitude of their children—they should praise God for it." By contrast, God limits the children of the rich to ensure that avaricious parents will not be prompted to even greedier acquisition for their children's sake; secondly, to place a limit on the oppression of the poor by the rich; and thirdly, to prevent rich children from being damned with their parents by inheriting unjustly held property.[15]

Parents then may merit eternal glory or eternal damnation in their children.[16] This was clearly a doctrinal question of some concern to parishioners, for Herolt returns to it repeatedly in similar terms:

> It is asked whether the labors parents have in raising and feeding their children are meritorious to them? I answer that, if parents bring up their children with the intention of their becoming good Christians and servants of God, then every single thing they do for them will

---

[13] R.6.4 (94^b-98^b).
[14] T.17.2 (K-M).
[15] T.108.3 (U-Y).
[16] D.4.3/5 (F), T.23.2/5 (O).

gain them merit—so long as they are in grace and without mortal sin. Thus as often as a mother breastfeeds her child, as often as she is disturbed by it, as often as she bathes or ministers to the child in any way, she merits every time.[17]

Several times he spells out the mundane parental tasks that earn such merit: "bathing, breastfeeding, washing, keeping watch, carrying, wrapping, lifting, feeding, informing, correcting." All are works of merit when done with right intention and in a state of grace. All the worry and toil the breadwinner undergoes to provide the children's food is similarly meritorious.[18] In later life, too, parents can merit eternal life in their children, for they always have a share in their children's good works, especially when they undertake vows of virginity or religion or works of penance; and parents are not to discourage their children from lives of religion.[19]

The Death of a Child

On the other hand, the terrible responsibility of parenthood is shown in how the sins of the parents are visited on the children. We have already heard birth defects, epilepsy, and retardation attributed to the parents' evident sin in breaching seasons of abstinence.[20] But parents may even be spiritually responsible for the death of children—indeed, deserve to have their children die, a fearful doctrine in an age when infant death was endemic. There are six reasons, Herolt says, parents deserve to have their children die.[21]

The first and most remarkable is that parents may lavish too much love and affection on their children. Too much love kills children spiritually.[22] If they love their children excessively, from their inmost heart, and feel more pleasure and love toward them than toward God, then "God sometimes in his goodness takes their children away" so that they may correct their priorities. In a curious variant on the old adage that "only the good die young," Herolt explains: "This is the reason why those children who are the most affable and prudent are the ones who die sooner—their parents love them with too much emotion, and after the world's fashion nurture them with too much care."[23] This fault sometimes translates itself onto the material plane. Inordinate love of a child—"to love a child more than God

---

[17] T.61.3 (U).
[18] D.4.3/5 (F), D.29.3/4 (G), T.23.2/5 (O), T.25.2/4 (F).
[19] Q.11.3.
[20] Q.29.1.
[21] D.23.3 (D), T.77.1 (A).
[22] T.16.1/2 (B).
[23] D.23.3 (D), T.77.1 (A).

or our salvation"—may lead a parent to retain or bequeath unjust possessions.[24] It is an act of mercy then when God sometimes takes the children of the rich in infancy.[25]

Cold comfort, this, for the recurring tragedy of the loss of babies in infancy. We might be inclined to wonder if the preacher's astringency was a pastoral device, a compensatory flattening of affect in an era that remembered more untimely death than most; but in other contexts, Herolt acknowledges the sharpness of parental, especially maternal, grief. One corollary of the fact that mothers love their children more, he says, is that they also grieve more at a child's death.[26] It is a huge consolation to a mother if she can help or support a dying child. (How great then was Mary's grief that she could not!)[27] Yet he has little sympathy for it. He is scathing about overweening grief and inconsolable mourning at the death of children:

> How great is the fatuousness of women who grieve inconsolably about the death of their children who have died after baptism and before losing baptismal innocence! It is especially fatuous for them to grieve that their children have passed from the company of men to the company of the angels, from the vale of tears to glory, from exile to homeland. They seem to be envious of them . . . they should rather rejoice that their children have so easily gained such glory for the merits of Christ's suffering![28]

It is a sure sign of a hard heart, he declares, to grieve for the death of loved ones or children but not for one's sins. Rather, we should imitate Christ's patience when he was struck and not complain to God about the loss of children.[29] Indeed, to murmur against God or the saints because of a child's death is mortal sin and a necessary subject for self-examination and pastoral questioning at the Lenten confession.[30]

We may note in passing Herolt's exposition of some other technicalities, scarcely designed to give this heartbreaking topic a more human face. An infant dying without baptism goes to the limbo of children, where it will never see God's face but suffers no sensible pain;[31] and this is a gratuitous act of divine mercy.[32]

---

[24] T.23.2/6 (Q).
[25] T.108.3 (Y).
[26] T.16.2 (E), T.116.0 (M).
[27] T.162.2 (L).
[28] D.23.2/9 (C); T.148.1 (S); cf. T.77.0 (X), where "parents" has been substituted for "women."
[29] Q.15.2-3.
[30] Q.19.2.
[31] D.1.11 (E), D.23.4/2 (F), T.41.14 (N), T.77.3 (C), Q.47.1.
[32] E.15.1/6.

Baptized infants who die in innocence share the lowest rank in heaven with deathbed penitents, since both have no actual merit of their own to add to Christ's.[33] But for similar reasons, extreme unction is not given to a dying child because it has committed no actual sin, nor does it have the capacity to receive unction with a devout disposition.[34] The one more human note in all this is the assurance that children who die in infancy will both recognize and be recognized by their families in heaven for the vision of God confers upon the insensible child the knowledge of all things.[35]

"But why," Herolt has a listener argue, "do baptized infants suffer illnesses and death? It seems quite without justice: since they are freed from all sin, they are not liable for any penalties, so they suffer unjustly!" There are two rejoinders. The first is highly theological, from Holkot: baptism removes the deprivation of the vision of God if an infant dies but not the penalties that attach to nature from the defect of original sin; hence, baptism does not absolve from liability to bodily pains and death. The second, from Albertus Magnus, is more paradoxical still: this, too, is mercy, for from the font of his kindness it is God's mercy to subject even the innocent to pains, so that others who see it may the sooner fear and be instructed.[36]

Parents may justly deserve to have their children die, not only for loving them too much, but also as a punishment for having failed to honor their own parents, for possessing property they have acquired unjustly (in which case, it is God's goodness that snatches a child out of danger), and for setting an evil example (in which case the child is mercifully preserved from the effects of imitating their perversity and evil). For less abstruse reasons, too, children may deservedly be taken away. A mother's refusal to breastfeed may cause an infant to die who might otherwise have lived, and parental negligence may lead to a child's death by drowning or fire. Herolt also transmits the old credulous fear that a baby sharing its parents' bed is in grave danger of being rolled on in sleep and suffocated.[37]

In another sermon, the motif "six reasons parents deserve a child's death" is given another form, equally guilt inducing, as "six groups of parents who kill their children spiritually." The two lists overlap: here, parents murder their own children's souls by aborting them in the womb, either deliberately or negligently; by loving them too much; by instructing them in evil; by failing to correct them when they go astray; by setting an evil example; and by amassing and bequeathing unjust possessions.[38]

---

[33] T.88.1 (L).
[34] D.27.1 (A).
[35] E.44 1.
[36] E.15.1/4.
[37] D.23.2 (D), T.77.1 (A).
[38] T.16.1 (A-C).

The Duty of Parents to Children

Sometimes, however, the list takes a more positive form: "six duties of parents to their children." A parent's first duty is to nurture children's disposition to God by urging them to offer God their innocence and purity; by giving instruction in the saving boons of the Lord's Prayer, the Creed, the Commandments, and the like; and by teaching them to attend church. Secondly, parents should inform children's behavior toward neighbors, teaching them to love them, to avoid causing them loss, and to forgive offenses. Thirdly, parents should inculcate a proper attitude to oneself, especially in keeping the body clean and chaste. The fourth parental duty is to give a good example; the fifth, to correct excesses; and last, to bequeath a just estate.[39]

Herolt's insistent theme is the liability of parents for their children's behavior. In the last judgment, parents will be required to give a strict accounting of how they dealt with the children in their charge;[40] and in anticipation of it, parents are to confess, and confessors to inquire about, failures to prevent children from sinning.[41] For all the sins of children redound to the parents if they fail to correct them.[42]

The correction of children thus has positive and negative moments. One of the constituent duties of marriage is "the due and honest education of children, preparing them for good and for the virtues, and correcting them if they go astray."[43] Positively, this takes the form of catechesis; but "it is not sufficient for parents to instruct them in good—they must also correct them when they transgress, since all the sins children perpetrate under parental obedience the parents will answer for at the last day."[44] Naturally, it is a sin—the alien sin of *jussio*—for a parent to order a child to do wrong; but it is equally a sin not to discipline a child for wrong. The alien sin of *consensus* when parents accept their children's excesses (for example, fathers and mothers who fail to disapprove their sons' and daughters' dancing) or the alien sin of *silentio* when, like Eli, they fail to censure their children's sins.[45] Parents have a particular responsibility to warn their children against theft, even of the most trifling things.[46]

---

[39] D.4.3 (C-G), D.29.317 (H), T.23.2 (H-Q).
[40] T.4.1/8 and 9 (Y).
[41] Q.19.3, Q.22.3.
[42] T.142.4 (X).
[43] D.29.3/7 (H), T.25.2/7 (L).
[44] D.4.3/5 (E), T.23.2/5 (L).
[45] T.144.1 (H) and .3 (J), T.145.7 (P).
[46] D.7.7 (D), T.104.7 (H-I).

But alas, many parents care little for the souls of their children—indeed, what is worse, they sometimes actually give them occasion to sin with clothes and costumes and rings, and they give them money for vaunting, drinking, philandering, dancing, jousting. They are putting swords in their children's hands to kill their own souls![47]

Far better for parents to give sinning children the bitterness of punishment and severity until they drive from them the poison of sin, as the bitter juice of rue repels venom.[48]

Herolt has practical advice about administering such discipline. It is a very dangerous practice, he believes, to use oaths and false threats to discipline children.[49] One must not curse a child in correcting it. He loves to retell Caesarius's story of the parents who swore at their son, "The devil take you!" and he did.[50] Mothers who raise children badly by cursing at them sin gravely against those who are also God's children.[51] Punishment must be tempered to a child's disposition: a good child who has erred out of frailty is to be disciplined gently and kindly but a recalcitrant child harshly and with rods.[52] Once again, it is generally the case that mothers are kindlier in this respect than fathers because they have more to do with the children.[53]

Faithfully performed, the parental task leads to godliness. The roots of goodness run deepest when implanted in early life. Herolt quotes with approval Aristotle's description of the child's soul as a *tabula rasa*. It is a well-prepared parchment whose first writing is almost impossible to erase, at least without vestiges remaining; it is a twig easily bent to left or right and grows in the direction it is bent. Hence, the crucial importance of a child's earliest training, which will indelibly incline him or her to good or ill. Christ's own circumcision is an object-lesson that we should begin to serve him in childhood; and accordingly, the prayer of an innocent child avails much for the living and the dead.[54]

Yet some aspects of a child's spiritual status must await rationality first and then discretion. Infants, as we saw, do not receive extreme unction partly because they do not have the disposition for devout reception. By the same token, children cannot make vows so long as their reason is not yet fully formed, and they remain under

---

[47] Q.12.1.
[48] R.7.2 (113^b).
[49] T.123.1 (F).
[50] D.4.3/5 (E), T.23.2/5 (N), etc. In other places, it is not parents and child, but a husband addressing a wife.
[51] D.23.2/8 (C).
[52] T.16.1/4 (C), T.23.2/5 (M).
[53] T.16.2 (E).
[54] T.20.0-3 (I-M).

parental authority.⁵⁵ And a child's first communion is to be delayed until it shows the signs of discretion and actual devotion, say at ten or eleven years of age.⁵⁶ The most pressing question, of course, is whether a child can sin mortally. The answer is that when a child has that use of reason that discriminates good from evil, and can know and understand what is prohibited by the commandments, then it becomes capable of mortal sin. But since people develop reason and discernment at different rates and degrees, the deciding issue is not age but discretion.⁵⁷

The Duties of Children to Their Parents

So far, we have heard the preacher address parents on their responsibility to their children; but children, of all ages, have answering duties to their parents.

The basic obligation is that of obedience.⁵⁸ Children who dishonor their parents by disobedience and impudence belie their profession of faith.⁵⁹ Love for one's parents is not only an expression of the universal obligation of love of neighbor;⁶⁰ but it is specifically demanded by the fourth commandment, and those who refuse obedience and honor to their parents in licit matters sin mortally by breaking the commandment.⁶¹

Such transgressors of the fourth commandment fall into several categories, and Herolt lists six. The first are those who are ashamed of their parents and are too disdainful to serve them, whereas "we are duty-bound humbly and reverently to serve our parents with all the strength of our body," including the simplest physical aid if it is needed. The second are those who bear hatred toward their parents in their hearts, not love; they secretly wish for their parents to die so they can inherit their estate and live as they wish without criticism. (Herolt here canvasses the Aristotelian view that parents tend to feel more love toward their children than children to parents, and acknowledges that it has some basis both in nature and experience, but hastens to add that there are exceptions, and ideally the love should be mutual.) A third group of transgressors are those who argue with their parents with harsh and acrimonious words, whereas the commandment requires that one should answer a parent civilly and accept their censure and correction with patience and humility. The Mosaic Law, the Wisdom literature, and (*a fortiori*) the Beatitudes all invoke the most terrible penalties on children who dare to curse their parents. The fourth group are those grown children who fail to support their indigent parents with the

---

⁵⁵ D.2.2/15 (Q).
⁵⁶ D.25.2/1 (H), T.47.1 (S).
⁵⁷ T.23.2 (I).
⁵⁸ T.59.3 (M).
⁵⁹ T.62.7 (B).
⁶⁰ E.9.1.
⁶¹ T.142.4 (X).

material necessities of life—poor recompense for the gifts of nature and nurture they have received from them. Even in his passion, Christ made provision for his mother's care, and even irrational creatures may be our example:

> It is said of the crane that when the mother and father have lost their feathers, the offspring forage for their needs until they grow new feathers or die.... And we read that when storks grow old, the young storks put the parents in their own nests and hold them against their breast, caress, and feed them as if they were chicks. Only vultures let their parents die of hunger!

The fifth and most inclusive category is those who disobey their parents, for honoring them must mean obeying them in those things that pertain to one's good and to salvation. It is an obedience we owe them for the threefold gift of salvation, formation, and education and embraces all such licit and salutary matters as going to mass and to church and hearing the Word of God or being silent or sitting down or going to sleep or getting up, and complying when parents forbid dancing or gambling or leaving the house at night or frequenting disreputable places. And finally, there are those who forget their parents after they die and fail to support them as they are duty-bound to do with masses, alms, pilgrimages, and prayers for their souls' release from purgatory.[62]

This last obligation, to support departed parents with suffrages, was of very practical concern to the mendicant orders and draws Herolt's special attention. Because Christ's harrowing of hell did not mean emptying purgatory, souls still must remain there until they are sufficiently purged; and we are therefore bound to support the souls of our parents by suffrages.[63] The assurance that we will do so is one of the crucial consolations the souls of our kinsfolk have in the pains of purgatory.[64] These suffrages may take the form of pious acts such as lighting candles, burning incense, sprinkling holy water, offering bread and wine, prayers, oblations, invocations of the saints, fasts, genuflections, and doing the works of holy mercy; or else they may take the practical form of shouldering the deceased's unfinished business, as by liquidating their debts, executing their wills (especially endowments for the repose of their souls, of course), fulfilling any penances imposed on them but unavoidably left incomplete, fulfilling unexecuted vows, and overlooking injuries and offenses the dead had done to oneself. But the greatest and principal suffrage is the celebration of masses for the dead.[65] Such suffrages

---

[62] D.4.1 (A), T.24.1 (S-U).
[63] T.146.5 (J).
[64] T.160.3 (F).
[65] T.160.5 (H-K).

have the additional benefit, by the way, that the souls in purgatory will in turn pray for us after they are freed.[66]

Thus parents have a right to expect sustenance and shelter in this life[67] and the support of their children's prayers after it. But failure to pray for our parents' souls is a refusal of filial submission and thus a mortal breach of the fourth commandment.[68] Five shafts of divine vengeance pierce the hearts of children who distress or fail to provide for their parents. They will be punished by impoverishment and loss of wealth; by the death or alienation of their own children; by physical debility—blindness, deafness, withering, and sundry illnesses; by the cutting short of their earthly life, for long life is the reward of honor to one's parents; and finally, the evil above all evils, by eternal death.[69]

But there are positive reasons too. Christ himself on the cross, by his care for Mary, teaches us to honor our parents by kindness in life and by provision at our death.[70] Three motives should induce us to honor our parents. The first is God's command, the only commandment with a promise attached, showing how greatly he is pleased when we keep it and displeased when we fail. The second, as we have seen, is the example of Christ, who honored his mother in her life by making her the mother of God, in her death by going out with all the company of heaven to meet her, and after death by placing her body and soul at his right hand. And third, we are prompted by the debt we owe our parents:

> From our parents we have received being, nurture, and instruction. Because we have received being from them, we should hold them in great reverence: "Honor your father, and do not forget your mother's groaning; remember that if they had not given you birth, you would not have existed" (Ecclus. [7:27-8]). Because we have received nurture from them, we should take great care of them, so that as they have diligently nurtured us in youth, we should nurture them with diligence in age: "Son, support your father in his old age, and do not distress him as long as he lives" (Ecclus. [3:12]). Because we have received instruction from them, we owe them great obedience: "Children obey your parents, for it is right that you should" (Ephes. [6:1]).[71]

The preacher is deeply troubled by the knowledge that many parents do not mold their children toward godliness, that their example (the most potent formative

---

[66] T.160.4 (G).
[67] T.116.2 (N).
[68] T.142.4 (X).
[69] D.4.2 (B), T.24.2 (X), cf. Q.19.3/4.
[70] Q.13.1, Q.42.1.
[71] Q.22.1.

force) is not always a good one, that fathers and mothers do not disapprove—indeed actively stimulate—the worldly pleasures of their young, and that they entangle their heirs in the webs of material greed. In the face of this threat to the very fabric of social cohesion, his austere prescription is tighter disciplinary control. There is only one relationship in life that may supersede the bond of duty between parent and child. It is not marriage, for though one has a duty to love one's spouse more than one's parents, one is bound to honor one's parents more than one's spouse.[72] Rather, it is the religious life.

Parents are not to discourage or impede their children from taking the vows of religion. Does not the decretal promise that "it avails to the parents' salvation if their offspring persevere in virginity"?[73] Even here, the obligation to provide for one's parents may possibly cause a person not to enter religion, if they are in very great need and there is no one else to support them—provided, that is, that one is capable of remaining in the world without danger of sinning. "But once religious profession is made, one is dead to the world. By this spiritual death, one's obligation is to God, and the care now expended on parents is dismissed, without sin or contravention of the precept."[74]

In every other case, the relationship envisaged by the preacher is lifelong. In a time when the bonds of family interdependence were so much more tenacious than now, there was none of our preoccupation with personal autonomy or adolescent passage to self-determination. It did not occur to churchmen to question that the fourth commandment was binding for life. One result is that, when Herolt speaks of "children," it is not immediately obvious what age-group he is addressing: a single sermon about parents and children may encompass all age-groups from cradle to grave, and it is only from the context that we guess the age of the "children" in a particular instruction. Accordingly, the real and perennial complexity of raising children, and the eager, impulsive testing and turmoil of youth, are foreshortened in an account where the infant spirit formlessly awaits the indelible impress of parental indoctrination where reason, discrimination, and accountability emerge in tandem at puberty, and where adolescent exuberance is feared and hated as the poison of sin. Herolt, after all, tells us very little about the lives of children.

---

[72] E.9.1.
[73] Q.11.3.
[74] E.9.1.

VIRTUE AND VICE IN SOCIETY

14

SOCIETY

Herolt flourished in an era when the church was still the most powerful institution in Western society. Ecclesiastical structures were the oldest, stablest, and most international institutions in European life. The church was the wealthiest and largest landholder, sometimes controlling half the land in a kingdom. Its bishops were a noble elite. It had a taxation system that reached into every corner of society, despite the resistance of secular rulers. In the clerical class, and monasticism in particular, the church had at its disposal Europe's largest, most unified, and most disciplined body of manpower. It was sedition to threaten the unity of the state religion, and it was a capital crime to contradict the doctrine of the Trinity. Pastorally, the clergy were in a position to exercise a powerful discipline over the public and private lives of their people.

The church enjoyed a far wider sphere of responsibility for the daily lives of citizens than did the state: all manner of regulations for which we now hold governments accountable in those days belonged to the church. Everyone assumed its right to supervise and regulate morality, family life, education, even commerce and warfare.

This power was not without its weak links. Politically, the papacy never regained the zenith of worldly power it had reached in the thirteenth century (though its greatest temporal splendor still lay ahead). The evolution of national self-consciousness in some regions had created resistant and countervailing centers of power. Herolt's first works saw the light of day during the Council of Constance, where national and lay power mandated the healing of an intractable papal schism that had scandalously threatened the catholicity of the Western church from within. Pastorally, and despite the efforts of the mendicant orders, the church's hold over the minds and hearts of the great neglected mass of rural lay folk was tenuous and superficial at best. And in the cities and along the conduits of trade, social and economic changes of a poorly understood and unforeseeably potent kind were disturbing the firm and settled ethical convictions sanctified by the church.

Occasionally, in an aside or an admonition, Herolt betrays the disquiet such changes evoked in the church's spokesmen. For the most part, nonetheless, the preacher offers a social ethic of an ostensibly timeless sort, indifferent to the fluctuations of cultural change, because founded on a God-given order whose disappearance is unimaginable. Though Herolt is well aware of the diversity of jurisdictions, and acknowledges regional variations in custom and law, he assumes as axiomatic the permanence of hierarchical order and of the feudal pattern of exchange where protection and provision from above are exchanged for ready obedience from below.[1]

The classic biblical justification for this view of society is the apostle Paul in Romans 13: "All power is from God, and one who resists authority resists the ordination of God." Herolt quotes it often. But it was Augustine of Hippo who had charged Paul's admonition with that deeply formative energy which shaped the social teaching of the Western church and the very institutions of European culture. Augustine declared that all order was attributable to God. He came gradually to the "profoundly pessimistic conclusion"[2] that the structures of human authority were a divine discipline, a necessary restraint on the wanton, chaotic self-indulgence of sinful mankind. It was a judgment that at once permitted a divine sanction on existing authority and a realistic recognition of the abuses by rulers of their power. At length, in a Christian society, it mandated the supervision of secular authority by churchly authority.

All these overtones sound when Herolt quotes from Romans 13 himself. The lesson of Christ's appearance before Pilate, he says, is this: secular authority is not to be despised but honored. "All power is from God, and one who resists authority resists the ordination of God" (Rom. 13). Hence the Lord said to Pilate, "You would have no power over me unless it was given you from above." Now, God gives power to rulers first so that they may restrain their subjects from evil, second so that they may compel them to good. For doing so they will have great merit in heaven: as 1 Tim. 5 says, "Let those that lead well be deemed worthy of double honor." So, too, it says in the decretals (21 q. 4: *"si ecclesia"*): "Rulers serve God by living uprightly and directing their subjects faithfully." Accordingly, authority is good and thus honorable. "Fear God and honor the king" (1 Peter 2). Augustine says, "God as

---

[1] E.3.1; E.30.2/2.
[2] Peter Brown, *Augustine of Hippo*, 238.

man was standing before Pilate the man, and no word of irreverence was spoken." So we too must stand before our rulers and willingly obey them in God's place.[3]

The greater a ruler's rank, the more honor he deserves—"the pope throughout the whole world, the bishop in his diocese, the rector in his parish; the king in his kingdom, the prince in his domain, the mayor in his city; the wife her husband, ... the servant his master and the maid her mistress, the religious his abbot or prior." Such honor is to be paid to them even if they are malicious, "not indeed for their malice, but insofar as they act as God's regents and have been appointed to his court."[4]

But the greater a person's power, the more perilous his abuse of it, since it entails scandal and even the ruin of others.[5] Those who are set in great honor should remember that they too will share a lowly grave.[6] There have been great and godly kings—David, the sainted emperors Henry and Oswald, King Louis of France—who though inwardly humble were greatly exalted both here and in heaven.[7] Judas Maccabaeus, Charlemagne, Henry, and Louis attest that one who wields the sword well may be sanctified by it, but the sword itself is not holy.[8] There are proud and ambitious men who actively seek high honor, leadership, and power over others in ways that belie their profession of faith.[9] Herolt roundly condemns "those rulers and governors who understand nothing of their power and rank except to swagger, and spend all day in tournaments, the hunt, drinking, dice games, and all the other worldly vanities, but never or rarely concern themselves with protecting the poor, widows, clergy, orphans, or religious, even though there is no other reason God has conferred their power on them except the defence of the church and the poor."[10]

The warning not to fail in the exercise of God-given authority is addressed not only to "you rulers and lords, you judges and potentates"; but in the same breath to "you husbands and family heads, you masters and mistresses." We have already examined the structures of power within the family; we are therefore well placed to understand the morality of public power. For the same relationship of God-given authority and submissive obedience that exists domestically between husband and wife, parents and children, and householders and their servants obtains socially between the ruling classes and their subjects. Whenever the preacher treats the question of mutual obligations between superiors and underlings, those

---

[3] Q.23.2/2.
[4] T.28.1/2 (F).
[5] Q.22.0.
[6] Q.40.1.
[7] T.31.1 (J).
[8] T.59.1/1 (H).
[9] T.62.4 (A).
[10] D.11.8 (L), T.59.1/1 (H).

in authority in church, state, and home are addressed together. The prelate and the paterfamilias, the monarch and the master exercise a like authority; and every subordinate, whether wife, child, manservant, maidservant, commoner, counsellor, or deputy, owes a parallel debt of obedience to his or her lord and master.[11]

Consequently, there is a striking degree of overlap between Herolt's model sermon on the mutual obligations of householders and domestics and his sermon on rulers and subjects.[12] Servants, maids, and attendants have three obligations to their masters and mistresses: first, to be loyal in handling their property, preventing loss, augmenting wealth, and avoiding timeserving, negligence, and larceny; second, to obey their lawful orders and not to provoke their displeasure; and third, to perform their labor and service with a right intention toward God and a due observance of pious exercises.[13] The duties of subjects to their rulers are likewise three: to be loyal, in body by not betraying them, in property by preventing loss, and in soul by giving no wicked advice; second, to obey all lawful commands within their jurisdiction; and third, not to withhold or retain any taxes, returns, or goods owing to rulers.[14]

The parallel continues with the reciprocating responsibilities of superiors. Masters and mistresses are obliged to provide adequate food and drink to their servants (unlike some who treat their underlings like beasts and without brotherly love); to be unpretentious, charitable, and benign to them (unlike some who are irascible, contemptuous, and unfriendly, like the master in Gregory's tale who snarled at a maid, "Come, you devil, take off my shoes!" and the devil did); and to correct them faithfully, for masters are accountable for their servants' faults.[15] *Mutatis mutandis*, the obligations of rulers to their subjects are precisely the same on a civic or national scale: to defend their territory and people, since they have been given the sword to guard the land and folk God has entrusted to them, to force men to live in peace, to defend the church, and to protect the helpless and needy; secondly, to be merciful to their subjects, if they wish God to be merciful to them, and especially to act justly in the matter of taxes and subsidies; and lastly, to be God-fearers and humble in dealing with other men. By contrast, subjects are punished now for their excesses, and no one tells a ruler the painful truth; yet God will be no respecter of persons at the judgment.[16]

Herolt is all too acutely aware that power corrupts, and that many rulers will have much to answer for in judgment, if not their own excesses, their failure to prevent those of their agents and deputies. Some tyrannical princes hold cheap the

---

[11] D.11.7-8 (K-L), T.59.3 (M), T.145.7-8 (P-R).
[12] T.33 and T.59.
[13] T.33.1 (A-C).
[14] T.59.3 (M).
[15] T.33.2 (E-H).
[16] T.59.1 (H-K).

lives of their subjects and kill to enforce their sway; they are not better than common murderers.[17] More frequently, the oppressive burden of exactions, levies, and taxes provokes the just complaint of the people against their rulers. Abuses of political power inevitably take the form of financial oppression above all. Herolt certainly affirms the duty of subjects "by ancient law" to pay taxes and tithes and to honor the public proprietorship of the ruler,[18] and he admits the occasional necessity for auxiliary subsidies and supplemental levies.[19] But too many rulers are sharks who protect the sprats only to swallow them themselves; they defend their people from outside attack only to despoil them with crushing burdens.[20] (As the knight says in one of Herolt's tales, underlings are just "sheep to be fleeced.")[21] Such tyrants are high on the list of common thieves;[22] and Herolt declares that, once begun, these oppressors of the poor find it excessively difficult to forgo their habit of exactions on their subjects and the poor and of extorting service from them.[23] Perhaps for this reason, Herolt states the curious principle that superiors may actually gain merit by forgoing exactions on their subjects; but less sanguinely, he also says that the subjects gain merit by sustaining exactions with patience.[24]

To be just, taxes and subsidies must remain within the assessments contained in the census.[25] Any further demands constitute extortion and theft. Except in certain stipulated cases, prelates and lords who impose stern and undue exactions on their subjects beyond the census are just as guilty of treason as a traitorous subject, for a lord owes the same faith to his subject as the subject to his lord. Unjustified levies, he says hopefully, must be reimbursed.[26] The exceptions are a small number of "rational causes" which may justify a moderate subsidy. Herolt lists four. The first is defense of the country from wrongful invasion by enemies (in which case subjects owe not only financial support but active military service). The second is ransom for the ruler himself if he is captured in the course of a just war. The third is when the ruler is required by his overlord or the pope or even his people themselves to go on crusade against heretics or pagans. And the fourth is the military outfitting of the ruler's son or the marriage of his daughter. These and

---

[17] T.142.5 (Y).
[18] T.59.3 (M), Q.40.2.
[19] T.59.1/2 (I).
[20] T.127.1/4 (H).
[21] D.7.1/2 (C), T.59.1/2 (K).
[22] D.7.1/2 (C).
[23] T.58.1 (F).
[24] T.150.2 (U) and 3 (Y).
[25] On public finances in the cities, see, e.g., Hermann Kellenberg, *Deutsche Wirtschaftgeschichte Bd I: Von den Anfangen bis zum Ende des 18. Jahrhunderts* (München: Beck, 1977), 202-10.
[26] Q.40.2.

similar expenses may be petitioned from the people in moderation and without coercion. To the objection that without compulsion no one would pay, Herolt rejoins that the ruler is commissioned to protect, not to despoil or extort, and that afflicting one's own servants is "devilish domination."[27] Exacting levies by force is an act of violence and the offspring of avarice.[28]

Of all the occasions for extra subsidies, the costliest and most burdensome is warfare. As we have just seen, military defense of one's territory and people is not only legitimate but a ruler's duty. He is "to exert himself manfully in defence of his subjects."[29] In practice, however, the recurrent warfare to which rulers commit their people may be anything but just. The first subject for the people's prayer at Rogationtide is "that God will restrain the wars that so often break out in spring."[30] "Now, alas," Herolt says, "it is quite common for the merchants and the peasants to discharge the entire cost of a war when they never gave any cause or occasion for it!" This unjust burden makes them martyrs of Christ.[31] Culpability for these depredations often rests as much on the shoulders of courtiers, counsellors, and deputies of rulers as on the incumbents themselves:

> It is sin when the evil counsellors of lords and princes advise wars, rapine, and extortion. Others urge fornications and thefts and the like. It is a sin when anyone at all gives advice that leads to fellow-citizens' loss, whether it is to impose a new tariff, or to make an old tariff heavier and larger, or to make harsher the census of paupers; similarly those in cities at whose advice new institutions are created at the expense of the poor and the commons. Such counsellors are guilty of all the crimes perpetrated or to be perpetrated on their advice.[32]

Sometimes abuses of the taxation system are also the fault of corrupt officials—tax collectors who on the one hand extort payments from the people and on the other cream off their own percentage before making returns to the prince.[33] Middlemen in the power structure often encumber their underlings in order to discharge their own obligations to overlords: "For debts owed to their lords they unjustifiably mortgage citizens and other subjects. It is theft in God's eyes when the property of the poor is thus unduly attached, while the prosperity

---

[27] D.7.1/2 (C), T.59.1/2 (J).
[28] D.17.2/3 (E).
[29] T.127.1/4 (H).
[30] T.64.0 (H).
[31] T.104.3 (F).
[32] D.11.2 (B), T.144.2 (J).
[33] T.59.3/3 (M).

of the principal debtors or the lords is spared."[34] Finally, however, it remains the solemn responsibility of a subordinate's chief to prevent derelictions and crimes on the deputy's part:

> So you rulers and lords who do not restrain your lieutenants, but leave them free to plunder poor folk—filching hens and geese and ducks and herds, feeding your horses by grazing them in their crops, stealing or raiding the fruit of their orchards and their vines, disparaging or beating or hurting or deriding the poor and cheating them—for all such deeds, if you fail to stop your underlings, you will be condemned.[35]

The principle that must control all the actions of the highest classes of society is this: true nobility consists in the virtues. A noble should be recognized by his virtues, not by the outward trappings of his rank. If clothes made the man—if noblemen were recognizable by "long tunics and huge sleeves and the large number of slits they wear in their cloaks"—then even craftsmen and peasants would be nobles because "nowadays they all want slits in their clothes!"[36] No, the source of nobility is the virtues: a noble is one whose virtue ennobles him.[37]

In particular, there are five principal virtues that ought to characterize the nobility. The first is generosity; the more generous a man, the nobler he is. Harshness, greed, plunder, and extortion of one's subjects are a sign of ignobility. But in practice, noblemen and the rich commonly despise the poor and look down on the lower classes for their want of nobility.[38] The second noble characteristic is gratitude—recognition of the blessings of God and of man. Nobles owe a practical debt of gratitude to the subjects who sustain them, for "noblemen themselves do not plough the fields or sow or reap or thresh, they do not work in the vineyards, they do not prepare bread or meat or fish or other food." It is others—farmers, butchers, tailors, cobblers, bakers—who feed and clothe them. The nobler a man really is, the more he will acknowledge their work; and those who disdainfully avoid the working classes show themselves ignoble. The third mark is mercy and compassion; a harsh and pitiless lord is no noble in God's eyes. The fourth is manliness and exertion in defense of one's subjects. And the fifth is magnanimity, an indifference to trivial and mundane things and a deep hunger for spiritual things. In the absence of these virtues, no one has any intrinsic right to be honored.[39] For

---

[34] T.104.3 (F).
[35] D.11.8 (L), T.144.8 (R).
[36] T.127.1 (E).
[37] E.7.3/1.
[38] E.7.3/2.
[39] T.127.1 (F-H).

nobles and commoners are all brothers: all come naked, all share one death. In this sense, there is no difference between a nobleman's grave and a peasant's.[40]

Thus while rank and power come high on the list of reasons to give honor in society, they are preceded by virtue first of all and gain their esteem because they share in God's own dignity. In theory then, honor is not simply identified with status. Who is to judge the justice of the powerful, the virtue of the nobility? Obviously the preacher has no wish to incite questioning on the part of the masses, to whom he recommends submissive obedience and the patient toleration of wrongs. That task falls instead to the priestly ministry, whose honor exceeds that of the angels and of "all kings, princes, knights, and nobles."[41] It is for the exercise of that prerogative, not the fomenting of dissidence, that the preacher lectures rulers on their duty and nobles on their virtue.

The institutional form of this prerogative is the liberty of the church—clerical immunity from secular jurisdiction and taxation.[42] Major excommunication is the penalty imposed on rulers for financial or legal impediments upon the church.[43]

There is a hint of a subtler form of clerical self-interest—the class consciousness of the urban clergy—in Herolt's ethical dilemma concerning the honor accorded wealthy leading citizens. A person is to be honored, he says, for holding a higher place in the community and for the greater contribution he can thereby make to it; and on Thomas's authority, the rich are to be honored because they can obtain those higher positions. But if someone were to be honored solely on account of his wealth, that would be flagrant respect of persons. So it becomes a matter of motive: if I judge in my heart that a wealthy man because of his wealth is better than a poor man because of his poverty, that is a sin; but if I honor the rich not for their material trappings but for their leading role in promoting the community, that is right and proper.[44]

It appears that the clergy's self-interest takes a double, if not ambivalent, form. The long defense of priestly liberties had the effect of creating amongst all the clergy a solidarity and cohesion that contributed greatly to their institutional power and practical effectiveness. Yet they remained part of the society in which they operated and reflected the assumptions of their social class. Accordingly, even when they repeated dogmas, laws, and sanctions of venerable antiquity, their adaptation of these rules to new secular interests rarely impeded the continuous course of social development in the long term.

In the short term, however, and perhaps especially in the realm of economic innovation, the conservatism of official church morality often lagged behind secular

---

[40] E.7.3/1.
[41] T.28.1-5 (E-H).
[42] T.111.1/3 (U).
[43] T.69.2 (K).
[44] T.28.6 (I).

developments. Thus Herolt threatens with major excommunication those rulers, princes, eminent personages, consuls, and rectors of cities who enact legislation requiring the payment of usury and also any scribes, guardians, provosts, magistrates and officials who make, write, dictate, promulgate, observe, or judge according to such statutes.[45] There are clear traces here of the classic running battle between moral arbiters and administrative pragmatists. Again, the making of certain loans on interest is no less usurious, Herolt argues, just because the lender happens to be a friendly society of citizens or a civic authority or council. Nor are town councils or community associations any more entitled than individuals to lend on mortgage without taking the produce of the land into account.[46] We shall return to this topic later.[47]

Thus issues that for modern European law arise in government regulation of the private sector arise for Herolt and his contemporaries in ecclesiastical regulation of the public sector and of social morality at large. Moreover, many of the modern rules of equity and citizens' rights before the law have their roots in the theories of the canonists. So it is not surprising to find the preacher explicitly laying down the law, commenting formally on matters of jurisprudence and legal ethics.

Justice, he insists in particular, is not for sale. Perversion of justice, all the way to judicial murder, may be perpetrated because of conflict of interest, when a judge has a personal stake in the outcome owing to kinship, friendship, or enmity with the parties. There must be no payment in advance prejudicing the outcome of a case: even though an advocate or legal expert may charge a fee, a magistrate must not sell his judgment, nor a witness his true testimony.[48] Even the advocate is not automatically entitled to his fee. Raymundus is Herolt's authority for asserting that an advocate may demand a moderate salary, not before the hearing by contract without penalty, but only after the case is finished. The amount to be paid is to be adjusted for the size of the case, the amount of work involved, and the customary local scale of fees. The penalty provisions make even this payment uncertain. So far from being remunerated, an advocate must make restitution to his client for any property lost because of poor advocacy if, for example, he fails to prevent unjust dispossession of a patrimony, or if a good case is dismissed or prejudiced because of his cavilling, unjustifiable delaying tactics, false allegations, or suborning of witnesses. An advocate is also liable for losses owing to any breach of faith, negligence, ignorance of the law, or inflation of his qualifications.[49]

---

[45]   T.69.2 (K), T.105.2/10 (R).
[46]   T.114.2/7 (C).
[47]   See chapter 20.
[48]   D.8.2/9 (E-F).
[49]   E.37.3.

A witness in a court case may not accept a fee for testifying but may be reimbursed for out-of-pocket expenses.[50] False testimony or perjury in a court of law seems to Herolt a pervasive and especially vicious form of lying. False witnesses kill the neighbor's soul, deny Christ by corrupting the truth, and cause irreparable loss to a fellow citizen's property, repute, or person.[51] The deliberate attempt to defraud another party by lying under oath is a mortal sin, as is the making of a false deposition before a judge or ruler.[52] We must especially avoid laying trumped-up charges against a defendant, lest we become like those who falsely accused Christ before Caiaphas.[53]

Yet church teaching condemns various supernatural devices designed to reveal or circumvent perjury. Herolt rejects judicial ordeals as breaches of the first commandment. The practice of confirming truth, establishing guilt, and resolving disputes by requiring someone to hold a bar of glowing iron or to plunge a hand into boiling water or to engage in a duel is strictly forbidden, in part because the performance of some sort of miracle is there demanded from God; in part because these tests are supposed to adjudicate hidden matters which are reserved to divine judgment; and in part, too, because this sort of test is not sanctioned but prohibited by divine authority. Accordingly, no assistance or advice is to be given to people who are tempting God by carrying out such ordeals. Rather they are to be restrained from doing so, for if they die in the process they will be damned eternally.[54]

This canonical prohibition recognizes that the capacity of a human court to determine the truth is severely limited. Two legal principles flow from this assumption. The first principle is that in a court of law all words and actions are to be interpreted in the most favorable light.[55] The second is that when a judge remains uncertain of the truth of some testimony, he has the discretion to require an oath in confirmation, on the assumption that a witness will fear to perjure himself solemnly. But Herolt is disquieted by the resulting practice of offering oaths voluntarily as a way of settling litigation. It creates a temptation to perjury. And since such an oath is *prima facie* evidence of truthfulness, it may place a plaintiff in the situation of accepting in law an oath that he knows for certain to be false or frivolous, thus paradoxically creating complicity in a wrong against himself, as well as a sin against God. Confronted with this situation, a litigant ought to withdraw his complaint and accept the loss rather than go along with a legal charade.[56]

---

[50] D.8.1 (D), T.133.2/4 (M).
[51] D.8.1 (A), T.96.2/1 (P), T.143.8/1 (D).
[52] D.8.1 (D), T.113.2/4 (M).
[53] Q.16.2/2.
[54] D.1.1/10 (J), T.41.6 (H).
[55] E.44.2/2.
[56] D.2.2/14 (J).

Two other matters display Herolt's technical interest in the law. One is the categories of justifiable and unjustifiable homicide; the other is the rule of inheritance. With the aid of Thomas and the canons, he carefully distinguishes four modes of killing. First, of course, a judge in fulfilment of his office may impose a sentence of death and the executioner carry it out. Capital punishment is licit, so long as the motive is removal of a rotten limb from the body politic and the protection of the common good; but if the motive of either the judge or the executioner is revenge or lust for blood, it is a sin even if the criminal is rightly condemned.[57] It ought to create the gravest difficulty for a judge to condemn a man to die because of the dignity of human nature.[58] Incidentally, once an execution has been carried out, the judge's licence is required before the body may be taken from the gallows for burial "lest any contempt of court be inferred"; but if that permission is granted, a hanged or beheaded criminal may be buried in a church cemetery so long as he had repented.[59] The second sort of homicide is killing out of necessity for self-defense. Here the distinction is to be drawn between avoidable and unavoidable necessity: if the need for self-defense could have been avoided, by evasion for instance, the killing is murder, but if unavoidable and performed more in sorrow than in anger, then it is no sin. The category of self-defense applies only to one's person and not to the protection of property. The third case is accidental death, which is culpable manslaughter where there has been criminal negligence, such as throwing a stone or javelin in a heavily frequented area, but no sin where due care has been taken but accidental death results, perhaps from archery in a private location or from felling a tree with the requisite precautions. And the fourth case is deliberate murder, which without distinction is always an enormity.[60]

There are seven ways, Herolt explains, to establish a legal right of inheritance. The first is the rule of proximation, the simple right of inheritance by blood relationship. The second is the rule of permutation or exchange between two heirs, when each formally relinquishes his right of inheritance in exchange for the other's right. The third is the purchase of an inheritance for cash. Fourthly, marriage creates a right of inheritance for a surviving spouse, since their property is legally held in common. Fifthly, a right of inheritance may be established by war, when a dispossessed heir regains a lost inheritance by the sword. Next, a hearing before a law judge may restore a disputed estate to a rightful heir. And finally, one may inherit by grace of adoption, when someone gratuitously adopts another as his heir.[61] Herolt is greatly exercised by the spiritual effects of unjust inheritance on both testators and beneficiaries. A strict accounting of the disposition of one's estate

---

[57] D.5.2/1 (C).
[58] D.5.2/9 (G).
[59] D.20.2 (F), T.89.7 (S-T).
[60] D.5.2/1-4 (C-D).
[61] T.159.3 (X).

will be demanded at the last judgment.[62] Herolt clearly feels that such a potentially controverted area of property law requires strict regulation. But it is perhaps the protection of the church's own large stake in the disposition of wills that animates his attack on executors who prolong the settlement of estates; they defraud the dead and offend God by their temporizing, he declares.[63]

From his very earliest writings, Herolt's frequent and precise citations of canon law reveal his competence in this field; but it is always a pragmatic, not a merely academic, concern. Whatever interest he displays in legal technicalities, he is far more interested in the maintenance of justice and equity in everyday social relationships. The will of God, he insists, is "that we should deal with our neighbor in equity—that in all our dealings we should follow the rule contained in natural law." All our words, deeds, and principles toward our fellow citizens must be marked by an outgoing honesty.[64] In terms of sheer quantity, a very large proportion of Herolt's preaching is devoted to encouraging neighborliness and to identifying and rebuking antisocial attitudes and behavior. If legal structures are a necessary safeguard against human sinfulness, nevertheless, the social fabric is maintained by neighborly solicitude. Though Herolt never questions the vertical order of authority and honor, the horizontal order of mutual benevolence and fraternal correction is far more central to his social ethic. His blindness to the web of tensions between the two orders, or the impossibility of modifying one without the other, may be the result of naiveté or the perennial incomprehension of the socially fortunate, but not any lack of the best intentions.

Incidentally, the social setting Herolt assumes for most of his moral commentary is an urban setting. The life of the mendicant orders in particular was bound up in inextricable ways with the cities, which were an essential environment for their growth and survival economically, intellectually, and religiously.[65] Yet Herolt is frank to admit that the honorable behavior he wants to encourage is harder to attain in the corrupting environment of the city. Christ wept over Jerusalem—over a city, not a village. Cities are far more dangerous, since worldly wisdom reigns in them more than the wisdom of God and resists godliness. In cities, people are more ambitious, voluptuous, luxurious, grasping than in villages; and more sins are perpetrated in cities because people live drunkenly and grow lukewarm in their lethargy—two states that increase the likelihood of sin—while people who live in

---

[62] T.3.2/4 (S).
[63] T.160.6/3 (O-P).
[64] T.102.2/4-5 (M).
[65] Cf. R. W. Southern, *Western Society and the Church in the Middle Ages: The Pelican History of the Church Volume Two* (Grand Rapids: Wm.B. Eerdmans Publishing Co., 1970), 272-99.

villages spend more of their time in unremitting work. They eat their meat and fall asleep, cutting short the opportunity for sin.[66]

Even physically, Herolt remarks, the pollution of cities is an unhealthy environment. The ancients lived longer because they did not crowd their cities and compounds so densely. "You can see this now in any city: there is a great stench in the streets, and from the odors many grow ill and die quickly." For the sake of public health, he declares, cities must be kept clean.[67]

In the chapters that follow, we shall examine in some detail the preacher's particular advice and reproof concerning social communication, conspicuous consumption, leisure, trade and property, and the outcasts of society. In the meantime, we may quickly review the underlying principles of civic behavior that should direct our intercourse in each of these areas. In spite of moral and physical pollution, the legal rule of construing actions in the most favorable light must also apply informally in one's judgment of a neighbor.[68] It is, after all, a simple application of the golden rule to grant someone else the same benefit of the doubt we allow ourselves.[69] It is a mark of the elect that they place the best possible construction on a neighbor's behavior, not merely outwardly but in the heart.[70] Herolt devotes an entire sermon to the sources and expressions of suspicion and unfounded judgment of a neighbor. It has various sources: The elderly tend to be suspicious because of the accumulated bitterness of a lifetime; dislike or jealousy of another inevitably jaundices one's judgment of him; and if the one judging is himself evil or perverse, he will automatically suspect others of a like malice. But the root cause is pride, since the truly humble hold others to be better than them. Herolt recommends a mental exercise: look to see if your neighbor has some good quality you lack; reflect on some defect in yourself that you do not see in your neighbor; or even if you can find no apparent good in the other, suppose that it is hidden inside him. Better to be mistaken often by having a good opinion of an evil man than to do someone an injustice. "The nectar a bee extracts from a flower it turns into honey, but the spider turns it into poison."[71]

Unless this rule is followed, suspicion will soon escalate to dangerous levels. There is an innocuous stage of prudent caution that is not really suspicion at all (the illustration that springs to Herolt's mind is the enclosure of nuns). Unbidden thoughts of a judgmental sort should be resisted. The danger arises when one first begins to doubt a neighbor's goodness from little signs. Next one decides that he certainly is bad on the basis of inadequate evidence or trivial faults. Then finally

---

[66] T.105.0 (before N).
[67] T.60.3/4 (P).
[68] E.44.2/2.
[69] D.30.2/3 (C-D).
[70] T.149.5 (F), T.154.2/3 (P).
[71] T.90.2 (D), E.3.2.

suspicion issues in defamation or actual violence or a definitive judgment that another person is intrinsically evil.[72] One of the most insidious forms of criticism, Herolt points out shrewdly, is animosity masquerading as sententious concern, a specious solicitude for another's "well-being" concealing hostile fault-finding.[73] The chief practical difficulty confronting the listener is that, as well as warning against censoriousness, the preacher also enjoins fraternal correction as the Christian's duty. Correction of subjects, employees, or children can be simply explained by the hierarchical principle, but correction of an equal clearly poses risks of a different sort.

No doubt Herolt is drawing on the long pastoral experience of the monastic chapter of faults when he speaks cautiously of the duty of fraternal correction. What makes such correction possible is the promise that judgment from firsthand observation of an undeniable fact is quite legitimate. Criticism in this case is no sin, so long as the fault observed cannot possibly be interpreted as good and the criticism is offered in hope of the wrongdoer's emendation.[74] Fraternal correction must proceed from charity, not from indignation or contempt; and its motive must be the utility of the one corrected, not a display of one's own power. It must be lenient, not clamorous, or else it will be not correction but confusion. Nevertheless, it remains a solemn obligation and must not be avoided for fear of vulgar reaction, timidity, or self-interest.[75] Fraternal correction is spiritual almsgiving, one of the spiritual works of mercy, but one must choose favorable circumstances to speak. And there are conditions, inner and outer, in which one should refrain from criticism. Herolt repeats the traditional monastic advice from Gregory's *Moralia*: consider whether you are yourself guilty of an equal or greater fault, if you have not ever been like the one to be reproved, that you may become like him in the future, what commendable features he also possesses, and the possibility that in spite of his apparent lapse he may be preferred to you in God's eyes.

The result of these reflections may be that reproof is far less appropriate than compassion, or even silence. There are five circumstances in which one should certainly refrain: if there seems no hope at all of correction; if the charge cannot be firmly substantiated; if a public authority such as a judge has taken note of the matter; if the critic himself cannot equal or surpass the good actions of the one criticized; or if it is a matter of correcting a mass of people, or an authority figure, the difficulty of both situations is likely to make the attempt counterproductive.[76]

---

[72] T.54.3 (T), T.90.1 (U-A), E.3.2.
[73] D.15.4/2 (G).
[74] T.90.1/7 (C).
[75] D.20.2/2 (K).
[76] T.63.2 (E).

The other side of the coin, of course, is that one must be willing to acknowledge and accept rebuke from a neighbor.[1] Since it is occasionally appropriate in correction to use somewhat insulting language, one should patiently endure the rebuff—that is, unless by doing so one encourages a bold and spiteful critic to abuse others too or endanger one's reputation or create problems for some third party.[2] As Herolt adds qualification upon qualification, a familiar process takes place: learned distinctions and pastoral discretion combine to turn a rather simple ethical injunction into an immobilizing mass of loopholes.

The underlying exhortation remains clear, however. Upright social behavior is peaceable, while intentional discord is mortal sin.[3] People who enjoy disputes are servants of the devil. By relying on clamor their contentiousness impugns the power of truth.[4] Too often, people are ready to rejoice in a neighbor's loss or be saddened by his prosperity, whereas the proper response is one of joy at his material and spiritual well-being[5] and willingness to share one's substance in his need.[6] One should always assume that a neighbor is worthy of respect. But in practice, many people despise their neighbors for their lack of status, for poverty, for handicaps or disfigurement, and for their sins.[7] Such a lack of compassion is a sign of pharisaic contempt[8] and springs especially from a life that is too secure and free of trials. One's brethren are disdained because they are subject to trials "that ought not to befall Christians" and treated with a hard-hearted, pitiless refusal of compassion and sympathy.[9]

To sow discord is to perform exactly the opposite mission to Christ's.[10] The chief sources of social dissension are identified over and over again as scandal, vindictiveness, contention, and above all slander, detraction, defamation, derision, and contumely (of which more shortly).[11] Any resort to actual physical aggression is fiercely condemned.[12] One who wishes to receive the heavenly prize "must not and cannot proceed by violence, but by virtue."[13] Though the fear of

---

[1] R.3.3 (33ᵇ).
[2] D.15.2/7 (C), T.63.2 (F), Q.33.1.
[3] E.8.4.
[4] E.10.4.
[5] D.14.2/2 (B) and .3/4 (F), E.4.1.
[6] T.150.4 (A), E.6.5.
[7] E.7.3.
[8] T.107.0 (H).
[9] T.40.2/4-5 (D).
[10] T.96.2/3 (R).
[11] See chapter 17.
[12] D.14.2/3 (D), T.95.8 (M), T.96.3 (T), T.131.3 (F), T.141.5 (N).
[13] T.31.0 (before I).

scandal—chiefly sexual scandal—is recognized as a potent brake on antisocial behavior, embarrassment is a dubious motive for avoiding sin.[14]

Our duty is to place the common good before the private good.[15] In practice, this means threading the narrow path between the opposing dangers of individualism on one side and conformism on the other. Individualism—the attempt to establish our own singularity by idiosyncratic language, behavior, or morality—is a symptom of self-aggrandizement and to be avoided at all costs. In the religious form of self-chosen spiritual exercises and austerities, it is an error of conscience.[16] One should conform to the social behavior of good men. But on the other hand, the desire to be like others in order to retain their approval is a snare of the devil.[17] The worldly wisdom of the majority systematically misrepresents goodness as priggishness but commends dissoluteness as social bonhomie—going along with the crowd in everything right or wrong, especially its merriments and amusements.[18]

Repeatedly, the listener is challenged to discover the happy mean between tolerance, compassion, forbearance, and selflessness in social relations and a flaccid, malleable, voguish conformity and abdication of responsibility. However much these exhortations bog down in hair-splitting distinctions and the casuistry of motive, a responsible concern for the good of fellow citizens and a pragmatic expression of love of neighbor are always clearly commanded. In its passage to the modern world, Christianity suffered a decline not only in its legal, political, and economic powers, but also in its capacity for such moral persuasion.[19]

In late-medieval preaching, the explicit motives of the social ethic are compassionate and humane and offer a noble ideal of a just, harmonious, and supportive community. But the doctrine is so deeply imbued with pessimism that the ideal is always shrouded in reproof. Guilt and merit before God form the implements of social control. The clerical guardians of morality come to embody less the community's aspirations than its self-hatred. There is a resulting tendency for civic ambitions toward freedom and advancement to become separated from the ethical models of the preachers, who in turn excoriate the resulting threat they see in secular morality.

The rift is compounded by the ulterior purposes of churchmen in protecting the power and privilege of an entrenched institution, in danger of becoming increasingly irrelevant to new forms of political and commercial power. They have compelling,

---

14 D.9.3 (A), T.51.2 (G), T.86.1/10 (C), T.100.3/7 (X), T.124.3 (N), E.8.3.
15 D.14.2/3 (B).
16 T.9.2 (N).
17 T.93.8 (Y).
18 T.144.4 (K).
19 Cf. R. H. Tawney, *Religion and the Rise of Capitalism*, 2nd ed. reprinted, (Harmondsworth: Penguin Books, 1980), 278-79. First published in 1937.

if unconscious, motives to affirm existing arrangements and to deplore change, embrace a social order in which authority transactions remain of a parent-child sort, and promote a personal ethic of motives and attitudes, adjudicated in the confessional, which leaves unchallenged the concentrated moral force of institutions. The forebodings are already present of a time when the traditional custodians of public probity by slow stages would lose their material and ideological ascendancy and with it their moral authority. No commonly agreed basis for compassion and honor has emerged to take its place.

15

WEALTH

The preacher's relative indifference to social and economic inequities, which may seem glaring to the modern hearer, is a corollary of that most firmly held of mendicant convictions—that the riches of this world are nothing in comparison with spiritual wealth. "Money is physical, but the soul is spiritual: you cannot fill a money chest with wisdom . . . and you cannot fill a soul with cash!"[20]

It is a classic theme whose rhetoric flows easily from the tongue of the mendicants. Many people want worldly wealth who cannot have it, but any man can have as much as he wants of God's spiritual wealth. No one can steal the heavenly riches; but temporal riches are snatched by fraud, theft, and plunder. The riches of the spirit are possessed in joy; but

> temporal things have an unavoidable entailment of bitterness—toil in acquiring them, fear in keeping them, grief in losing them, anxiety in spending them, yet life is very miserable if they remain unspent!

When worldly wealth is given away, it is gone, but spiritual wealth is multiplied by distribution. The soul is adorned by spiritual riches but soiled and tainted by temporal. Nothing is more precious than spiritual wealth, but

> worldly wealth is all but worthless except to fill mouth and belly and to cover a body's nakedness; and after death it is totally worthless—it cannot keep a body from the worms or preserve a man in life.[21]

Herolt borrows from Augustine three reasons why riches are called "the mammon of iniquity." Wealth often makes a man iniquitous. It deceives its possessor in this present life, promising security and giving fear, promising satisfaction and giving hunger, promising stability and giving sudden ruin. And all too often, it is

---

[20] D.17.1/5 (B).
[21] E.45.2.

acquired by plunder or other illicit means.[22] In sermon after sermon, Herolt expands on each of these motifs but most of all on the gnawing anxiety of possession. Too much concern about earthly prosperity removes a person's intrinsic peace of mind, his calm service of God, and his pursuit of salvation. The disquiet of mind that springs from this inordinate desire for gain is the offspring of avarice.[23] Even in the absence of any wish to make gains illegally, too much desire and love for possessions are a direct breach of the ninth commandment, since they readily supplant God and salvation.[24] That is why Christ teaches us to pray, "Give us this day . . ." for he wants to rid us of superfluous and excessive anxiety about our temporal needs.[25]

There is a direct antithesis between devout trust in God's providence and anxiety over things. God demands confidence in his material sustenance, and the Holy Spirit's gift of piety instils such reliance; but those who do not share it amass and hoard income unjustly and feverishly. In their preoccupation with earthly and transitory business their minds are suffocated, and they display the restless tossing and turning of dying men.[26] Even among so-called believers, there are all too many who belie their faith by overweening concern for possessions, always fearful that they will be in need—"as if they were on the brink of starvation!"[27] But the effect is the very opposite, for precisely such anxiety is one reason God withdraws his favor.[28] It extinguishes the love of God and the sweetness of divine grace.[29]

Yet scholastic subtlety and pastoral practicality combine to make the contrast a little less stark. While the injunctions of the Psalms, the Sermon on the Mount, and the Fathers against material anxiety are all duly recited, the antithesis is qualified.

Is it always a sin for a Christian to be anxious about temporalia? No. Anxiety about worldly provision is twofold. There is a permissible (indeed necessary) level of concern about it, given the constraints of earthly existence: of course, a man should devote as much toil and care to sustaining himself as his human frame demands, if he is to survive and serve God. But the acquisition of goods must be proportioned to this goal and therefore moderate, "enough and no more." Any excess above this standard of sufficiency is overweening anxiety, "a solicitude that perturbs the mind" in the words of the Gloss.[30] Illicit temporal anxiety thus betrays itself two ways:

---

[22] T.104.0 (before F).
[23] D.17.2/2 (D).
[24] D.9.5 (A), T.118.5 (J), T.143.9 (G).
[25] D.21.2/4 (H), T.65.2 (R).
[26] T.73.2 (A), T.118.5 (J), T.122.1 (R), T.129.2/8 (Q).
[27] T.62.1 (X).
[28] T.72.8 (U).
[29] T.94.3 (D).
[30] E.3.1.

excessive zeal in obtaining income at the expense of spiritual service and excessive fear of inadequate material support.[31]

For the mass of Christians who do not take vows of poverty but remain in the world, the question immediately arises: how much is "enough"? How to decide what wealth is excessive? The preacher offers a concise three-point test. Excess is anything over and above what is needed to maintain "a person's honest station." The need of the person is simple, basic physical sustenance. The need of one's station is reasonable means to obtain a livelihood (a plough for a farmer, for instance, or a horse for a soldier). The need of an honest station is the wherewithal to perform those tasks of skill and virtue that befit one's social status. Anything beyond these three needs is to be given to the poor. "But I have children and friends to take care of, not just myself!" Apply the same three rules to your dependants too. "I am alone, and I am afraid of being left in need by my future infirmities." What you possess is not granted for a length of time—for a day or a year—but for leading an upright life, so distribute your surplus to the needy. (If, however, you gather an annual crop, then of course retain enough to last the year.)[32]

"Enough and no more" seems a simple test until we find that "honest station" is broad enough to encompass widely differing class and economic circumstances. The legitimate needs of social respectability include appropriate household staff, furnishings, and clothing.[33] Moreover, wealth confers on some an honorable capacity for leadership and community advancement.[34] Wealth is not evil in itself. It may be dangerous and deceptive, but it is not intrinsically ungodly.

So Herolt's sermon "On seven classes of the rich"[35] describes four classes of wealthy people who will be damned but three who will be saved. The prosperous damned includes those who have acquired their riches by fraud or injustice, especially traders, but also robbers, extortionate rulers, usurers, and gamblers.[36] Secondly, there are those whose riches are gained justly but who indulge their own pleasure in their use, spending irresponsibly on themselves rather than on the poor and the salvation of souls. Such rich people are also wont to place their children at risk by overindulgence and pampering.[37] Their most glaring fault is their refusal to provide for the poor. It is a sign as grave as theft.[38] The biblical Dives was not condemned for his wealth but for his abuse of it in showing no pity to the beggar

---

[31] E.30.1/2.
[32] E.29.3/4.
[33] E.29.3/4.
[34] T.28.1/6 (I).
[35] T.82.
[36] T.82.1 (C), T.104 passim, T.141.2 (K), E.45.3.
[37] T.16.1/2 (B), T.82.2 (C).
[38] E.29.3/4.

Lazarus.[39] Like Dives, some rich people would still feed their pigs and their dogs before they would feed the poor.[40]

> Specially hateful are those rich folk who have great, wide houses and would rather let them go empty than receive paupers inside them for God's sake; whereas it is praiseworthy for any rich man to have at least one pauper in his house, so that he may give to that poor man whatever food or drink he leaves on the table himself, and thus be able to merit eternal life.[41]

A third group of rich men who will be damned are those who keep hold of property they are duty-bound to restitute—wealth illicitly acquired either by themselves or by others; losses caused to others by bad advice, false testimony, or jealous interference; or lost property they have failed to return to the rightful owners.[42] Two special instances receive strong emphasis: the duty to repay debts on time and the danger to both testator and heirs of estates comprising unjust wealth.[43] Fourthly, even if the rich have gained their wealth legally, they will still be damned if they hang onto it with too much tenacity and insatiable cupidity. Once again, the symptom of this fatal condition is failure to give to the poor, not now from lavish self-indulgence but from miserly hoarding:

> They let bread, meat, and grain rot before they are willing to give it away to the poor, and this from excessive meanness because they are afraid they will go short themselves. Sometimes such people are even afraid to eat for their own needs! They are like the toad, of which we read that it lives on dirt, but if it lifts its head from the ground it grows frightened that it won't get any more, so it doesn't dare eat more dirt than it can touch or gather with one foot.[44]

But your wealth is not your own to hoard avariciously, and as we shall see, the alms the pauper seeks is not yours but his.[45]

By contrast, there are three sorts of rich people who will merit eternal life: those who are merciful and humble and show compassion to the lowly; those who, for God's sake, forgive a neighbor's borrowings if he is in need or delay collection

---

[39] T.82.2 (C), Q.16.1.
[40] D.20.1/2 (A).
[41] T.89.3 (Q).
[42] D.7.11 (L), T.82.3 (D), Q.36.3, E.45.1/1.
[43] D.5.3/6 (N), D.23.3/3 (D), T.133.2/8 (O), T.150.4 (A), Q.42.3.
[44] T.82.4 (E), T.118.1/6 (J), T.141.2/4 (K).
[45] T.103.1/2 (R), T.150.1/2 (N), E.45.3, and see chapter 16.

of legitimate debts; and those who observe abstinence and poverty in the midst of plenty. It will count as a sort of spiritual martyrdom

> when you lie on a hard floor though you have two or three beds, or drink water when you have wine, or eat the gravy rather than the meat... similarly, if a man keeps himself from the conjugal act on sacred days and nights, and abstains from dancing and other worldly delights, and wears humble clothes when he is wealthy enough to have costly garments; or if he abstains from eating fruits such as apples and pears; and so on. As often as a rich man for God's sake deprives himself in this way of something to eat or drink and gives it to a poor man for the love of God, he merits eternal joy and an eternal crown.[46]

Herolt even offers an entire sermon on how to gain merit by means of worldly possessions—by almsgiving, patience in the face of exaction or theft, willingness to forgo dubious gain, generosity to neighbors for God's sake, and restitution of unjust possessions to the rightful heirs.[47]

The saying in the Gospel about the virtual impossibility of a rich man's entering heaven does not apply then to the godly rich—were not David, Jacob, Abraham, Emperor Henry, Louis of France, and many other rich men saved?—but does apply to those who abuse their wealth for carnal indulgence and above all to those whose wealth is ill-gotten.[48] However, the social behavior of the rich suggests that in practice the dangers of affluence outweigh its special opportunities for merit. The life of prosperity contrasts so starkly with Christ's example:

> Christ was born in a stable; a greedy man is not content with only one house. Christ was placed in a hard manger and on straw, wrapped in rags; a voluptuous man wants soft and sumptuous beds. While Christ lived in poverty, the Christian strives to amass great wealth, ignoring the word of the gospel that it is difficult for a rich man to enter the kingdom of God.[49]

The rich like to puff themselves up and glory in their money and power and the elegance of outward appearance.[50] Even in church, rich people hold aloof from genuflecting or prostrating themselves like poor folk because it is beneath their

---

[46] T.82.5-7 (E-F).
[47] T.150 passirn.
[48] E.41.1/1.
[49] T.15.2/3 (Q).
[50] T.31.1/3 (J).

dignity. They do not want to dirty their expensive clothes or tire their delicate bodies; the long points of their shoes get in the way, and they do not want to court embarrassment by bending in disgracefully short garments. And anyway, they do not think they have much need for God.[1]

The chief dangers of wealth are deceptive security, ambiguity in one's standing before God, the temptation to corruption, and a divided will at the hour of death.

Riches seem to offer security and satisfaction; but a life of ease, free of all trials, expels the fear of God and creates in its place pride, indolence, self-satisfaction, contempt of others, and a lack of compassion.[2] "If someone is rich, let him reflect that he is on his way to death, and of all his riches he will take nothing with him but the sack!"[3] In reality, we must thread a narrow path in this life between too much anxiety and too much attachment, between too much adversity and too much prosperity.[4]

At first sight, prosperity seems to be a sign of God's favor; and indeed, an increase in material well-being is promised to the generous giver.[5] But the very opposite may be the reality, the preacher warns. God often grants his temporal benefits to evil men as a reward for good works done in mortal sin. That is, reprobates, who can earn no eternal merit, must nevertheless be treated justly for any good they happen to have performed, and their reward takes the form of material success. The implication is that continual prosperity is a sign of God's anger. One can almost go so far as to say that constant good fortune is a means of distinguishing the children of the devil from the children of God. The sinner who always prospers but fails to reform is marked for damnation.[6]

Though material blessing ought to prompt a man to conversion, in practice wealth may be fatal to his salvation because it offers opportunities to sin.[7] The corrupting effect of wealth may produce two contrasting reactions. On the one hand, some people spend virtually their whole lives—talk, occupation, care, and love—in accumulating and conserving profits; they are slaves of wealth.[8] On the other hand, riches make for indolence—a fault Herolt believes is especially characteristic of wealthy women. Rich women, he says, should spin and not sit idle.[9] Opulence and abundance of temporal possessions are an occasion for sin in

---

[1] T.21.3 (X).
[2] T.40.2 (D).
[3] Q.40.1.
[4] T.136.2 (G).
[5] T.103.3/1 (A).
[6] T.92.2/1 (L), T.108.1 (Q), T.149.1 (B).
[7] D.17.4/7 (O).
[8] T.114.0 (before A).
[9] D.20.1/4 (C).

women: a field needs correct watering, a metal tool needs proper use, and a human body needs appropriate toil.[10]

Finally, at life's end, wealth greatly increases the bitterness and peril of the death struggle. In that last battle, when one must abandon all worldly preoccupations and yield oneself wholly to God, the demons will use property to distress one's mind and evoke faithless regret.[11] Death ought to make utterly plain the contemptibility of all the things people seek after in the world:

> The king of France, in the toils of death and despaired of by his doctors, had all his princes and prelates called to him, and he said: "Look, I who am the richest, noblest, and most powerful of men, for all my wealth, power, and friends cannot extort a truce of a single day or a single hour from death. What good then are all these temporal things?" And so saying he provoked all the bystanders to tears.[12]

But such insight eludes all too many of the rich when they come to die. Herolt tells contrasting stories about two usurers on their death beds. One has all his wealth displayed to him and declares, "Since you do not wish to die with me, I commend you to the devil!" But the other refuses the priest's advice to make restitution on the grounds that he would have nothing to leave to his sons and dies "fearing temporal poverty more than eternal."[13] Even after death, the rich man is at a disadvantage: "Temporal goods multiplied here harm a man after death because of the strict accounting he must render of his property"—how he acquired it to the last penny, how he spent it to the least farthing, and how he disposed of his estate.[14]

All these spiritual dangers are endured for wealth, but wealth can provide us little but food and clothing; it cannot satisfy mind and soul. The cupidity of man is infinite, but nothing less than God can satisfy the capacity of the soul. Earthly possessions are empty; they cannot enter the essence of the soul:

> Wine still in the jug does not fill a man's belly or slake his thirst. Money still in a purse or chest does not fill a man's heart or slake the thirst of his avarice. Only the grace of God entering the heart can extinguish the heart's thirst; but money sharpens the thirst of avarice.[15]

---

[10] Q.37.1.
[11] T.134.2/5 (Y).
[12] T.118.2/1 (K).
[13] T.108.3 (Z), T.118.2/1 (L).
[14] D.17.4/5 (M), T.3.2/4 (R).
[15] D.17.1/5 (B), T.94.1 (B).

These familiar and repeated moral themes provide a rationale for the church's involvement in the economic functioning of society. They justify the church's role as a redistributive agency by insisting on almsgiving and restitution as essential to penance, as a regulatory force in its strictures on usury and fraudulent trade, and as a conserver of the *status quo* in its conviction that the real effects of economic behavior are to be found in intention and disposition, not in adjustment of the social structure.

It scarcely needs to be said that the church itself held an ambiguous position in performing these roles. In practice, this social ethic carried overtones of the class outlook and professional self-interest of the clergy who propounded it. Not only in its curial and episcopal superstructure, but even in its mendicant branches, the church was both executor and beneficiary of many of these arrangements. It adopted a sacrosanct posture as the repository by right of alms, endowments, tithes, bequests, votive offerings, and conscience money. Its personnel were accounted able to handle huge resources (by definition not "temporal possessions") with an incorruptibility beyond ordinary men by the church's own account. The contrast between the human reality and the institutional ideal was unmistakable. But the moral power of the doctrine was also unmistakable.

16

THE POOR

There is only one form of "usury without sin"—to give alms to the poor.[16] Almsgiving is an investment that yields a hundredfold return to the giver.[17] Unlike worldly wealth, spiritual riches are multiplied by distribution. To give in charity is to have more, like lighting one lamp for another.[18]

Such exhortation, of course, is addressed to the haves rather than the have-nots; the poverty-stricken themselves are not the audience Herolt anticipates for his sermons. The perennial status of the poor is assumed, rationalized, and to some extent justified. Although the miseries of abject poverty are sometimes acknowledged, the preacher's strongly held convictions about mendicant spirituality, the imitation of Christ, and the role of suffering and charity in the system of merit combine to idealize the state of the poor and dampen any expectation of change.

The sermon on the seven classes of the rich[19] is paired with an identically structured sermon on the seven classes of the poor.[20] In this case, too, four classes of the poor are damned and three are saved.

It is both wicked and stupid, Herolt declares, for a poor man to complain against God because of his poverty. "What obligation does God have to you? What has he ever received from you? God has already given you more than you are worthy of or ever deserved: created you from nothing . . . redeemed you with his blood . . . allowed you a body with its members."[21] It is reprehensible to argue against God, since he does not make some rich and some poor without a reason. He has a special purpose in depriving paupers of property now. It is a sign of his greater delight in the poor that he withholds worldly wealth here to grant them eternal wealth later.[22] If the birth rate among the poor is higher than among the

---

[16] Q.9.1.
[17] D.13.2/1 (C).
[18] E.45.2/4.
[19] T.82; see chapter 15.
[20] T.81.
[21] T.81.1 (A).
[22] T.108.1 (P).

rich, fertility is a sign of God's love, so they should not complain.[23] Christ showed his love for the poor by assuming utter poverty himself in his birth, way of life, and death. Especially in death, he was *pauper, pauperior, pauperrimus*. He chose his apostles not from rich men but from poor fishermen. It should be a consolation to paupers that they are imitating Christ.[24] Patience in poverty is a way of taking up his cross and following him.[25]

But all too many of the poor try to alleviate their penury by recourse to petty dishonesties—stealing food or fuel, dealing in shoddy goods, and selling themselves in prostitution.[26] Instead of patiently resigning themselves to their humble estate in order to be exalted later, they envy the rich, the worldly goods they have obtained from God. When they see the rich extorting usury, gambling, dressing ostentatiously, and eating and drinking gluttonously, they would gladly imitate them if only they had the means. That makes them "paupers not of Christ but of the devil." A proud pauper is doubly reprehensible because, unlike the rich man, he has no excuse for his pride! But envy is both self-destructive and fruitless, and the failure of resignation will damn the soul.[27]

By contrast, the poor who will be saved include the indigent who would gladly be better off if God so willed but are not prepared to acquire means against God's justice, so they accept alms and bear their poverty patiently. Such paupers are duty-bound to pray for those who give them alms.[28] The working poor who succeed in feeding themselves by honest and upright labor will also be saved.[29] But the outstanding examples of poverty in the preacher's list are those who are gladly and voluntarily paupers, and cherish their poverty so much that, even if they could gain wealth without sinning, yet they choose for God's sake to avoid or forgo it. These are the "good paupers," who laudably humble themselves now so that they may be exalted in the future. They have the triple merit that they despise worldly things, are humble in spirit and intent, and yearn for heavenly things. As in the monastic vow of poverty, this spiritual transaction gains as it were a right to a heavenly inheritance by the legal principle of exchange.[30]

For God has three kingdoms, the preacher says—a heavenly, an earthly, and an infernal kingdom; and he gives the infernal realm to the demons, the earthly realm to the rich, and the kingdom of heaven to the poor.[31] The rich have their glories

---

[23] T.108.3 (U).
[24] T.11.3 (D), T.15.2/3 (Q), T.27.2 (B), E.7.3.
[25] Q.35.2.
[26] T.81.2 (A).
[27] T.81.3-4 (B).
[28] T.81.5 (B).
[29] T.81.6 (B).
[30] T.31.1/4 (K), T.81.7 (B), T.159.3/2 (X), S.40.1.
[31] S.40.1.

here, and rot; the poor are abject here, but are carried in honor to the banquet of the highest king.[32] But because God wants both sorts of people to be saved, he has arranged matters so that each class may welcome the other into its realm—the rich may receive the poor on earth by their alms, and the poor prepare a heavenly welcome for the rich by their prayers.[33]

In the sermon books, Herolt devotes far more time and energy to one side of this equation than the other. His inability to distinguish clearly between the voluntary poverty of the monk and the involuntary poverty of the chronically poor, his conviction that the presence of the poor is part of a divine order whose apparent inequities will be resolved in heaven, and his sense of the social outlook of his audience all lead him to address the moral obligations of the rich rather than the consolation of the poor. He cannot be described as complacent about inadequate provision for paupers, but he is not so much concerned about their plight as about the spiritual danger to the well-to-do if they fail to give alms.

There is, needless to say, a pragmatic aspect to this emphasis. Potential donors own the money and goods needed by the poor, who by definition have nothing to offer in exchange. So the chief appeal, in a welfare system funded by individual charity, must be addressed to the propertied classes. Very occasionally, Herolt commends the generosity of the merely poor to the totally indigent: such generosity in the midst of one's own poverty is a spiritual martyrdom that opens heaven. God honors the small gifts of the poor more than the large gestures of the wealthy because of their pure intent; and when a poor man is saddened that he has no gift at all to give to a pauper, God will regard the intention to be just as generous as an alms.[34] "If you do not have a coin to give, give a crust of bread, and if you do not have that, give a cup of cold water."[35] Yet most of his exhortation is directed to the upper classes and appeals far more to their duty and self-interest than to their compassion.

Such an appeal ought not to be necessary, he says, since God grafted into our hearts a natural impulse to succor the deficiencies of the poor. We can see this impulse at work even amongst the animals, and "those who see the wants and needs of their neighbors and have no compassion are more hardhearted than beasts."[36] We must always be ready to hear the cry of the poor.[37] Alms should therefore be given freely, and three things should induce us to do so.

First, the one who seeks alms from you is Jesus Christ in the guise of the pauper, and you should consider it is to him that you give it.[38] "A pauper is to be received

---

[32] P.P.: 49 "Pauperes" (441).
[33] S.40.1.
[34] D.3.5/3 (R), T.13.1/2 (S), T.150.1/1 (S).
[35] T.103.2/1 (S).
[36] Q.9.1.
[37] E.24.2/2.
[38] T.103.1/1 (R), T.150.1 (M).

and consoled just as if Christ knocked at the door hungry, thirsty, naked, blind and halt and homeless."[39] Alms is sent to God by the hand of the pauper. It is "a glad giving of presents to the beloved."[40] The hand of the pauper is the treasury chest of Christ: whatever the poor man accepts, Christ has received.[41]

What Christ asks you for in the pauper's guise belongs to him, not to you. If an earthly overlord placed his property in your care, and when he asked for part of it you refused, would he not be justly indignant? It is a clear sign of inner pride not to recognize that all possessions come from God and are owed back to God in the poor:[42]

> A pauper begged an alms from a certain rich noblewoman, and she gave him a denarius with the words, "I have now given you more than God ever gave me." The pauper answered, "But you have so much, and such good things that God has given you!" "He did not give them to me," she replied, "but put them in my charge so that I could support the poor from them, and render an account of how I spent or retained every single denarius."[43]

Thirdly, Christ asks for your benefit, not his own. This, in fact, is the heart of the appeal, though it reduces the needs and feelings of the wretched pauper him or herself to a mere appearance.[44] Herolt quotes with approval the words of John Chrysostom: "Do not think that God would have made the wealthy for the utility of the poor, whom he is quite able to sustain without the wealthy; but he made the poor for the utility of the rich, who would have become altogether too fruitless and sterile unless paupers had been created."[45] Any sense of outrage that God permits the poor, the weak, and the crippled to go on living in wretchedness is a stupid questioning of God's purpose, the preacher says: God allows the poor to love so that the rich may have a means of meriting eternal life by their alms.[46]

For almsgiving is a means a purchasing a heavenly inheritance.[47] Alms are rewarded temporally, spiritually, and eternally.[48] Even though a temporal reward is not the principal motive or intention of almsgiving, Proverbs 3 and Luke 6 are

---

[39] T.33.1 (B).
[40] T.64.1/4 (I), T.119.3/5 (U).
[41] D.13.2/1 (B), T.103.2/4 (T).
[42] D.13.2/1 (B), T.103.1/2 (R), T.150.1 (N).
[43] T.150.1 (P).
[44] T.103.1/3 (R).
[45] T.150.1 (O).
[46] T.109.4 (D).
[47] T.159.3/3 (X).
[48] T.150.1 (R).

authorities for promising a growth in temporal goods as a result, as is a story told by Peter Damian about a poor man and his wife who had a single denarius to buy food to eat with their bread on a fast day, but on the way to market the man was asked for alms by a pauper and gave him the coin. When they sat down to their meal of dry bread, a strange visitor appeared and placed on the table twenty solidi, wrapped in linen cloth, and said that his master had sent them.[49]

More importantly, almsgiving is rewarded by the remission of sins. It is one of those simple acts of piety by which venial sins are extinguished.[50] Generosity in alms leads to forgiveness and the infusion of grace.[51] Consequently, almsgiving is routinely imposed as one of the forms of satisfaction in sacramental penance.[52] It leads to increase in grace: God must be merciful to him who is merciful to his neighbor.[53] Adducing St. Laurence as an example of one who was always merciful to the poor, the preacher gathers a catena of texts (from Matthew, Luke, John, James, Aristotle, Ambrose, Basil, and Gregory) to demonstrate that mercy shown leads to mercy received.[54] Even an alms given in a state of mortal sin is a "habilitation for grace" because the pauper who receives it will implore God's mercy on the donor.[55] Because paupers are bound to pray for benefactors who have given to them, worked for them, and shared their reward with them, by almsgiving one gains many intercessors and friends before God.[56] Those ungrateful poor who accept alms but do not pray faithfully for the givers grieve the souls of the dead.[57]

Almsgiving opens heaven, prepares a man's heavenward path, and shows him the gate of paradise. It leads him to a good end and escorts him in death when all his friends desert him.[58] In return for his gifts, he will be given "good measure" (that is, angels at his departing), "pressed down" (Christ, the Blessed Virgin, the angels and saints will receive him with gladness and honor), "shaken together" (the Blessed Virgin and the saints and angels will share all their merits and joys with him), and "running over" (Christ, and the glorious Virgin Mary, all patriarchs, prophets, apostles, evangelists, martyrs, confessors, virgins, and holy saints and elect will give him perpetual thanks that he showed mercy to an indigent man).[59]

---

[49] T.150.1 (R).
[50] D.12.6/7 (Q), T.110.3/7 (S).
[51] T.121.7 (P), T.150.1 (R).
[52] Q.35.3.
[53] T.103.3/3 (A).
[54] S.31.2.
[55] T.92.2/3 (M).
[56] T.81.5 (B), T.103.3/4 (A).
[57] T.160.6 (P).
[58] T.14.1/8 (I), T.103.3/5-7 (A-C).
[59] T.150.1 (R).

The opposite side of the coin is that failure to support the poor leads to outer darkness. Characteristically, it is not clear whether this failure is a failure of compassion or of duty. Everyone without exception is under obligation to support a neighbor materially when he is in desperate straits.[60] In such extreme necessity, almsgiving is a commandment, in other circumstances a counsel.[61] Tightwads and misers who hoard their property greedily and do not use it to support the poor may be damned on this account, for in God's eyes they are thieves.[62] Such hoarding when the poor are in need is a mortal sin against the ninth commandment.[63] Withholding essential food from the poor in need is spiritual murder and breaches the fifth commandment as well.[64] Herolt agrees sadly with Guillaume Péyraut that there are no Jewish beggars because the Jews support each other in times of need, but among Christians so few people have the true love of God the Father in them that many beggars are found in utter penury.[65]

In spite of his virtual indifference to the personal experience of individual paupers, Herolt does reserve special outrage for class oppression by those rich and powerful members of society who not only neglect the duty of support, but actively oppress the poor for their own ends. They include tyrannical rulers who persistently impose financial exactions on the poor or extort labor from them;[66] heartless counsellors who advise the erection of new civic edifices in great cities at the expense of poor commoners;[67] middlemen who encumber the poor and attach their goods in order to repay their own debts to overlords or to finance their wars ("alas, this is now common, and the poor people are rightly regarded as martyrs of Christ if they sustain it patiently!");[68] avaricious employers whose harsh and grasping demands lead to the forced labor and even death of the poor and needy;[69] and in general all those who keep back the people's money, a sin of great gravity that howls continually in God's ears for vengeance.[70] God's justice will shorten the years of the ungodly that oppress the poor and the weak.[71]

But such denunciations of blatant political injustice are far less frequent than the reproof of private miserliness. Some rich men hang onto their possessions

---

[60] E.24.1/1.
[61] E.29.3/2.
[62] T.150.1 (P).
[63] D.9.6 (B).
[64] D.5.3/7 (O).
[65] E.29.3/1.
[66] T.58.1 (F).
[67] T.144.2 (J).
[68] D.7.3 (C), T.104.3 (F).
[69] D.17.2/1 (C).
[70] T.104.4 (F-G).
[71] E.35.2/1.

with such tenacity and insatiable cupidity that they would rather let meat or grain rot before they would give it away to the poor.[72] They are like toads, Herolt says, and tells a series of stories about people so proud that they cannot stand having paupers near them: a rich man who could not abide the clamor of the poor either in plenty or in famine, so he moved to a lakeside and hid in a back room and told his servants to say he was not there (an armed angel cited him to judgment), a priest who so loathed lepers that he built a wall and heard confessions and administered the sacraments through an opening in it (he contracted the disease only in those parts of his body he kept away from them), a servant so disdainful of beggars that he would not carry alms out to them (he became a leper himself), a toll gatherer notorious for never giving alms, and a clever beggar who got food from him anyway when he could not find a stone and threw wheat at him instead (even this unwilling gift yielded enough grace to lead the toll-gatherer to a life of sanctity).[73]

Just as a certain philosopher advises that every man should possess one friend and one enemy—the friend to tell him the truth and the enemy to keep him vigilant—so "any rich man should at least have one pauper in his house, to give that poor man to eat or drink what he himself leaves on the table, so that in this way he can merit eternal life." But many are still so mean that instead they drive paupers away from their homes. "Those rich people are especially reprehensible who have great, wide houses and would rather let them go empty than have paupers in them for God's sake!"[74] Instead of this mean-spirited arrogance, Herolt gives specific instructions about the manner in which alms should be given.

First, they are to be given abundantly. If we are to show mercy to the extent of our ability, it must be with real feeling and willingness, since God regards the intention and the feeling far more than the amount.[75] Secondly, the right priorities must be followed. Charity must begin at home. Just as no one could plausibly claim to be merciful who had no pity on his destitute mother, so no one can claim that his almsgiving makes him merciful if he has no pity on the mortal illness of his own soul. One who wants to give alms must begin with himself, and first clothe his soul in love for God and neighbor. Mercy must be shown first of all to the soul, and only then to the body.[76]

Next, alms must be given with gladness and sweet words. The Lord loves a cheerful giver because cheerfulness "fattens up" an alms.[77] "God will repay you wearing the same expression you showed to others in your gift." Many sin against

---

[72] T.82.4 (E).
[73] T.81.7 (B), T.82.4 (E), T.150.1 (N).
[74] D.20.1/3 (B), T.89.3 (Q), T.103.0 (before R).
[75] D.3.5/3 (R), T.103.2/1 (S).
[76] T.73.2/2 (B), T.103.2/2 (S).
[77] Perhaps an allusion to the Vulgate text of Proverbs 15:17, *"Melius est vocari ad oleum cum charitate quam ad vitulum saginatum cum odio."*

this requirement by adopting an austere demeanor in word, gesture, and facial expression when approached by the poor.[78]

Alms should be given speedily. Too many people make paupers wait long at the door and let them cry out. But the preacher's chief concern is not the heartlessness of unnecessary delay, but the widespread practice among the rich of fulfilling their almsgiving duty by posthumous bequests in their wills. "Alms are to be given in a man's lifetime," Herolt insists. "An alms given in life is like a lamp throwing light ahead of a man as he walks—it stops him falling in the ditch; but alms given after death are like a lamp a man carries behind his back!" He tells a cautionary tale of a rich man who made a will on his deathbed leaving bequests to priests and religious for his soul's repose; but when they came to collect their legacy, his only son refused to pay on the ground that "if he is in hell, no prayers avail for him; if in heaven, he does not need them; and if in purgatory, he shall be purged of his last sin, for I'll not give a thing for his soul!"[79]

Almsgiving should be with humility and good intent and not with false pride. Noblemen and the rich commonly despise paupers, Herolt says, but the poor are to be honored as Christ honored them. One should always reflect that, but for God's will, he too would be disfigured, blind, deaf, or leprous, and show the same compassion he would like to receive.[80]

Herolt offers an image of the range of almsgiving he regards as fitting. Some givers, he says, place their alms in God's hands—that is, they give unasked to widows and orphans who are ashamed to beg and those they recognize to be in need. Some place their alms under God's feet; they give hospitality to mendicants, pilgrims, and paupers for God's sake. Some place their alms in God's lap, with gifts to lepers, the blind, and captives. Some place their alms in God's mouth, by gifts to priests who daily consume the body of Christ or to adorn the house of God where the sacrament is consecrated. Some place alms on God's heart; they forgive the injuries and offences committed against themselves and their property. And some clothe Christ by offering gifts for the souls of the dead in purgatory.[81]

None of these attitudes to giving will be enough, the preacher warns, unless the donation is made from justly acquired property. An alms made from the "patrimony of Christ," the poor box administered by priests, is good; an alms from one's own patrimony is better; but an alms made from the fruits of one's own effort is best. It is therefore a fitting way to mark saints' days to make gifts for the poor by manual labor, as St. Elizabeth of Hungary did by spinning wool alongside her maid so that she could give clothing to the poor from her own work. But God is not pleased by alms given from the proceeds of seizure or theft, which should rather be restituted;

---

[78] E.7.2; T.103.2/3 (S).
[79] T.103.2/4 (T).
[80] T.103.2/5 (T), E.7.3.
[81] E.7.2.

and alms from the proceeds of usury are acceptable only if the donor has enough remaining from other sources to repay the interest he extorted.[1]

Whatever the spiritual incentives to generosity, in practice a more mundane and prudential calculation prevails. As we have seen, in cases of real need, almsgiving is a precept and failure to give support is a mortal sin; but in other cases, it is a pious counsel. There are therefore practical considerations applying to both parties.

On the part of the giver, alms should be given from any surplus that remains after adequate provision has been made for one's own dependants, who are one's first responsibility as right reason demands. The precept implies that such excess must be given to the poor, for while the title to material possessions is assigned to their owners, in another sense they belong to those who can use them. But what constitutes "adequate provision" for one's own household, and how is "excess" calculated? People are entitled to retain the simple physical necessities, adequate means to make a reasonable livelihood, and those practical possessions (such as furniture, clothing, and household goods) that permit them to maintain a virtuous, honest, and socially useful life. Anything over and above these legitimate needs is excess and is for the poor. Anxiety about possible future demands on income for oneself or one's children is no excuse for retaining current surplus, which is to be distributed to those who need it now. Rich men who fail to do so commit a sin as grave as theft.[2]

On the part of the recipient, he must be sure that he needs the alms, or else it is theft. Not every occurrence of need invokes the pious duty of giving, but only such need as cannot be alleviated by other means. A discriminating judgment is therefore to be exercised in choosing eligible recipients and fitting circumstances. "Extreme necessity" is not always to be interpreted literally, since then aid might be given only when it was too late to be of use; but it is to be taken to include "extremely probable signs of future necessity," and therefore to include those with no visible means of support who are too infirm, poverty-stricken, or disabled to be able to work. It also includes those clerics and religious who steadfastly serve God and show their zeal for souls by fulfilling the canonical hours, saying mass, and hearing sermons and confessions. In short, alms are to go to the deserving poor and not to the rich. May a rich and healthy man, it is asked, go on pilgrimage as a mendicant? No, Herolt insists, because such a vow is prejudicial to the poor who have a right to the alms and possess no alternative means of support.[3]

There are two circumstances when alms are certainly not to be given. The first is if you believe your gift will encourage immorality, such as gifts to actors or whores. The second is if your own motives are mixed, and your purpose is not kindness but some ulterior motive, such as the hope of entertainment from actors. Yet in spite

---

[1] D.7.15 (BB), T.103.2/6 (U-X), S.43.1/8.
[2] D.5.3/7 (O), E.29.3/2-4.
[3] D.5.3/7 (O), T.103.2/7 (H), T.121.2 (H), T.150.1 (Q), E.29.3/5.

of these cautions, it remains proper to give alms to an evil man considered not as the sinner he is but as a person in dire need.[4]

Finally, Herolt says, the church's precept to give alms is a shorthand for urging all the faithful to perform the "six works of mercy" of Matthew 25.[5] He quotes Augustine's comment that if someone knew no other part of Holy Scripture but this, it would be enough for salvation. The "six works" are to feed the hungry, give drink to the thirsty, receive strangers to hospitality, clothe the naked, visit the sick, and minister to those in prison.[6]

One of the surest signs of predestination is compassion, and the sign of true compassion is practical support.[7] The works of holy mercy are a principal form of the service God requires of Christians.[8] Such "training courses" are the soul's preparation to receive the gifts of the Spirit, and the Pentecostal gift of healing is displayed in our works of mercy to the poor—above all to the sick (for there is greater mercy in visiting the sick than in all the others).[9] By our works of mercy to the needy and poor, we imitate the example of Mary in feeding the infant Christ, or of St. Elizabeth in ministering to the sick at her hospital by the Wartburg. These tasks are the most fitting activity for Christian widows.[10] They are suffrages to support the souls of the departed in purgatory.[11]

"By nature, all animals preserve a mutual mercy towards their own kind—how much more should man, who is made in God's image?" the preacher asks,[12] and he tells a story to impress on his hearers how gladly God accepts works of mercy done to the poor in his name:

> A farmer lived with his wife in a large, isolated hall in a village. It was their custom each Friday to invite a pauper in order to commemorate and revere Christ's passion. If there was no pauper nearby, they postponed their meal until one should come. But as it happened, one Friday they could find no pauper at all; so the man said to his wife, "Prepare the meal, and I shall go out and see if I can find a poor man." He went out, and saw a poor man lying in the muddy street of a public square not far from the house. He went up to him and invited him to come. When the poor man reached the house,

---

[4] T.103.2/7 (Y).
[5] Q.35.3.
[6] D.20.1/1-6 (A-D), T.89.1-6 (O-R).
[7] T.149.6 (G).
[8] T.155.2 (T).
[9] T.67.5 (D), T.68.2/7 (G), T.128.2 (O).
[10] T.17.2/3 (K), T.116.1/6 (S), S.43.1/8.
[11] T.160.5/10 (H).
[12] T.89.0 (O).

the wife said to him, "I shall wash your feet, because they need it so badly, and then we shall eat." She took a dish of water and washed his feet, and she found that he had two large nail prints in his feet; and said to her husband, "This poor man has wounds in his feet, just like the Lord Jesus!" Then the Lord Jesus spoke: "On other days you have welcomed me and given me hospitality in my members; but today you have received me in person. And I promise you that in this present world you will have life's necessities, and after this life I will welcome you to life eternal."[13]

---

[13] T.89.3 (T).

17

SPEECH

The tongue is set in a slippery place, to show how easily it can bring our downfall, and it is doubly enclosed within teeth and lips because of its capacity for mischief. The tongue is never tamed.[14] Nothing does as much damage to social relationships as the sins of speech. The preacher returns to the subject time and time again, sprinkling his sermons with the apothegms and clichés of a hoary homiletic tradition, and drawing the subject together with a succinct *sermo communis* "On Speaking."[15] We shall follow his own outline here.

Speech is an act of reason, a unique capacity of rational creatures. It cannot therefore be morally neutral, but every spoken word is either meritorious or culpable.[16] So there are four things to be observed, Herolt says, lest we offend in our tongue and our words: *what* we say, *to whom* we say it, *when* we speak, and *how* we speak.[17]

What are we to say? Peter tells us to speak as if in God's words, and Paul tells us to let no bad language pass our lips but only edifying words. These injunctions are directed against those who speak scurrilous, harmful words, betraying the turpitude hidden within the speakers. "A pig is known by its tongue, whether it is clean or dirty outside; a man by the words he utters."[18]

Herolt often expands on what he means by "scurrilous, harmful words." One of his lists reads "disgraceful language, lying, mockery of the good, curses, oaths."[19] Another catalogue lists "useless chatter, hurtful, scandalous gossip, blasphemy, cursing, swearing without reason, lying, scurrilous lustful talk, mockery and detraction."[20] Again, he outlines "eight modes of verbal offence:" false testimony, derision, sowing of discord, fraudulent speech, disturbing neighbors with

---

[14] E.28.2/3.
[15] T.139.
[16] E.16.3/5, E.24.2/1.
[17] T.139.1 (before K).
[18] T.139.1/1 (K).
[19] T.19.3/4 (F).
[20] T.62.5 (A).

contentious and inappropriate talk, scandalizing them with wanton, lascivious language, provoking them to anger, and damaging reputations.[21]

It is this last topic of defamation that most exercises Herolt. Detractors are the devil's dogs, yapping at their prey until they have bitten it; they are pigs wallowing in the mire of slander, serpents lying coiled and striking without warning. Character assassination is worse than murder; the theft of the good name is worse than any material robbery, all but impossible to restore; and the tongue of the slanderer is worse than hell because it devours the good with the bad.[22]

Defamation and detraction take various forms. When someone's hidden wrongs are publicized to embarrass him or bring him into disrepute, the destructive motive makes it a sin even if the allegation is true. Evil reports are often passed on in embroidered form. Wrongdoings are attributed falsely; this is the gravest form of slander. But it is also detraction enviously to deny a neighbor's inner goodness, or to belittle his obvious outward goodness, or to twist his good qualities into bad by attributing an ulterior motive. In fact, Herolt says, the best way to avoid detraction is to say nothing at all about a neighbor in his absence.[23]

Heeding slander is often as bad as propagating it. "Both speaker and hearer of slander carry the devil on their tongues."[24] Failure to discourage detraction of the good and innocent traps many people.[25] A growing pleasure in hearing others denigrated is a sure sign of spiritual death, just as the approach of physical death is signalled when gold placed on the tongue tastes not bitter but sweet.[26] So we must circumcise our ears against breeding detraction.[27]

At the Easter confession, the penitent is to confess the mortal sin of defaming a neighbor or of listening willingly to a slander, and the confessor is to question him or her on the point.[28] Priestly absolution for the sin of slander is not effective, even if accompanied by contrite tears, unless the slander is retracted and restitution made to the one defamed for loss of reputation.[29] No spiritual progress can be made until this restitution is made.[30] But it is Herolt's experience that most detractors are quick to backslide into their defamatory ways.[31]

---

[21] T.96.2 (P-T).
[22] D.5.4/1 (P); T.91.1 (E-F); A.D.: 1, 2 "Detractores" (115^b).
[23] D.5.4/2 (Q), T.91.2 (G-H).
[24] D.5.4/3 (R), T.91.3 (I).
[25] Q.16.1/3.
[26] T.129.2/7 (Q).
[27] T.19.3/3 (F).
[28] Q.19.2, Q.22.3.
[29] T.91.2/3 (G), Q.26.2.
[30] E.41.1/1.
[31] T.58.4 (F).

The confessor is particularly concerned with this form of antisocial speech because it contravenes so many commandments at once. Detraction is a form of murder, the killing of souls.[32] It is the offspring of envy, its frequent motive,[33] and of gluttony because overindulgence dulls the discretion and loosens the tongue.[34] To take someone's honor is worse than theft or plunder.[35] And of course it is a direct contravention of the commandment against false witness.[36] It is a characteristic mark of hypocrites that they are detractors of good men and adulators of evil men, misconstruing the deeds of others for the sake of favor and gain.[37] Whispering campaigns to sow discord between friends and neighbors are an aggravated and specially malicious form of detraction.[38] And perhaps most despicable of all is the subterfuge of falsely speaking well of someone in the deliberate hope of eliciting a negative response. "This is a double sin, both fraud and an invitation to obloquy."[39]

Closely allied with slander are the verbal sins of mockery and insult. It is all too easy for venial jousting to slip over into mortal derision (Herolt recites Thomas's rules for telling the difference).[40] One must refrain one's tongue from derisory speech.[41] In particular, to mock good men in the service of God is to join those who derided Christ and spat in his face;[42] but the godly should tolerate derision patiently as Christ did.[43] Banter readily becomes outright insult. Abusive raillery—"You're a thief, or adulterer, or usurer, or liar!" or "You're blind, or crooked, or mangy!"—may claim to be jest, but in fact it taunts and pummels the neighbor with his vices and shortcomings.[44] Incidentally, a technical distinction is drawn between insult and contumely; an insult is any reference to another's defects but contumely also attributes guilt, so that "You're blind!" is merely an insult, but "You're a thief!" is contumely. But in practice, the terms are used interchangeably, for either robs a man of his honor, which is his most precious possession.[45] Biblical precedent requires one exception, however: since Christ called his disciples "fools," and Paul called

---

[32] D.5.3/3 (K), E.43.2/2.
[33] D.14.3/5 (F).
[34] D.18.4/1 (L).
[35] D.8.5 (H).
[36] D.8.7 (L), T.143.8 (D).
[37] T.100.2/1 (R).
[38] D.14.3/2 (E).
[39] T.143.8/5 (F), E.22.1/4.
[40] D.8.2 (E), T.96.2/2 (Q), T.143.8/3 (F).
[41] E.25.2/1.
[42] Q.20.2/2.
[43] Q.25.2/2.
[44] T.143.8/6 (F).
[45] D.15.2/7 (C), T.95.7 (J).

the Galatians "stupid," reproachful language is apparently acceptable in correction, so long as it is used with discretion and moderation.[46]

There are, as it were, three provinces in the world, Herolt says, each with its own provincial dialect. The heavenly dialect comprises prayer, thanksgiving, and talk of God; the earthly dialect speaks of mundane affairs; and the infernal tongue spews curses, swearing, and blasphemy.[47] The reprehensible sin of blasphemy takes various forms. In angry self-vindication, contumely is first directed against God by irreverent swearing by Christ's head, or his hairs, nose, eyes, or other parts, even by Christ's bowels or lungs or heart or liver (one who so swears is deposed if he is a cleric, anathematized if a layman); secondly, by abominable execration and profanity, such as oaths by dung, or the private parts, and the like; thirdly, by swearing unnecessarily by the five wounds of Christ, or by his death, passion, or precious blood. Every such oath if uttered deliberately is a mortal sin, even if it happens a hundred times a day. Indeed, Herolt tells us, there are some countries where such oaths are treated so stringently that an offender loses an ear or his tongue or a finger; and he approvingly relates the example of King Louis of France who ordered a blaspheming Parisian cauterized on the lips with a burning iron and when his nobles demurred replied that he would be glad himself to bear such an unbecoming penalty in his lips all his lifelong so that Christ would not be blasphemed in his realm. Anyway, the preacher says, sometimes God himself punishes such people in the very member in which they have blasphemed their redeemer. What of inadvertent blasphemy? There is some difference among the canonists on the point. Heinrich of Vrimaria says such oaths are venial if they tumble out without reflection in the course of conversation; but Thomas says this is only so if the speaker fails even to notice the meaning of his own blasphemy in an attempt at colorful speech. If he does register the words' meaning, it is mortal sin; and if he is trying to gain himself a reputation as a fearsome fellow, it is demonic:

> Some people say, "If I don't swear, no one will be frightened of me! No one will consider me to be anything!" So in order to be fearsome and to be thought more of, they swear and blaspheme God. 0 wretched man! Where you are looking for honor, you will find eternal confusion![48]

Then there are people who although they do not blaspheme persistently yet name Christ's blood and his death habitually and emptily, as when they say in the vernacular *"Heyliges blut, es gat den also ubel!"* (Holy blood, it turned out so badly for him!) or *"Heylige martel, wie ist es dir geschehen"* (Holy victim, what has

---

[46] D.8.5 (J), D.15.2/7 (C), T.63.2 (E), T.95.7 (J).
[47] T.139.1/1 (L).
[48] D.2.2/5 (D), T.123.1 (A-C), Q.17.2/2.

happened to you?). There are some, again, who swear not by the creator but by creatures, saying things like *"bocks blut. bocks lychnan, bocks lung, bocks leber, bocks mag"* ("goat's blood, body, lung, liver, stomach"), or from bad habit they swear meaninglessly "by the living God," "by the holy God," "by all the saints." This sort of swearing is also mortal sin if used deliberately, whether seriously or in jest. If it is a slip of the tongue, again it is a mortal sin if one becomes aware of it and its meaning, but venial if it is unintended and unnoticed.

> If you do intend to correct yourself thoroughly and to speak your words simply according to the gospel's precept (saying "yes, yes" and "no, no"), and if nevertheless you then do swear from a slip of the tongue, you should immediately be contrite for it and say one "Hail Mary, blessed virgin," and she will seek grace for you from her Son, that by it you may take better care not to relapse again.[49]

Blasphemers are especially evil people; they are worse than the Jews, for they slew Christ once in unbelief but blasphemers do so every day in full knowledge of who he is. They are worse than dogs, since even dogs do not bite their own masters and benefactors. They are worse than the creatures, who all praise their creator, but blasphemers dishonor God with the very member made for man's honor and God's praise—the tongue. Blasphemy is the diabolical sin, the language of hell: "Such men learn here to blaspheme God, the labor of the damned, so that they may practise how to do it in the future!" And blasphemy, the sin against the Holy Spirit, is scarcely remitted and even fails to yield any utility or pleasure. God often visits the blasphemer with sudden death, the preacher warns.[50]

Cursing receives the same stern treatment as blasphemy. It is distinguished from it mainly by definition, since cursing has the additional character of "pronouncing evil against someone or something either by imprecation or wish." The cases Herolt describes in his dissuasion include gamblers who curse God when they are not winning at dice: "they project devilish guilt onto the divine innocence"; people who curse irrational creatures when they are upset, "betraying the enormous stupidity of cursing brute animals even though they cannot understand"; husbands who curse their wives, and parents their children; people who curse themselves for bodily infirmity, loss of possessions, or other temporal difficulty; paupers who curse God for their poverty and affliction; and others who curse the divine purpose, as farmers who curse a rain-bearing wind. "It is specially stupid for a mortal man, ash and worm, to set his mouth against heaven by murmuring against his creator and blaming him for his acts." It is even a mortal sin to curse the devil, for though

---

[49] D.2.2/5 (D), T.123.1 (D-F), T.142.2 (S-T).
[50] D.2.2/5 (D-E), T.123.2-3 (G-H), Q.17.2/2, A.B.: 3 "Blasphemantes" (113ᵃ).

he is evil in will, he is good in his essence as God's creature, and it is therefore a sin to wish him evil.

Since a curse wishes for evil, it is intrinsically repugnant to love of neighbor and, therefore by definition and biblical precedent, a mortal sin. Blasphemous cursing can be absolved only by the bishop or his penitentiary, and the severe canonical penalties for the sin are outlined, with a proviso that in judging a soul a discreet priest may mitigate their rigor. And it may be found that because of the pettiness, inadvertence, or impulsiveness of a trivial curse, it is only a venial sin after all: "the frame of mind is the chief factor in assessing verbal sins."[51]

Cursing takes on a specially destructive form when it is used either deliberately or in rage to provoke another to anger. Herolt enjoins particular caution against provoking the elderly and others known to be volatile, and above all against cursing and provocation between husbands and wives and within the family circle.[52] The content of our conversation in society must also exclude all wanton, lascivious, scurrilous, and lustful talk. Such language scandalizes and corrupts one's neighbors. Those who use it often claim that flirtatious talk is only superficial and jesting, but the mouth betrays what is in the heart.[53] Some women, and even maidens, delight to speak suggestively, reprehensibly displaying their shamelessness. Words, looks, and laughter may be only venial if they are genuinely innocent jests; but even jests may convey a mortal intention to arouse.[54]

The content of our speech, in short, must be free of all deceptiveness. Those who speak deceitfully to their neighbors repeat Judas's kiss. They have "honey in the mouth and poison in the heart (*mel in ore et fel in corde*)."[55] But those who are in the Spirit speak in new tongues:

> They reject the old tongue which the devil and evil men introduced from the beginning . . . . For the old tongue is an angry, harsh response to neighbors, especially in cursing them and provoking them to wrath . . . . And the old tongue is blasphemy and swearing . . . use of shameless and lustful language . . . detraction and denigration of the neighbor's repute . . . speaking lying words to a neighbor's loss . . . idle and useless chatter . . . pleasure in talking about mundane and transitory things . . . . But the new tongue is to speak meekly, modestly, and truly; to inform, warn, and correct the neighbor in fraternal admonition; to pray gladly, give thanks to

---

[51] D.2.2/10 (F), T.95.7 (L), E.22.2/1.
[52] D.15.2/7 (C), T.67.2 (A), T.95.7-8 (M).
[53] D.8.8 (M), T.96.216 (T), E.16.2.
[54] D.19.2/6 (F), T.86.6 (A), E.16.2.
[55] D.8.4 (G), T.96.2/4 (S), E.22.1/4.

God, willingly confess, and for the rest to speak good, honest, and edifying words.[56]

Our second consideration must be with whom we speak, and here the Wisdom literature is the preacher's guide. With a fool, speak few words; it is fatuous for a wise man to speak much with a stupid one. With an angry or litigious person, speak soft words, and do not excite them to even greater rancor. It is generally a mark of prudence to yield victory to the verbose. With old people, speak with reverence, and avoid provoking their rage. With someone wise, speak few and brief words, for they will suffice.[57]

The third consideration is when to speak. Ancient wisdom and monastic discipline combine to teach us that there is a time for silence and a time when something needs to be said but never a time when everything needs to be said. Failure to exercise discretion in speaking aptly or keeping silence is like a city without a wall or with its gates open in time of war. It is like a ship without a rudder. It is like a house without a door so that anyone who likes can come in and out at will, even pigs and dogs. In fact, the critical place for the protection of a house or a camp is the entrance: capture the entrance and you hold the camp. So it is critically important to keep a guard on the lips.[58]

The fourth consideration is how to speak. Our discourse should be simple, prudent, and honest, without cachinnation or clamor but sweet and rational.[59]

To follow these four rules, we need to imitate the example of Christ's own manner of speaking, which was marked by its truth, usefulness, and moderation.[60]

Truthfulness is specially pleasing to God and lying specially hateful. Lying is a diabolical sin, for the devil provoked man's first sin with a lie. It defiles the mouth; to lie is to let flies swarm disgustingly in the mouth. It makes liars into counterfeit coins, which outnumber the genuine coins—truth-tellers—by a thousand to one. Lying is so potent a poison that it kills the soul of the speaker himself and offends both God and man.[61] As the tongue becomes dry, spotted and black at the approach of death, so a lying tongue signals the onset of spiritual death.[62] There are forms of untruth, Herolt admits, that are merely verbal: preventive lying (*mendacium officiosum*), for example to preserve property by lying to a robber, or virginity by claiming to be married, or life by denying the whereabouts of the intended victim, is pardonable, as is some humorous untruth (*mendacium jocosum*) designed to raise

---

[56] T.67.2 (A).
[57] T.139.1/2 (M).
[58] T.139.1/3 (N).
[59] T.139.1/4 (N).
[60] T.15.2/6 (T), T.139.2 (O).
[61] D.8.1 (B), T.133.1 (J).
[62] T.129.2/5 (Q).

the spirits of someone sad and burdened in mind, or intended as a mere figment to please and amuse. But to speak against the truth of faith—to assert that Christ was not born of a virgin, for example, or to deny the veracity of Scripture—is destructive lying (*mendacium perniciosum*) and a mortal sin.[1] In social interaction, the most damaging forms of lie are false testimony, defamation, insincere oaths, broken promises, and misrepresentation in trade.[2] Accordingly, Herolt advises, one who wishes to be truthful should avoid cupidity and fear of others, the chief occasions of lying.[3]

Christ never spoke a useless word, and we must follow him in this, for mere truth without utility is not enough. It is an indication of this need for usefulness, Herolt suggests, that on its way to the light our speech must pass through six stages: it begins in the lungs, proceeds to the heart, passes through the throat, crosses the tongue, the teeth, and the lips before it is finally expressed. Again, the preacher feels impelled to warn against the deceptiveness of jest as a means of masking the uselessness or offensiveness of conversation.[4]

Christ's words also remained moderate, for truth and utility are inadequate without moderation. Like the rich man who prudently counts his cash before spending it, forethought before speech is conducive to wisdom.[5] Christ demands this wisdom and discretion in the soul that is his spouse.[6] This is a topic close to Herolt's heart; he loves to commend silence or economy of speech and to pillory loquaciousness. Moderation in words, he says, is a prime virtue; it is the sure sign of the virtuous man that he speaks few words, and those honest and useful.[7] By contrast, talkativeness is a sign of foolishness, and it makes one odious to one's hearers.[8] By using few words, we guard our souls, but using many makes them vulnerable. Verbosity is an impediment to spiritual growth, and the vice of loquacity is incompatible with devotion and piety.[9] Even our own physical makeup should teach us this lesson: our tongue is enclosed, and whereas we have two ears for hearing and two eyes for seeing, we have only one mouth for speaking to teach us moderation.[10] Silence is observed in cloisters because it is the material of peace. And we have Christ's own example of silence before Pilate and Herod: six times during his interrogation he remained silent, to teach us to preserve silence and

---

[1] D.8.1 (D), T.133.2/1-3 (L-M).
[2] T.133.2 (N-P).
[3] D.17.2/5 (F), T.133.1/2 (K).
[4] T.139.2/2 (P-Q).
[5] T.139.2/3 (R).
[6] T.157.2/3 (H).
[7] T.139.3/1 (S), E.44.2/2.
[8] D.18.4/1 (L), T.139.3/4 (S), Q.33.2.
[9] T.18.4(S), T.139.3/3 (S).
[10] T.139.3/2 (S), E.24.2/1, E.28.2/3-4, Q.32.2.

speak few words.[11] And finally, in the judgment we will render to Christ a strict account of every idle word that has passed our lips. "Oh, how many idle words you have spoken without reason or necessity in your lifetime!"[12]

Herolt has gleaned from pulpit tradition a medley of epigrams, verses, and stories to impress his admonitions on the minds of hearers. On deceit:

> *qui mel in ore gerit et me retro pungere quaerit,*
> *euis amicitiam nolo mihi sociam*
>
> (He who has honeyed lips and tries to stab me in the back,
> I can do without *his* friendly company!)[13]

On dissolute talk after overindulgence:

> *post vinum verba,*
> *post imbrem nascitur herba*
>
> (Words follow wine as weeds follow rain.)[14]

On the virtues of saying little, Seneca: "The taciturnity of stupid men will be taken for their wisdom," and "Reticence is the sentry of the soul."[15] Cato: "It never hurt anyone to be silent; but talking did!"[16] And the three philosophers who were asked to explain their silence:

> There were three philosophers who were earnestly asked why they were so untalkative. The first, Socrates, replied, "I have often regretted speaking, but being quiet, never." The second said, "No fool can stay silent." And the third said, "We are born with one mouth and two ears, so we should listen much and speak little."[17]

And, of course, there is a wealth of stories, especially from monastic tradition, commanding silence and rebuking verbosity, such as St. Agathon who carried a stone in his mouth for three years until he learned silence, or St. Theodonas who

---

11   T.139.3/6 (S), Q.32.2.
12   D.8.8 (M), D.12.3/1 (M), D.18.4/1 (L), T.4.2/3 (P), T.139.3/7 (S), Q.32.2.
13   T.96.2/4 (S).
14   D.18.4/1 (L).
15   Q.32.2/2.
16   T.139.3/3 (S).
17   P.L.: 18 "Lingua" (261), E.24.2/1.

remained silent in his cell for thirty years.[18] There are the inevitable macabre tales of dire warning, like the ribald fellows who cut up a chicken and said, "Neither Peter nor Christ could put it back together again" and were immediately smitten with leprosy, or the woman whose tongue never decomposed after her death as a sign of her misuse of it,[19] or Gregory's story of a blasphemous child:[20]

> A citizen of Rome dearly loved his five-year-old son, who whenever anything thwarted his will immediately and habitually cursed the Lord's name. One day, when the father was holding the child in his arms, the boy cried out, "Black men are coming to take me away!" The father replied, "Don't be frightened, my child." The boy said again, "You cannot see the black men who want to take me," and began to tremble. Then demons in the form of black men appeared and snatched the child violently from his father's arms and tore the boy's body into pieces.

If God thus avenged the sin of blasphemy in a child of five, what will he do in adults?

---

[18] T.18.4 (T); P.L.: 15, 16, "Lingua" (257, 258); E.24.2/1.
[19] P.B.: 8 "Blasphemia" (27); P.L.: 19 "Lingua" (262).
[20] T.123.3 (H).

18

FOOD AND DRINK

"Of all creatures large of body, man has the smallest mouth and the shortest teeth, and his mouth is not stooped to the ground."[21] Even our own physical nature teaches abstemiousness in food and drink. The fact that we have two ears and two eyes but only one mouth should teach us not only moderation in speaking, but temperance in eating and drinking.[22]

Enjoyment of our food, the preacher assures us, is no sin.[23] Our sustenance is the good gift of God.[24] But rarely are people content with sufficiency; they eat and drink to excess and fall into the mortal sin of gluttony. Gluttony makes a god out of a creature: the glutton worships his voracious belly.[25] The parallels between the actions of the gormandizer and the customary rituals of religion prove that this is idolatry.

A sacral being has a holy day on which he is celebrated; the gluttonous celebrate their holy days in the taverns, but they devote far more time to eating and drinking that they do to church attendance. Worshippers construct temples and build altars, ordain ministers, and burn incense; the temple of the glutton is the kitchen, his altar the table, his priests are the cooks, his burnt offerings roast meat, the fumes of his censers the smell of his delicacies.

In the lives and miracles of the saints, some make the blind see, but gluttony makes people blind drunk; some saints heal the lame, but winebibbing makes men stagger; some saints make the dumb speak, but sottishness slurs the speech; some saints make the sick well, but gluttons make themselves sick; some saints enlighten, but gorging makes fools out of wise men; some saints raise the dead, but people die from excess.

In a way, gluttony is even worse than pagan idolatry, for at least the heathen deck their idols with gold, silver and gems, "but the belly the glutton takes for his god is just like a privy!"[26]

---

[21] E.11.2.
[22] E.28.2/3.
[23] D.18.3/5 (J).
[24] T.98.0 (before F).
[25] D.1.1/24 (V), D.18.1/1 (A), T.98.2 (G), E.50.2, Q.30.2.
[26] D.18.1/1 (A), E.50.2.

Gluttony creates a haven for the devil, a foothold where the habit of overindulgence offers him secure tenure. It harms a man in body and soul—in body by generating illnesses like leprosy, dropsy, and paralysis, and by shortening life; and in soul by vitiating its powers, inducing a forgetful memory, a befuddled intellect, and a feeble will.[27]

The abuses of food and drink take several common forms: eating too soon, too preciously, too eagerly, too fussily, too lavishly.

First, it is wrong to take food before the proper time, unlike those, for instance, who tuck into their breakfast before they have even said a single *Paternoster* or given a thought to reverencing God. The soul is nobler than the body and should be fed first.[28]

A second abuse is to crave food that is too delectable. Herolt produces three curious reasons for censuring this fault: first, the stomach is an unclean vessel, and to put costly foodstuffs in it is merely to pollute them; secondly, it pits two against one—the body and delicate foods versus the spirit (we have concupiscence enough without fuelling it with dainties); thirdly, it habituates a person to eating nothing but fine foods—a special danger in the upbringing of children—and creates a propensity for backsliding into gluttony.[29]

It is reprehensible to eat too much: we must strike a balance between too much, which harms the body and suffocates the mind, and too little, which debilitates the body. Those who indulge their voluptuousness in food and drink anticipate their own death by inflicting sickness on themselves.[30] It is swinish to eat too avidly—to be so preoccupied with desire for food that like an animal one omits to think of God before eating. So pause before eating, and say at least one Lord's Prayer and make the sign of the cross and think of the poor. Remember the nun who ate a little lettuce in the cloister garden before prayers and ingested a devil with it or the *conversus* in a certain city who drank some wine without permission or the sign of the cross and with it drank a demon. And at table, let the conversation be of good, upright, and godly topics; and avoid scurrilous, dirty, or defamatory talk. When we speak of edifying things, the angels surround our meal, but vicious and slanderous talk brings demons to dance about the table.[31]

It is intemperate to eat too often: two meals a day are plenty for a healthy man. According to the physicians, Herolt claims, eating too often is quite harmful because piling food on top of undigested food already in the stomach blocks the digestive tract and impairs the power of digestion. Exceptions here may be made

---

[27] D.18.1/2-3 (A-B), cf. A.G.: 5 "Gulosi" (117ª).
[28] D.18.2/1 (C), T.98.1/1 (F).
[29] D.18.2/2 (C-D), T.58.6 (F), T.98.2 (G).
[30] D.18.2/3 (D), T.98.1/3 (H), E.35.2/1.
[31] D.18.2/4 (E); T.98.1/4 (H).

for laborers doing hard physical toil and for growing children who need to be fed more often.[32]

The preacher is scornful of those who devote too much effort and attention to the preparation of food. Some people spend all day preparing meals but can scarcely ever spare time to hear a single mass. Or they require their servants to spend so much time in the kitchen that they cannot listen to sermons. Paraphrasing Hugo's *Claustralium*,[33] Herolt mocks gourmets who "obsess about decoctions and frying pans and varieties of condiments— something soft, something hard, a bit of cold, a bit of hot, now raw, now cured, now roasted, a little pepper, a little garlic, a little cinnamon, a little salt—as fussy as the wonted cravings of a pregnant woman!" Their standards are hardly ever met; they complain however much trouble their wives or maids have taken: "Too much salt! Over fried! Too soft! Too tough!"[34] (These trenchermen apparently never set foot in the kitchen themselves.)

Overeaters also eat a damaging variety of dishes at their meals. Herolt quotes five proofs from Macrobius of the physical dangers of this deplorable gluttony. Animals are often healthier than men because they instinctively eat only simple, natural food, and only enough to satisfy their wants. Physicians urge recuperating patients to eat simple, wholesome food because it is more assimilable, and it is easier to diagnose an illness in a patient on a simple diet. Observation yields the same conclusion: if one watches two drinkers of similar complexion, and one of them mixes his drinks while the other imbibes the same quantity of a single liquor, the first will succumb quicker. Finally, since nature is uniform in operation, different dishes will be digested differently: the more digestible foods will be processed quicker, and the residue will stay in the stomach to interfere with later digestion.[35]

All these abuses lead men and women into one or other of the transgressions that constitute the mortal sin of gluttony and are a standard part of the interrogation of the penitent in confession.[36] The most obvious, and the easiest to police, is any breach of church regulations on fasting. This consumption of "illicit and prohibited foods" is said to be like Adam's sin in paradise, but the standard is more mundane. Meat, eggs, and milk products are forbidden in Lent. Meats are generally forbidden in all fasts because on the whole they are more delicious than other foods and cooperate more with the humors of lust, and they are therefore excluded on Fridays and also by widespread custom on Saturdays. Local usage determines additional abstinence in various other fasts, and one is bound to observe the regional practice. On fast days, there is to be no eating before the prandial meal, no moving the meal

---

[32] D.18.2/6 (E).
[33] Hugo de Folieto, sometimes wrongly attributed to Hugo of St. Victor, *De Claustro Animae*, 2.19, (MPL 177, 1072-73).
[34] D.18.2/5 (E), T. 8.1/2 (G).
[35] D.18.2/7 (F), T.60.3 (P), T.98.1/5 (J-K).
[36] Q.22.3.

forward in time, and no eating after it. Full or partial exemption from these rules is granted for growing children, pregnant women if there is a risk to the fetus, the elderly, and the sick. But pilgrims, laborers, and beggars are exempt only in emergency. Where adjoining fasts fall on a Thursday and a Saturday, it is permissible to honor the Friday fast merely by eating simple fare.[1]

However, it is just as easy to commit a mortal sin with foods that are not prohibited by canon law. If self-love leads some people to refuse to fast, pleasure in delicious food and convivial company leads others to place feasting before the self-love they owe God, and to eat food they know is harmful to their strength and incompatible with their nature just because it tastes good. Long sittings and elaborate meals and carousing for pleasure and camaraderie all too often lead to sickness and even death.[2] Delight in food becomes a specially heinous sin when the appetite for delectation is allowed to become the final and principal cause of eating, whereas God should be the final and principal cause of all our actions. To enjoy food is a natural response, and not sin; but when it is an end in itself, it is gluttony.[3]

Even wholesome and natural foods are an occasion for mortal sin when they are deliberately eaten to excess. Overeating from ignorance, inadvertence, or constitutional weakness is only venial sin; but nausea, vomiting, or loss of reason is taken as *prima facie* evidence of the mortal sin of gluttony.

The chief culprit, of course, is alcohol; and Herolt embarks on a long discussion of drunkenness where, somewhat uncharacteristically, he adds his personal opinion to the views of the canonists on the subject. The doctors commonly hold that inebriation is categorically a mortal sin when the drinker certainly knows the liquor to be intoxicating, and yet deliberately and willingly drinks too much. If he is unaware of its potency, or overdoes it unintentionally, it can be venial. But Thomas says there are three aspects to intoxication: if the user is unaware of a drink's power to inebriate, it is no sin; if he knows its power, but does not think he can become drunk, it is venial; if he knows its power, but would rather get drunk than abstain, it is mortal. "I believe," Herolt adds, "that inebriation is less of a sin in those who have weak heads and get drunk very quickly on a small amount of liquor; yet I do not presume to say that it is not a mortal sin in such people." In fact, if a person realizes he has a weakness for strong drink, yet repeated experience does not prompt him to break the habit, perhaps it is an even greater sin.

Such technicalities aside, drunkenness is an especially detestable sin, not only in itself, but because it is the catalyst for so many other sins, and above all because

---

[1] D.7.1/2 (M), D.18.3/2 (H), T.39.2-4 (L-P), T.99.2 (M-N), T.141.3 (L), T.154.1/1 (K), Q.5.1.
[2] D.18.3/3 (H), T.99.2/3 (N).
[3] D.18.3/5 (J), T.99.5 (P).

it robs a man of the reason that alone sets him apart from the brute beasts.[4] Such sottishness produces loss of sight, fogging of vision, a staggering gait (*"Ach, how many drunkards cannot even get home on their own two feet!"*), slurred and babbling speech, confusion of mind, bickering and brawling, sickness, and ultimately death.[5]

Consciousness of these dire effects is the best remedy against abuses of food and drink, Herolt suggests. The evils that flow from crapulence should be enough in themselves to deter us from excess. The memory of death should make us aware that by stuffing our bodies we are merely being "cooks for the worms."[6] And we shall give a strict account in judgment of every bite and drop that passed our lips without reason, need, or utility.[7]

Then we should keep before our mind's eye the poverty and wretchedness of Christ and the three times in the Gospels he went hungry—in the wilderness, at the cursing of the fig tree, and on the cross when he said, "I thirst." The Christian should remember the vinegar and the gall whenever bitter or insipid food is set before him, and be content.[8] The example of Christ and the saints commends to us the virtues of abstemiousness. Throughout his life, Christ never ate any meat except the Passover lamb; John the Baptist lived on locusts and wild honey; Martha ate no meat, eggs, cheese, fish, or anything cooked but only herbs, apples, and roots for seven years before her death. Such abstinence leads directly to a healthy body and mind:

> A sober and abstinent person lives delightedly in his sleeping, waking, working, and praying, and is properly disposed for every physical and spiritual demand, as well in mind as in body . . . . But indulgence of the flesh generates infirmities. That is why the rich are so often debilitated and ill—it is the variety of dishes that does it.[9]

But abstinence prolongs life, as the example of the patriarchs shows. From Adam until the flood, men did not eat meat, fish, or artificial foods but vegetables, herbs, and fruit, and it was only with Noah that wine drinking was introduced. The longevity of religious in cloisters proves the same truth.[10]

The Holy Spirit's gift of understanding expels gluttony because then we understand that we should use God's creatures of food and drink for his honor and our sustenance.[11] Otherwise gluttony is used to hiding beneath a facade of

---

[4] D.18.3/4 (J), T.99.2/4 (O), E.11.2.
[5] E.50.2.
[6] D.18.6/1-2 (P-Q).
[7] D.18.6/5 (T), T.3.2/3 (R).
[8] D.18.6/3 (R), T.15.2/4 (R), Q.42.2/2.
[9] E.11.2.
[10] D.18.1/3 (B), T.60.3 (O), E.11.2; E.35.3/1.
[11] T.3.2/3 (R), T.73.6 (G).

liberality—"God made everything for us to enjoy!"—but it is against nature and the order of providence for one man to try and swallow everything. It hides, too, behind a false show of necessity; but there is a difference between sufficiency and superfluity. Nature is content with a little; it is custom that makes many things necessary. Gluttony can even masquerade as an appetite for plain food, when it is craved and consumed in vast quantities. For it is not the food that makes the sin but the appetite: Esau craved a mere dish of lentils and lost his birthright, whereas Elijah in the desert was fed with meat but remained faithful. It was not wine that Adam took in the garden—just an apple.[12]

But the most graphic incentives to moderation in eating and drinking are the visions of the two great eternal banquets, the feasts of heaven and hell. Whatever strictures the preacher applies to feasting and serving too many courses at banquets, his image of heavenly delights nevertheless stands in the great naïf tradition of the grand festivity. At the heavenly feast, all the guests are noble, for we shall all be kings and queens; the banquet is prepared at infinite expense, for it cost Christ's death; and all the dishes are grand, lavish, sweet-tasting, and costly, for all the joys and rewards of the saints in heaven are the courses at this never-ending board.[13] At this feast we shall enjoy the noblest of service, for Christ—not an angel or St. Peter or some other saint—will wait on us. The seating pattern will show a perfect order, for there will be places set for all the saints, patriarchs, prophets, and apostles and seats of honor for the martyrs and confessors and virgins. And Mary will have a special seat of her own at her Son's right hand. At last our every desire will be perfectly satisfied at this noblest of tables, where we will sit at the self-same board as God, our host.[14]

But hell, too, will hold a feast, an infernal banquet that will serve three courses, accompanied by the bitterest of drinks and the saddest music in the universe. For the damned, the first course will be perpetual hunger and thirst, the second the death of their own flesh, and the third their flesh either decocted by the frigidity of hell or roasted by its undying flames. Sulphur and fire will be the wine they drink (Psalm 11:7 here provides the traditional exemplary symbol of the drunkard in hell helplessly clutching a flaming goblet of brimstone).[15] And for music:

> Just as at great feasts it is the custom to sound diverse instruments of music, so at those infernal feasts or weddings three sorts of music will resound: the gnashing of teeth ... the ululation of demons ... and the wailing of all the damned together.[16]

---

[12] D.18.5 (O).
[13] D.18.6/6 (V), T.53.6 (P), T.84.0 (J), E.11.2.
[14] Q.26.1.
[15] T.62.3 (Y), T.99.2/4 (P).
[16] T.101.3 (E).

19

AMUSEMENTS

Can fun and games be virtuous? Yes, says the preacher, if and when the body needs recreation and the soul needs rest and solace. After all, one cannot work all the time.[17]

It is just as well that Herolt introduces his model sermon on fun and games with this assurance. Otherwise, the listener might be forgiven for inferring that the church frowned on merriment in general and on the commonest forms of merriment above all. Whenever he turns to the details of popular conviviality, Herolt seems dour and censorious; yet in principle he admits there is a middle path of virtue where lightheartedness and play are not only permissible but wholesome. He even describes recreation as the spice of life:

You find three sorts of people. There are some who are like food without any seasoning at all—they never joke or play, but are always dour and stiff. But it is against human reason for anyone to appear so grave—say by showing no delight in anything—that he robs others of their pleasure. As Seneca says. "Rule yourself wisely so that no one thinks you harsh nor scorns you as mean." But there are others who are like food with too many spices and too much salt—people who play to excess. And there are some who are like food seasoned to perfection—they use play in a virtuous way.

Fun must have three characteristics to be virtuous. First, it must be simple, innocent, and harmless. Some people care so little for the feelings of others that they actually seek out peoples' defects to poke fun at them. That sort of joke is not virtuous.

Secondly, fun must be circumspect. The chosen amusement must be appropriate to one's status: different jokes or games are suitable or unsuitable, decorous or indecorous for a cleric, a prelate, a religious, a secular, for woman, youngster, man, wife, servant, or virgin. One must first consider person, situation, and dignity and attempt nothing that may degrade oneself or one's status, avoiding above all the slightest hint of unseemliness. The time, too, must be appropriate: a perfectly innocuous joke may be quite out of place at a time of sadness or devotion. Then one

---

[17] T.22.0 (A).

must consider the circumstances: different sorts of jokes are fitting before laymen and clergy, the elderly and the young, superiors, equals, and subordinates.

The third essential of virtuous fun is the avoidance of excess, either in frequency or in length, unlike those reprehensible people who "spend the greater part of their time in sport and jest and laughter and other worldly vanities like games of dice or chess or cards."[18]

Apart from his general affirmation of the legitimacy of recreation, we hear very little about what innocent merriment might look like but much about the frivolous depravity of almost every popular form of merrymaking. None of them arouses his ire more than the dance.

Dancing

The two sins most indulged on holy days, he protests, are drunkenness and dancing.[19] He devotes the central part of his exposition of the third commandment (on Sabbath observance) to a tirade against dancing, and he repeats much of it with elaboration in a sermon for Quinquagesima.[20] The profusion of sermonic devices and exemplary stories churchmen marshalled against dancing are clear evidence of its popularity as a form of entertainment. Dancing attracted the gaiety of the young with an energy that successfully competed with the solemnity of holy days and, of course, never more successfully than in Shrovetide. It is no coincidence that Herolt provides sermons "on worldly pleasures" and "on dancing" for the eve of the pre-Lent carnival.

Those who dance on feast days, he declares, sin worse than those who work on them.[21] How foolish to deprive oneself of the saints' intercession by scorning their feasts; how incongruous to seek eternal rest by refusing to be quiet and by exertion of the body and mind in the dance.[22] Sometimes, he says, there is a veritable plague of dancers around churches and church yards, impeding the godly folk who want to serve God; and he passes on one version of a classic tale:

> A priest in Saxony, celebrating the divine office in the church of a great saint, heard girls and boys dancing outside, and they were disturbing him and the others in their prayers; so he called down a curse on them that they should not be able to stop their dancing and singing. The result was that they went on and on for a whole year, without eating or drinking but dancing and drinking endlessly, until first they sank up to their knees in the ground, and then up to their

---

[18] T.22.1 (A).
[19] D.3.2/3 (K).
[20] D.3.3 (L-O), T.37.1-3 (P-X).
[21] Q.19.2.
[22] D.3.4 (L).

thighs. Everyone who visited the place saw this amazing affliction from God, and no one was able to go to their aid or free them from their affliction until St. Gilbertus, then bishop of Cologne, came to the place. He saw the divine affliction and felt compassion for them, and enjoined the people to fast and pray together for them, and thus he absolved and liberated them. Some of them died soon after; but some lived a long time, and the tremor of their limbs displayed their penalty until the day of their death.[23]

As far as they can, Herolt declares, dancers crucify the Son of Man afresh. He justifies this judgment by a detailed analysis of dancing technique itself. There are five actions, he says, demanded by the art of dancing well. The first is to leap high in the air; but the higher one leaps in the dance, the deeper one falls into hell.[24] "Dancer, if only you realized how every brash movement is a leap into the depths of a cesspit!"[25] Especially those who take a lead in the dancing at carnival jump straight into hell.[26] The second action is to fling the arms wide to enlarge the circle; but by so doing, dancers ridicule the extending of Christ's arms on the cross and thus deride the mercy of God. Thirdly, dancers toss the head back and shout loudly and thus show their contempt for the Christ who hung his head on the cross, their shouting a bestial mockery of his crying out with a loud voice. Fourthly, they link arms and hands firmly with each other to preserve the order of the dance; and it signifies how the devil holds dancers firmly in his grip and power. Finally, dancers decorate themselves prettily—their heads with silks and caps and veils, the rest of their bodies with diverse costumes as an apt sign of how dancers become deformed, blackened, and like devils in hell:

> For the more they decorate themselves with assorted ornamentation and variegated costumes and colors, the more diverse, and varied the pains they will earn in hell—each superfluous tunic and each motley color will have its special punishment in hell, a particular pain attached to each color in turn, one for red, another for yellow, and so on.

Moreover, decorated headdress does despite to Christ's crown of thorns, trailing sleeves to the robes in which he was mocked, gold and silver cummerbunds to the rope of his bondage.[27] At the sounding of the third thunder in judgment, the nail prints in Christ's feet will be displayed to all dancers.[28] "Christ bore the cross and

---

[23] T.37.3 (A).
[24] D.3.3/5 (M); T.37.1/1 (P).
[25] T.36.2 (K).
[26] E.13.2/5.
[27] D.3.3/5 (M-O), T.37.1 (P-R), cf. P.C.: 7 "Chorea" (35).
[28] T.5.3 (F).

spent all his strength in suffering to redeem you, and you spend all your strength in dancing!"[29]

But, the parishioner objects, people danced a hundred years ago, why not now? A hundred years ago, the preacher rejoins, men were peopling hell by their misdeeds just as they still do: precedent is no excuse.[30] Indeed, biblical precedent points in exactly the opposite direction. Look at the vengeance wreaked by the Levites on the children of Israel when they danced before the golden calf. Salome danced before Herod and demanded the Baptist's head, demonstrating how much power a dancing woman has to separate even those who like John have God's grace from their head, namely Christ.[31]

Beware especially of women who set aside their veils and let their hair down for the dance.[32] There are many forewarning precedents in the church's memory too: the girl in Canterbury who sang and danced with such beauty that she enticed the hearts of many, but was snatched up from the midst of the crowd by a malign spirit and thrown to a twisted death; the youth who heard a preacher inveigh against the dance as the gate of hell and answered, "No, it is the gate of consolation and happiness!" and in the very next dance fell down and killed himself on the sharp stones; the vain and wanton woman, killed accidentally in the dance by a young man's staff, whose body awaiting burial was savaged by a foul demon in the guise of a huge black bull; the village near Cologne where a silk-clad ram was offered as a prize to the best dancer, and when the priest's dire warnings went unheeded, the whole village was razed by a destructive thunderstorm; and various horrid visions vouchsafed to the godly of dancers in hell squashed into spiked iron cells, endlessly burned by sulphurous fire, torn by dragons, and chewed to the bone by hellish wolves.[33]

To avoid the bonds prepared in hell for hands and feet that have been the agents of dancing and leaping, and the curses the damned will then pronounce on their own errant limbs,[34] Christians should circumcise their feet from the illicit movements of the dance,[35] and in penance confess each instance of "offending God by dancing."[36] Otherwise, on the last day Christ himself will demand account of each step and each leap of the dancer, and how many dances one has danced, and he will adjudge them evil.[37] So the conscientious confessor will make strict inquiry of

---

[29] T.15.2/2 (P).
[30] T.37.3 (U).
[31] D.3.3/1 (L), T.37.3 (X).
[32] D.13.3/2-3 (G-H).
[33] D.3.4 (L), T.37.3 (X), T.154.1/1 (G), P.C.: 9-12 "Chorea" (37-40).
[34] T.5.5 (J), T.37.1 (P), T.125.6 (S).
[35] T.19.3/5 (F).
[36] Q.19.2.
[37] T.3.2/3 (Q).

the penitent about dancing,[38] and where he detects a contravention will impose an appropriate castigation such as coming barefoot to church.[39] The monk, incidentally, who sets aside his habit in order to jump or dance is to be excommunicated if he does so in the presence of laymen but not if only clergy are present.[40]

The sinfulness of dancing consists not only in its mockery of the passion but also in the number of mortal sins it commits: *pride*—"people do not dance out of humility!"; *lust*—dancing inflames participants and onlookers alike to evil desire by movement and adornment and the touching of women; *envy*—the participants vie for admiration and are jealous of each other's costumes; and *avarice*—people aspire to a finery and beauty that is beyond them.

Moreover, dancing contravenes the sacraments. The dance breaches the sponsor's vow in baptism to renounce the devil and all his pomps, for "when people enter the dance, they enter the pomps or processions of the devil": the fact that the regular motion of the dance is to the left betrays it as the devil's procession. Dancing reverses confirmation, since the devil's sign of pride adorns the brow in place of the sign of the cross. It contravenes penance, in that it shatters the peace made with God in the Lenten shrift and advances instead in the vanguard of the devil's army. And it contravenes marriage by its often intentional success in arousing adulterous desires.[41] In short, dancing contradicts the profession of Christian faith, for it takes such joy in the pleasures of this present age.[42]

But it is not only the dancers themselves who are contaminated by this shameless folly. The onlookers sin as much as the dancers by giving occasion and by not condemning what they see; they participate in the dance by their attitude and approbation. Remember that St. Damian's sister suffered fifteen days in purgatory merely for not confessing that she had overheard some dancers singing sweetly.[43] Parents who urge their children to dance are guilty of the alien sin of *iussio*; parents who merely fail to forbid their children to dance, or enjoy it when they do, are guilty of the alien sin of *consensus*.[44] Innkeepers who provide space for dancers to make merry commit *recursus*, another alien sin, and will answer for it at the judgment seat of Christ.[45]

As we have noticed already, the pre-Lent carnival was the occasion of the year's most uproarious dancing and festivity, and therefore was the focus of the preacher's sharpest concern. Custom, Herolt says, makes even great sins seem trivial:

---

[38] Q.22.3.
[39] T.156.4 (C).
[40] Q.32.2/2.
[41] D.3.3/2-3 (L), T.37.2 (S).
[42] T.62.6 (A).
[43] T.37.3 (T-U).
[44] T.144.1 (H) and 3 (J).
[45] T.4.1/8 (Y), T.144.5 (M).

the carnival is the clearest example of it.[46] That, he explains, is why the church chooses to chant the story of the flood throughout the week from Sexagesima to Quinquagesima, and on Quinquagesima, to read the terrible story of the destruction of the Five Cities; it is supposed to draw her sons away from the vain, drunken sprees and worldly joys characteristic of this season of *CarnisPrivium*.[47] For the same reason, the liturgy anticipates holy week and reads the story of the passion just before Lent begins. "But alas! At this season of Shrovetide our Lord is ridiculed by people who sin more in these few days than in all the rest of the year."

Festivity

Dancing is only one of a series of debaucheries hallowed by custom. The preacher attacks festive indulgence in "foolish amusements," the gluttonous eating and drinking of the carnival, the lustful acts and unclean thoughts provoked by it.

He solemnly intones against what he sees as the dire social and spiritual consequences of fancy dress costumes and masquerades. Men take off their own clothes and put on women's clothing and vice versa. It is not lawful, he insists, for a woman to wear man's clothing, a topic of some perplexity for medieval churchmen, since hagiographical tradition does provide a few laudable examples of women saints who cross-dressed as men; but Herolt stays with the prevailing judgment that it is culpably perverse, since Deuteronomy forbids it, the Gloss identifies it with pagan superstition, and Thomas insists that "exterior attire must match the status of the person in accordance with common custom."[48] He cannot regard such burlesque as innocent escape, but he declares that revelers who wear clothing of the opposite sex are idolaters, those who dress up in animal skins show themselves bestial, and worse, those who disguise themselves in demon costumes prove that they are slaves of the devil. Nor, of course, does he see any levelling virtue in the Shrovetide pantomime in which common people masquerade as emperors, kings, popes, and bishops but accuses the mummers of "setting aside all God's honor" and threatens them with punishment here and in future.[49]

Tournaments

Among the upper classes, carnival is a time for mounting tournaments, and this too Herolt censures but with a more prosaic account of his reasons. The only

---

[46] T.131.4/3 (J).
[47] E.12.0, E.13.2.
[48] Thomas Aquinas, S.T. 2/2 q.169. See also Marina Warner, *Joan of Arc* (Harmondsworth: Penguin, 1983), 147ff.
[49] E. 13. 2.

way a tournament may escape condemnation as a mortal sin is if it is designed solely to teach skill at arms and contravenes no prohibited season. But tournaments at carnival are a breach of ecclesiastical prohibition; and anyway, some canonists ban them altogether because they threaten the death of both body and soul. Some members of the nobility waste all their days in jousting and use them to seek for themselves an illegitimate honor. But under canon law, jousting carries heavy penalties. In the church's eyes, one who kills another in the lists is guilty of murder, and the one who is killed is not to be buried in hallowed ground.[50]

The physical harm done by tournaments is at least confined to the upper classes; sometimes the amusements of the rich inflict damage and loss on other members of the community. "Hunters who cause damage to crops with their horses, dogs, and retainers sin gravely and are bound to make restitution," the preacher insists,[51] and he recites the inevitable string of fearful examples of knights and nobles who became addicted to the hunt: the powerful lord who demanded that his subjects ride to hounds with him every day, driving them into poverty by forced neglect of their families and fields, who disappeared without a trace as he chased a wild beast; the two cruel sons of a pagan emperor who tortured and slew the Christians they trapped in their hunting nets but then killed each other in the crossfire from their bows as they tried to down a stag; the German noble whose passion for hunting caused him to neglect the mass, despite his wife's devout admonitions, until he was repaid by the birth of a monstrous child with the head and drooping ears of a hound; and the knight, chaste, upright, hospitable, and good living but addicted to fowling, who was displayed in purgatory lacerated on the face, shoulders, arms, and hands by the bites of the birds and dogs he had used for his sport.[52]

Gambling

But the amusement which, after dancing, draws the preacher's most energetic censure is one that knows no boundaries of class, namely gambling.

It is a little startling to find Herolt's sermon on gambling assigned to the feast of Christmas, until he explains that "nowadays, alas, it has become the custom for many people to spend this most sacred of nights in gambling."[53]

Just as each step and gesture of the dance has its anti-Christian interpretation, so now Herolt tells us the baneful significance of each throw of the dice. If the player throws one eye, it means the kingdom of heaven will be taken from him; two eyes are his body and soul, eternally damned; three eyes, the Holy Trinity will be hidden forever from the gambler's vision; four eyes, he will be eternally separated from the four orders

---

[50] T.28.2/2 (K), T.59.1/1 (H), E.13.2/6.
[51] Q.40.2.
[52] T.22.3 (C-E), P.V.: 1 "Venatio" (588).
[53] T.12.0 (F).

of the new testament saints—apostles, martyrs, confessors and virgins; if he throws five eyes, the salvation that flows from the five wounds of Jesus will be frustrated; six eyes, his omission of the six works of mercy will bring him to the judgment.[54] The twenty-one total points on each die correspond to the twenty-one Hebrew letters in which God gave the scriptures to the faithful, so the dice player has no excuse for not knowing God's will.[55] A similar interpretation is appropriate for other games of chance too, Herolt says, whether the markings are carved on tiles or pictured on cards.[56]

The preacher provides an even more elaborate list of the mortal sins involved in gambling—eighteen of them in one version of the list, sixteen in another. The gambler is first of all an idolater: the fact that he is so much more generous with his wagers than with his almsgiving shows that he has made the dice his god. Next, the typical gambler is guilty of execrable swearing and blasphemy against God and the saints, especially when he is losing, he curses God for his losses. Thirdly, he breaks the solemnity of sacred days and nights. He breaches the fourth commandment by disobeying his parents' presumed prohibition against gambling; the fifth if he kills an opponent over a trifling bet, as sometimes happens. To support their habit, not a few bettors are reduced to theft, which not only breaks the sixth commandment but may even lead to their hanging. Seventh, gamblers often boast that they won when in fact they lost—false witness. Eighth, their motivating impulse is desire for gain, which is greed, the root of all evils. The ninth sin is mercilessness for a gambler is quite willing to take the shirt off his opponent's back, and if bystanders agree to divide up the clothing won and lost on dice games, they share the guilt. Wagering is also the worst form of usury, since illicit profit is taken not in a year or a month but the very same day. It shows contempt to the prohibitions of mother church and causes scandal to one's neighbors. It leads to sins of omission, since the time wasted in gaming could have been spent in pious works. The actual process of gambling involves deliberate fraud, lying, false oaths, disloyalty, and deception and leads inevitably to anger, threats, and hatred.[57]

Since gamblers' winnings are the fruit of such a battery of sins, most obviously of avaricious desire for gain, the church regards the proceeds as unjust property that must be restored.[58] Herolt quotes Guillaume of Lyon: "Anyone who gambles from greed sins mortally: if he wins he wins hell, and if he loses he loses heaven, and whatever profit he has made must be given away for God's sake on the advice of his confessor." He cannot escape by claiming that what he wins one day he loses the next.[59] Confessors are to ask penitents how often they have gambled from avarice

---

[54] D.7.1/17 (JJ), T.12.1 (G).
[55] D.7.1/17 (KK), T.12.2 (H).
[56] D.7.1/17 (OO).
[57] D.2.2/10 (F), F.7.1/17 (KK-LL), T.12.2 (H-J).
[58] D.7.1/17 (MM), T.12.3 (L), T.104.13 (L), T.141.2 (K).
[59] Q.42.3.

and specifically how much has been won and lost.¹ Absolution will be withheld unless restitution of winnings is made, whether large or small; and Herolt quotes from the canonists a set of elaborate rules for this restitution.

If the bet was won from a minor, it must be repaid to his father; from a married woman without her own income, to her husband; from a religious, to his superior or monastery; from a priest, to the poor, using one's confessor as agent; from the handicapped, to their guardians. "But if these sorts of people win, they are not bound to make restitution to you, because you don't deserve to have it back—you were trying your best to despoil them!" If the loser was reluctant to take part, but was pressured to join the game either at the beginning or in progress, then restitution is to be made to him; but if he was a willing participant, the takings are to go to the poor. Hustling is forbidden as fraud—"if, for instance, a player represents himself as unskilled in the game, or someone easily deceived, when in fact his own intention is to deceive." And of course it is fraud to use weighted dice, to throw good dice dishonestly by sleight of hand, to call false numbers, to miscount the money, and so on. In all these cases, the mark is to receive his losses back. But where there is no coercion or fraud, and the game is between willing participants using property that is their own to spend, the overriding logic is that neither winner nor loser is entitled to the stakes:

> One is not bound to make restitution to the other, but neither is he entitled to keep it himself. The reason is that since the game is a form of looting no one can licitly acquire anything for himself by it, and therefore cannot keep his winnings; but neither must he give it back to the other, because he too was trying his best to loot his neighbor, and does not deserve to get it back.

The beneficiaries then are to be the poor, through the policing agency of the confessor.² Habitual gamblers almost always backslide after penance, however, and will suffer at judgment when the lots that were cast for Christ's raiment will be displayed to their confusion.³

Other contributors to games of chance share in the guilt, whether they are the craftsmen who make loaded dice, innkeepers who attract trade by hosting gambling games, spectators who hold the stakes, adjudicators of betting disputes, or merely drinking companions.⁴ The chief target of Herolt's assault is dice, but the same principles apply to wagers on games of checkers (*bretsypil*), cards (*cartenspil*), chess (*schachzabelspil*), and hazard (*feglen*). Is there any legitimate way of enjoying

---

1   Q.19.2, Q.22.3.
2   D.7.1/17 (MM-NN), T.12.3 (L).
3   T.5.3/14 (G), T.58.2 (F).
4   D.2.2/10 (F), T.55.5 (X), T.145.6 (O).

these games? Yes, he replies, so long as four conditions are met: there must be no incongruity of persons (for instance, no priests may be involved), or of matter (only trivial bets for something to eat or drink are permissible), or of time (not at times of mourning, penitence, or communion), and finally, the game itself must be played according to the rules![5]

But gamblers should not be looking for ways to legitimize their addiction; rather, they should open their eyes to the dissuasions that lie all around them.[6] Not least among them are the case histories the preacher can produce from his storehouse of examples—Caesarius's story of the knight of Soest, whose passion for dice drew him into a fatal losing game with the devil; the man who lost his clothes in a dice game and in anger shot an arrow into the air as if to strike God in heaven, and repented when it fell back at his feet stained with blood; the player who lost everything he had except one denarius, which he threw away with curses, and the demons retrieved it and claimed his soul; or the drunk who was shaking the dice bowl to see who would pay for the wine. "Let three pay!" he said, but the game was suddenly interrupted when he fell down dead. "I concede the game!" the other player said.[7]

Other forms of recreation or entertainment receive little treatment at Herolt's hands. He mentions actors only in passing as he disapproves the low life of the taverns.[8] He seems to be ambivalent about music. On the one hand, he affirms the godly virtue of singing morning hymns, refers often to the church's hymnody, and speaks glowingly of the sweet sound of angels and saints continually making music to God in heaven. The use of harps, organs, and diverse musical instruments in the Corpus Christi procession prefigures that heavenly praise of Christ. Mothers, too, sing sweetly to their children, a practice Herolt warmly recommends.[9] However, others sing illicit songs to attract worldly honor. The custom at great feasts of sounding diverse musical instruments becomes for the preacher an image of the cacophony of hell, and he counsels solemnly against hiring "disreputable people like pipers, lutenists, and trumpeters" for wedding celebrations.[10]

In general, Herolt says, worldly merriment, inappropriate jollity, jests, and gestures displaying levity of mind may lead to mortal sin if they involve some intrinsically evil act, like seductive jokes or illegal dancing or jousting or vindictive derision or proud displays; if they cause harm, provocation, or scandal to a neighbor; or if the participants take too much pleasure in them and overdo them.[11]

---

[5] D.7.1/17 (OO), T.12.4 (N).
[6] D.7.1/17 (MM).
[7] T.12.5 (O), T.60.4 (Q), P.L.: 20-22 "Lusores" (263-265).
[8] Q.42.3, E.26.3.
[9] T.2.2 (K), T.17.2/9 (M), T.78.114 (E), T.84.5 (K), R.6.4 (98a).
[10] T.26.8 (T), T.28.2/2 (K), T.101.315 (F).
[11] T.36.2 (J-M), T.86.6 (A), T.139.2/2 (P), T.148.8 (F).

Lighthearted jocularity is only venial if it does no harm and is not directed against love of God and neighbor;[12] and it may even be a positive good if it is intended to relieve some grief or trial in oneself or others:

> For too much sadness dries up devotion, and performance of the virtues is smothered, for it does not agree with a man to do something good when he feels too downcast inside. And if the human mind is always preoccupied with serious matters, it grows tired and sluggish. So if time and place permit, it is right to take rest and recreation. But beware of superfluity and excess: as Aristotle says (Ethics 9), "A little delight suffices to season life as a little salt suffices to season food." It follows that those people who chase after too many worldly joys and physical recreations are reprehensible indeed.[13]

---

[12] T.32.2/4 (N), T.110.1 (M).
[13] T.36.2/5 (N).

20

TRADE AND COMMERCE

"In the commerce of buyer and seller, it is difficult for sin not to intrude," the decretals say, and the preacher has a wealth of evidence to prove it.[14] From canonists, confessors, and common knowledge, he draws together a catalogue of the rogueries, sharp practices, and market manipulations that seem endemic to trade.

It need not be so, he insists. Those who claim that it is impossible to engage in trade without lying are wrongheaded. He repeats a story from Caesarius to make the point:

> Two burghers of Cologne confessed, among their other faults, to two classes of sin, lying and false swearing. Intrinsically, they are certainly great sins, yet these days they are regarded as trivial, almost nonexistent, as a result of mercantile practice. "Domine," they declared, "we could buy or sell almost nothing at all unless we were free to lie, use oaths, and sometimes swear falsely!" The priest said to them, "Those are very serious sins, and forbidden by the Savior, who said 'Let your yes be yes and your no no.'" They replied, "We cannot keep this precept in our business!" The priest said, "Take my advice and everything will be all right. Do not lie, do not swear, but make your recommendation match the price you expect." And they promised to try it for a year—the period the priest proposed to them. As a result Satan, who is always opposed to human salvation, sabotaged them, and that year they were hardly able to sell anything. When the year was up they went back to the priest and said, "Our obedience to you this year has cost us dearly—people shunned us and we could sell nothing in the absence of swearing!" Then the priest said, "Do not be afraid—it is a trial. Remain firm in your hearts, so that no adversity, no poverty may deflect you from your purpose, and the Lord will bless you." Prevailed on by his words, they promised that they would keep his counsel and the divine command for the

---

[14] T.133.2/9 (P), citing *de pe.* dist. 5, "qualitas."

rest of their lives, even if it meant they had to beg. It was a wonderful thing, but the Lord immediately put a stop to the trial imposed on them, and brought them more customers than frequented the other merchants. In a short time they became so rich that they marvelled, and went back to their confessor to thank him for the fact that by his counsel they had been exonerated from such grave sins, and moreover had become materially wealthy in the process.[15]

In spite of the alleged payoff, few of Herolt's contemporaries seem to have entrusted their business success to strict observance of the golden rule: "It is the will of God that we deal with our neighbor in equity, and in all our dealings follow the rule enshrined in natural law and taught in the gospel by Christ himself.... This rule must specially be observed by merchants, laborers, farmers, and artisans."[16] In practice, however, each one of these groups declares its avarice by its deceits. Christ had to drive the money changers from the earthly temple, and there are twelve principal classes of merchants who will be ejected from the heavenly temple into the abyss of hell.[17]

Tricks of the Trade

The first, as we have seen, are those who buy and sell with lying and deceit, even if they know no other way to conduct business. It is perjury if someone swears that his merchandise is better quality than it really is, or that the customer agreed on a higher price for it than he did, or that "I paid more for it in such and such a city," inflating the wholesale price.[18] It is also blasphemy when a vendor swears by God that he will not let an article go for less than such and such a price when in fact he intends otherwise; and likewise when a buyer insists, "I'm not prepared to go higher than so and so, by God!" while really intending to go higher.[19] This sort of deception is the mortal fruit of avarice if it works to the other's disadvantage: "It is a matter for great grief that always, every day, so much money is made in business, in buying and selling, at the loss and ruin of the other party."[20]

But fraud and avarice in trade go far beyond mere verbal falsehood. Material deception is also rife, and the second group condemned is those merchants who are delinquent in value. They deal in false specie or give false measure—the clothier with too short an ellwand, the peddler with rigged scales, the wineseller with an

---

[15] T.133.3 (Q).
[16] T.102.4 (M).
[17] D.17.1/11-12 (O-S),.T.106.1-12 (A-G).
[18] D.2.2/3 (C), D.7.14/1(O), T.106.1 (A), T.123.1/6 (F).
[19] T.123.1/6 (F).
[20] D.17.2/5 (F).

undersized jigger, and their like.[21] Herolt spells out the varieties of such trickery. Some people keep two sets of weights, one for buying and another for selling. Others have weights that are accurate enough, but they deliberately misread them or manipulate them fraudulently, like taverners who fill up the measure with froth or hucksters who rest their finger surreptitiously on the scale. Others, more cunning still, keep accurate measures but take steps to add weight to the merchandise at selling time by dampening wool or linen, for instance, or taking pepper down to the cellar and rolling it from one side to the other in the dust to make it heavier, or watering down wine or otherwise adulterating their wares. Such frauds must make restitution, or else the archangel Michael will demand a full accounting on the last day.[22]

Another device, less active but certainly more common in the marketplace, is the practice of hiding inferior goods beneath a layer of better quality wares. This is culpable in itself, but compounded when sellers swear the whole collection is the same quality as the visible layer. Another variant is to display high quality merchandise but actually supply inferior.[23] A more reprehensible sharp practice is to misrepresent flawed and defective items as good. It involves the seller in a double risk, not only deception but also the potential to cause the buyer actual harm—if, for instance, he misrepresents a lame horse as swift, or a rickety house as sound, or rotten food as fresh. However, Herolt does admit some legitimacy to the principle of *caveat emptor*. If a fault is hidden, the seller is bound to declare it and adjust his price, but if it is obvious—a one-eyed horse, for instance—he is not obliged to stress it, since the buyer may prefer to take a flawed item for the sake of a lower price.[24]

The principle of transparency extends even to the place where business is conducted. Herolt condemns traders who choose obscure locations and shun the broad light of day for their shady dealings; they are up to no good.[25]

Usury and Credit

But these obvious and age-old tricks of trade are now accompanied by more sophisticated market manipulations based on finance. These are matters of special concern to the preacher, who finds usury adopting the subtle guise of accepted trade practice. He condemns traders who increase their prices when they sell on credit: if the price to the buyer at term is higher than the market price on the day

---

[21] D.17.2/6 (G).
[22] D.7.14/2 (P), T.82.1 (C), T.106.2 (B), Q.41.3, E.8.1/1.
[23] D.2.2/3 (C), D.7.14/4 (Q), T.106.4 (C).
[24] D.7.14/6 (Q), T.106.6 (D).
[25] D.7.14/8 (Q), T.106.8 (E).

of the sale, the difference is usurious and must be repaid.[26] In particular, merchants exploit credit arrangements by buying low for cash and then immediately selling high on credit, taking a profit for their entrepreneurship even though they perform no labor and add no value to the goods. The church sanctions a reasonable profit for middlemen if and only if they contribute to the corporate work involved in delivery of the goods; any profit out of proportion to this added value is usurious.[27]

Herolt is acutely conscious that financial practice represents a growing challenge to canonical definitions of usury, not least in the recent statutes of many mercantile cities. So he vigorously restates the church's hard line against every form of usury, and he outlines the way he is certain the church can enforce its view. The church adheres to a policy of attacking usury on several fronts at once. The first remedy is an ecclesial process against any civil administration that allows or enforces usurious contracts. Automatic major excommunication awaits "all authorities—rulers, rectors, consuls, judges, and officials—who make, write, or dictate statutes which compel anyone to pay usury, or prevent anyone from seeking repayment, or who observe such a statute and judge in accordance with it." Secondly, through its pastoral authority the church urges the victims of usury to seek redress and restitution and enjoins repayment on all usurers (and their heirs) on pain of damnation. Canon law prescribes four punishments for public usurers: automatic excommunication; withholding of communion, even at death; exclusion from the oblations; and exclusion from burial in hallowed ground. (They are to be buried, Herolt says, "beneath the gibbet.") Thirdly, if moral persuasion fails, the church will invoke social sanctions against any usurer who will not repent and call upon the magistrate or prelate to enforce compliance.[28]

After a rhetorical set piece in which the usurer is colorfully portrayed as worse than a thief, a Jew, the traitor Judas, and every sinner, worse than death and hell themselves, Herolt goes on to describe all the blatant and subtle, public and private modes of usury. First, of course, usury means "advancing a loan on the contractual condition of receiving back a greater amount": this is express usury. But secondly, those who lend without an express contract, yet only in the hope of receiving back more than the capital, commit "usury of intention" in God's eyes, and any such extra return is usurious. Thirdly, if one lends property against a certain term, and at the due date will not extend the credit further unless some payment is forthcoming, the church regards this as usury. Fourth, as we have seen already, it is usury to sell goods on credit for a much higher price than they cost the vendor. "In general, anything that accrues beyond the capital is usury," the decretals say. Similarly, it is usury to buy for ready cash and then, by offering credit either to the original vendor or someone else, to resell immediately in a market dearer than

---

[26] D.7.14/3 (O), T.106.3 (C).
[27] D.7.14/7 (Q), T.106.7 (E).
[28] D.17.15 (X,EE), T.69.2/9 (K), T.105.2/10 (R), T.114.1 (B) and 3 (D).

the goods are or could be worth. Sixth, Herolt regards trade in futures as usury: to buy commodities—wine or grain—while they are still growing, at a price far more modest than one would conceivably pay at harvest or vintage. This is especially reprehensible when it takes advantage of the producer's cash flow needs, "as when rights to the harvest are bought from farmers in Lent when they are in straitened circumstances, though the price at harvest would unquestionably be much higher." However, if the buyer fully shares the farmer's risk by buying futures before the growing season begins, or at sowing, that is not usury.

Herolt's seventh instance conflicts even more directly with widespread practice: it is usury, he says, to accept a mortgage or advance a loan on a piece of land while failing to compute its produce in the capital value. But, the listener objects, friendly societies of citizens themselves lend money on this basis, as do town councils and business syndicates. No matter, Herolt says, they are all usurers, whatever their authority. Eighth, anyone who lends a neighbor old grain in the expectation of being repaid later in new grain is engaged in usury because he expects and receives back a better product than he gave.

The perennial economic predicament of the peasant farmer gives rise to many dubious transactions: Herolt's ninth case illustrates their desperate expedients (and the advantage taken by their creditors). It is usury to advance money to the poor for future delivery of sheep or cattle they may not really have. Such advances are usurious unless the buyer believes honestly and in good faith that the seller actually has the animals to sell. Finally, it is usury to lend money on a contract guaranteeing that the other party will later lend money in return. Paradoxically, however, though it is wrong to induce anyone to accept a loan under usury, the canonists hold that anyone who is prepared to pay it may borrow at usury, not only in extreme need, but also where utility dictates it.[1]

If usurers take unfair advantage of the plight of the needy, so do other traders. Some buy goods or shares below market value from people whose circumstances force them to sell; some sell at inflated prices to those who can barely afford the cost. For example, someone may purchase debenture stock guaranteeing a perpetual fixed return; but because he knows the seller has been forced to unload, he pays only a fraction of the capital value—"one florin in nine." Or a cunning salesman may charge forty florins for a horse hardly worth thirty florins to someone with an income of fifty florins.[2] Grain merchants buy cheaply during a glut and wait to resell until shortages have forced up the price.[3]

Just as traders in commodities deprive farmers by buying cheaply before harvest, so dishonest merchants knowingly make contracts with craftsmen for the supply

---

[1] D.7.15 (Y-DD), T.82.1 (C), T.114.2 (C), T.143.7 (B).
[2] D.7.14/5 (Q), T.106.5 (C).
[3] Q.41.3, E.8.1/1.

of goods for a fixed cash price at a given date, even though the craftsmen's costs at that date may be much higher, and thus deprive them of their livelihood.[4]

In addition to all these forms of business manipulation, several more blatant practices come under inevitable church censure: the sale of goods that have no legitimate purpose but are useful only for sinning—poisoned swords or arrows, potions, false weights, loaded dice, trinkets designed to seduce; the pursuit of business on holy days (with suitable exceptions for trade in perishables) or, at the other extreme, observance of "Egyptian days," the two days each month popularly held to be inauspicious for trade; and of course fencing—dealing in stolen goods (the preacher outlines the five sins fences commit, and the four remedial actions they should take).[5]

All these classes of merchants and financiers then will be lost unless they repent and restore ill-gotten profits. But commerce is not the preacher's only target: the suppliers know all the crooked tricks of the trade too. Herolt gives details of the commonest dodges. In the food business, he mentions dairymen who water down their milk and butter; butchers who disguise bad meat; bakers who use inferior ingredients in their loaves. Innkeepers commit a special group of sins: they serve food and drink on Sundays and feast days to people who should be in church; they adulterate the wine—a heinous crime—for it leads to illnesses and miscarriages and is tantamount to murder; their cellarers typically give short measure; they serve prohibited foods; they entertain low life; and they charge by what the custom will bear, not by cost. The rag trade, too, has its ploys: cobblers singe their boot leather to make it seem better tanned; cloth makers weave beyond the needed length and, after payment, pull out the surplus; tailors devise newfangled, vain, and superfluous styles; clothiers choose dark locations to hide the flaws in their stuff and measure with short ellwands. Other occupations act the same way: smiths falsify the worth of their wares by mixing in base metals; carpenters and day laborers who are paid piecework take three days to do the work of two; domestics purloin from the households they serve.[6]

Work Practices

In general, the preacher says, it is required of all workers that they toil faithfully, with patience and tranquillity, according to the statutes of their city, abstain from work on holy days, produce licit goods for licit uses and not invent newfangled items, and accept suitable payment within the customary range and not seek overpayment. The godly intention of their work should be to make a modest

---

[4] D.7.14/9 (Q), T.106.9 (E).
[5] D.1.2/7 (H), D.7.14/10-12 (Q, S), T.106.10-12 (F, G), T.117.2/3 (D), T.142.1 (R).
[6] D.7.10 (K), T.4.1/7 (X), E.26.3, E.41.1/1.

living, curb the sin occasioned by idleness, and have the wherewithal to contribute to the needy.[7]

His ideal, however, is threatened by the pressure moneymaking imposes on the workforce. Master craftsmen pressure their employees to produce counterfeit work; merchants and retailers teach their shop assistants the tricks of giving short measure. These are striking examples of the alien sin of *iussio*. The alien sin of *participatio* is committed by those who in bad faith buy stolen or alienated property, or by magistrates and public suppliers who allow the staples of bread and wine to fall into short supply to drive up the price.[8]

Against all these abuses of trade, the church brings its battery of cautionary tales, threats of judgment, confessional questioning, and above all the demand for restitution at the Lenten penance.[9] Yet in the last analysis, it is not business, but its circumvention, that the scripture reprehends:

> In itself, business is good and necessary. For God has ordained that no country is wholly self-sufficient but must be mutually dependent. So businessmen are the ministers of all when they undergo the attendant dangers of robbers, rivers, and fire. There are many worthy merchants of this sort, as illustrated by the account in the *Lives of the Fathers* of a devout hermit who asked God to show him someone who was his equal, and God showed him a trader selling his merchandise with fairness and equity. But alas! There are also many who fraudulently deceive their neighbors.[10]

The cleansing of the temple proves that it is God himself who avenges all such abuses.[11]

---

[7] T.55.1-7 (U-Y).
[8] D.11.1 (A) and .6 (J), T.144.1 (H), T.145.6 (O).
[9] E.8.1/1, Q.22.3, Q.41.3.
[10] E.15.3/1.
[11] E.15.3/3.

21

THE JEWS

Commerce and wealth are not intrinsically evil; only unjust acquisition and the abuse of trade are evil. In everyday practice, the inevitable question arises: "What then of our dealings with the Jews who live and trade among us?"

Herolt's answer, like so much medieval anti-Semitism, is a tangle of ancient prejudice and modern pragmatism. The Jews are at once outcast and protected by grudging privilege, a protection, however, kept so brittle by bigotry and churchly contempt that the least outbreak of popular hysteria could shatter it and find a scapegoat in the Jews.

So Herolt's first answer seems to be: "Christians must have no dealings with Jews at all—they are to be shunned." But it gradually emerges not only that there are customary dealings with the Jews, but also that there are church rules to regulate those dealings.

At first then, the emphasis is on the almost-total segregation of the Jewish inhabitants. They bring it on themselves, Herolt says: "Just as the Jews once held aloof from Christ's disciples and segregated them from their fellowship and communion, so now we must treat the Jews."[12] But it is not only that the historical tables have been turned; the Jews deserve rejection because they reject the faith. Even though they were instructed by the law and the prophets, they ignored and overlooked Christ.[13] They still have no excuse because now the faith is preached throughout the world;[14] and since faith is the foundation, all Jews—together with pagans and heretics—are by definition in a state of damnation and at judgment will be condemned immediately.[15]

The corollary is a series of shunning actions which canon law instructs Christians to take toward Jews. Herolt lists ten attitudes Christians must adopt.

Christians must not eat with Jews or invite them to meals or buy food from their cookshops. (Confessors regularly ask penitents at the Lenten shriving whether

---

[12] T.69.0 (G).
[13] T.21.1 (R).
[14] D.23.4/3 (F), T.77.3 (D).
[15] T.5.2/4 (E), T.142.1 (O), E.21.2/1.

they have bought food from Jewish shops.)[16] During illness, Christians must not seek health care from Jewish practitioners nor obtain medicines from them.

Jews must not be permitted to hold public office amongst Christians because (the decretals say) they might use their office as an opportunity to vent their anger.

At all times, Jews must be forced to wear a costume that will plainly distinguish them from Christians. Just as the Samaritan woman recognized that Christ was a Jew by the distinctive fringes on his clothing, so now the church requires Jews—males and females alike—to wear recognizably non-Christian attire.[17]

On the liturgical days of lamentation and Passiontide, Jews must not be abroad in public; and on Good Friday itself, they must not even open their doors or windows.

Jews may not employ servants or maids of Christian name, since there is no justification—including employment—for any Christian's frequenting a Jewish home. By the same token, Jews may not have Christian midwives or wet nurses. But the preacher recognizes that this injunction has been hard to enforce among the laity, so he underlines it with categorical threats:

> If such Christians are not prepared to withdraw from [Jewish employers], they are to be excommunicated. As long as such Christians are in the service of Jews and lodging with them continuously, they are precluded from receiving the sacraments of the church and participating in all the blessings available in the church. If they die thus, they are to be buried in a dung heap or a field, and by no means in a holy place, nor is any sacrament of the church to be administered to them.

Christians must not lease their homes to Jews for the practice of usury. If they do so, they will be guilty of whatever sins the Jews commit in them.[18] It is one of the nine "alien sins" to allow sins to be perpetrated in one's home by evil men.[19]

Christians must not retain even the smallest gift, in money or kind, given them by Jews. This is clearly the matter of greatest practical concern, since more time is devoted to this prohibition than to any other, and reflects well-entrenched business practices. Following the authority of Thomas Aquinas in a letter to the Duchess of Lotharingia, Herolt distinguishes between *receiving* and *retaining* money or gifts

---

[16] Q.19.2.
[17] Q.24.1.
[18] T.144.5 (M).
[19] D.7.16 (GG), T.105.2/1-8 (P). A transcription of sermon T.105 "On the Jews" may be found online at *http://www.uni-trier.de/uni/fb3/geschichte/cluse/pred7.htm* (Dr. Christoph Cluse of the Arye Maimon-Institut für Geschichte der Juden in Trier).

from Jews. A Christian may licitly accept gifts, since the Jewish donors have no right to retain them, having extorted them by usury in the first place. The Christian may even retain amounts that the Jews may have extorted by usury from himself or from his ancestors (no doubt a useful qualification). But in the normal course of events, property extorted from other people may not conscientiously be retained but must be restored to the rightful owners, if they can be identified and located. In principle, the Jews themselves are duty-bound to make such restitution; but since they cannot be trusted to do so, Christians must achieve the same purpose by accepting gifts and passing them on as repayments. Where the rightful recipients are unknown, Jewish gifts are to be applied to some other pious use on the advice of the diocesan. In practice, this generally means selling gifts in kind and applying the proceeds to the poor with the help of one's confessor. Herolt mentions several typical categories of Jewish gifts, some very valuable and some relatively cheap, offered as considerations: costly presents such as geldings or silver goblets or cheaper gifts of fowl (including the customary Jewish tribute of a fowl to one's master on St. Martin's Day). Whatever their value, so long as the donors have no income other than from usury, the recipients must expend all these gifts for the poor. Questions about accepting Jewish gifts are to form part of the confessor's examination and instruction concerning restitution at the Lenten shrift.[20] The consequences for those who dare to keep and use such presents are these:

> If anyone accepts anything of this sort from Jews and dies without making restitution, he (and his heirs who keep those gifts and knowingly use them) will be damned. The same is true of anyone who eats the fowl Jews give their masters at the feast of Martin.

Even if amounts received from Jews have been earned legitimately, Herolt warns, they may still bring bad luck:

> One should be aware that people often experience misfortune in goods they have received from Jews, even if they have acquired them through their own labors. Such people rarely, if ever, become rich![21]

Making the *bona fide* reception of gifts from Jews permissible, and their disposition a matter of conscience, allows some practical latitude to widespread social practices, while also ensuring that at least some resources are redistributed from Jewish financiers to the Christian poor. But formal legitimation of the Jews' financial role is fiercely resisted.

---

[20] Q.22.3, Q.42.3.
[21] D.7.16 (GG), T.105.2/9 (Q), T.143.7 (C), T.145.6 (O), S.3.2/9.

The tenth shunning action is that Christians in positions of statutory authority must not give any judgment that forces anyone to pay interest to Jewish usurers (or to any other, for that matter). "All authorities—rulers, consuls, judges, officials—who enact, draft, or dictate statutes compelling anyone to pay usury (or to refrain from seeking repayment), or who observe such a statute and judge in accordance with it, automatically incur sentence of major excommunication."[22]

Whatever concessions are made to the realities of commercial life, the social behavior toward Jewish neighbors encouraged by such preaching only reinforces attitudes of extreme discrimination. Even the explicit concessionary statements, however humane they sound, imply the legitimacy of anti-Semitic prejudice.

So when Herolt asks whether it is licit to engage in commerce with the Jews, he answers: of course, since the church allows them to live in our cities, and they could not survive unless they could buy the necessities of life. But then, as the canonists point out, it would be a shame if they were to buy even necessary food and drink with money they should not have (namely, the proceeds of usury). Accordingly, Christians should not sell them goods for money unless they earn it legitimately by working or are no longer in a position to repay ill-gotten gains. But to sell them bread, meat, fish, and other foods so that they can consume such delicacies to excess ("as is common with Jews") is not only illicit for a Christian, but it is also a contradiction of neighborly love because it provides an occasion of damnation.

Similar answers are given to parallel questions about working for Jews for a wage or even gambling with Jews. Where there is any suggestion that the money involved has been acquired by anything but honest labor, the rule of restitution supervenes, and any commerce becomes illegitimate. It is also implied that anything but marginal subsistence on a Jew's part is *prima facie* evidence of usury.[23]

In this, as in so many other cases of racial prejudice, it was all too easy to represent discrimination as simple realism. The Jewish minorities in European cities were outsiders, politically, ethnically, culturally, and religiously. They were observably different in language, appearance, dress, and custom. Their reputation for acquisitive skill, though a stereotype, was not wholly unjustified: Jewish businessmen shared an ethnic loyalty, a capacity for hard work, and a freedom from canonical restraints on dealing in venture capital that often yielded a competitive advantage and certainly maintained a tradition of commercial acumen and financial shrewdness. But prejudice turned these potentially admirable skills into their opposites: Herolt speaks of the "sloth, infidelity, and malice" of the Jews.[24] Fear

---

[22] D.7.16 (GG), T.105.2/10 (R).
[23] E.15.3/2.
[24] T.21.1 (R). On the vicissitudes of the Jewish commercial community in Herolt's own city of Nürnberg, see Gottfried Michelfelder, Die Wirtschaftliche Tägtigkeit der Juden Nürnbergs im Spätmittelalter, in *Beiträge zur Wirtschaftsgeschichte Nürnbergs*

of what was alien led to an insistence on segregation, which in turn reinforced the fear. A central element in maintaining this loop of hatred and allowing the self-perpetuating anti-Jewish mythology to flourish was the church's representation of the Jews as *religiously* despicable.

In exposition of the Gospels, and especially of the passion, the Jews *en masse* are portrayed as enemies of God and haters of Christ. Only twice does Herolt make any distinction amongst Christ's Jewish contemporaries. The vices of the scribes and Pharisees, as leaders and great men, were more grievous than those of the little people; and a few individuals who had been recipients of Christ's miraculous power did not join the Jews' insistent clamor for his crucifixion.[25] But in general, Christ found himself placed among three sets of Jews, the malicious, the vainglorious, and the fearful;[26] and their treatment of him was violent, ignominious, and bitter.[27]

> What great injuries and contumelies he sustained from the Jews, who called him now demon-obsessed, now Samaritan, now a flesh-eater and winebibber, now blasphemer, now a seducer of the people, and uttered many other blasphemies against him, and moreover often looked for opportunities to injure him, trying now to stone him, now to cast him from the top of a mountain.[28]

They tried to entrap him with words of adulation, and when they failed they falsely accused him, repaying his good with their evil.[29] They spat in his face; what could be more coarse, despicable, ignominious and vituperative?

> Oh what blind jealousy of unhappy Jews! who did not shudder to defile and befoul with their basest spit so lovable a face, and not only with the simple spit of saliva, but as a token that they cast their filthiest execrations in his face.[30]

The desire of all nations showed the Jews his face, and those vilest of men covered it with a veil.[31]

Bd I. *Beiträge zur Geschichte und Kultur der Stadt Nürnberg* Bd 11/I. (Nürnberg: Im Selbstverlag des Stadtrats zu Nürnberg, 1967), 236-260.
[25] Q.22.0; Q.32.2.
[26] Q.35.0.
[27] Q.13.2.
[28] Q.6.2.
[29] Q.23.2, Q.34.1, Q.35.1, Q.36.1.
[30] Q.20.2.
[31] Q.22.2.

This is the standard, unquestioning approach of Christian homiletic tradition to the Gospel narrative, and it does not preoccupy Herolt very much except in the *Passionale* that forms one third of his *Quadragesimale* and in his remarkable Good Friday narrative.[32] But its force is not merely historical. Its essential link to contemporary anti-Semitism is displayed by the peroration to Herolt's sermon *"On the Jews"*[33] where he declares: "Finally, we should be aware that to this very day the envy of the Jews against Christ and the catholic faith is still such that if they dared and could they would gladly persecute Christ and the Christian faith." He goes on to tell a story about some Jews who on Good Friday made a wax image of Christ, fastened it with nails to a cross, and speared it on a lance. The Blessed Virgin appeared and demanded of the Christians why they tolerated the fact that still, in their city, on that day, the Jews crucified her son. The Christians broke into the homes of the Jews, took them captive, and discovered the image of the crucified.[34]

The story has a twist in its tail, however. Wondrously, when they broke in, the Christians found that the wounds of the wax image were bleeding; and at this miracle, many Jews were converted to Christian faith. The expectation of ultimate Jewish conversion persists as a ground for toleration, in spite of everything said about their malice. In light of all the Jews did and would still like to do to Christ, why does the church permit them to live? "Because," Herolt says on the authority of Psalm 58, John 10, and Jeremiah 23, "all Jews must be converted at the end of the world."[35]

The impulse to seek Jewish conversions leads to some canonical principles to control proselytising. Christians should in general have contact with unbelievers only if they themselves are strong in the faith and have a realistic hope of achieving conversion. Jews may not be compelled or harshly coerced to receive the faith but must be led by the authority of scripture, reasons, and sweet words. They may not be given rewards for receiving faith, but they may be drawn to receive it by gifts and promises, especially if it allays their fear of a life of poverty among Christians, or if the gifts are a simple benevolence to Jewish captives to ease their conversion.[36] The children of Jews are not to be baptized against the will of their parents if they are below the age of discretion. But if they have attained the age of discretion, they may accept Christian faith and be baptized even in defiance of their parents' wishes. (Herolt gives it as his own opinion that it is not a sin to baptize a dying Jewish infant even without parental consent.)[37]

There are several other reasons why the church does not persecute Jews. God did not want the Jews totally consumed but merely dispersed to honor the patriarchs

---

[32] S.14.1.
[33] T.105.
[34] T.105.3 (U), cf. P.P.: 44-46 "Passio Christi" (436-438).
[35] T.105.1/5 (O).
[36] E.40.3/2-4.
[37] D.7.16 (HH), D.23.4/3 (F), T.77.3 (D), T.105.3 (S), E.40.3/5.

and prophets from whom they descended; to revere Christ and his apostles who were born Jews; to confirm Christians' faith, since the Jews possess the Old Testament books from which we draw testimony about Christ; and to give a constant reminder of Christ's passion whenever a Christian sees a Jew.[1]

The preacher allows that some unfaithful Christians are worse than Jews.[2] Worldly haters of prelates are like the Jews who hated Christ. A Christian usurer is worse than a Jew because a Jew will not take usury from a fellow Jew.[3] Unworthy communicants are worse than Jews because the Jews crucified Christ ignorantly, but the Christian knowingly.[4] Blasphemers are worse than Jews because the Jews crucified Christ only once.[5] But, of course, these admissions simply reinforce the categorical assumption that a Jew is a standard of pejorative comparison.

Ultimately, the preacher's message is that Christians are right to treat the Jews and their belief with contempt:

> The Jews are not willing to believe that Christ is Son of God and of the Virgin Mary and the world's redeemer, even though they possess this knowledge from their own scriptures, from the sayings of the prophets who announced Christ. But the Jews themselves falsely expound sacred scripture and say that Messiah is still to come; but they *were* deceived and they *are* deceived.

As if to illustrate the point, Herolt then borrows from Caesarius a tale of sorrow and deceit which is chilling in its disdain and moral confusion:

> There was a young man, a student, who slept with the daughter of a Jew, and she conceived from him. And the student took a reed and crept up to the Jew's home by night, and spoke through the reed through the window of the room where the Jew lay with his wife, and said, "Rejoice and glorify God, for the Lord has visited your people. For your daughter is pregnant and will bear the true Messiah who was promised in the law and the scriptures!" The student did this three times. When the parents saw that their daughter was indeed pregnant, they attached their faith to the words the youth had intimated, and announced it to other Jews, who were all filled with joy and glorified God, and held the girl in great honor. When the time came for her to give birth, all the Jews gathered to witness so

---

[1] D.7.16 (FF), T.105.1 (O).
[2] E.29.1/1.
[3] T.114.1 (A).
[4] D.26.2/3 (B).
[5] Q.14.2.

grand a sight. At length the girl, with great grief, delivered not a son but a daughter. When the Jews saw it, they realized they had been deceived and were all thrown into turmoil, and one Jew rushed up in the heat of his anger, seized the youth and smashed his head against a statue. So all the Jews who lived there withdrew in confusion and indignation.[6]

---

[6] T.105.1/3 (O).

THE LAST THINGS

22

DEATH AND JUDGMENT, HEAVEN AND HELL

We shall all die. The brief time remaining to every man and woman is a moment, perhaps less. Our whole life is a race toward death; all run it alike—noble or ignoble, rich or pauper, young or old. Like the sun which no sooner rises than it takes its course to sink again beneath the earth, the moment we are born we begin our race to death. For those in mortal sin, it is an uninterrupted training for hell, a mad rush to an eternal penalty; for those in grace, it's a single daily regimen for the kingdom of heaven.[7]

Nothing is more certain than death, and nothing is more uncertain than the hour of death. Like most fifteenth-century sermonists, Herolt repeats and amplifies the long catalogue of warnings from Augustine, Gregory, Jerome, Bede, Isidore, and most of all Bernard, on the inevitability yet unpredictability of death.[8] Bernard said, "It is certain that you will die. It is uncertain when, how, or where. Since death awaits you everywhere, if you are wise you will await it everywhere."[9]

When a person dies, he passes hence alone, with no help but God. He goes naked and is buried and eaten by worms. His sins follow him unless he has repented here, and if he has not repented, God condemns him, the angels separate him from the good, and the demons torture him perpetually in hell. The demons, therefore, gather like vultures about his death struggle to await their due; he goes hence to a region totally unknown to him, knowing nothing of what awaits him, or whether he will spend his first night in heaven, purgatory, or hell. The time of grace and negotiation is lost to him forever, and death deprives him of all the joys of the world—"so leave them now for those merits that last!"[10]

Physically, nothing is more terrible than death. The preacher dwells long on its horrors. With ghastly vividness, he details the signs and symptoms of terminal illness and its accompanying terror. The face contorts, the eyes cannot bear light, the

---

[7] E.11.1, cf. T.59.2 (L), T.65.2 (Q), T.73.3 (C), S.15.2, E.4.2.
[8] E.g., T.54.1/1 (Q), T.93.6 (T), T.128.1 (J), T.153.1 (A), &c.
[9] T.9.0 (E).
[10] T.115.1-7 (F-L).

nose and lips constrict, the teeth grind in agony, black spots appear on the tongue, reflexes fail and tastes distort, pain grows in intensity, and the body thrashes to and fro, causing biting of the tongue and tearing at the face, the eyes turn inward, veins break in the skin, the body rattles in grief, and the soul separates.[11] Then dissolution follows in all our members, we are eaten by worms and putrefy, snakes hatch from our marrow, and we return to dust and ash.[12]

Yet these physical terrors pale beside the spiritual horror awaiting one who has not "learned to die well."[13] The chief source of this dread, of course, is uncertainty about one's destination. As we have seen, this anxiety is inescapable for those who have led dissolute, reprobate, and unrepented lives and is mitigated by the hope and humility of the contrite who have lived in grace. Herolt gathers contrasting stories about the deaths of evil and upright people, the one in wretchedness, the other in joy; but he also tells sobering stories of those who seemed to die in devout peace but were later found in hell.[14]

In the hope of winning this greatest battle for the soul, the demons crowd around a deathbed. Herolt quotes a piece of wry doggerel about the "vultures":

Post hominis mortem tria quaerunt avide sortem
Vult vermis carnem; sathan animam; posteritas rem

(At a man's passing, three pant for a share:
his meat the worm; his soul the fiend; his loot the heir![15])

The demons devote more energy to tempting and squeezing us in our death struggle than at any other time. Why? They do not want anyone, good or bad, to make a good end; their purpose is to impede any natural desire for the good. They know that if a person can evade their power in this struggle, he or she will never fear them again, and a demon does not want to lose someone he has had living in sins for decades! But if a demon gains a soul in the death agony, he will never lose him again, unlike other times when he may lose him by penance.

What are the temptations the demons use to afflict the dying? Doubts about the faith, memories of past deeds to provoke despair, intolerance of pain to drive the mind beyond its limit; and if these strategies do not succeed, then vain complacency

---

[11] T.97.7 (O), T.129.2 (Q), T.134.1/2 (U), Q.30.0, E.49.1/2.
[12] D.18.6/1 (P), T.115.2 (H), E.38.2/3, A.M.: 8 "Mors" (120b).
[13] T.115.7 (M).
[14] E.g., "Mors malorum": T.115.4 and 5 (J); P.M.: 56-63 (335-342); "Mors proborum": T.9.3 (P); T.78.4 (H); T.115.1 (G); T.134.2 (X); P.M.: 64-70 (343-349); ambiguous: T.134.3 (A); T.156.3 (B); &c.
[15] T.115.4 (H).

about life's achievements or a tenacious preoccupation with mundane possessions and involvements—a futile reluctance to leave honors, wealth, wife and family, the pleasures of the flesh, or the joys of the world.[16] For many, especially the rich, this last is an ironically potent weapon. Material attachments disquiet the mind and fill it with bitterness, but they are useless at death. They do not guard the body from worms nor buy a single moment longer in life nor ransom the soul from the demons; they merely make the dying worse from regret.[17]

But those who place Christ before them at the hour of their death, and retain their trust in his mercy, may see the cloud of demons conquered, confused, and retreating and in their place a great company of angels to shield them from demonic assault, show reverence to their human souls, and lead them in happiness to their celestial fatherland.[18] It is therefore a source of security to surround one's deathbed with good and godly company, to receive the *viaticum*, and to recall one's sins (against pride), one's good deeds (against despair), and above all the divine mercy.[19] For such good people, death is called a sleep because they depart in hope of rising, rest sweetly and unshaken, and arise renewed.[20]

But for most, the physical and mental anguish of the deathbed is only the last and sharpest crisis in a lifelong spiritual confrontation with death—a death which flowed from the sin of humanity in its beginnings, horrible not only because of its universality, demons daily awaiting the separation of soul from body, and physical corruption, but especially because once expelled from the body the soul has lost its opportunity and can never return to merit. It must now be judged and see whether it has done good or evil.[21]

What destination awaits the soul? Herolt scornfully rejects the superstition that the soul cannot depart or find rest until the church bells stop pealing, or spends the first night with St. Gertrude, the second with the archangel Michael, and only then goes to its appointed destination.[22] He implies that the soul discovers immediately whether it is in heaven, purgatory, or hell.

Heaven, Purgatory, and Hell

Under the Old Testament, he explains, there were four places beneath heaven where departed souls could go. They were the limbo of the fathers, the limbo of children, purgatory, or Gehenna.

---

[16] T.134.2/1-7 (S-Y).
[17] T.94.5 (D), T.118.2/1 (L).
[18] T.78.4 (H), T.158.3/3 (N), Q.42.1, P.M.: 64 "Mors proborum" (343).
[19] D.13.7/1(Q), T.56.9 (B), T.78.2 (G).
[20] Q.31.1, A.M.: 12 "Mors bonorum" (121ª).
[21] E.49.1/2.
[22] D.1.13 (M).

The *limbo patrum* was where the souls of the faithful departed went before the passion. It was nearest to heaven, and in it there was no sensible pain, but neither was there any vision of God. When Christ "descended into hell," this is where he descended, smashed it, let the fathers out, and opened heaven. It exists no longer.[23]

The next place is purgatory, in which the souls of the faithful who have not yet fulfilled their penance by worthy satisfaction are purged by fire.

Below purgatory is the *limbo infantium*, for children who have died without baptism in original sin, a place dark inside and out, lacking divine grace or the vision of God, but without sensible pain. (How can that be just and merciful? It is a perfect combination of both, since it is of God's mercy that these infant natures are kept in being, though they would never have had any capacity for grace; and besides, it is better for them than for any human being in the world!)[24] And in the lowest place is the inferno of the damned.

In three places then—earth, purgatory, and hell—souls are vexed by the fires of tribulation. How do they compare? Herolt charts the similarities and differences: On earth, tribulation is light, transitory, punitive but meritorious, and purging. In purgatory, tribulation is heavy (not light), transitory, punitive but not meritorious. In hell, tribulation is heavy (not light), eternal (not transitory), and disfiguring (not purging)[25]

The preacher's strategy is almost exclusively to use exemplary tales to convey his graphic picture of the lake of purgatorial fire and its agonies, while addressing the congregation directly on the advantages of penitential satisfaction over the pains of purgatory in intensity, duration, and effect.

Purgatory is reduced if one serves God from youth.[26] Illnesses and trials are permitted here because they shorten purgatory later.[27] We are freed from future labor and pain by what we undergo here.[28] But it is not simply that the same quantum of penalty may be discharged here or there. Herolt outlines the calculus by which the light sufferings of this life are highly magnified in purgatory:

> How long, according to divine justice, must one spend in purgatory to discharge the penalty for one mortal sin? It is probably enough to be punished in satisfaction of each mortal sin for as many years as there are days in seven years. This is the reason: in the present,

---

[23] D.22.5 (L-M), T.146.5 (J), Q.37.2, Q.47.0, E.20.3/2.
[24] D.1.1 (E), D.23.2/9 (C) and .4/2 (F), T.41.14 (N), T.77.2 (C), T.105.3 (T), T.160.1 (A), Q.47.1, E.15.1/6.
[25] E.12.1.
[26] T.20.5 (O).
[27] T.29.3 (X), T.134.2/3 (U), E.24.1/2.
[28] T.153.3 (C).

by strict justice, a seven-year penance should be imposed for each mortal sin (Decretal 32 q. 2). But in purgatory, a day corresponds to an earthly year.... Ezekiel 4[:6] speaks of "a day for a year": a day in this time of grace and mercy for a year in the later time of justice. The children of Israel prove it: for their sinfulness, they wandered forty years in the desert to reach a promised land they could have reached in forty days if they had not sinned.... Since, then, there are 365 days in a year, seven years amount to 2,555 days. This is the number of years which, by mere justice, one must burn in purgatory for a single mortal sin.[29]

One should not despair on this account, the preacher hastens to add, for this is the sum on the basis of untempered justice; but God is merciful, and in practice contrition, the shame of confession, satisfactions, good works, vicissitudes, and infirmities patiently borne all dilute the penalty of purgatory. So do prayers and suffrages for the departed, which may dramatically shorten the sufferings of loved ones.[30] So too do indulgences, but they are effective only for those who receive them in contrition and grace.[31] Nonetheless, the scale of time and intensity remains unimaginably altered:

> A sinner laid low by a grave and lingering illness asked God to release him from this world. When he had prayed for this repeatedly, an angel appeared to him and said, "I have been sent to expedite your petition. Choose what you prefer: either to spend two days in purgatory, or to sustain your illness for two more years." Joyfully, the man chose to die, and after his death the angel led him to purgatory. A short hour later, the angel appeared to him. When he saw him, the man said, "Who are you?" He said, "I am the angel of God who brought you here." He replied, "Go away—you are no angel of God! Angels do not lie, and you lied to me—you said I had to spend only two days in purgatory, and I've been here for years already." But the angel told him, "Don't you know that you haven't been here for even an hour yet?" Then the man said, "Please take me back to the world—I'm ready to bear my infirmity for as long as God likes, so long as I don't have to come back here!" And by divine disposition that is what happened: he was taken back and patiently bore his illness for two years and passed away.[32]

---

[29] T.156.4 (C).
[30] T.146.5 (J), T.156.4 (D), T.160.5 (H-K).
[31] T.13.1/3 (B).
[32] T.134.2 (X).

This story is quoted from Humbert's *Tract on the Sevenfold Fear*. Herolt knows another version of it from Guilelmus[33] and others with exactly the same theme—a day in purgatory far worse than a month's illness and a horrible tale of a penitent criminal asking his young cousin to dismember him with shears limb by limb in place of the pains he would otherwise endure in purgatory,[34] or comparisons like this:

> If all the coals in the whole world were gathered into one pile, and they were all burning, and a man were to stand in the middle of the pile, he would not experience so much pain as a soul burning in purgatory.[35]

Or this:

> In the tribunal of the present church, satisfaction is made easily, but the punishment is severer in purgatory's court—for one venial sin a man will bear a harsher penalty in purgatory than St. Lawrence suffered on the gridiron.[36]

Or this:

> Suppose a soul were to burn in purgatory for thirty years, and an angel came and said, "You have a choice whether you want to be punished here for just one more day," or to return to the body and discharge the remaining day in your flesh, but it would mean that your punishment forced you to live in the body for ten more years, the ground on which you trod was full of iron spikes which would pierce your feet, and you would have bread and ashes to eat, gall and vinegar to drink, a hair shirt to wear, and you would lie on the ground and have a hard stone under your head for a pillow"—then that soul would gladly choose to return to the body and endure that punishment for a hundred years rather than stay one more day in purgatory![37]

The exemplary tradition included many stories of people who had indeed been sent back from purgatory to discharge penalties on earth. To Herolt, the prodigious self-abnegation of these returning souls proves that sceptical people fear the purgatorial fire all too little because they do not find it described in scripture,

---

[33] P.P.: 88 "Poena purgatoria" (472).
[34] T.128.1/6 (M), .P: 89 "Poena purgatoria" (473).
[35] P.P.: 82 "Poena purgatoria" (466).
[36] D.12.4/1 (M).
[37] T.160.1 (B).

or do not believe what they hear, or have experienced nothing of it—or even because they substitute their own superstitions about weekend furloughs from purgatory.[38]

However misguided these illusions, there are consolations which assuage the excruciating pain of purgatory, he says. First, the good angels visit those in purgatory and comfort them, and let them know of those still on earth or in heaven who are praying for them. Moreover, those in purgatory are certain of their eternal blessedness. They are worthy souls who have been judged to be in grace and love and, therefore, can take joy in an assurance we cannot know on earth. As Thomas said, in heaven there is certainty without expectation, on earth there is expectation without certainty, but in purgatory there is both certainty and expectation. Finally, they are consoled by the hope of the suffrages of their relatives and friends and the prospect that their sufferings may be readily shortened by them (which incidentally places those who benefit from these prayers in debt to those who have offered them when their turn comes).[39]

Of course, only those whom the preacher describes as "moderately good" go to purgatory. There are "good and perfect and innocent people" who fly immediately to heaven, five classes of them, Herolt says: those who die in baptismal innocence or retain it unsullied; those in grace who attain a plenary indulgence, for they have no penalty to liquidate; those who have sincerely entered an approved religious life and have lived according to its rule; martyrs for the faith; and those contrite souls who through penitential works have made full satisfaction for all their sins.[40] Sinners, meanwhile, "go down to hell in a moment," as Job [21:13] declares.[41]

The Torments of Hell

So graphically have the terrors of death and purgatory been portrayed that one wonders what more could be said about hell, but the task is not beyond the preacher's skill. "If you must suffer such great pains in purgatory on account of the least sin, oh how great then is the pain in hell which will be everlasting and never-ending!"[42] Accordingly, Herolt gathers even more patristic authorities and exempla to paint his image of infernal torments, an image drawn for our instruction, he says, for God calls us by threats of hell sharper than one can imagine: hopelessness, no redemption, no mitigation of pain, but eternal darkness, undying worms, inextinguishable fire.[43]

---

38 D.1.13 (N), P.P.: 84 "Poena purgatoria" (468).
39 T.160.3-4 (F-G).
40 S.24.2.
41 D.1.13 (N), S.24.2.
42 R.1.4 (19ᵇ).
43 T.74.1/7 (J), E.2.2/6.

There are five differences between earthly fire and hell fire. The heat of fire here is to the heat of hellfire as a mere picture to its reality. This fire burns only from outside but penetrates from inside and out; it burns both body and soul. This fire gives light; hellfire burns in outer darkness. Earthly fire consumes what it burns, but the fires of Gehenna do not; fire is extinguishable, but hellfire never goes out.[44] Indeed, the more damned there are in hell, the greater the horror because the fiercer it burns.[45]

The fire is only the first of nine goads to the sufferings of the damned—a ghastly mirror of the nine choirs of angels in heaven.[46] The pit or dungeon of hell is so deep than the damned have fire above them and below them, a fire deeper than the distance from heaven to earth.[47] Alongside unimaginable heat, hell inflicts intolerable cold. One who returned from the brink of death described how, after his soul left his body,

> a shining figure had led him beyond the sunrise to a valley of infinite hugeness, where there were two swamps, one full of worms and blazing flames, the other of ice and outsized hailstones, and they were full of souls which, when they could bear the vehemence of the fire no longer, would resort to the icy cold, then back to the fire.[48]

A third horror is the egregious stench of bodies in the sulphur pit and flame. The fourth is perpetual hunger and thirst, so famishing that if they could the damned would gladly eat frogs, toads, and snakes; but they cannot for this infernal banquet has courses of tantalising hunger, the guests' own flesh boiled and roasted, and the bitterest drink from goblets of brimstone.[49]

The fifth torment is the horrid vision of demons. While there are stories of demons deceitfully taking innocuous guises here on earth, they are revealed in all their appalling gruesomeness to the damned. Those who have glimpsed their frightfulness, their horns, and their protruding eyes like reeking furnaces have recoiled in horror, and would do anything to escape that sight again, or have been destroyed by it.[50]

---

[44] T.101.2 (D).
[45] D.12.2/3 (K).
[46] T.125.1-9 (O-A).
[47] T.101.4 (G).
[48] P.P.: 73 "Poena inferni" (457).
[49] T.101.3 (E), with biblical proof texts from Job 24[:19], Ps. [11(10):7], Ps. [59(58):7], Isa.9[:20], Luke 6[:25], the Apostle [Rom.8:13], and Rev. 16[:10]; cf. exemplum in T.99.2/4 (P); T.125.2-4 (O-Q).
[50] T.125.5 (R); P.P.: 74, 75 "Poena inferni" (456, 459).

The sixth torment is bondage and darkness. The preacher is at his most lurid when he narrates the grotesque punishments inflicted by a depraved demonic hoard—punishments devised to match the sins committed in the flesh, in accordance with the rule: "The instruments of sin are the instruments of punishment" (Wisdom [11:17]). The demons rejoice at the damnation of sinners because they provide raw material for them to drain their cruelties, and unlike a human enemy, a demon wants to go on tormenting forever.[51] Here are scenes from some of the exemplary stories in the *Storehouse* and the *Sermons*:

> A knight burning in hell, sitting on a fiery horse, holding a falcon on his hand ... The horse was a devil who galloped with him through fire for the pride he had taken in riding' and falconry ... and the falcon was another devil which was eating his hand, his arm, his muscles, and caused him such grief that he wished it would tear his heart from his chest.[52]

> A great prince borne down ablaze and sitting in a throne of fire, and in front of him were beautiful women poking fiery faggots in his face—he was burning as far as his genitals—and beating him with whips: this had been a powerful and lustful prince ... Demons were tearing the skin off another and rubbing and spattering him with salt, and roasting him over a fiery pit: this had been a cruel overlord, an oppressor of his subjects and exactor of the poor ... [53]

> Horrible demons carrying a vat of fire, in which they had cast a burgher recently dead and another man's wife. They were burning and boiling as if in a metal pot, swimming in pain like peas in a pot of oil, both crying "Woe! Woe! Woe!"[54]

Like the lake of fire, the bath is a recurrent image—the dissolute Udo in his brimstone bath, the emperor Nero inviting his counsellors to join him in a bath of molten gold[55]—but there are particular features of the earthly bathhouse weirdly and cruelly reproduced in hell. The cinctures of earth are the hammers of fire with which demons twist and beat the damned. In hell, too, there are masseurs—demons who lacerate and punish the damned with iron hooks. The razors of hell cut off

---

[51] T.87.3/5 (S), T.125.6 (S).
[52] P.P.: 76 "Poena inferni" (460).
[53] P.P.: 66 "Poena inferni" (450).
[54] T.85.3 (Q).
[55] T.62.3 (Y), P.P.: 70 "Poena inferni" (454).

the damned from every good they could have hoped for in heaven or earth.[56] The hands and feet especially are bound because they have been so swift to do evil. And while the inferno is the place of outer darkness, there is just enough light amidst the fetid smoke and fumes for the damned to see the causes of their grief.[57]

The wretched screaming and weeping of hell are the seventh of its horrors. The music of the infernal banquet is made by the gnashing of teeth (Matt. 13[:42]), the ululation of demons (Isa. 16[:7]), and the wailing of all the damned together (Zech. 12[11])—the saddest music in creation.[58]

"If only one tear were shed for each pain a damned soul will suffer in hell fire, more tears would be shed for each lost soul than all the vases in the world could hold."[59] Ultimately, however, it is the inward spiritual tortures of hell which are most wretched. The eighth horror is eternal death, the state of perpetual sadness without consolation. Death is threefold, of nature, guilt, and hell, but only the death of hell is eternal and irreversible.[60] There are only evil souls in hell, sinners cut off from mercy or penitence, so twisted by unalloyed envy and loss that they even wish their parents, families, wives, and children damned. Their wills are corrupted; they are stuck in evil unable to will good. They long endlessly for surcease but do not know how to achieve it.[61]

The final ineluctable punishment of hell is eternal separation from God, the Blessed Virgin, and all the saints and angels. Until the judgment, the damned see the glory of the blessed, and it reinforces their sense of bitter deprivation; after the judgment, they will no longer have even this distorted sight (though their pain will not diminish).[62] 7 No prayer avails, or is to be made, for those in hell: "even if the blessed Virgin and all the saints were to pray for one lost soul until the last day, Christ would heed her not at all." They will have no good from God nor a drop of God's mercy.[63]

Judgment

If, as the preacher has told us, the departing soul knows instantly after death whether it is in heaven or purgatory or hell, then in one sense the judgment occurs at the departure. There are two judgments, Herolt explains, a particular judgment and a general judgment—the particular at death, when good and evil alike see

---

[56] T.101.4 (G).
[57] T.125.6 (S-T).
[58] T.125.7 (U).
[59] E.33.3/3.
[60] D.18.6/1 (Q), Q.18.2, E.35.2.
[61] T.87.3/6 (K), T.125.8 (X), E.35.2/3.
[62] T.87.3/4 (I), E.33.3/4.
[63] T.87.3/2 (H), T.1011 (B), T.125.9 (A).

the Christ who was crucified (the evil to their confusion), and the general, or last, judgment when all will be judged for what they have done in the body.[64]

Except for the traditional Advent sermons on the last things, Herolt devotes relatively little energy to describing scenes of final judgment. When he does mention it, the message is almost always the same: the judgment is so fearful because we must give strict account before Christ and all creation of every single thought, word, deed, possession, expenditure, legacy, time, example, office, skill, duty of care, status, and failure for all the years, months, weeks, days, hours, and minutes we have lived.[65] Nothing will be hidden—vindictive or perverse thoughts, illicit sexual acts, gluttonous debauches, outbursts of rage, mean or ruthless deeds, and dishonesties great and small. Christ will interrogate, demanding account of each idle word, lewd step, and false measure in as much fine detail—and in the selfsame prosaic, almost-banal terms—as a stringent and shrewd parish confessor. The questions Herolt places in the mouth of Christ are word for word with his recommendations to priests for rigorous examination at penance.[66]

Where will the last judgment happen? In the vale of Jehosaphat (Joel [3:2]), in the air above the place where Christ ascended to heaven. It will happen at the end of the age, but exactly when, no one knows (Mt. 24[:36]), in spite of those who quote proof texts suggesting midnight or dawn. It would be fitting, Herolt says, if it happened on a Sunday, as many believe, but no one can be sure.[67]

Fifteen signs will precede Christ's coming to judgment, tradition teaches. The sea will rise forty cubits then sink into the abyss. All the beasts and monsters of the seas will gather at the surface and bellow to heaven. The oceans and all waters will catch fire, plants will sweat blood, and birds will gather and fly backward and forward keening. Then all the buildings on earth will collapse. Bolts of fire will cross the firmament from west to east. The rocks will smash together and break in pieces. The whole earth will quake; mountains and hills will crumble to dust. Men will come from the caves, mad and unable to speak to each other. All the graves from sunrise to sunset will be opened, and the skeletons will stand above the tombs. The stars will fall, and all those still living will die and be raised with the already dead.[68]

Then seven thunders will sound. At the first thunder, the resurrection trumpet will call up all the dead. Each group in the hierarchies of heaven and hell will come with their forerunners—Adam with all the God-fearing faithful, Abraham with the patriarchs, Isaiah with the prophets, David and all good kings, Peter and the

---

[64] T.3.1 (O).
[65] T.3.2 (P-S) and T.4.1 (U-B), cf. T.53.4 (O), T.138.5 (H), T.139.3 (S), E.2.2/4, E.39.2/5.
[66] Cf. T.4.1/7 (X) and Q.22.3.
[67] D.3.1/4 (B), T.3.1 (O), T.117.1/12 (B), T.162.1/7 (G).
[68] T.6.1 (L-M).

apostles and evangelists, Stephen and Lawrence with all innocent martyrs, Nicholas and Martin with confessors, Katherine with the virgins, Elizabeth the widows, Anna the faithful spouses, and the queen of heaven herself leading all obedient priests and religious. And then Lucifer, Satan, Asmodeus, Beelzebub will come with all the host of hell—Cain with the murderers, Judas the traitors, Pilate unjust judges, the child-slayer Herod with all evil rulers, Barrabas with thieves, Lamech adulterers, Nemroth usurers, Gehazi false traders, Simon leading all the simoniacs, Athaliah the killers of children, and Jezebel the whores.[69]

At the second thunder all these hosts appearing for judgment will be divided into four groups: those saints who sit at the feet of Christ and confirm his judgment, the faithful who are judged and saved, the reprobate who are judged and lost, and those beyond grace who are immediately consigned to the devil (such as Jews, heretics, and pagans who did not receive the faith).[70]

The third thunder will sound, and Christ will display his wounds universally in the judgment—his scars to ingrates, thorn marks to the proud, spear wound to the angry and envious, the nail prints of his hands to the grasping and his feet to dancers, the cross to the indolent, his lashes to the lustful, the cloaks he wore before Pilate and Herod to fussy overdressers, his blindfold to tricksters and lying traders, his bonds to the libidinous, gall and vinegar to gluttons, spittle to those who paint their faces, beard hairs to those who curl and trick out their hair or uncover their heads seductively, the soldiers' lots to gamblers, and Judas's pieces of silver to those who acquire wealth unjustly.[71] But good and upright people will also see his wounds and will understand how mercifully they were redeemed by his passion; heaven is aware of their sins, but it is to their honor that they arose from them and truly repented.[72]

When the fourth thunder sounds, all the witnesses testify against the sinner. The chief accuser is the sins themselves, with reinforcement from the devil eagerly reciting each transgression, and the world and all creation will cry out in testimony.[73]

The fifth thunder is prelude to the wails of the damned:

> Woe to you, my cursed feet! What have you set to my account that by evil step and illicit leap you have barred the door of heaven to me? Now we enter the gate of hell, which because of you will never be opened again. Woe to you, hands! Why have you destroyed the crown of glory for me by evil touch? Now, because of you, I shall be lowered into the fire whence I shall never escape. Woe to you,

---

[69] T.5.1 (D).
[70] T.5.2 (E).
[71] T.5.3 (F).
[72] T.57.8 (E), T.87.2 (G).
[73] T.5.4 (H).

accursed heart! What have you set to my account that by your evil thoughts and delights you have destroyed for me the joys of heaven? Now begins your grief, which no gladness will ever follow. O cursed tongue, how many evils have you done to me by uttering so many foul words? Therefore my mouth will cry out for a thousand years and more, and no one will come to help. O cursed eyes that never shed a single tear for my sins before a priest, now begins your unbearable weeping before demons, and you will mourn a million years and never find a comforter.[74]

The sixth thunder is when Christ the judge calls the elect to himself and pronounces sentence on the damned, saying to those on his left hand, like the king in the parable, "Depart, depart, depart . . ."[75] And by the seventh thunder, we understand the multiplicity of the pleas of the wicked after this life and the greatness of the joys awaiting the good in heaven.[76]

For at last those on Christ's right hand will enter with joy the place for which we have been created and redeemed, our true country, the homeland where our hearts will find their resting place. The principal cause of humanity's creation in the world is heavenly bliss and beatific vision.[77]

As God has goaded us by terror of hell to abandon our wilful aversion, so too he allures us to grace by lavish promises of eternal fruition and ineffable joys with the angels, saints, the Blessed Virgin, and all the company of heaven.[78]

If these inducements pose any risk that a person might make a false penance (as some anecdotes suggest[79]) out of fear or desire rather than contrite love for God, Herolt is sure that both these emotions, fear and love, are good for the soul. Horses put down two hooves at a time to move faster, so the preacher's vocation is to evoke both the horror and the yearning.[80]

The Joys of Heaven

Accordingly, the sermon on the ninefold terrors of hell is matched by a sermon on the ninefold joys of heaven.[81] Like hell, too, heaven is pictured as a banquet, a great feast whose guests are all kings and queens, the costliest of feasts because it was

---

[74] T.5.5 (I), T.37.3 (Q).
[75] T.5.6 (K).
[76] T.5.7 (K), cf. T.53.5-6 (P).
[77] T.65.2 (Q), E.4.3, E.42.1/3, E.44.1, E.50.3/1.
[78] T.74.1/6 (I).
[79] E.g., T.156.3 (B).
[80] T.4.0 (before U), cf. D.20.2/1 (H), &c.
[81] Cf. T.84 and T.101.

prepared at the expense of Christ's death. There the divine host lavishes on the elect new gifts and precious courses, each worth the labor of thousands of years.[82]

The first heavenly joy will be eternal youth, without any aging at all. All the elect will be raised as if at the age of thirty-three, as Christ at his resurrection, whether they were a day old or a hundred years old.[83] Even an infant who was baptized and had then died, so insensible that it could not discern good or evil, is made so efficaciously wise in heaven that it knows more of God than all the philosophers and teachers in creation. "How then would its parents recognize it?" some say. But the elect see all things clearly: without recognition of love, how could there be perfect joy?[84]

The second celestial joy will be perpetual health without debility or even the capacity to suffer. For now at last the soul will have perfect control of the body. The glorified body can no more suffer than the sun's rays. It will be brilliant, subtle, agile, and immortal; and no sword or dagger, no fire or cold, and no hunger or thirst can harm it. Each transformed body will rise at the size to which it would have grown if it had attained its ideal size without impediment but not therefore all at the same size.[85]

The third course at the heavenly banquet will be wealth without poverty, an abundance of all we need. Here on earth, there is nothing which can truly satisfy our deep yearning: Honors, pleasures, and riches cannot fulfil the human heart, unless we come to God and find our rest there—just as an impression in wax matches only the original seal which formed it. Our treasure is in heaven.[86]

The fourth joy is perpetual peace, which flows from the fulfilment of our heart's desire, for joy is to desire as rest is to motion: as joy is full when no yearning remains, so in our homeland our movement of yearning will find its resting place.[87]

The fifth joy will be the music at the divine feast, the sweet sound of angels and saints continually singing the praises of God. No earthly song, no instrument of music however ravishing, can even begin to compare with the sweetness of that heavenly chorus.[88] It is in anticipation of that future bliss, and the honor Christ will receive in heaven, that strings and organs and a diversity of instruments are sounded in procession in high liturgical feasts.[89] Thanksgiving is the occupation of the blessed in heaven.[90]

---

[82] T.84.0 (I), cf. T.53.6 (P).
[83] D.22.12 (V), T.50.3 (C), T.84.1 (K), T.147.12 (O), E.20.3/7, E.50.3/2.
[84] E.44.1.
[85] T.50.3 (C), T.84.2 (K).
[86] T.84.3 (K).
[87] T.84.4 (K), EI.4.3.
[88] T.84.5 (K).
[89] T.78.1/4 (E).
[90] T.112.1/7 (M).

The next great gift of God to his guests is the due reward and joy that each of the elect will have of his or her own merits. Where one is seated at the heavenly feast depends on the merits one has attained in grace: "It is a certain and indubitable truth of Christian faith to hold that the least in merits will be placed with the lowest ranks in heaven, those of moderate merit in the middle ranks, and the highest with the highest ranks of the angels." Though all the saints will dwell in unsullied bliss, yet one spirit will be more blessed than another in heaven, according to the merits they have accrued for their good deeds. There will be those who (so to speak) are rewarded only a little—for example, those baptized children who died in infancy and have only Christ's imputed merits or deathbed penitents. Others will be rewarded much because they were swiftly converted, served God from their youth up, and exceeded the penance they owed. And those special saints who lived in great abstinence, or never sinned mortally, will be rewarded with superabundance; they are closest to God by the fervor of their contemplation and the flame of their love.[91] Nothing is more precious than the prize, the heavenly crown, and the good which "eye hath not seen nor ear heard."[92]

Yet there is no envy or backbiting on account of these gradations of bliss, for the seventh gift is the joyous society and communing of all the elect. Love, which begins here, will be perfected there; and all will love their neighbors as themselves, delighting to see their gladness and freely sharing each merit and joy. It is the company of heaven which is the "good measure, pressed down, shaken together and running over" of the promised reward—the sublime company of patriarchs, prophets, apostles, evangelists, martyrs, confessors, virgins, and all the saints and angels who await us there.[93]

Chief among this company, and the eighth font of heavenly joy, is the Blessed Virgin Mary, in whom we shall rejoice above all the saints as the queen of heaven and earth, of angels and men. She is *illuminatrix*, the lamp of the supernal city, its dawn, sun, moon and star, and light of the world.[94] She deserves all honor and cannot be praised enough.[95] Above all, she is the bearer of God, the mother of the creator, but thus also the mother of goodness, grace, mercy, wisdom and knowledge, mother of beauteous love, mother of us all.[96] All grace comes through Mary: she may even be called the "neck" which joins Christ the head to his body the communion of saints because she is the channel and

---

[91] T.84.6 (L), T.88.1-9 (L-N), E.42.3/2, E.51.3.
[92] E.11.1/3.
[93] T.84.7 (M), cf. T.66.1 (T), T.150.1 (R), E.11.1/3.
[94] D.21.4 (H), T.162.1/9 (J), Q.4.3, Q.32.2.
[95] T.161.0 (S), T.162.0 (before D), E.18.2/4, Q.18.3.
[96] D.1.24 (X), D.4.5/3 (Y), T.161.0-3 (S-A), E.14.3, E.25.3/2.

dispense of grace, the *mediatrix* who is our advocate before Christ and whom Christ cannot refuse.[97]

Her unique qualification to be our intercessor before Christ, and thus to be the source of mercy on all alike, is that she is so approachable. Herolt quotes John of St. Geminiano:

> The sun does not shine on the earth unless its rays pass through the air—the air is closer to the earth than the sun. So the sun of righteousness, Christ our Lord God, does not send the rays of his grace except through the glorious Virgin, who is incomparably closer to every creature than God himself.

Her maternal tenderness toward all justifies our trust that she will help us in every need and condone our weakness even, the exemplary tradition suggests, importuning her son to temper his strict justice at her softening pleas for mercy for wayward sinners. "Those whom the Son loses through justice, his mother brings back by mercy and indulgence."[98] Herolt retails many such stories,[99] especially on those occasions when the calendar pays special honor to the Virgin; yet it is quite clear that he himself holds to a richly Christocentric piety and does not intend that his hearers should imagine any contrast between mother and son in showing compassion.

> If you are upright, rejoice, for from her whose feast we celebrate today has arisen the sun of righteousness, and he is the giver and augmentor of grace. If you have been led captive by some sin or confront grave temptation, take comfort and quickly celebrate the feast of the blessed Virgin's birth, for her son has been made our redemption.[100]

In the midst of an eloquent tribute to her efficacious aid, Herolt interpolates a long excursus explaining that the merits of the saints, including Mary's, avail only at God's good pleasure.[101] Rather, such is her piety and humility that biblical statements about Christ's accomplishment for us are fittingly applied to her honor too.[102]

Herolt is characteristically thorough in the rich materials he makes available for Marian preaching—four common sermons for her feasts in the *de tempore*

---

[97] D.2.2/5 (D), D.21.4/3 (O), T.161.0 (S) and .4 (B), T.163.3/3 (M), Q.32.2, E.25.4.
[98] T.exemplum (B), M.96.
[99] E.g., T.161.4 (C); M.2, 9, 10, 12, 47, 51, 59, 71, 96, 99.
[100] T.161.0 (S).
[101] T.161.1 (T), S.1.2.
[102] E.g., Q.11.3, Q.18.3, Q.25.3, Q.32.3, Q.39.3.

collection, five of the festal sermons *de sanctis*, each of the Saturday homilies in the *Quadragesimale*, and a special collection of a hundred stories about her sustaining miracles.[1] With deep piety, he urges her devotion, albeit with the veneration of *hyperdulia*, not the worship of *latria*, which is owing to God alone.[2] But beyond the times especially dedicated to her devotion, Herolt speaks of Mary relatively little and then chiefly in relation to the birth or passion of her son. While Mary is an example to all, and her graces are available to all, there is sometimes an implicit suggestion that deeply affective attachment to the Blessed Virgin is more appropriate for women.[3] The preacher's portrayal of Mary as the exemplary woman is fraught with deep-seated paradox—a model by nature unique and unattainable.[4] A similar tension in the character of Mary's innocence was the subject of protracted doctrinal controversy among Herolt's contemporaries: was she pure because by grace she refrained from sin in spite of common human fallibility or because she was uniquely kept from sin by the miracle of her own immaculate conception? The Dominican Herolt maintains the view of Lombard and the Angelic Doctor that Mary was conceived in original sin, so emphasizing her human affinity with us in the vicissitudes of life and the uniqueness of Christ's mediation and sacrifice;[5] but he is also prepared to accept the Scotist compromise that Mary was preserved and kept from any taint of sin, mortal, venial, or original, from the moment of her conception. Because she was divinely cleansed in body and soul from original sin, she was immune from weakness, ignorance, and malice and therefore unable to sin so that she could be pure enough to receive in herself the faultless mirror of Christ and create no impediment to the Spirit's work of incarnation.[6]

At the heavenly feast, the Blessed Virgin sits at Christ's right hand as queen of heaven, noblest in place, adornment, and companionship.[7] For the faithful, her company is next to the highest joy of all. "As the day is ravished with joy by the sun's presence, so all the court of heaven rejoices in my lovely presence."[8] There can be no doubt that Herolt is earnestly committed to her devotion and commends it to his listeners, yet compared with the heart-felt, spontaneous ardor of his preaching of Christ and his passion, the Marian passages have a customary

---

[1] T.161, 164; S.5, S.11, S.25, S.32, and S.34; Q.4, Q.11, Q.18, Q.25, Q.3.2, and Q.39; and the *Promptuarium Discipuli de miraculis beatae Mariae virginis*.
[2] D.1.24 (X), E.25.3/2.
[3] E.g., D.21.4/5 (Q), T.11.3 (D), T.61.2 (T), T.162.1/9 (J), R.3.5 (39^b), R.6.0 (86^a).
[4] See chapter 12.
[5] D.22.3 (H), T.146.3 (E), S.5.1.
[6] D.21.4/1 (N), T.1.2 (E), T.162.1/1 (D), T.163.2/1-2 (Q), S.5.1, S.11.1, Q.18.3.
[7] T.162.1/8 (H).
[8] M.14.

and wonted flavor. The soul of this disciple's spiritual energy is the contrite desire for God himself, here known imperfectly *ex auditu*, there perfectly *ex visu*. The last and the highest of heaven's joys, in which all the others consist, is the open vision of our father God as he is in himself.[9]

The ninth joy is above all the others, and without it all the earlier joys are nothing. It is the joy we shall have when we see God. This will be the *summum bonum*—to see God's own face: the longing of every will is fulfilled in the divine vision. Augustine says in Book 22 of *The City of God*, "God himself will be the goal of our desires, for he will be seen without end, loved without weariness, praised without flagging. Whatever man desires he will have when he looks into the mirror of the trinity. One who sees God sees everything, and knows whatever occurs in earth, heaven, or hell . . ." As Gregory says, "What do they not see, who see him who sees all?" This vision of God is our entire reward and wholeness—that we shall see God face to face. "Show us your face, Lord, and we shall be saved" (Psalm [80:4]). "This is life eternal, that they should know you the only true God and Jesus Christ whom you have sent" (John 17[:3]). The soul's longing is given to man for this very reason, that he should struggle to attain to where he may see God. As the psalm says, "My soul thirsts for God, the living fount: when shall I come and appear before the face of God?" (Psalm [42:2]).[10]

With so great a consummation, this thirst should spur the yearning soul to any lengths to attain God's presence. As a figure in one story exclaims, "If there was an iron column covered with the sharpest razors and spikes set up from earth to heaven . . . I would let myself be dragged up and down it to judgment day, now climbing, now descending, if I could thereby attain the glory of God I have lost by my pride."[11] But the preacher has no illusions that most of his hearers will turn from their sins and worldly preoccupations and strive toward heaven. In a life of St. Bernard, Herolt learns that thirty thousand people died in the same hour as the saint. Of them, one devout hermit went up with Bernard to heaven, three went to purgatory, and all the rest went down to hell.[12]

These sobering odds explain the unsubtle, even heavy-handed, means the preacher must use to goad the reprobate majority by gross physical terror to sense their shame and turn from their fatal road or to coax untutored beginners by artless images of bliss to examine their mundane lives and live better. Herolt's purpose, and his advice, is that simple preachers in the parishes should set aside the cultivated language and recondite opinions of illustrious scholars and study how to preach simple things to simple folk.[13]

---

[9] T.84.9 (N), E.42.1/3, E.44.1.
[10] T.84.9 (N), cf. D.18.6/6 (V), D.30.7 (M), T.53.6/4 (P).
[11] T.84.6 (L).
[12] T.149.9 (L).
[13] S. preface.

Yet there is no doubt of Herolt's own wide learning or his profound spirituality. In the last analysis, what draws Herolt's energy and passion is not so much the preacher's stock in trade of sins and good deeds, punishments and rewards, even though these subjects inevitably occupy most of his massive homiletic collection. He is at his most spontaneous and moving when he is addressing those who have committed themselves to the life of the spirit. With them he shares his heartfelt conviction that the heavenly vision is simply the culmination of a union with God which can take place here, in the quiet, diligent, contrite life of the virtues—above all, of obedience, friendship, patience, humility, and love.[14] Our unity with God is the answer of our hearts to his love shown to us in Christ: "God loved us so ardently that he loved us above all creatures—indeed, above himself."[15] We may speak of his power, wisdom, goodness, and justice; but when we see him as he is, we shall know that in himself our God is mercy:[16]

> God is the *summum bonum et infinitum*, and so merciful and ready to receive the sinner to grace and to forgive him his sins that never would a faithful mother who had carried her only child in her womb be so swift to stretch forth her hand if she saw her child fallen into the fire. So Christ is ready to receive the contrite person to grace and to forgive his sins . . . . When the sinner considers the goodness of God, how it stands in need of nothing from us, and so has mercy on us from his own infinite goodness, then the heart of the sinner melts, because he knows that he can never be fully cast away from God.

---

[14] E.g., T.18.3 (R), T.119.1 (S), T.157.2/4 (H), E.44.2, R. passim.
[15] E.16.1/4.
[16] T.29.1/1 (O).

Appendix 1

HEROLT'S SERMON BOOKS

Johann Herolt's collection of sermons and homiletic guides circulated widely in manuscript in the middle decades of the fifteenth century, and after the invention of printing, edition after edition was published in the years after 1470. He was one of the most published authors of the incunabular period. Some of his works are readily accessible, but others still exist only in single manuscripts. Here is an outline of this remarkable body of sermon books for parish use.

1416: *Liber discipuli de eruditione Christifidelium.*

Herolt's first work, in thirty long chapters, contains the basic materials for catechetical preaching: the Ten Commandments; the nine alien sins; mortal and venial sin; the seven mortal sins; the six works of mercy, physical and spiritual; the Lord's Prayer; the angelic salutation; the Apostles' Creed; the seven sacraments; and the seven gifts of the Holy Spirit. The book concludes with a tabular index showing how various sections of the catechism may be rearranged to form well-rounded Sunday sermons. Even though it is a young man's book,[17] it already displays the thoroughness of Herolt's preparation for his task. Over sixty different classical, patristic, and scholastic authorities are precisely quoted in more than twelve hundred citations, and the sermons also contain 104 exemplary stories drawn

---

[17] Nicolaus Paulus, "Johann Herolt und seine Lehre," *ZkTh* 26, 419-20, demonstrates convincingly on internal grounds that the 1416 date is reliable, in spite of the fact that three related München MSS [Clm 8842 (1457), Clm 4700 (1460), Clm 18410 (1472)] give the date as 1446 in their *Explicit*, and that some printed editions adjust the date to 1444. The best evidence for the early date is to be found in the exposition of the sixth commandment [D.6.6 (E)], where according to the earliest manuscripts Herolt says, "From Abraham to Christ was 2676 years; from Christ to the present, 1416 years have passed; and added together this makes 4092 years." Furthermore, the *Explicit* of the MS in the Nürnberg Stadtbibliothek (Cent. II, 47, f. 1ᵛ-124ᵛ) reads: "*Et sic est finis huius libri qui intitulatur liber Discipuli de erudicione Xpi fidelium collectus anno domini 1416.*"

from a number of major collections of exempla.[18] Thirty-eight fifteenth-century manuscripts of the work are known.[19] The book was published in seven different printed editions between 1472 and 1500[20] and at least five times in the early sixteenth century.[21]

1418: *Sermones discipuli de tempore. Sermones communes eiusdem discipuli omni tempore predicabiles. Sermones communes discipuli de sanctis.*

This is the centerpiece of Herolt's library of preaching materials. Although it was completed only two years after *de eruditione*, it is a massive compilation of pulpit themes and traditions, crafted with remarkable skill, thoroughness, and consistency. It contains 136 *de tempore* sermons—two or more model sermons for each Sunday and dominical holy day for the whole liturgical year from Advent I to Trinity 25. These are followed by twelve sermons (T.137-148) suitable for preaching at any season: they contain catechetical instructions on thoughts, words, deeds, the mortal sins, the Decalogue, alien sins, the creed, and the sacraments. The common of saints (T.149-164) contains sixteen sermons suitable for preaching on commemorations of any apostle, martyr, confessor, or virgin, the angels, all saints, souls in purgatory, and the Blessed Virgin Mary. Finally, eight exempla about Mary are appended. Many manuscripts and most printed editions also include an elaborate alphabetical index of subjects and a series of other tables summarizing catechetical themes and canonical prohibitions for ready reference.

A substantial proportion of the catechetical book *de eruditione* is reworked in the *sermones de tempore*. Parts of some chapters form the basis for entire Sunday sermons. Other sections are quoted or adapted as one part of a three-point sermon. Sometimes the *de tempore* version is a précis of materials treated at greater length in the catechism. Although the materials are often identical in the two books, Herolt

---

[18] For an assessment of the *de eruditione* and a comparison with other fifteenth-century catechisms, see Johannes Geffken, *Der Bildercatechismus des funfzehten Jahrhunderts und die catechistischen Hauptstücken dieser Zeit bis auf Luther* (Leipzig: T. O. Weigel, 1855), 22, 34, 54-55, 60, 63, 69, 80-81, 87, 97-98.

[19] The MSS and printed editions of D are listed in the bibliography below. See also Thomas Kaeppeli, OP, *Scriptores Ordinis Praedicatorum Medii Aevi* (*SOPMA*), vol. 2 (G-I. Rome: ad S. Sabinae, 1975), 450-51: 2386.

[20] Hain 8516-22. The edition on which I have chiefly relied is the first printed edition (Strasbourg: Georg Husner, about 1476), Hain 8517.

[21] Köln: C. de Zyrickze, 1504, 1509; Strasbourg, 1509; Hagenau: H. Grau, 1516, 1521.

sometimes reworks a quoted passage in order to make a different or clearer point or to make it more suitable for ordinary pulpit use.

There is a consistency and orderliness about Herolt's shaping of his materials that is consciously designed to make these model sermons congenial to use. The heading of each sermon gives the name of the Sunday or holy day, the biblical location of the text for the sermon, and a thematic title. Only rarely is there any direct explication of the scriptural text. Rather, the subject of the sermon is briefly introduced with a very short protheme, often with a classical authority or an illustration from everyday experience. This is directly followed by a summary statement of the numbered points to follow: "In this sermon, there are three things to be said." Each sermon is normally self-contained, but on several occasions when his subject demands it, Herolt continues a topic from one Sunday to the next, usually striving for some symmetry between the two instalments. The standard number of sections in each sermon is three but not infrequently expands to five, seven, twelve, or even twenty-four points to accommodate traditional motifs and mnemonic devices. The preacher carefully reminds the listener of the theme as he proceeds, clearly announcing the arrival of each new numbered part: "As to the third part of this sermon," or "the fifth class of rich people," or "the fourth grade of humility," and so on. However, each major point may then be subdivided into a series of subsections, themselves carefully numbered and identified. Sometimes there are up to four levels of nested subpoints, complicated still further by an occasional excursus on some practical question of pastoral discipline; but the apparent complexity of this form is on the whole shrewdly paced so that the listener is not baffled by the ramification of the theme. Certainly by comparison with many of his contemporaries, Herolt is a model of lucidity in his use of the method of elaboration, division and subdivision enjoined by the *ars praedicandi*.

Herolt's enterprise in the *Sermones* is a thorough, even exhaustive, coverage of all the themes that the committed preacher will address to the people in exhortation, admonition, and appeal.

Over two hundred manuscript copies of this work have been located, apart from many copies of individual sermons.[22] Usually in combined editions with the *Sermones de sanctis* and the *Promptuaria exemplorum* of 1434, the *Sermones discipuli de tempore* was printed forty-eight times between 1474 and 1500;[23] it was republished a score of times in the early years of the sixteenth century,[24] and

---

[22] The MSS of T are listed in the bibliography, including a number of additions and amendments to Kaepelli's listing in *SOPMA* II, 451-54: 2387.

[23] Hain 8473-8505 (but not 8483); Copinger 2921-27; Reichling 207, 549, 1223, 1536, 1750. Not noted by Hain-Copinger-Reichling is an edition at Paris: Jean Morand, 1500.

[24] The sixteenth-century editions of T are listed in the bibliography.

it formed the major part of the editions of Herolt's works published in Venice and Mainz in the early years of the seventeenth century.[25]

1430: *Additiones ad sermones discipuli*

This manuscript, never printed separately, contains a small number of supplementary sermons for special occasions, such as passion sermons for Good Friday, at the dedication of a church, on indulgences, for the New Year, and on the twelve fruits of the mass. They were later incorporated into the *sermones de sanctis*. Accordingly, only a handful of manuscripts exists[26] containing the additions alone; for the most part, the text is to be found in manuscripts and printed editions of the *de sanctis* sermons.[27]

1434: *Sermones de sanctis*

In his preface, Herolt says that after he had completed the *de tempore* set he was asked to make a collection of saints' day sermons and "persuaded by fraternal charity I have complied." The result is forty-eight sermons providing materials for the feasts of each apostle, the saints named in the Roman rite and those celebrated throughout Germany, together with additional sermons for the major dominical and Marian holy days, and incorporating the additions mentioned above. The standard form of the saint's day sermon is: part 1, the dignities or privileges of the saint; part 2, "something for our instruction" on an appropriate point of Christian commitment arising from the saint's example; part 3, circumstances in which the saint is to be invoked, as illustrated by examples drawn from the legend of the saint. Eighty-four manuscript versions of the *de sanctis* sermons have been found in thirty-seven locations.[28] Most of the many printed editions of the *Sermones Discipuli* listed above incorporate the *Sermones de sanctis*, but four separate printed editions also appeared by 1500 and several more in later years.[29]

---

[25] Venetiis: P. M. Bertranus, 1606; Mainz: B. Gualteri, 1612.

[26] E.g., Bamberg, Theol. 36, 376^v-395^v (1430/5) (not listed in *SOPMA*); München, Staatsbibl. Clm 7476, 198-215 (wrongly listed in *SOPMA* as Clm 7474); Clm 12004, 2-179; Vorau, Stiftsbibl., 112, 71^v-72^v ("sermo de cogitationibus" only).

[27] On the basis of the München Staatsbibl. Clm 15135, Paulus gives the date as 1435; but the testimony of the Nürnberg MSS Cent. III, 82 ("A.D.1434") and Cent. IV, 82 (c.1434) is decisive for the earlier date.

[28] The MSS of S are listed in the bibliography and (with three omissions) in *SOPMA* II, 454-55: 2388.

[29] Copinger 2928-30; Reichling I, 150; Hain 8483. In combination with the *Promptuaria*, the *sermones de sanctis* were also reprinted at Lyons: Jn de la Place,

1434: *Promptuarium exemplorum Discipuli secundum ordinem alphabeti*

Herolt's conviction of the power of exemplary stories to communicate the preacher's message graphically and memorably was already displayed in his early books by the inclusion of 104 exempla in the *de eruditione*, 283 in the *sermones de tempore*, and 52 in the *sermones de sanctis*. The alphabetically arranged "Storehouse of Examples" adds 632 narrations, legends, histories, and fables.[30] The subject headings illustrate almost every major theme the preacher will address[31] and a thorough alphabetic index accompanied the work from the beginning.

1511; Nürnberg: J. Koberger, 1514; Lyons: de Sabino, 1534.

[30] The number of exempla counted here must necessarily be approximate, since neither the manuscripts nor the printed editions are uniform in the number of stories they contain. Some later manuscripts progressively add further stories to the original compilation, and the numbering of the exempla changes accordingly. The usual number of exempla in most of the incunabular editions is 632 (Though in most cases only 628 are given at length. Since the other four appeared in both the *Promptuarium* and the *Sermones*, the full story has been replaced by a cross-reference). The following editions, for example, include the 632 numbered exempla: [Köln: Ulrich Zell, 1477] (Copinger 2932); [Strasbourg: The R-Printer (Adolf Rusch) after 1478] (Hain 8473); Nürnberg: Anton Koberger, 1481 (Hain 8482), 1483 (Hain 8487); Strasbourg: [Martin Flach], 1492 (Hain 8307); &c. But some later-printed editions include additional stories: the editions at London: Julian Notary, 1510 and Rouen-Caen: P. Olivier. M. Angier, 1518, contain 643 *exempla*, while B. Elers, *Discipulus Redivivus*, Augsburg: Wolf, 1728, has 634. Meanwhile, the number of cross-references to the *Sermones* incorporated into the *Promptuarium* increases from about 220 in early MSS to over 290 in some editions (in other words, to incorporate the entire *index exemplorum* of the *de tempore* sermons).

In the absence of a critical edition, I have adopted the numbering of the majority of incunabular editions, in which the number of exempla under each letter of the alphabet is as follows:
A: 19, **B:** 9, **C:** 43, **D:** 12, **E:** 43, **F:** 18, **G:** 27, **H:** 9, **I:** 56, **L:** 43, **M:** 70, **N:** 4, **O:** 31, **P:** 133, **R:** 15, **S:** 21, **T:** 26, **U:** 47, **X:** 1, **Y:** 5

[Note that this differs from the list given by J. Th. Welter, *L'Exemplum dans la littérature religieuse et didactique du Moyen Âge* (Geneva: Slatkine, reprints 1973; Paris-Toulouse 1927), 400 n. 10, which is based on other printed versions.]

[31] Abstinentia, Accidie, Adulterium, Amicitia, Aqua benedicta; Baptismus, Blasphemia; Caritare, Charitas, Chorea, Confessio, Conformatio, Consilium,

Forty manuscripts of the *Promptuarium exemplorum* have been identified.[32] Almost all of the many printed editions of the *Sermones de tempore* and *de sanctis* also include this and the following *Promptuarium*, but it was published separately on only two occasions.[33]

1434: *Promptuarium Discipuli de miraculis beatae Mariae virginis*

The six miracle stories of the Blessed Virgin Mary which ended the *Additiones* of 1430 are now joined by ninety-four further legends and stories to make up one hundred instances of "how the Blessed Virgin sustains men, women, and children in life, death, and after death in all needs and dangers." The "Storehouse of Miracles" was combined with the ordinary and festal sermon books and the "Storehouse of Examples" to form the great handbook for preachers that was repeatedly published from the 1470s onward.

Thirty-seven manuscripts of this work are known (many of them side by side with the *Promptuarium exemplorum*).[34] Separate editions comprise three printings

---

Consuetudo, Contritio, Correctio fraterna, Crux sancta; Damnatur multi, Decimae, Desperatio, Detractio, Discretio; Ebrietas, Elemosyna, Ecclesia, Eucharistia, Excommunicatio, Excusatio, Exemplum; Festa, Fides, Filii at filiae; Gaudia celi, Gaudia mundi, Gratiarum actio, Gratia spiritus sancti, Gula; Hospitalitas, Humilitas; Jejunum, Jesus, Indulgentia, Infirmitas, Innocentia, Invidia, Ira, Judei, Judex justus, Judex iniquus, Judicare temerarie, Judicium dei, Jurare falsum; Labor, Lacrimae, Laus humana, Loqui, Lusores, Luxuria; Maledicare, Matrimonium, Misericordia dei, Misericordia opera, Missa, Mors malorum, Mors boni, Mulier, Mundus, Murmuratio; Nativitas Xpi; Obedientia, obsessus, Opera, Oratio; Patientia, Parentes, Passio Xpi, Paupertas, Pax, Peccare, Pena inferni, pena purgatorii, Penitentia, Perseverentia, Predestinatio, Prelati, Prosperitas, Pulchritudo; Res injuste acquisitae, Religiosus, Requies, Ridere; Sepultura, Servire deo, Societas, Somnia, Sortilegia, Spernentes proximos, Superbia spiritualism Tempestas, Temporalia, Tempus, Temptatio, Trinitas; Venatio, Verbum dei, Vetula, Vidua, Virginitas, Virtutes, Unctio extrema, Voluntas, Voluptas, Votum, Usura;Xpianus; Ymago, Ypocrita.

[32] The manuscripts of P are listed in the bibliography and also (with five omissions) in *SOPMA* II, 455-56: 2389.

[33] Copinger 2931-32.

[34] The manuscripts of M are listed in the bibliography and also (with two omissions) in *SOPMA* II, 457: 2391.

in Cologne in the 1470s[35] and one modern edition (the first printing of any of Herolt's writings for two hundred years), a translation into English under the title "Miracles of the Blessed Virgin Mary."[36]

1434: *Promptuarium Discipuli de festis sanctorum intimandis diebus dominicis*

Alongside the two other *Promptuaria* in many manuscripts, and dating from about the same time,[37] is this calendar of saints' days in each week of the year from January to December. It was compiled, Herolt says, "from martyrologies and certain legends of the saints" and was designed to help the parish priest announce each Sunday the saints' days for the coming week. Though it was no doubt useful to the clergy, and continued to be copied by hand for forty years, it was not of interest to the printers. There are thirty-four extant manuscripts,[38] but it was never published as a printed book.

1435: *Quadragesimale Discipuli*

A collection of forty-five Lenten sermons, one for every day from Ash Wednesday to Good Friday.[39] There is a completely regular pattern to this book of systematic Lenten preaching. Each sermon is divided into three distinct parts, with the theme of each part continuing from one sermon to the next.

For the ferial, or weekday, sermons, part 1 is a brief tropological homily on some feature of the Gospel text; after introductory remarks in the first week, part 2 begins a daily history of the passion in thirty-three articles from Gethsemane to Christ's death and explains how we are to imitate each example of his patient suffering; part 3 is a detailed treatise on the three parts of penance (contrition, confession, and satisfaction)—an instruction for the Lenten shrift of Holy Week in preparation for an Easter communion. (This part, Herolt says, is inspired by

---

[35] Copinger 2933-35.

[36] *Miracles of the Blessed Virgin Mary*, translated with a preface and notes by C. C. Swinton Bland and an introduction by Eileen Power (Broadway Mediaeval Library, London: G. Routledge and sons, 1928).

[37] For this date, Nürnberg Stadtbibliothek MS Cent. III, 82, f. 74-112 is dated 1434-35, and München Staatsbibliothek Clm 15135, f. 79-122v is dated 1435.

[38] The MSS are listed in the bibliography and also (with three omissions) in *SOPMA* II, 456-57: 2390.

[39] The last sermon is numbered 47 because the user is urged to add the two Good Friday sermons from the *de tempore* set (T.48 and 49) to make a total of three passion sermons for that day.

Nicolaus von Dinkelsbühl's recent Tract on the three parts of penance, but in fact is quite distinct.).[40] Often an exemplum is added.

In the Sabbath, or Saturday, sermons, the first two parts remain the same; but the instruction on penance is replaced by a discourse in honor of the Blessed Virgin Mary, explaining why Saturday is dedicated to her and how the unity between Mother and Son is so great that the biblical statements about Christ's deeds should also be understood of Mary's grace.

The Sunday sermons are longer and have more of the character of the *de tempore* sermons. The opening exordium explains the name given to each Sunday in Lent, the tropological theme drawn from the day's Gospel is expounded more fully, the passion narrative is omitted but the treatise on penance continues, and the last part of the sermon is a narrative exemplum. (Of the forty-one exemplary stories used in the *Quadragesimale*, only one is new[41]—all the others are references to exempla already used in the dominical sermons or the *Promptuaria*.)

Even though this Lenten handbook is an important supplement to the basic homiletic set, its publishing history is rather different. Indeed, it achieved its widest circulation only in the sixteenth century. Twenty-two fifteenth-century manuscript copies exist.[42] It was printed only once or perhaps twice in the fifteenth century,[43] but from 1500 on, it was printed at least ten times in the sixteenth century (twice by itself, but usually bound with the *Sermones* and *Promptuaria*). It was especially popular in France. New editions also appeared in the two following centuries.[44]

1436: *Der Rosengart*

This little book is exceptional in several respects. It is Herolt's only work in the vernacular German. It survives in a single manuscript, preserved in Nürnberg from

---

[40] Nicolaus Prunczlein von Dinkelsbühl (c. 1360-1433), *Tractatus de tribus partibus penitentiae*, printed in 1516 as *Nicolai Dünckelspühel tractatus hoc volumine contenti*: I. *De dilectione dei et proximi*. II. *De preceptis decalogi*. III. *De oratione dominica*. IIII. *De tribus partibus penitentie*. V. *De octo beatitudinibus*. VI. *De septem peccatis mortalibus, etc*. VII. *Confessionale*. VIII. *De quinque sensibus*. Argen[torati]: Joannes Schottus, 1516. See also Alois Madre, *Nicolaus von Dinkelsbühl: Leben und Scriften*. Beitrage zur Geschichte der Philosophie und Theologie des Mittelalters XL, 4 (Münster, Westph.: Aschendorff, 1965), 180-87.

[41] Q.7.2.

[42] The MSS of Q are listed in the bibliography and also (with four omissions) in *SOPMA* II, 457-58: 2392.

[43] Hain 8514-15.

[44] The sixteenth- and seventeenth-century editions of Q are listed in the bibliography.

the library of the Dominican sisters at St. Katharine's. It is a partial reconstruction from verbatim notes of a series of Advent sermons delivered to the nuns of St. Katharine's by Herolt himself in 1436, when he was cursor of the Katharinenkloster. In place of the rather didactic and literal style of the sermons to parish laity, Herolt here adopts a delightfully figurative style, ordering his materials around the ancient image of the enclosed garden.

The hearer is led to the entrance of a walled garden on a high mountain, and then each feature of the rose garden—the wall, the entrance gate, the groundwork, the trees, branches, birds, and flowers—colorfully sustains a passionate discourse on the monastic virtues of godly fear, diligence, humility, patience, and obedience. However elaborate the allegory and winsome the style (replete with verses for each birdsong and lore about the medicinal virtue of each herb and flower), the content remains wholly consonant with the most heartfelt themes of the sermon books, from which Herolt freely draws quotations, images, and outlines and thus gives us perhaps our best glimpse of how he hoped his materials could be adapted for the pastoral needs of diverse audiences.

Before the elaborate outline of the garden allegory has been fully exploited, Advent has given place to Christmas. The nativity sermon urges the sisters to take the infant Jesus from Mary and carry him into the garden to sing and play with him, present him gifts of bright clothing and nourishing food (devotion, chastity, fervent desire, perseverance, and joy), and give him a Christmas garland of roses plucked from the garden of virtues. Imitation of Christ's suffering and removal from sin is the theme of a more somber sermon on the Circumcision ("when Jesus was born there was peace in the world, so the angels announced peace; but now we preachers cannot announce such peace, for the world is filled with discord and afflicted on every hand"); but the garland motif returns with Herolt's eloquent description of his New Year's gifts—a garland of red and white roses for the spiritual, blue and white lilies and lily of the valley for the virgins, cool damp sweet-smelling violets for the widows, the green rue that expels poison for married folk, and a garland of nettles and thistles to prick and burn the crude mortal sinners and turn them from their sins.

The manuscript has many lacunae, and has been partly revised by a second hand, but enough of Herolt's authentic voice survives to make *Der Rosengart* an invaluable counterpoint to his more formal homiletic handbooks.[45]

---

[45] *Der Rosengart* is to be found only in the Nürnberg Stadtbibliothek, Cent. VII, 57, f. 2-144. Part of the text (f. 2-20v) has been transcribed in Dietrich Schmidtke, *Studien zur dingallegorischen Erbauungsliteratur des Spätmittelalters. Am Beispiel der Gartenallegorie* (Hermaea NF 43). Tübingen: Max Niemeyer, 1982, Textanhang 448-54. See also Schmidtke's remarks on 103-06. I shall shortly publish a complete transcription and translation of *Der Rosengart*.

1437: *Postilla discipuli super evangelia dominicalia et de sanctis secundum sensum litteralem*

Brief historical, etymological, and exegetical comments on the whole text of the Gospels appointed to be read on each Sunday and festival. This *Postil*, and the two companion works that follow, are quite unlike the rest of Herolt's output, to the extent that a serious question must be raised about whether he was indeed the compiler.

There can be no doubt at all that the manuscript tradition (including some of the earliest manuscripts) plainly ascribes the authorship to Discipulus and even to Johann Herolt by name.[46] Furthermore, since the sermon books rarely make any exegetical or historical commentary on the literal meaning of the biblical text, preachers may well have felt the need for such a convenient short collection of textual comments: clarification of literal difficulties in the text for the day was enjoined by the manuals of preaching method.[47] Strong arguments thus exist for accepting the *Postils* as part of Herolt's library of sermonic aids.

The case against Herolt's authorship rests on three internal features of the text itself: first, it displays none of the distinctive marks of Herolt's style, so recognizable in the sermon books; secondly, the list of authorities cited in the *Postils* contrasts strikingly with the consistent pattern of authorities quoted in the other works;[48] and thirdly, there are not a few passages where the literal meaning of the biblical text is understood in one way by the *Sermones* and quite another way by the *Postils*. These

---

[46] For example, the Bamberg Staatsbibl. Theol. 36 (1445-47), f. 314 is headed *Incipit postilla discipuli*, while an old index on the binding lists the work as *postilla hiroltz*; the Eichstätt Staats- u. Seminarbibl. (Hochschulebibl.) 482 (not before 1455), f. 244 is headed *Postilla . . . fris hiroldi OP*; Berlin, Staatsbibl. Lat. qu. 746, f. 159; Karlsruhe, Landesbibl. Aug. 92, f. 148v; all four MSS at Klosterneuburg, CCl 407, 457, 459, and 548; München, Staatsbibl. Clm 13568 (1437), f. 142 v, 26826 (xv), f. 1, 26880 (xv), f. 318; and Würzburg Univ. Bibl. M. ch. f. 135 (1458), f. 277 all attribute the Postil to Discipulus; &c.

[47] See Th. M. Charland, *Artes praedicandi: contribution à l'histoire de la rhétorique au moyen âge* (Ottawa: Institute d'études médiévales d'Ottawa, 1936).

[48] The authorities most often quoted in the *de eruditione* and *sermones* are (in descending order of frequency): Augustine, Gregory, Bernard, Thomas, the Decretals, Aristotle, Chrysostum, Jerome, Guilelmus of Lyons, Isidor of Seville, Ambrose, Hermann de Schilditz, Henricus de Vrimaria, Raymundus, and about fifty other authors.
The corresponding list for the *Postils*: Lyra, Gorran, Vincentius, Thomas, Augustine, Chrysostum, and about thirty others.

objections could possibly be dismissed on the grounds that the enterprise of compiling literal notes on the text is a very different enterprise from constructing model sermons, and that the *Postils* are more obviously an unmodified collection from other recent commentators (especially Nicolaus of Lyra and Nicolaus of Gorran).

It is true that Herolt himself, in a single reference in his last work, calls the commentary *Postilla discipuli*;[49] yet the likelihood remains that these materials were compiled under Herolt's supervision, but not by him personally. This conjecture would account for the anomalous features I have described. Whether Herolt was directly responsible or not, these *Postils* contain almost no instruction in faith and life; and for this reason (as well as uncertainty about the authorship), I have omitted them from this account of Herolt's preaching.

An additional complexity attaches to the *Postil* on the Gospels, which is extant in at least twenty manuscripts.[50] Together with the *Postil* on the Epistles, it was printed in a staggering 110 or more editions between 1472 and 1500 and many times thereafter.[51] It was, in short, one of the most popular biblical aids of the period. But it was published not under Herolt's name or *nom de plume* but attributed to the nonexistent "Guillermus Parisiensis."[52] It appeared from the very first edition with a preface purporting to be by this pseudonymous compiler.[53] The printed editions differ from the earlier manuscripts in the following ways. The MSS announce the location of the pericope in the Gospels and then proceed directly to verse by verse comments, but the printed "Guillermus" always inserts a short "history of this gospel" (that is, a precise account of where the discourse or narrative fits into the chronology of Jesus' life). Secondly, the printed editions impose a greater regularity on the citation of sources, especially by the addition

---

[49] A.X.: 1 (f. 130a); see footnote 39 below.

[50] The MSS of this Postil are listed in the bibliography and also (with a few inaccuracies) in *SOPMA* II, 458-59: 2393.

[51] Frederick R. Goff, "The Postilla of Guillermus Parisiensis," *Gutenberg-Jahrbuch* 34 (1959), 73-78, counts 105 incunabular editions as certain, and up to six out of 17 "indeterminate editions" as probably authentic. A complete listing is to be found in this article by an eminent bibliographer.

[52] I have found one edition, however, where the name Discipulus has survived into the printed version: the *Postilla super epistolas et evangelia* [Germany: printer of Lotharius, 1474] (Hain 10209) heads the Common of Saints gospels, "*Incipit postilla Discipuli de fmuni sanctorum.*"

[53] The information given about "Guillermus Parisiensis" in, for example, Quétif-Echard, I (1719), 868, or C. G. Jöcher, *Allgemeines Gelehren-Lexicon*, Leipzig: J. F. Gleditschen, 1751, 4/1978, is clearly based on the preface to the *Postil*, not on independent information.

of unde ("whence") before an author's name. Thirdly and most importantly, in the printed editions fifty-one of the sixty-five expositions have been augmented by brief sermon outlines, based on a word or theme in the text, and introduced at the end of the literal commentary by the words, "Concerning this present gospel, where it says . . . (circa *presens evangelium ubi dicitur* . . .)." More than half these additions are excerpts from the sermons of the thirteenth-century Dominican preacher Hugo de Prato Florido, but there is a score or more of unidentified sources.

The practical effect of the additions is to turn the literal *Postil* into a concise preaching manual. The process by which the original text was expanded is most plainly visible in the Munich manuscript Clm 26826, where the bare commentary on the literal sense has first been written in full, then the same scripter has incorporated all the sermonic outlines in eleven inserted sheets and sixty-one marginal additions.[54] While it is possible that this scripter copied these additions later from the printed book, it is also possible that this manuscript, which originated in Herolt's own cloister, is the source of the added materials. What is certain is that the sermon outlines were already attached to the *Postilla discipuli* ten years before it was printed as the *Postilla Guillermi Parisiensis*, for Herolt's 1463 *Applicationes* (see below) refers the reader to a passage in the *Postil* which belongs to the additional insertions, not to the original text.[55] Further, the added material contains one cross-reference to an exemplum in Herolt's *Promptuarium*.[56] In spite of its rather mysterious history, this *Postil* (together with its companion on the Epistles) "must be regarded as one of the earliest "best sellers.""[57]

1439: *Postilla discipuli super epistolas dominicales et de sanctis secundum sensum litteralem*

This is the companion volume to the *Postil* on the Gospels. The pattern of literal commentary (based largely on Nicolaus of Lyra, supplemented by Nicolaus

---

[54] München, Staatsbibl. Clm 26826 (xv), f. 1-114v. According to f. 1, this book first belonged to the Dominican monastery in Nürnberg (Herolt's own cloister) and later to the Regensberg Dominicans. It is not precisely dated.

[55] A.X.: 1 (f. 130ª) refers the reader to a fuller treatment in the Postil of the theme of Christ's fierceness under the old covenant compared with his meekness under the new. This is to be found in the Postil's appended sermon for Advent 1, between two excerpts from Hugo de Prato.

[56] The additional material for Pentecost 16 contains a cross-reference to *Promptuarium discipuli* P.: 97: *Mulier quaedam flet super filium defunctum inconsolabiliter.*

[57] Goff, "Postilla," 73.

of Gorran and relatively few other authorities) is exactly the same as the earlier *Postil*, but in this case no supplementary material appears either in the manuscripts or in the *Postilla* of Guillermus Parisiensis. Some misunderstanding exists on this point, however, because some libraries (followed by Fr. Kaeppeli in the *Scriptores Ordinis Praedicatorum*) have confused this work on the literal sense with a later, undoubtedly authentic, work of Herolt's, the *Sermones discipuli super epistolas dominicales* (see below).

The confusion stems from the fact that the *Incipits* of the two books are (not surprisingly) very alike, since they are based on the same text; but in content, the two books could not be more unlike. As we shall see, the *Sermones* are a fully worked set of preached expositions in Herolt's own characteristic style, whereas the *Postilla* is a spare exegetical commentary on the grammar and literal meaning of the text and raises the same doubts about Herolt's authorship as the other *Postil*.

Only fifteen manuscripts of the *Postil* on the Epistles are known to exist,[58] but it achieved huge circulation as part of the pseudonymous *Postilla of Guillermus Parisiensis*.

Undated (but probably 1439): *Postilla discipuli secundum sensum litteralem super officium missae et super epistolas et evangelia per Quadragesimam*

This work completes the set of *Postils*, but unlike the two previous parts, it was not incorporated in the *Postilla* of Guillermus Parisiensis and was not published as a printed book. It consists of brief literal commentaries on the Psalm, Introit, Collect, Epistle, and Gospel for each mass in Lent, sometimes also including a short concord of the Epistle and Gospel for the day. Its sources are the same as before (notably Lyra, Gorran, Thomas, and the glosses), and like the other *Postils*, it shows no compelling signs of Herolt's authorship. Seven manuscript copies have been located.[59]

---

[58] The MSS of the *Postilla super epistolas* are listed in the bibliography. In *SOPMA* II, 459: 2394, this work is conflated with the MSS for the *Sermones . . . super epistolas dominicales* (see note 46 below).

[59] The MSS for this Postilla are listed in the bibliography and (with one omission) in *SOPMA* II, 460: 2395.

1441:[60] *Sermones discipuli super epistolas dominicales*

This rich set of sermons on the Epistles appointed for each Sunday and dominical feast is an authentic work of Herolt's maturity and throws fresh light on the preaching enterprise as he saw it. The *Epistle Sermons* are certainly not "insignificant," as Cruel judged.[61] Though they never enjoyed the circulation of Herolt's major handbooks, they reveal more of Herolt himself as a theologian and teacher than his earlier productions. This is partly because of the method employed. Instead of stating a chosen theme and then elaborating it (as in the *de tempore* sermons), here Herolt allows the apostle's words to suggest the subject matter. The resulting themes are treated in Herolt's now-familiar style; but the topics sometimes follow each other in an apparently unsystematic way, their unity provided by the tenor of the biblical text or its aptness to the season. This greater expository freedom and the occasional injection of an explicit personal opinion suggest that this round of sermons may have begun not as a series of models for others to imitate but as sermons Herolt himself preached.

By the same token, his deliberate and self-conscious avoidance of theological subtleties in the other books is not so apparent here: he does occasionally allow himself to speculate about some of the controversial scholastic issues of the day (though always in a pastoral mode). With this greater freedom come a more graphic style and a livelier treatment of many of the central topics of his preaching. Of the fifty-two exempla in these sermons, fourteen are not in the earlier collections, thirty-eight are references to the *Promptuarium*, and three to the *de tempore* sermons.

The original form of this work contained fifty-one sermons, as do the printed editions. But several manuscripts also include five additional sermons (for Ascension, Trinity, Corpus Christi, Trinity 20, and Trinity 25) for a total of fifty-six sermons altogether.

---

[60] I prefer this date on the basis of manuscripts in the Bamberg Staatsbibliothek (Theol. 14 (1448/61), f. 135v) and Koblenz Landeshauptarchiv (Best. 701 Nr. 189, f. 236) whose *explicits* gives 1441 as the date of the collection. R. Cruel, *Geschichte der deutschen Predigt im Mittelalter* (Detmold: Meyer, 1879), 480, gave the date as 1440 but did not cite a precise source. In response, Nicolaus Paulus, *ZkTh* 26 (1902), 424-25 and note, preferred the date 1444 on the basis of the edition printed at Strasbourg: G. Husner, 1478 (Hain 8510). A 1444 date is also supported by a manuscript in the Köln Historisches Archiv [GB f° 115 (1460/80), f. 87], and by the earliest known edition [Strasbourg: G. Husner, 1473] (IGDI, III, 4699), but the testimony of the Bamberg and Koblenz MSS is persuasive.

[61] Cruel, *Gesch. d. deutschen Predigt im MA*, 480.

Nineteen extant copies of the manuscript are listed.[62] As a printed book, the Epistles appeared ten times in the fifteenth century but has not been reprinted since.[63]

1463: *Applicationes ad sermones secundum proprietates rerum naturalium*

Herolt's last extant work was prepared twenty years after the last of his other known writings and only five years before his death. It survives in only one manuscript in Munich[64] and was never printed. Yet it is unquestionably Herolt's work, and many of the materials so colorfully gathered here were used earlier to illustrate the sermons in the earlier books. The *Applicationes* is an alphabetical collection of 151 illustrations of the vices and virtues drawn from the world of nature—more than a hundred birds, beasts, fish, precious stones, metals, plants, herbs, and natural phenomena.[65] Each illustration describes some familiar or exotic

---

[62] The MSS of the *Sermones discipuli super epistolas dominicales* are listed in the bibliography. In *SOPMA* II, 459: 2394, Kaeppeli does not distinguish between this work and the *Postilla super epistolas*, and his listing should therefore not be relied on. It is not always possible to tell from the catalogues which of these manuscripts contain the longer or shorter versions; but I do know that fifty-six sermons are to be found in the MSS at Bamberg, Klosterneuberg, Luxembourg, Marburg, and Salzburg.

[63] Hain 8509-13, Copinger 2936- 2939, IDGI III 4699.

[64] München, Staatsbibl. Clm 8132 (1474), f. 111-131ᵛ, tabulae f. 132-133ᵛ. The *expliciunt* carries three dates: 1463 is the year of collection *"ex diversis libris doctorum katholicorum"*; at the end of the *expliciunt*, the date 1467 is given; and 1474 is the date when the copyist (Rudolf Haschober, chaplain in Straubing) made this version, presumably from a 1467 copy of the 1463 text.

[65] The subject headings (and the applicationes for each) are as follows:

Abstinentia (5)	Bird, lion, peacock, snake, wolf
Accidia (1)	Sleep
Adulatores (1)	Scorpion
Amicitia (1)	Earthquake
Amicus (1)	Hawk
Anima devota (2)	Woman, maiden
Anima (3)	Eagle, hawk, pregnant woman, sun, wind
Avari (3)	Gryphon, snake
Baptismus (2)	River Jordan, water spring
Blasphemantes (1)	Crow
Boni (4)	Falcon, god tree, lion, sheep
Caritas (5)	Deer, fire, potter's clay, root, sun
Confessio et contritio (2)	Absinth, burning coal
Conscientia (2)	Bee
Cor (1)	Root
Detractores (2)	Dog, snake
Dilectio (2)	Feet, juniper
Elemosyna (1)	Eagle
Eucharistia (1)	Fish
Excommunicatus (1)	Rabid dog
Exemplum malum (2)	Basilisk, rose and thorn

Fides (1)	Mustard seed
Gaudium (1)	Swan
Gaudia et ludi (1)	Dolphin
Gratia (2)	Lark, young raven
Gulosi (1)	Vulture
Heretici (2)	Lion cubs, panther cubs, viper, whale
Hominis dignitas (1)	Brute beasts, cattle, fleas, horse, viper
Homo (2)	Dust, straw
Humilitas (1)	Magnet
Infirmitas (1)	Elephant, lion, medicine
Ingrati (1)	Pelican
Injuria (1)	Dove
Iracundus (1)	Dog
Judices (1)	Dog
Justitia (1)	Iron
Lacrimarum compunctio (2)	Rain, water
Leges (1)	Spider's web
Luxuria (5)	Clouds, fire, goat, horse, worm
Mali (1)	Tares
Maria (3)	Olive, palm tree, vine
Matrimonium (3)	Brute beasts, elephant, stork
Mors (2)	Snake
Mors bonorum (1)	Sleep
Mortis memoria (3)	Ash, peacock, tails
Mundus (2)	Desert, sea, wind
Obedientia (1)	Camel
Operis intentio (1)	Root
Opera meritoria (1)	Eagle
Opera bona (2)	Eagle, root
Opera Christi (1)	Mountain
Orare (1)	Wild ass
Patientia (1)	Gold
Pagsio (2)	Pepper tree snake
Passio Christi (1)	Mountain
Pauperes (1)	Hen, stork
Peccator (3)	Ass, bad servant, children
Peccatum (4)	Absinthe, old age, thorn, thunder
Peccati delectatio (2)	Bear, mouse
Penitentes (2)	Stork, sturgeon
Penitentia (3)	Ass, lion, phoenix
Pena (1)	Abeston, salamander
Perfecti (1)	Heron
Perseverantia (1)	Leopard
Predicator (1)	Cock
Prelati (4)	Crow, eagle, head, tree, whale
Proficit homo (1)	Tree
Prosperitas (1)	Smoke
Prudentia (3)	Ant, snake, hedgehog
Raptores (1)	Gryphons
Religiosi (1)	Bees
Sacerdotes (1)	Stars
Societas bona (1)	Olive
Superbus (1)	Dragon
Superbia (2)	Moth, peacock
Sapere (1)	Gnat
Temporales divitiae (1)	Brier, fruit tree, snake
Temptatio (3)	Cat and mouse, roebuck, toad
Tribulatio (2)	Balsam, rue, snake, toad
Verbum dei (1)	Food

characteristic of the object chosen and then makes a series of figurative applications of these characteristics to the foibles of everyday life, the dangers of sin, or the winsomeness of virtue. Herolt's delightful collection is worthy to stand alongside other bestiaries and the earlier collections of natural sermon illustrations so beloved of his order, and it is a pity it has received little attention.

Most of the entries contain cross-references to exempla in the other books (121 references to the *Promptuarium*,[66] 2 to the *de tempore*, 1 to the Epistles, and 1 to the *Postil* additions).

Vidua (1)	Dove
Virgines (1)	Pearl
Virginitas (3)	Bee, cedar, moth, rose, snake, viola
Virtuosi (3)	Hare, meadow, olive
Vita contemplative (1)	Nutmeg, sapphire
Xristus (3)	Lamb, light, unicorn
Ypocrita (1)	Nutshell, swan

[66] Interestingly, to a version of the *Promptuarium* (presumably Herolt's own copy) containing at least 657 stories, 25 more than the most commonly printed set.

Appendix 2
ABBREVIATIONS, EDITIONS, BIBLIOGRAPHY

Herolt's works are cited as follows:

D = *De eruditione Christifidelium*
T = *Sermones de tempore*
S = *Sermones de sanctis*
P = *Promptuarium exemplorum sec. ordinem alphabeti*
M = *Promptuarium de miraculis beatae Mariae virginis*
Q = *Quadragesimale*
R = *Der Rosengart*
E = *Sermones super epistoles dominicales*
A = *Applicationes sec. proprietates rerum naturalium*

Most of Herolt's sermon books have clear numerical divisions, and some are indexed by letters interpolated in the text; but they are not consistent, and in the absence of any modern edition, there is no uniform way to locate passages.

To make it possible for readers to consult many diverse manuscripts and early editions, I have used a notation that applies very readily to the large sermon books, less simply to the shorter, less ordered works. These examples illustrate how to interpret the notes:

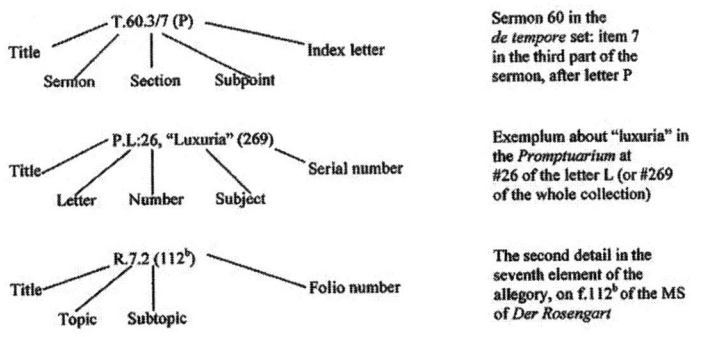

T.60.3/7 (P) — Sermon 60 in the *de tempore* set: item 7 in the third part of the sermon, after letter P (Title / Sermon / Section / Subpoint / Index letter)

P.L:26, "Luxuria" (269) — Exemplum about "luxuria" in the *Promptuarium* at #26 of the letter L (or #269 of the whole collection) (Title / Letter / Number / Subject / Serial number)

R.7.2 (112^b) — The second detail in the seventh element of the allegory, on f.112^b of the MS of *Der Rosengart* (Title / Topic / Subtopic / Folio number)

Other Abbreviations

AFP *Archivum Fratrum Praedicatorum.* Rome: S. Sabina, 1930 ff.
AOP *Analecta sacri ordinis fratrum Praedicatorum.* Rome, 1893 ff.
Copinger Copinger, Walter A. *Supplement to Hain's Repertorium bibliographicum or collections towards a new edition of that work*, 2 parts. London: Henry Sotheran, 1895-1902.
du Cange du Cange, Charles Dufresne. *Glossarium Mediae et Infimae Latinitatis.* Edited by D. P. Carpenter and G. A. L. Henschel. Paris, 1842.
Hain Hain, Ludwig F. T. *Repertorium bibliographicum in quo libri omnes ab arte typographica inventa usque ad annum M.D.; typis expressi ordine alphabetico vel simpliciter enumerantur vel adcuratius recensentur. Indices uberrimi C.Burger.* Leipzig: Harrassowitz, 1891.
IDGI *Indice generate degli incunaboli delle biblioteche d'Italia a cura del Centro Nazionale d'Informazioni Bibliografiche.* Rome: Ministero dell' Educazione Nazionale, 1943-48.
MOPH *Monumenta Ordinis Praedicatorum historica.* Rome: In Domo Generalitia, 1896 ff.
PRE *Realencyklopädie für protestantische Theologie und Kirche*, begrundet von J. J. Herzog, Aufl. 3 hrsg. A. Hauck (21 vols, 1898-1908 and Register 1909, Erganzungen und Nachträge, 2 vols, 1913). Leipzig: J. C. Heinrichs, 1898 ff.
QF *Quellen und Forschung zur Geschichte des Dominikanerordens in Deutschland*, begrundet von Paulus von Lod. Leipzig: Harrassowitz, 1907 ff.
Reichling Dietrich Reichling, *Appendices ad Hainii-Copingeri Repertorium Bibliographicum. Additiones et emendationes*, 7 pts. Monachii.: J. Rosenthal and Monasterii Guestphalorum: Theissinger, 1905-14.
SOP Echard, Jacobus, and Jacques Quétif. *Scriptores Ordinis Praedicatorum Recensiti, notisque histories et criticis illustrati.* Paris: Ballard et Simart, 1719-21. Reprinted in the Burt Franklin Bibliographical and Reference Series No. 16. New York: Franklin, 1959-61.
SOPMA Kaeppeli, Thomas, OP. *Scriptores Ordinis Praedicatorum Medii Aevi.* Rome: Sabina, 1970 ff.
ZkTh *Zeitschrift für katholische Theologie.* Innsbruck: Rauch, 1877 ff.

Editions of Works by Johann Herolt

The most complete earlier listing of manuscripts is given in Thomas Kaeppeli, OP, *Scriptores Ordinis Praedicatorum Medii Aevi*, vol. 2, G-I (Roma: ad S. Sabinae, 1975), 450-60: 2386-2396. Because of some omissions and inaccuracies in that guide, the version of Kaeppeli's list given here contains those corrections I have been able to identify.

1416: *Liber discipuli de eruditione Christifidelium*

Manuscripts
Admont 617 (xv), f. 1-92^v.
Bamberg, Staatsbibl., Theol. 62 (xv), f. 98-212; Theol. 95 (xv), f. 193-294.
Basel, Univ. Bibl. A VI 1 (1442), f. 1-192^v.
Colmar, Bibl. municip. 103 (297) (xv), f. 106^v-162.
Colmar, Bibl. du Consistoire 1934 (xv), f. 85-256^v.
Düsseldorf, Landes—u. Stadtbibl., B. 104 (xv), f. 134-194.
Erlangen, Univ. Bibl. 547 (xv), f. 231-305; 570 (xv), f. 1-220.
Gotha, Landersbibl., Chart. A 18^a (1435).
Graz, Univ. Bibl. 321 (xv), f. 51-156^v; 582 (1442), f. 1-172; 636 (xv), f. 1-80.
Harburg (Schloss), Fürstl. Oettingen-Wallerstein'sche Bibl. II, 1, fol., 30 (xv), f. 1-182.
Karlsruhe, Bad. Landesbibl., Ettenheimmünster 29 (1453), f. 1-147^v.
Köln, Hist. Archiv, GB f. 176 (xv), f. 230-34 (on the Ten Commandments).
København, Kongel. Bibl., GL. kgl. S. 1591 4° (xvi), f. 126^v-29^v (on the twelve articles of faith).
Kremsmünster L (xv), f. 2-214.
Liège, Univ. 34 (xv), f. 9-74^v; 261 (xv).
München, Staatsbibl., Cgm 651 (extracts); Clm 4700 (1460); 7453 (xv), f. 318^v-97^v (on the nine alien sins); 8842 (1457), f. 37-117^v; 14113 (1461), f. 167-272^v; 17618 (xv), f. 38-210; 18410 (1472), f. 4; 27018 (1461).
München, Univ. Bibl. 2° 669, 67^v-142.
Nürnberg, Stadtbibl., Cent. II, 47 (xv), f. 1^v-124^v ("collectus a. 1416").
Olomouc, Univ. knihovna I 172 (xv).
Stuttgart, Württemb. Landesbibl., HB IV 10 (xv), f. 318-47^v; HB IV 30 (1444); Theol. 4° 186 (xv).
Vatican, Pal. lat. 418 (1428), f. 15-221^v; Vat. lat. 10057 (xv), f. 134-224; 10059 (xv), f. 13-155^v.
Vorau, Stiftsbibl., Cod. 238, f. 102^v-08 (on the Ten Commandments, abbreviated).
Walberberg, Dominikanerkloster 42 (xv).

Printed Editions

Seven incunabular editions are listed in Hain 8516-22.
Sixteenth-century editions were printed at Köln: de Zyrickze, 1504, 1509; Strasbourg, 1509; Hagenau: H. Grau, 1516, 1521.

1418/30: *Sermones discipuli de tempore. Sermones communes eiusdem discipuli omni tempore predicabiles. Sermones communes discipuli de sanctis.*

Manuscripts

Augsburg, Staats—und Stadtbibl., Fol. 528 (xv).
Bamberg, Theol. 36, f. 176^v-395^v (*additiones* 1430/35).
Basel, Univ. Bibl. A I A (xv), f. 24^v-344^v; A X 68 (xv), f. 2-83; A XI (xv), 4a.
Berlin, Staatsbibl., Theol. fol. 20 (1468), f. 27-363; Theol. fol. 235 (xv), f. 2-222; Theol. fol. 374 (xv), f. 1-66^v; Theol. qu. 79 (xv), f. 15-274.
Beromünster, Stiftsbibl. C. 30 (1449).
Brno, Univ. knihovna R 361 (1456), f. 1-358.
Brussels, Bibl. Royale 1412 (xv), f. 1-297^v.
Budapest, Országos Széchényi Könyvtár, Clmae 506 (xv).
Cambridge, Univ. Libr Mm. V. 39 (1455).
Chicago, Univ. Libr. 790 (xv).
Donaueschingen, Fürstenberg. Hofbibl. 279 (1469), f. 1-228.
Einsiedeln 711 (xv), f. 1-210; 712 (xv), f. 1-200.
Engelberg 236 (xv).
Erlangen, Univ. Bibl. 566 (xv), f. 1-355; 567 (xv), f. 1-347 (incl. *additiones*), 347^v-57 (tabula); 588 (1438-47), f. 79-101 (extracts): 590 (xv), f. 105 ^{v} (extract).
Frankfurt a. M., Stadt—u. Univ. Bibl., Praed. 53 (xv), f. 1-136^v; Barth. 76 (c.1449); Leonh. 5 (1451), f. 1-320^v; Carm. 9 (1454-55), f. 136-278^v.
Gdansk, Bibl. Gdanska Polskiej Akad. Nauk, Mar. F. 189 (xv), f.1-236^v, 241-292.
Giessen, Univ. 757 (xv); 759 (xv).
Göttweig 297 (xv); 310 (c.1461); 312 (xv).
Graz, Univ. Bibl. 743 (1460); 945 (xv), f. 1-204^v; 1375 (xv), f. 192-255^v.
Hamburg, Stadt Univ. Bibl., Theol. 1097 (1443), f. 1-226 ("pars aestivalis").
Harburg (Schloss), Fürstl. Oettingen-Wallerstein'sche Bibl. II, 1. fol., 148 (xv), f. 1-185; II, 1, fol., 188 (1459), f. 1-264.
Herzogenburg 34 (xv), f. 1-232.
Innsbruck, Univ. Bibl. 233 (1438); 566 (xv), f. 1-282.
Karlsruhe, Bad. Landesbibl., Reichenau Pap. 15 (xv), f. 25-308^v, 313-380; Pap. 107 (xv), f. 1-687; St. Blasien 99 (1451).
Kassel, Murhardsche Bibl. d. Stadt u. Landesbibl. 2°Ms. Theol. 45 (xv).

Klagenfurt, Studienbibl., Pap. 165 (1437-41).
Klosterneuberg 456 (xv), f. 1-413^v; 457 (xv), f. 1-240; 458 (xv), f. 1-307; 459 (xv), f. 7-135; 460 (xv), f. 1-271; 509 (xv), f. 1-355; 548 (xv), f. 1-212.
København, Kongel. Bibl., Gl. kgl. S. 74 (1469-70), f. 103-286.
Kön, Hist. Archiv W 150 (xv); GB f°. 165 (xv); GB f°. 176 (xv), f. 1-230.
Kremsmünster CXCIV (xv); CXCV (xv).
Lambach 64 (1463); 87 (xv); 98 (xv); 257 (xv); 313 (xv).
Liège, Univ. 98 (xv); 199 (xv).
London, British Museum, Add. 19909 (xv).
Lüneburg, Ratsbücherei, Theol. 2° 33 (xv), f. 22-247^v; Theol. 2° 93 (c. 1462), f. 2-380^v.
Luzern, Zentralbibl. 30 fol. (xv).
Mainz, Stadtbibl. I 47 (xv), f. 195-252^v; I 177 (xv) (*Serm. comm. de sanctis*, illegible).
Maria Sall 25(xv), f. 1-89.
Melk 409 (1470), f. 2-338; 1868 (before 1441).
München, Staatsbibl., Clm 2792 (1461), f. 1-164^v; 2793 (xv); 2794 (1462); 3093 (1456), f. 1-245; 3315 (xv); 3316 (xv); 3441 (1445); 3753 (xv), f. 1-222 (*pars aestivalis*); 3766 (xv), f. 143-166; 4754 (1454), f. 25-377; 5172 (1453); 5177 (xv), f. 127-189^v; 5232 (xv), f. 1-188; 5611 (xv), f. 1-376; 5925 (xv), f. 231-247; 6966 (xv), f. 1-532; 7453 (xv), f. 110-213^v; 7477 (xv), f. 1-340, tabula 341-44; 7529 (1463), f. 1-122; 7718 (xv), f. 1-4^v; 8343 (xv), f. 1-464; 8843 (xv), f. 27-465; 8860 (xv), f. 1-1251; 8861 (1455), f. 1-185; 8887 (1441), f. 26-112@; 9723 (xv); 11448 (xv), f. 35-99; 11449 (1462), f. 102-217; 11450 (xv), f. 213-254 (*commune de sanctis cum exemplis*); 11461 (xv), f. 155-178^v; 11883 (xv), f. 1-272; 12004, f. 1-204^v; 13420 (c. 1454), f. 332-402^v; 14128 (xv), f. 11-399, 400-406 (*casus*); 14351 (1450), f. 1-383; 14551 (xv); 15001 (xv), f. 1-255 (*pars*); 16177 (xv), f. 1-193; 16504 (xv), f. 1-292^v; 16507 (1433-36), f. 1-182^v; 16508 (xv), f. 1-193; 17235 (xv), f. 175^v-220; 17248 (xv), f. 1-312; 17632 (c. 1467), f. 34-306^v; 17786 (1456), f. 1-271; 18021 (xv), f. 219-257 (*"de adventu domini"*); 18228 (1439), f. 2-209^v; 18229 (xv); 18308 (xv), f. 1-164^v, 173-195^v; 18419 (xv), f. 205-296 (*"commune sermonum"*); 19533 (1444), f. 1-384; 19534 (1448), f. 1-230; 19543 (c.1461); 23758 (xv), f. 356-402 (*"de peccatis"*); 23'794 (1465-66), f. 36-323; 23844 (xv) (*"mixti"*); 26707 (1452); 26896 (xv); 27423 (1462), f. 1-241 (part only, with interpolations); 28468 (1448), f. 1-290.
New Haven, Yale Univ. Library, Beinecke Libr., Marston 141 (1444), f. 15-239, (a *Manuale* containing a selection of sermons, one for each Sunday); Marston 196 (xv).
Nürnberg, Stadtbibl., Cent. VII, 15 (xv), f. 102^v-110.
Olomouc, Kapitulni knihovna 114 (1450); 276 (1461).
Ottobeuren O. 27 (xv), f. 62-132.

Opava, Slezská stud. knihovna 37 (1455), f. 1-358.
Pommersfelden, Gräfl. Schönborn'sche Bibl. 181 (xv), f. 15^v-80.
Prague, Narodni Mus. XXI. D. 6 (xv); XIV. C. 10 (1444).
Prague, Státne (formerly Univ) knihovna, VI. E. 10 (xv), f. 85-100 (*"Tabula"*); XII. A. 14 (xv), f. 1-63.
Quedlinburg, Kreis—u. Stadtbibl. XXV (xv).
Rein 70 (1469).
Rottenburg, Priesterseminar 1 (xv).
Salzburg, St. Peter a. III. 14 (xv), f. 41-70; a. VII. 7 (1465), f. 25-30^v; b. XI. 9 (1438).
Salzburg, Studienbibl. M. II. 169 (xv); M. II. 315 (xv).
St. Florian 240 (xv), f. 1-206^v; 305 (xv); 307 (xv); 310 (xv); 364 (xv); 372 (xv).
St. Gallen, Stiftsbibl. 327 (xv); 1038 (xv); 1065 (xv).
Schlägl 135 (xv), f. 1-288; 218 (xv), f. 142-189^v.
Schwaz, Franziskanerkl. Q I/1. 14 (1448).
Sélestat 73 (1465-77), f. 1-332; 76 (1438-9).
Strasbourg, Bibl. Nat. et Univ. 77 (xv), f. 217.
Stuttgart, Württemb. Landesbibl., HB I 138 (c.1437-9), f. 1-384^v; Theol. fol. 185 (xv), f. 2-246^v; Theol. fol. 255 (xv); Theol. fol. 325 (xv); Theol. fol. 334 (xv).
Trier, Seminarbibl. 94 (xv), f. 25-401.
Trier, Stadtbibl. 265 (xv), f. 198-291; 317 (xv); 335 (xv).
Tübingen, Univ. Bibl. Mc 8 (1437); Md 4 (1468).
Vatican, Pal. lat. 455 (1438), f. 1-222; 458 (xv), f. 149-168; Vat. lat. 10059 (xv), f. 246-254.
Vienna, Nat. Bibl. 3725 (xv), f. 263; 3771 (xv), f. 5-84; 4140 (xv), f. 189-337; 4745 (1442-46), f. 1-95^v; 4918 (xv), f. 1-128, 158^v-184^v.
Vienna, Schottenkloster 49 (xv), f. 13-352^v; 50 (xv), f. 5-408^v; 341 (xv), f. 1-409^v; 381 (xv), f. 1-392^v.
Windsheim, Ratsbibl. 73 (1456); 110 (xv), f. 3-372.
Wolfenbüttel, Herzog August Bibl., 34. 3. Aug. fol. (xv), f. 1-405^v; 143 Helmst. (xv).
Wroclaw. Bibl. Uniw. I F 691 (xv), f. 109-143; I F 695 (1443), f. 1-311; I F 696 (xv), f. 1-179; I F 697 (xv), f. 33-485^v; I Q 274 (xv), f. 1-369^v; I Q 391 (xv), f. 1-406^v; I Q 392 (1470).
Zürich, Zentralbibl. C 36 (xv), f. 2-180^v.

Printed Editions

Forty-eight incunabular editions are listed in Hain 8473-8508 (but not 8483); Copinger 2921-27; Reichling 207, 549, 1223, 1536, 1750. Not noted by Hain-Copinger-Reichling is an edition at Paris: Jean Morand, 1500. Microfilm copies of some incunabular editions are available from General Microfilm Company (Watertown, Mass.) in *German Books Before 1601*, Rolls 197/1; 204/1 and 2; 279/1; 334/6; 411/2; and *French Books Before 1601*, Rolls 109/3; 111/3; 207/6.

Sixteenth editions include: Lyons: Claudius Duvost, 1502; Nürnberg, A. Koberger, 1502; Strasbourg: M. Flach, 1503, 1509 (not listed by Benzing); Brixen: Angel. Britan., 1504; Köln: Quentel, 1504, 1510; London: Julian Notary, 1510; Rouen: Petrus Violette, 1511; Paris: Nic. de la Barre, 1513; Lyons: Joh. Huguetan, 1514, 1518; Hagenau: H. Grau, 1514; Lyons: Bernard Lescuyer, 1514; Caen-Rouen: Michael Angier-Pierre Olivier, 1518; Köln: s.n., 1518; Paris: s.n., 1519; Nürnberg: Joh. Stuch, 1519, 1520; Lyons: Joh. Huguetan, 1520; Lyons: Antoine du Roy, 1529; Lyons: s.n., 1541; [Louvain: Joh. de Westphal], s.n. and s.d.; Venice: M. Sessa, 1598 (see also Panzer, *Annales Typographici* X, 295, and Benzing, *Bibliographie Haguenovienne*, 136).

Seventeenth editions were published at Venice: P.M. Bertranus, 1606; Mainz: B. Gualteri, 1612.

An online edition of sermon 105 "On the Jews" [Trier: C. Cluse, Arye Maimon-Institut für Geschichte der Juden, n.d.] is at *http://www.uni-trier.de/uni/fb3/geschichte/cluse/pred7.htm*.

1430: *Additiones ad sermones discipuli*

Manuscripts

The *Additiones* are usually found incorporated into the MSS and editions of the *de tempore* and *de sanctis* sermons. I know of only a few MSS containing the additions alone:
Bamberg, Theol. 36 (1430/35), f. 376ᵛ-395.
München, Staatsbibl., Clm 7476 (xv), f. 198-215.
Vorau, Stiftsbibl., 112 (xv), f. 71ᵛ-72ᵛ (*"sermo de cogitationibus"* only).

1434: *Sermones de sanctis*

Manuscripts

Arras 631 (xv).
Bamberg, Staatsbibl., Theol. 15 (xv), f. 1-101; Theol. 16 (1466), f. 1-79ᵛ; Theol. 17 (c.1470), f. 65-171; Theol. 131 (1446-56), f. 1-61; R. B. Misc. 201 (xv), f. 11ᵛ-108.
Basel, Univ. Bibl. A.X. 68.
Berlin, Staatsbibl., Theol. fol. 144 (1468), f. 303-400; 175 (xv), f. 249-304; Theol. qu. 271 (xv), f. 129-324.
Cambrai 595 (xv)

Colmar, Bibl. du Consistoire 1940 (xv), f. 1.
Cues 121 (1456), f. 108ᵛ-201ᵛ.
Donaueschingen, Fürstenbergische Hofbibl. 279 (1469).
Einsiedeln 48 (xv), f. 1-60.
Erlangen, Univ. Bibl. 558 (1461), f. 139-231; 568 (xv), f. 1-74ᵛ.
Frankfurt a. Main, Stadt—u. Univ. Bibl., Carm. 9 (1454-55), f 44-125ᵛ.
Giessen, Univ. 757 (xv); 758 (xv).
Göttweig 297 (xv); 310 (c.1461); 313 (xv).
Graz, Univ. Bibl. 743 (1460), f. 250ᵛ-297.
Harburg (Schloss), Fürstl. Oettingen-Wallerstein'sche Bibl. II, 1, fol., 149 (xv), f. 1-71.
Innsbruck, Univ. Bibl. 566 (xv), f. 288-378.
Klosterneuburg 509 (xv), f. 357-439ᵛ.
Köln, Hist. Archiv W 191 (xv), f. 62-158.
Lambach 69 (xv), f. 1-87.
Liège, Univ. 98 (xv); 199 (xv).
Lüneburg, Ratsbücherei, Theol. 2° 33 (xv), f. 262-281.
München, Staatsbibl., Clm 3589 (xv), f. 1-96ᵛ; 3766 (xv), f. 1-96ᵛ; 4708 (1469-72), f. 144-210; 4751 (1473), f. 56ᵛ-121ᵛ; 5212 (1449), f. 217-289ᵛ; 5612 (1465), f. 1-69ᵛ; 5865 (xv), f. 403-423; 5901 (xv), f. 47-150; 7453 (xvl, f. 1-109; 7529 (1463), f. 125-208; 7551 (1461), f. 1-123; 8377 (xv), f. 1-72'; 9730 (xv), f. 162-235; 11448 (xv), f. 100-171ᵛ; 11461 (xv), f. 1-154ᵛ; 11466 (xv), f. 149-180; 15135 (xv), f.1-69ᵛ (with some *sermones communes*); 16168 (xv), f. 181-296; 16482 (1457), f. 1-81; 16485 (xv), f. 105-152; 17235 (xv), f. 222-310ᵛ; 18230 (1468), f. 1-98ᵛ; 23792 (xv), f. 70-174; 26685 (1446), f. 116-199; 26823 (xv), f.,149-215; 26896 (xv); 26932 (1467), f. 163-249; 28204 (1455), f. 1-105ᵛ; Cgm 4357 (xv).
Nürnberg, Stadtbibl., Cent. III, 82 (1434), f. 1ᵛ-73; Cent. IV, 82 (c.1434), f. 2-137ᵛ; Cent. VII, 63 (xv), f. 9-50ᵛ, 68ᵛ-84, 96ᵛ-143.
Oxford, Bodleian Libr., Laud. Misc. 380 (xv), f. 101.
Paris, Bibl. Nat., lat. 3297 (xv), f. 1-126.
St. Paul im Lavanttal, Hosp. chart. 84 (xv)
Schlägl 113 (1448), f. 1-118.
Sélestat 61 (xv); 73 (1465-77), n. 3.
Strasbourg, Bibl. Nat. et Univ. 29 (1459), f. 2-96.
Trier, Seminarbibl. 94 (xv), f. 1-23.
Uppsala, Univ. C 414ᵃ, f. 1-237.
Vatican, Vat. lat. 10059 (xv), f. 234ᵛ-246.
Vienna, Nat. Bibl. 3631 (xv), f. 13-123; 4264 (c.1467), f. 1-85ᵛ; 4918 (xv), f. 129-158.
Vienna, Schottenkloster 246 (xv), f. 1-12ᵛ, 85-189ᵛ.
Vorau, Stiftsbibl. 358 (xv), f. 1-132ᵛ.

Windsheim, Ratsbibl. 74 (1456), f. 6-83; 102 (xv), f. 73-192ʳ.
Wroclaw, Bibl. Uniw. I F 745 (c.1460-1), f. 1-76'; I F 746 (c.1463), f. 1-51ʳ.

Printed Editions

The *Sermones de sanctis* were incorporated in most of the printed editions of the *Sermones discipuli* listed above. In addition, four separate editions appeared in the fifteenth century: Copinger 2928-30, and Reichling I, 150 = Hain 8483.

A few more editions appeared in the early sixteenth century in conjunction with the *Promptuaria*: Lyons: Jn de la Place, 1511; Nürnberg: J. Koberger, 1514; Lyons: de Sabino, 1534.

1434: *Promptuarium exemplorum Discipuli secundum ordinem alphabeti*

Manuscripts

Aarau, Katonsbibl., Wett. 26 fol. (xv).
Bamberg, Staatsbibl., Theol. 15 (xv), f. 163-267ʳ (*"collectum a.d.1444"*), 267ʳ-275 (*tabula*); Theol. 17 (1470), f. 171-315, 315-325ʳ (*tabula*).
Basel, Univ. Bibl. A.VI.31 (xv), f. 69-182ʳ.
Berlin, Staatsbibl., Lat. fol. 914 (xv), f. 137-233; Lat. qu. 705 (xv), f. 6-157.
Berlin, Deutsche Staatsbibl., Magd. 208 (xv), f. 1-207.
Brussels, Bibl. Royale 5076-78 (xv), f. 3-227.
Cambridge, Univ. Libr. 1147 (xv), f. 185-207.
Colmar, Bibl. de la Ville 933 (xv) l, f. 40-70ʳ.
Colmar, Bibl. du Consistoire 1940 (xv), f. 181.
Cues 121 (xv), f. 202-258.
Donaueschingen, Fürstenbergische Hofbibl. 279 (1469).
Eichstätt, Staats—u. Seminarbibl. (Hochschulebibl.) 418 (xv), f. 3-118.
Einsiedlen 48 (xv), p. 181-394.
Erlangen, Univ. Bibl. 568 (xv), f. 76ʳ-173.
Frankfurt a. Main, Stadt—u. Univ. Bibl., Carm. 9 (1454-55), f. 281ʳ-454ʳ.
Giessen, Univ. 758 (xv).
Graz, Univ. Bibl. 668 (xv), f. 25-150.
Koblenz, Staatsarchiv 701/168 (xv).
London, British Museum, Add. 19909 (xv), f. 163.
Melk, Stiftsbibl. 207 (xv), f. 1-85.
München, Staatsbibl., Clm 5614 (xv), f. 1-153; 8132 (1474), f. 1-80; 8344 (xv), f. 1-112ʳ; 28204 (1455), f. 199ʳ-334ʳ.
Nürnberg, Stadtbibl., Cent. III, 82 (1434-35), f. 113-179.

Poznan, Bibl. Raczynski 140 (xv), f. 139-148 (*"primum de gaudiis celi"* [f. 143], *"de Udone"* [f. 148]).
Prague, Metrop. Kap. E. XI (xv), f. 346-356.
Salzburg, Studienbibl. M. II. 304 (xv); M. II. 367 (xv), f. 1-79.
Sélestat 61 (xv).
Vienna, Nat. Bibl. 1535 (xv), f. 1-103.
Wolfenbüttel, Herzog August Bibl. 42. 13 (1444), f. 241-358 (*"collecti a.d. 1434"*).
Wroclaw, Bibl. Uniw. I F 678 (xv), f. 298-307^v; I F 696 (xv), f. 180-230; I F 697 (xv), f. 471^v-4851; I F 745 (xv), f. 132-256; I F 746 (xv), f. 81-182^v; I Q 262 (xv), f. 217^v-346^v; I Q 337 (xv), f. 109-232.

Printed Editions

The *Promptuarium* was almost always included in the printed editions of the *Sermones Discipuli* listed above. Two separate editions are listed by Copinger: 2931-32.

A seventeenth-century edition is contained in B. Elers, editor, *Discipulus redivivus: seu sermones Discipuli quadragesimales et festivales, cum Promptuaris exemplorum: opus ante trecentos annos a . . . sacerdote Ordinis Praedicatorum conscriptum; . . . collectum a . . . B. Elers &c*, Augsburg: Wolf, 1728.

1434: ***Promptuarium Discipuli de miraculis beatae Mariae virginis***

Manuscripts

Bamberg, Staatsbibl., Theol. 15 (xv), f. 282-303^v; Theol. 16 (c.1463), f. 80-97; Theol. 17 (c.1470), f. 326-349.
Berlin, Staatsbibl., Lat. qu. 705 (xv), f. 166-195.
Colmar, Bibl. du Consistoire 1940 (xv), f. 312 (*"collectum a.d. 1434"*).
Donaueschingen, Fürstenbergische Hofbibl. 279 (1469).
Eichstdtt, Staats—u. Seminarbibl. (Hochschulebibl.) 418 (xv), f. 120-143.
Einsiedeln 48 (xv), p. 408-445.
Erlangen, Univ. Bibl. 568 (xv), f. 180-200.
Frankfurt a. Main, Stadt—u. Univ. Bibl., Carm. 9 (14,547.5), f. 455-493.
Giessen, Univ. 758 (xv).
Göttweig 248 (xv), f. 41^v; 478 (xv).
Koblenz, Staatsarchiv 701/168 (xv).
London, British Museum, Add. 19909 (1473), f. 239.
Mülhausen, Gymnasialbibl. 18 (xv).
München, Staatsbibl., Clm 5614 (xv), f. 166-197'; 8132 (1474), f. 89-108'; 14590 (xv), f. 153-193; 16168 (xv), f. 298^v-331^v; 28204 (1455), f. 106-131; Cgm 634 (xv), f. 76-76^v (79 only).

Nürnberg, Stadtbibl., Cent.III, 82 (1434-35), f. 180-197; Cent. IV, 82 (c.1434), f. 138-164ᵛ
Salzburg, Studienbibl. M. II. 304 (xv); M. II. 367 (xv), f. 83ᵛ-103.
St. Florian 335 (xv), f. 146-174.
Sélestat 61 (xv).
Stuttgart, Württemb. Landesbibl., Theol. fol. 329 (xv), f. 208-234.
Vorau, Stiftsbibl. 358 (xv), f. 234ᵛ-240.
Windsheim, Ratsbibl. 102 (xv), f. 193-221.
Wroclaw, Bibl. Uniw. I F 695 (xv), f. 311-313; I F 696 (xv), f. 230ᵛ-241ᵛ; I F 745 (xv), f. 63-289; I F 746 (xv), f. 185-202; I Q 262 (xv), f. 347-370ᵛ; I Q 351 (xv), f. 205-214.

Printed Editions

This *Promptuarium* was incorporated in most printed editions of the *Sermones Discipuli*. It had three separate printings in the fifteenth century (Copinger 2933-35), and an English translation appeared in 1928: *Miracles of the Blessed Virgin Mary*, translated with a preface and notes by C. C. Swinton Bland and an introduction by Eileen Power. Broadway Mediaeval Library. London: G. Routledge and Sons, 1928.

1434: *Promptuarium Discipuli de festis sanctorum intimandis diebus dominicis*

Manuscripts

Bamberg, Staatsbibl., Theol. 15 (xv), f. 105-150, 150ᵛ-152 (*tabula*); Theol. 17 (1470), f. 8-61, 62-63 (*tabula*); Theol. 96 (xv), f. 1-24.
Basel, Univ. Bibl. A. XI. 44 (xv).
Berlin, Deutsche Staatsbibl., Magd. 32 (xv), f. 329-357.
Colmar, Bibl. du Consistoire 1940 (xv), f. 121.
Einsiedeln 48 (xv), p. 83-181.
Erlangen, Univ. Bibl. 568 (xv), f. 209-251.
Frankfurt a. Main, Stadt—u. Univ. Bibl., Carm. 9 (1454-55), f. 10-44.
Giessen, Univ. Bibl. 758 (xv).
München, Staatsbibl., Clm 1224 (xv), f. 137-170; 4708 (1469-72), f. 229-289ᵛ; 8344 (xv), f. 1-112ᵛ; 8862 (1467), f. 1-83ᵛ; 9733 (xv), f. 97-138ᵛ; 11461 (xv), f. 179-210ᵛ; 15135 (1435), f. 79-122ᵛ; 16168 (xv), f. 332-370; 23834 (xv), f. 131-229ᵛ; 23847 (xv), f. 425-491ᵛ; 23867 lxv), f. 1-67; 28204 (1455), f. 137-195ᵛ.
Nürnberg, Stadtbibl., Cent. III, 82 (1434-35), f. 74-112.

Sélestat 73 (1465-77), f. 332-387.
Stuttgart, Württemb. Landesbibl., Theol. fol. 71 (xv); Theol. fol. 329 (xv), f. 1-51.
Uppsala, Univ. C. 414ª (xv), f. 239-358.
Vatican, Vat. lat. 10060 (xv), f. 212-255.
Vorau, Stiftsbibl. 358 (xv), f. 133-234.
Windsheim, Ratsbibl. 98 (xv), f. 323-376^v; 102 (xv), f. 1-71.
WolfenbUttel, Herzog August Bibl. 33. 6. Aug fol. (xv), f. 62-109^v.
Wroclaw, Bibl. Uniw. I F 745 (xv), f. 85-129; I F 746 (xv), f. 52-79.
Printed Editions: none

1435: *Quadragesimale Discipuli*

Manuscripts

Basel, Univ. Bibl. A. VIII. 13 (xv).
Berlin, Staatsbibl., Lat. qu. 746 (xv), f. 318-386.
Colmar, Bibl. du Consistoire 1934 (xv), f. 1-75^v (*"collectum a.d. 1435"*).
Eichstdtt, Staats—u. Seminarbibl. (Hochschulebibl.) 433 (xv), f. 295-383.
Erlangen, Univ. Bibl. 568 (xv), f. 257-317.
Harburg (Schloss), Fürstl. Oettingen-Wallerstein'sche Bibl. II, 1, fol., 51 (1441).
München, Staatsbibl., Clm 5613 (xv), f. 1-86^v; 7453 (xv), f. 224-311; 7551 (xv), f. 124-213; 11449 (1462), f. 1-99; 11457 (1473), f. 180-279; 17285 (xv), f. 112-300; 17286 (xv), f. 1-188; 23869 (xv), f. 1-98^v; 26787 (xv), f. 1-150^v (*"collectum a.d. 1435"*); 26813 (1443), f. 1-78.
München, Univ. Bibl. 2° cod. MS 129 (xv), f. 1-96.
Stuttgart, Württemb. Landesbibl., Theol. 4° (xv).
Vatican, Vat. lat. 10060 (xv), f. 128-192^v.
Wolfenbüttel, Herzog August Bibl. 42. 13. Aug fol. (1444), f. 1-81^v.
Wroclaw, Bibl. Uniw. I F 282 (xv), f. 134-189'7; I F 696 (xv), f. 243-273^v; I Q 315 (xv), f. 1-67.

Printed Editions

The *Quadragesimale* was printed only once (or perhaps twice) in the fifteenth century (at Reutlingen: Joh. Otmar, 1489): Hain 8514-15.

Sixteenth-century editions include: Rouen: Petrus Violette, 1500, 1513; Lyons: Claude Duvost. 1502; Paris: Nic. de la Barre, 1513; Lyons: B. Lescuyer, 1514; Hagenau: Henr. Grau, 1517; Rouen-Caen: Petr. Olivier and Michael Angier, 1518; Nürnberg: Joh. Stuch, 1520; Lyons: Antoine du Roy, 1529; Lyons: s.n., 1541; Lyons: s.n. and s.d.; Venice: J.A. Bertranum. 1599.

Later editions appeared at Mainz: B. Gualteri, 1612; B. Elers, editor. *Discipulus redivivus.* Augsburg: Wolf, 1728.

1436: *Der Rosengart*

Manuscript

Only at Nürnberg, Stadtbibl., Cent. VII, 57 (1436), f. 2-114.

Printed Edition

A short part of the text (f. 2-20^v) has been transcribed in Dietrich Schmidtke, *Studien zur dingallegorischen Erbauungsliteratur des Spätmittelalters. Am Beispiel der Gartenallegorie.* Hermaea NF 43. Tübingen: Max Niemeyer, 1982, Textanhang, 448-54.

I shall shortly publish a transcription and translation of the whole manuscript.

1437: *Postilla discipuli super evangelia dominicalia et de sanctis secundum sensum litteralem*

Manuscripts

Bamberg, Staatsbibl., Theol. 16 (c.1463), f. 99-153; Theol. 36 (1445-47), f. 314-376^v (*"Incipit postilla discipuli,"* and indexed on the binding as *"postilla hiroltz"*).
Berlin, Staatsbibl., Lat. qu. 746 (xv), f. 159-274, abbreviations f. 275^v (*"discipuli"*).
Eichstdtt, Staats—u. Seminarbibl. (Hochschulebibl.) 483 (not before 1455), f. 244-300 (*"Postilla . . . fris hiroldi OP"*).
Kahlsruhe, Bad. Landesbibl., Reichenau Pap. Aug. 92 (1491), f. 7-1481 (*"discipuli"*).
Klosterneuberg CC1 407 (1454), f. 407-461; 457 (1453), f. 265-296^v; 459 (1449), f. 135-184; 548 (1450/60), f. 229^v-256^v (all *"discipuli"*).
Marburg, Univ. Bibl. 49 (1449-50), f. 108-175^v (*"discipuli"*).
München, Staatsbibl., Clm 5192 (1481), f. 125-302 (includes additions, plus the "Guillermus" preface f. 303-303^v); 13568 (1437), f 1-142^v (*"discipuli"*); 26826 (xv), f. 1-112, 116-164^v (plus marginal and interleaved additions); 26880 (xv), f. 318-389 (*"discipuli"*).
Uppsala, Univ. C. 414^a (1474), f. 584-613 (*de sanctis*), 613-133 (*commune sanctorum*).
Vatican, Vat. lat. 10059 (xv), f. 157-234 (*"collecta a.d. 1437"*).

Windsheim, Ratsbibl. 44 (xv), f. 95-239.
Wroclaw, Bibl. Uniw. I F 282 (1461), f. 193-261.
Würzberg, Univ. Bibl., M. ch. f. 135 (1458), f. 277-354, 356 (*Discipulus*).

Printed Editions

A complete listing of 105 certain incunabular editions, six probable and eleven "indeterminate" editions is given in Frederick R. Goff, "The Postilla of Guillermus Parisiensis," *Gutenberg-Jahrbuch* 34 (1959), 73-78.

Microfilm copies of some incunabular editions are available from General Microfilm Company (Watertown, Mass.) in *German Books Before 1601*, Rolls 278/2, 280/1, 299/2, 321/8, 335/15, 374/70 444/4, and 451/5.

1439: *Postilla discipuli super epistolas dominicales et de sanctis secundum sensum litteralem*

Manuscripts

Berlin, Staatsbibl., Lat. qu. 746 (xv), f. 1-122.
Göttingen, Univ. Bibl., Theol. 127 (1474), f. 167-219.
København, Kogel. Bibl., Kall 306 4° (1478), f. 1-126.
München, Staatsbibl., Clm 5192 (1481), f. 2-113 (a manuscript copy of the printed *Postilla Guillermi*); 9721 (xv), f. 319-388 (*"collecta a.d. 1439"*); 12029 (xv), f. 1-59 (*"collecta a. 1439"*); 15182 (1445), f. 235-343ᵛ (*"collecta a.d. 1439"*).
Prague, Státní knihovna I. C. 26 (not before 1485), f. 75-128 (*"cum glossis germ."*).
Uppsala, Univ. Bibl. C 414ᵃ (1474), f. 359-541 (*epistolas per circulum anni*), f. 541-583 (*de sanctis*).
Windsheim, Ratsbibl. 44 (xv), f. 1-81.
Wroclaw, Uniw. Bibl. I F 282 (1469), f. 84-133.

Printed Editions

Not separately published, the Epistles formed part of the *Postilla Guillermi* listed above.

Undated (probably 1439): *Postilla discipuli secundum sensum litteralem super officium missae et super epistolas et evangelia per Quadragesimam*

Manuscripts

Berlin, Staatsbibl., Lat. qu. 746 (xv), f. 277-317.
Eichstdtt, Staats—u. Seminarbibl. (Hochschulebibl.)433 (xv), f. 229-295.
Paris, Bibl. Nat., lat. 10703 (xv), f. 1-87.
Uppsala, Univ. Bibl. c 414ª (1474), f. 633-44 (part only: breaks off in *dom. prima in xl*).
Vienna, Dominikanerkl. 55/288 (xv), f. 1-67ᵛ.
Wroclaw, Uniw. Bibl. 1 F 282 (1469), f. 261ᵛ-302; I F 746 (xv), f. 206-247ᵛ.

Printed Editions: none

1441: *Sermones discipuli super epistolas dominicales*

Manuscripts

Kaeppeli, SOPMA II, 459: 2394 does not distinguish this work from the *Postilla super epistolas*, and his list conflates two different sets of MSS. The following contain the *Sermones*:
Bamberg, Staatsbibl., Theol. 14 (1448/61), f. 2-135 (contains 56 sermons), tabula f. 136-142ᵛ (*"collecta Anno do. 1441"*).
Eichstdtt, Staats—u. Seminarbibl. (Hochschulebibl.) 755 (xv), *tabula* f. 4-6, *sermones* f. 7-115.
Klosterneuberg, Stiftsbibl. 400 (1457), f. 266-444 (contains 56 sermons), *tabula* f. 445-53ᵛ.
Koblenz, Landeshauptarchiv Best 701 Nr. 189 (xv), f. 1-236, tabula f. 237-52 (*"collecti anno 1441"*).
Köln, Hist. Archiv GB f° 115 (1460/80), f. 1-87, tabula f. 87ᵛ-91ᵛ (*"anno domini 1444"*); W 191 (1479), f. 1-61.
Luxembourg, Bibl. Nat. 130 (1467), f. 60-205 (contains 56 sermons).
Mainz, Stadtbibl. II 28 (xv) (*"Sermones Discipuli super epistolas Pauli"*); II 95 (xv) (*"anno 1444 collecta"*).
Marburg, Univ. Bibl. 56 (1464), f. 1ᵛ-226ᵛ (contains 56 sermons), tabula f. 226ᵛ-236.
Poznan, Bibl. Raczynski 140 (1462), tabula f. 39ᵛ-43, sermones f. 43ᵛ-139.
Prague, Metrop. Chapter E IX (xv), registrum f. 228-32, sermones f. 231-346.
Salzburg, Bibl. St. Peter b. VIII 7 (xv), f. 2-135 (contains 56 sermons), *tabula* f. 136-142.
Uppsala, Univ. Bibl. C 414ª (1479), f. 647-880, registrum f. 880-91 (*"collegit frater Theodoricus de Norinberga ordinis predicatorum"*).
Wolfenbüttel, Herzog August Bibl. 50. 2. Aug. fol. (1467-72), f. 1-72ᵛ; 42.13. Aug. fol. (1444), f. 81ᵛ-240ᵛ (*"collecti anno Domini 1444"*).

Wroclaw, Bibl. Uniw. I F 528 (1457-61), f. 195-303ᵛ; I F 696 (xv), f. 274-329ᵛ (*"collegit frater Theodoricus Heroldus de Nuremberga ordinis predicatorum"*); I Q 297 (xv), f. 1-128, *tabula* f. 136.

Printed Editions

Ten incunabular editions are listed in Hain 8509-13; Copinger 2936-2939; IDGI III, 4699.

1463: *Applicationes ad sermones secundum proprietates rerum naturalium*

Manuscript

München, Staatsbibl. Clm 8132 (1474), f. 111-131ᵛ, *tabulae* f. 132-133.

Printed Editions: none

Select Bibliography

Barth, Hilarius M., OP. *Regensberg: Dominikanerkirche.* (Schell Kunstführer Nr. 48). 2. völlig neu bearb. Auflage. München u. Zürich: Schell, 1973.

Bock, Friedrich. "Das Nürnberger Predigerkloster. Beitrage zu eiher Geschichte." *Mitteilungen des Vereins für Geschichte der Stadt Nürnberg 25.* Nürnberg: Schrag, 1924, 147 ff.

Brown, Peter. *Augustine of Hippo.* Berkeley and Los Angeles: U. of California Press, 1969.

Caplan, Harry. "The Four Senses of Scriptural Interpretation and the Medieval Theory of Preaching." *Speculum* 4 (July 1929), 282-90.

Caplan, Harry. *Medieval artes praedicandi: A Hand-List.* Ithaca: Cornell University Press, 1934.

Charland, Th. M. *Artes praedicandi: contribution à l'histoire de la rhétorique au moyen âge.* Ottawa: Institute d'études médiévales d'Ottawa, 1936.

Cruel, R. C. *Geschichte der deutschen Predigt im Mittelalter.* Detmold: Meyer-Klingenberg, 1879.

Eis, Gerhard. "Lupold von Wiltingen. Eine Studie zum Wanderanhang der Katharinenlegende." *Festschrift für Wolfgang Stammler.* Berlin-Bielefeld: Schmidt, 1953, 78-91.

Forbes, T. R. *The Midwife and the Witch.* New Haven: Yale University Press, 1966.

Franz, Adolph. *Der Magister Nikolaus Magni de Jawor. Ein Beitrage zur Literatur—und Gelehrengeschichte des 14. und 15. Jahrhunderts.* Freiburg im Breisgau: Herder, 1898.

Fries, Walter. "Kirche und Kloster zu St. Katharina in Nürnberg." *Mitteilungen des Vereins für Geschichte der Stadt Nürnberg 25.* Nürnberg: Schrag, 1924, 1 ff.

Geffken, Johannes. *Der Bildercatechismus des funfzehnten Jahrhunderts und die catechetischen Hauptstücke in dieser Zeit bis auf Luther. 1: Die Zehn Gebote.* Leipzig: Weigel, 1855.

Goff, Frederick R. "The Postilla of Guillermus Parisiensis." *Gutenberg-jahrbuch* 34 (1959). Mainz: Gutenberg-Gesellschaft, 1959, 73-78.

Haupt, H. "Geisselung (kirchliche) und Geisslerbruderschaften." 3rd ed. *Realencyklopädie für protestantische Theologie.* Edited by A. Hauck, vi (1899), 432-44.

Jöcher, C. G. *Allgemeines Gelehren-Lexicon.* Leipzig: J. F. Gleditschen, 1751.

Keppler, Paul. "Zur Passionspredigt des Mittelalters, II." *Görres-Gesellschaft: Historisches Jahrbuch* IV/2 (1883). München: Herder, 1883, 161-188.

Lecoy de la Marche, A., *La chaire français au moyen âge.* Paris: Renouard, 1886.

Lewis, C. S. *The Discarded Image.* Cambridge: Cambridge University Press, 1964.

Loë, Paulus von, OP. *Statistisches über die Ordensprovinz Teutonia. (QF 1)*. Leipzig: Harrassowitz, 1907.

Löhr, Gabriel M., OP. *Die Teutonia im 15. Jahrhundert. Studien und Texte vornehmlich zur Geschichte ihrer Reform. (QF 19)*. Leipzig: Harrassowitz, 1924.

Löhr, Gabriel M., OP. "Über die Heimat einiger deutschen Prediger und Mystiker aus dem Dominkanerorden." *Zeitschrift für deutsches Altertum und deutsche Literatur* 82/1-2 (1948). Weidemann: Berlin-Frankfurt, 1948, 173-78.

Löhr, Gabriel M., OP. "Das Nürnberger Predigtkloster im 15. Jahrhundert. Beiträge zu seiner Geschichte." *Zeitschrift des Vereins für Geschichte der Stadt Nürnberg* (1947), 223-32.

Madre, Alois. *Nicolaus von Dinkelsbühl: Leben und Schriften (Beitrage zur Geschichte der Philosophie und Theologie des Mittelalters* XL, 4). Münster, Westph.: Aschendorff, 1965.

Meyer, Johannes, OP. *Buch der Reformacio Predigerordens. I, II und III Buch (QF 2), IV und V Buch (QF 3)*, hrsg. B. M. Reichert, OP. Leipzig: Harrassowitz, 1909, 1908.

Meyer, Johannes, OP. *Liber de Viris Illustribus Ordinis Praedicatorum. (QF 12)*, hrsg. Paulus von Löe, OP. Leipzig: Harrassowitz, 1918.

Michelfelder, Gottfried. *Die Wirtschaftliche Tätigkeit der Juden Nürnbergs im Spätmittelalter,ll Beiträge zur Wirtschafisgeschichte Nürnberg*, I (*Beiträge zur Geschichte und Kultut der Stadt Nürnberg*, 11/I), hrsg. vom Stadtsarchiv Nürnberg. Nürnberg: Selbstverlag des Stadtsrats, 1967, 236-60.

Miles, Margaret. *Augustine on the Body* (AAR Dissertation Series 31). Missoula: Scholars' Press, 1979.

Moeller, Bernd. "Piety in Germany Around 1500," *ARG* 56 (1965), 5-30, and also in Ozment, *The Reformation in Medieval Perspective*, 50-75.

Oberman, Heiko A. "Facientibus Quod in se est Deus non Denegat Gratiam: Robert Holcot O.P.and the Beginnings of Luther's Theology," *HTR* 55 (1962), 317-42, and also in Ozment, *The Reformation in Medieval Perspective*, 27 ff.

Oberman, Heiko A., ed. *Forerunners of the Reformation: The Shape of Late Medieval Thought Illustrated by Key Documents*. New York: Holt, Rinehart & Winston, 1966; Philadelphia: Fortress Press, 1981.

Oberman, Heiko A. *The Harvest of Medieval Theology: Gabriel Biel and Late Medieval Nominalism*. Cambridge: Harvard University Press, 1963; 2nd revised edition, Grand Rapids, W. B. Eerdmans Pub. Co., 1967.

O'Malley, John. *Praise and Blame in Renaissance Rome: Rhetoric, Doctrine & Reform in the Sacred Orators of the Papal Court, c1450-1521*. Durham: Duke University Press, 1979.

Owst, G. R. *Preaching in Medieval England: an introduction to sermon manuscripts of the period c. 1350-1450*. Cambridge: Cambridge University Press, 1926.

—. *Literature and Pulpit in Medieval England: a neglected chapter in the history of English letters & of the English people*. Cambridge: Cambridge University

Press, 1933; 2nd revised edition Oxford: Blackwell, and New York: Barnes & Noble, 1961.

Ozment, Steven E. *The Reformation in Medieval Perspective.* Chicago: Quadrangle, 1971.

Pannekoek, A. *A History of Astronomy.* London: George Allen & Unwin, 1961. Translated from *De Groei van ons Werenbeeld,* Amsterdam: Wereld-Bibliotheck, 1961.

Panzer, Georg Wolfgang. *Annales Typographici ab anno MDI ad annum MD XXXVI continuati.* Nürnberg: Zeh, 1802, reproduced Hildersheim: Olms, 1964.

Paulus, Nicolaus. "Johann Herolt und seine Lehre," *ZkTh* 26 (1902), 417-447.

—. Untitled note on Herolt's sepulchre. *ZkTh* 27 (1903), 366-68.

Petry, Ray C. *No Uncertain Sound: Sermons That Shaped the Pulpit Tradition.* Philadelphia: Westminster, 1933.

Petry, Ray C., "Emphasis on the Gospel and Christian Reform in Late Medieval Preaching," *Church History* XVI/2 (June,1947), 75-91

Richstatter, Karl, SJ. *Die Herz-Jesu-Verehrung des deutschen Mittelalters.* 2. Aufl., München-Regensberg: Kösel und Pustet, 1924.

Roth, Dorothea. *Die mittelalterliche Predigttheorie und das Manuale Curatorum des Johann Ulrich Sargant.* Basel: von Helbing & Lichtenbahn, 1956.

Schmidtke, Dietrich. *Studien zur dingallegorischen Erbauungsliteratur des Spätmittelalters. Am Beispiel der Gartenallegorie.* Hermaea NF 43. TUbingen: Max Niemeyer, 1982.

Schneyer, Johannes B. *Geschichte der katholischen Predigt.* Freiburg i. Br.: Seelsorge Verlag, 1969.

—. "Repertorium der lateinische Sermones des Mittelalters," *Beiträge zur Geschichte der Philosophie und Theologie des Mittelalters* XLIII/1-4 (Munster, 1973).

—. "Winke für die Sichtung und Zuordnung Spätmittelalterlicher Lateinische Predigtreihenl" *Scriptorium* XXXII/2 (1978).

—. *Die Unterweisung der Gemeinde über die Predigt bei scholastischen Predigern: Eine Homiletik aus scholstischen Prothemen.* München-Paderborn-Wien: Schöningh, 1968.

Siebert, H. "Die Heiligenpredigt des ausgehenden Mittelalters," *ZkTh* 30 (1906), 470-91.

Siggins, Ian D. K. "The Catholic Preachers of Luther's Youth." *Luther: Theologian for Catholics and Protestants.* George Yule, ed. Edinburgh: T&T Clark, 1986, 2nd edition 1989.

Siggins, Ian D. K. *Luther and His Mother.* Philadelphia: Fortess Press, 1981. Reissued Eugene: Wipf & Stock, 2003.

Smalley, Beryl. *The Study of the Bible in the Middle Ages.* Oxford: Clarendon Press, 1941.

Southern, R. W. *Western Society and the Church in the Middle Ages.* The Pelican History of the Church Vol. 2. Grand Rapids: Wm B. Eerdmans Publishing Co., 1970.

Stammler, Wolfgang. *Die Deutsche Literatur des Mittelalters Verfasserlexicon*, Bd II. Berlin & Leipzig: de Gruyter, 1936. Second fully revised edition ed. Kurt Ruh, Bd III/4. Berlin & New York: de Gruyter, 1981.

Tawney, Richatd H. *Religion and the Rise of Capitalism*. Second edition reprinted, Harmondsworth: Penguin Books, 1980 (1937).

Tentler, Thomas L. *Sin and Confession on the Eve of the Reformation*. Princeton: Princeton University Press, 1977.

Thomas, Keith. *Religion and the Decline of Magic*. New York: Charles Scribner's Sons, 1971.

Walther, Wilhelm. "Das sechste Gebot in Joh. Herolts Preigten," *Neue kirchliche Zeitschrift* 3 (1892), 485-99.

Warner, Marina. *Alone of All Her Sex: The Myth and Cult of the Virgin Mary*. New York: Alfred A. Knopf, 1976.

Weber, G. Anton, "Johann Herolt. Ein Beitrage zum Bilde, das N. Paulus gezeichnet." *ZkTh* 27 (1903), 362-66.

Welter, J-Th. *L'Exemplum dans la litterature religieuse et didactique du Moyen Âge*. Geneva: Slatkine Reprints, 1973 (reprint of editions at Paris-Toulouse 1927).

Wilms, Hieronymus, OP. *Geschichte der deutschen Dominikanerinnen 1206-1916*. Dülmen i. W.: Laumann, 1920.

Wilson, E. F., ed. *The Stella Maris of John of Garland. Edited Together with a Study of Certain Collections of Mary Legends made in Northern France in the Twelfth and Thirteenth Centuries*. Cambridge, Mass.: Medieval Academy of America and Wellesley College, 1946.

Würfel, Andreas. *Toden-Kalender des St. Katharina Klosters in Nürnberg mit der Priorin und des Convents Insiegeln. Benebst einer Anhang merkwurdiger Urkunden herausgegeben von Andreas Würfel, Pfarrer in Offenhausen*. Altdorf, 1769.

Zawart, Anscar, OFM. *The History of Franciscan Preaching and of Franciscan Preachers 1209-1927, A Bio-bibliographical Study*. Franciscan Studies 7. New York: Wagner, 1928.

Index

A

Abstinence 128
Accidie 69
Albertus Magnus 103, 110, 126, 171, 175, 184
Almsgiving 75, 206, 214, 217, 218, 221, 222, 223, 224, 227, 252
Amusements 255
Anger 68
Animals and birds, examples from 110
Anselm 40
Aristotle 99, 103, 142, 148, 173, 177, 186, 187, 222, 255, 302
artes praedicandi 11
Astrology 98
Augury 33
Augustine 19, 40, 49, 53, 63, 99, 121, 125, 143, 173, 194, 210, 227, 273, 290, 302
Avarice 70, 211

B

Barth, Hilarius M 10
Beginners, proficients, and perfecti 38
Benedict of Nursia 126
Bernard of Clairvaux 45, 46, 49, 126, 147, 160, 273, 290, 302
Bishops 85
Black Death 100
Blasphemy 232
Body 115, 126, 274
  as insufferable encumbrance 125
  cadaver 125
  of damned in hell 131
  of the elect recreated in beauty 122, 131
  prompts to virtue 122

Brethren of the Common Life 1, 2
Bromyard, John 12
Brown, Peter 121, 194
Business practices, deceitful 257

C

Caesarius 86, 186, 254, 256, 269
Caesarius of Heisterbach 47
Castigation 50, 130
Cato 237
Charlemagne 195
Childbirth 28
Children 190
  care of 172, 180
  death of 173, 184
  duties to parents 187
Chrysostom, John 33, 49, 160, 221
Church 82, 193
  as body of Christ 81
  one, holy, and catholic 80
Cities 204
Cluse, Christoph 264
Concupiscence 124, 147
Confession, priestly 60
Conrad de Grossis 5
Constance, Council of 23, 80, 193
Contrition 38, 39, 42, 46, 52, 53, 54, 55, 57, 58, 59, 61, 62, 75, 79, 122, 128, 141, 152, 168, 277, 299
Correction 206
Creation 97
  renewal of 101
Cursing 233

D

Damian, Peter 222
Dancing 250

331

Death 275
  remembrance of 54, 62
  struggle 20, 28, 33, 216, 274, 275
Defamation, slander 230
Despair 20, 36, 47, 49, 54, 55, 56, 61, 68, 76, 77, 127, 274, 275, 277
Dreams, divination 25, 26
Drunkenness 242, 246
Duns Scotus 178

E

Echard, Jacobus 5, 303, 312
Egyptian days 24, 99, 261
Elizabeth of Hungary 225, 227
Envy 67
Erasmus, Desiderius 2, 13
Eve 161
  curse of 160, 162
  sin of 160
Exactions, levies, and taxes 197
Excommunication 85, 201, 259

F

Faith 22
Fall, effects on creation 101
Fasting 241
Festivity 250
Filthy talk 145
Flamocheti, Guido 9
Food and drink 244
Food and drink, abuses of 240
Forbes, T R 170
Franz, Adolph 29
Freedom of the will 34
Fries, Walter 6, 8
Fun and games
  frivolous depravity 246
  virtuous 245

G

Gambling 233, 254
George, Bishop of Bamberg 8
Gery, Robert 4
Gluttony 70, 125, 239, 242

God's strange work and proper office 40
Grace 40, 46
Gregory the Great 19, 25, 49, 65, 99, 156, 206, 222, 238, 273
Guilelmus Durandus 278
Gwichtmacherin, Gertrud 7, 9

H

Healing, cures 28
Heaven 45, 51, 58, 74, 75, 79, 80, 90, 93, 153, 164, 184, 219, 244, 254, 273, 279
  joys of 290
Heinrich of Vrimaria 136, 232
Hell 19, 39, 40, 45, 67, 74, 78, 86, 91, 105, 107, 131, 140, 146, 154, 160, 164, 165, 188, 230, 244, 247, 248, 252, 254, 257, 273, 274, 276, 279
  torments of 282
Henkel, Nikolaus 104
Henry, Emperor 195, 214
Henry of Hassia 99
Heresy, heretics 23
Herolt, Johann 4
  life of 3
  name variants 7
  pastoral purpose 10
  preaching style 2, 10
Hinnebusch, W A 7
Holkot, Robert 41, 184
Hugo de Folieto 241
Human nature 113
Humbert de Romans 278
Humility 43, 164
Hunting 251
Hus, Johannes 23

I

Immerdorfer, Ulrich 9
Incubi 144
Influence of the spheres 98
Isidore of Seville 49, 104

J

Jacob, E F 3
Jacobus de Voragine, Legenda aurea 29
Jacques de Vitry 18
Jauer, Nicolaus 29
Jerome 19, 49, 273, 302
Jews 233, 270
  conversion of 268
Joannes Januensis 115
Johannes of Erfurt 143
Johann of Werden 104
Judas Maccabaeus 195
Justice and mercy 40

K

Kaeppeli, Thomas 7, 294, 305, 307, 312
Katharinenkloster 3, 6, 43
Kellenberg, Hermann 197
Kindling of sin 124

L

Last judgment 285
Law and legal practice 204
Lewis, C S 98
Life, brevity of 103
Limbo of children 275
Löhr, Gabriel 5, 6, 7
Louis of France, King 195, 214
Lust 73, 143
  sinful even without act 143
Luther, Martin 2, 3, 13, 135, 294

M

Macrobius, Ambrosius Theodosius 241
Majority of people unjust and evil 102
Manichaeism 75, 121, 131
Mankind, common condition of 115
Mardach, Eberhard 5
Marriage 158
  celebrations 152
  clandestine 151
  community property 157
  mutual obligations of husband and wife 157
  remarrying 158
  sexual duty 155
Mary, Blessed Virgin 45, 129, 189, 222, 290
  model for women 164, 181
Mary Magdalene 175
McCulloch, Florence 104
Merit 46, 51
Meyer, Johannes 4, 5, 7, 306
Michelfelder, Gottfried 266
Midwives 169, 180
Miles, Margaret 121
Miracles 19, 20, 239, 289
Mockery and derision 231
Monastic life 92, 190
Monastic possessions 90
Monastic virtues 92
Music and singing 254
  at the heavenly feast 286
  of infernal banquet in hell 282

N

Nider, Johannes 6, 8, 89, 103
Nobility 199

O

Oberman, Heiko A 2, 41
Observant reform 3, 5
Ordeals 36, 202
Oswald, St 195
Owst, G R 12

P

Pannekoek, A 98
Panzer, G W 4
Papacy 85
Parents
  duties of 181
  duties to children 185
Patriarchs, longevity of the 128
Paulus, Nicolaus 4, 135, 293, 296, 306, 312
Penance 38, 39, 47, 53, 54, 55, 60, 62, 79, 89, 93, 127, 136, 138, 140,

141, 182, 217, 222, 248, 249, 253, 276, 277, 283, 299, 300
  at life's end 54
Peter Lombard 57
Poor
  classes of the 218
  complaints against God 218
  good paupers 219
Pope Boniface IX 5
Pope Eugene IV 8
Pope Martin V 90
Pope Sixtus IV 91
Poverty 224
Preaching 19, 21, 44
Predestination 47, 48, 227
Pregnancy and childbirth 167
Prelates, worthy and unworthy 86
Pride 66, 124
Priesthood
  dignities of 88
  social status 200
Priests, unworthy 89
Ptolemy 98, 99
Purgatory 273, 276, 279
Pythonesses, soothsayers, and spellbinders 25

Q

Quétif, Jacques 5, 303, 312

R

Raymond of Capua 5
Recreation 245
Regensberg 10
Reproductive theory 121
Rulers
  honor to 195
  oppression by 196
  subjects duties to 196

S

Sacraments, abuse of 29
Satisfaction 61
Schneyer, J B 4

Seneca 48, 237, 245
Servants 196
Sex 148
  adultery 139
  aphrodisiacs 148
  arousing desire 146
  before and after the fall 135
  enticing desire 146
  fantasies 145
  fornication 136
  incest 142
  practical remedies 147
  prostitution 137
  sodomy 142
  violation of clerical celebacy 141
  violation of virginity 137
  within marriage 155
Sin 79
  mortal 76, 124
  nature of 64
  venial 75
  venial and mortal sins 60
Social behavior, principles of 207
Society 209
  model of 194, 195
  principles of behavior 205
  social virtues 199
Sorrow for sin 52, 56
Soul 121
Southern, RW 204
Speculation 20
Speech 238
  provincial dialogues of 232
Stammler, W 4
Staupitz, Johann 13
Suffering, inevitability of 130
Suffrages 188, 277
Superstition 32, 35, 144, 153, 168, 170, 275

T

Tawney, R H 208
Tentler, T L 79
Thomas Aquinas 41, 76, 119, 175, 232, 242, 250, 264

Thomas, Keith 99, 170
Tournaments 250
Trade and commerce 262
Trades 199

U

Universe, Ptolemaic model of 98
Usury 201, 260, 264

V

Virgins 174
Virtues 51

W

Walther, Wilhelm 4, 135
Warfare 198
Warner, Marina 159, 250
Wealth 217
  anxiety about 211
  dangers of 215
  miserliness 223
  negative effects of 210
Wealthy, classes of the 212

Werewolves 32, 110
Widows 158, 173
Witchcraft 170
Women 179
  adornment of 176
  characteristics 159
  characteristics 176, 178
  humility in 164
  labor pain 180
  nagging 165
  old crones 170
  pain of labor 160
  pregnancy and childbirth 167
  property of 176
Work practices 262

Z

Zwingli, Huldrych 13

Get Published, Inc!
Thorofare, NJ 08086
06 November 2009
BA2009249